Peer Gynt, Oslo, 2005

Shakespeare's Sonnets, Berlin, 2009

Einstein on the Beach, New York City, 1976

A Space for Mozart [Mozarts Geburtshaus], Salzburg, 2005

Video portrait of Isabelle Huppert by Robert Wilson, 2005

Time Rocker, Paris, 1997

The Threepenny Opera, Berlin, 2007

"Self-Portrait," Polaroid photograph by Robert Wilson, 50 × 60 cm, 1999. Courtesy Sacha Goldman Collection

Robert Wilson
from Within

Marina Abramović
Laurie Anderson
Pierre Bergé
Anne Bogart
Charles Chemin
Daniel Conrad
Giuseppe Frigeni
Gao Xingjian
Philip Glass
Sacha Goldman
Jonathan Harvey
Isabelle Huppert
Stefan Kurt
Joseph V. Melillo
Ivan Nagel
Jessye Norman
Yvonne Rainer
Jacques Reynaud
Marc Robinson
John Rockwell
Carlos Soto
Viktor & Rolf
Serge von Arx
Rufus Wainwright
Jörn Weisbrodt
Robert Wilson

Edited by Margery Arent Safir

THE ARTS ARENA
THE AMERICAN UNIVERSITY OF PARIS   Flammarion

Der Freischütz, Baden-Baden, 2009

Contents

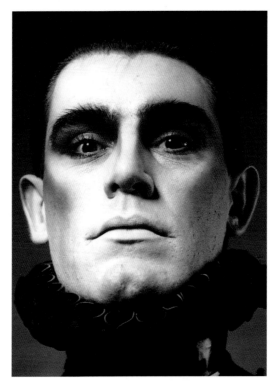

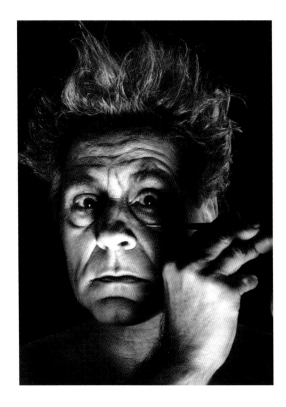

The Forest, Berlin, 1988

1433 – The Grand Voyage, Taipei, 2010

Lulu, Berlin, 2011

KOOL – Dancing in my Mind, New York City, 2009

Happy Days, Luxembourg, 2008

Death Destruction & Detroit II, Berlin, 1987

Einstein on the Beach, New York City, 1976

Les Fables de La Fontaine, Paris, 2004

T.S.E.: come under the shadow of this red, Gibellina, Italy, 1994

Things have a life of their own, you only have to awaken their souls[1]

Improbable Ancestors I

"Would I find La Maga?"[2]

Why would I keep transforming in my mind a Uruguayan-in-Paris singer of Hugo Wolf songs into a Texan sometimes-in-Paris admirer of Richard Wagner, Lucía (the singer's real name) into Robert, La Maga into El Mago, the opening question of Julio Cortázar's experimental novel *Hopscotch* into the opening of this book on Robert Wilson?

Perhaps because it is my language, literature, the one I know how to speak. And yet I know there is something there. Robert Wilson has read *Hopscotch*; he liked it. Hopscotch, a child's game. A hopscotch is a structure. Ten rectangles. A journey from 1 to 10, a desire from 1 *for* 10. In most of the Western world, 1, the point of departure, is Earth and 10, the longed-for point of arrival, is Heaven. Flat on the ground, horizontal, it is nonetheless a vertical journey. A metaphysical child's game.

"For me a horizontal line is space, and a vertical line is time," Wilson says. "It is this cross of time and space that is the basic architecture of everything."[3] When offered an American ballet company, George Balanchine famously responded, "But first a school." Robert Wilson says, "But first a structure."

The father can be guilty instead of the mother in a Wilson piece. It doesn't matter. Ivan Nagel says that you can change the story in Wilson's work, but not the structure.

•

Wilson: "Balanchine is a classical choreographer, so everything is based on classical pattern and mathematical analyses that are classical in their construction. One of the things that fascinates me about Balanchine – if you see Balanchine, you see 17 women standing in a line and you think they are all doing the same step, but no; if you see it long enough and look close enough, you see that each one is slightly off the beat. And if you take one of the last works he did, *Mozartiana*, the compositions are very simple. You've got five girls, two girls, one girl. The mathematics are very, very simple, like Mozart or like Shakespeare. I mean you look at Mozart's *Magic Flute*, and it would seem very simple, but it's very complex. If I or anyone else tried to do something with such simple mathematics,

1
These words are spoken by the world-wandering gypsy, wizard and sage, possessor of secret knowledge, all-knowing writer of prophecies, for some magician, for all and above all the repository of time, past, present, and future – Melquíades, – on the opening page of Gabriel García Márquez's celebrated novel, *One Hundred Years of Solitude*, Gregory Rabassa, trans. (London: Picador, 1978), 9. Translation MAS.

2
Julio Cortázar, *Hopscotch*, Gregory Rabassa, trans. (New York: Pantheon Books, 1966), 3.

3
Robert Wilson, "From a Distance," interview with Margery Arent Safir, in *Balanchine Then and Now*, Anne Hogan, ed. (Lewes: The Arts Arena and Sylph Editions, 2008), 111–19. Unless otherwise indicated, all Wilson quotations are from this interview.

The Threepenny Opera, Berlin, 2007. Traute Hoess and Jürgen Holtz

St. John's Passion, Paris, 2007

the CIVIL warS – Knee Plays, Minneapolis, 1984

it would be boring. The classics are...the avant-garde. The avant-garde is rediscovering the classics, so you're rediscovering what you were born knowing. Socrates said the baby was born knowing everything, and it's the *recovery* of knowledge that's the learning process.... [I]n the 1960s, we thought Balanchine was revolutionary, but he's a classic. Man has always been discerning the same mathematics....The only things that remain over time are the classics."

•

The first volume of this series was on Balanchine, and Robert Wilson himself contributed to it. Balanchine surrounded himself with people who spoke his language; but still, they were all dancers. What stands out in this collection is how little the individuals have in common aside from Robert Wilson and how much in common their observations of Robert Wilson have. John Rockwell says that whether Wilson is director, set designer, or lighting director, his is the dominant voice in a production. It is said often that whatever Robert Wilson touches becomes his work; it is possible that this book, despite other intentions, is yet another example.

•

Ah, but it's precisely that vampirism, that charming, genteel, intelligent vampirism that delights and fascinates. One can go back and find things very early in Wilson's life and career that already look like Robert Wilson; some of it his, some not. Sacha Goldman shows pictures of Wilson's first home and its garage in Waco, Texas. It is astounding to see this small town garage of Wilson's childhood already looking like a Wilson stage set: Of course the other way of putting it is that Wilson's stage set re-creates the garage in Waco, Texas. Somehow, it's more fun to imagine the garage existing because Robert Wilson drew the picture, a kind of Kabbalistic logic with images in the place of words and numbers. The garage in Waco *is* because Wilson imagined it. In Jorge Luis Borges's short story "Tlön, Uqbar, Orbis Tertius" what began as a man-made fantasy of another planet ends up invading our reality. "Things have a life of their own," Melquíades would have it. "You only have to awaken their souls."

Everyone in Waco saw that garage, but only Wilson carried it with him and transformed banal matter into the stuff that dreams are made of. The magic is in the transformation, seeing what we all see but seeing it in a different way, taking it deep inside the self and transporting it outside of its habitual context so that we can see it as he sees it: Perhaps to him, what he sees is simple reality, whereas to us, who must learn to see, it is magical. That's what magical realism is.

•

Improbable Ancestors, II

"Oh, let me come in, let me see some day the way your eyes see," Horacio Oliveira says of La Maga. Oliveira is an Argentine writer in Paris who has come to understand that what he is looking for cannot be found in books. "There are metaphysical rivers," he tells us. "I describe and define and desire those rivers, but she swims in them....And she doesn't know it, any more than the swallow."[4] I don't assign such innocence to Robert Wilson; but still he swims in those rivers that the rest of us can only talk about, or at best watch, resigned, looking out from the shore. That's one of the reasons why speaking about Robert Wilson and his work is difficult. Serge von Arx says, "It seems almost contradictory to write about it." The journey may be doomed to failure, but what fun and how many beautiful sights along the way: islands of images sitting in the midst of those metaphysical rivers, saying it all and graciously tolerating our more inadequate means of doing so, trapped as the rest of us are in a binary language, where the weakness of reason is inevitably, and sadly, still called "madness."[5]

•

Along the way in *Robert Wilson from Within* we meet a giant frog, a revisionist Wizard of Oz, a child magician, a Buddhist teacher, a giant-eater, a great theater artist, an artist *tout court*. All of them are Robert Wilson, of course. All of them, even added together, are not all of Robert Wilson. "Ay, there's the rub," as Hamlet, one of Wilson's appropriated stage characters, might say. Wilson, for *nous les autres,* the rest of us, and perhaps for Wilson himself, is something phenomenological in that he is, yes, a phenomenon/phenomenal, but also in that he is an experience. He is to be lived more than talked about or studied, which might explain what he's doing in live theater. "Why wear glasses if you don't need them?" Oliveira tells the book-challenged La Maga.[6]

I look at Wilson's stage and I hear Cortázar's definition of the fantastic: viewing through the interstices, the cracks, in everyday reality. A coffee pot boils at the same time that the doorbell rings and a cat is run over, and in that conjuncture, something – for an instant – becomes visible, something that may have nothing to do with the coffee, the doorbell, or the cat: Another dimension of reality opens its doors, and, if we are fortunate, allows us to catch a glimpse of its messages. Sadly, it is only an instant. The doors close (or the curtain falls) and we return to our impoverished binary vision of the world. "And yet," Cortázar concludes, "I will never put in doubt the reality of the messages."[7] Even if we cannot grasp that rainbow and keep it in our hand, how much more beautiful the world is knowing that it's there. Even if the rainbow hides a razor's edge.

POEtry, Wilson's work with Lou Reed, is based on the horror-filled and fascinating life and work of that master of the grotesque and arabesque, Edgar Allan Poe who, like Wilson, is revered as a genius in France, and often ignored or misunderstood in his native America. When I think of Wilson I think of Poe, a most brilliant intellect and imagination constantly

4
Cortázar, 96.

5
Ibid., 75.

6
Ibid., 25.

7
Julio Cortázar, "The Present State of Fiction in Latin America," Margery Arent Safir, trans., in *The Final Island*, Jaime Alazraki and Ivar Ivask, eds. (Norman: University of Oklahoma Press, 1978), 30.

fighting the battle between double-edged extremes, both seductive and terrifying: order and chaos or reason and madness, which is much the same thing. His imagination, unbridled in the content of his stories, is reined in by the strict rigor of his prose and his dramatic construction. One can almost feel the reins' taut pull. The attraction of the void and the terror of the abyss. There is in Poe the terror of truly letting go and of unleashing the demons, and thus the need constantly to tame them. Everything gets reduced to what can be grasped by the mind, controlled, whether the unfathomable distance to the moon in Poe's hoax "Hans Pfaall" or the size of the universe in his cosmology *Eureka*. At a time when astronomers and cosmologists still debated about a finite or infinite universe, Poe declares the universe finite, necessarily. The terror would be too great the other way. And for Wilson? Borges credits Poe with being the father of the detective story, others the father of science fiction, both genres about discovery and imagination. Borges says that no one of Poe's stories is flawless, but that taken as a whole the work of Poe is the work of a genius.[8] And Wilson?

In art, "grotesques" are ornamental arrangements of arabesques interwoven with garlands and small, fantastic human and animal figures, often designed in symmetrical patterns around an architectural framework. In fiction, characters are usually considered grotesque

8
Jorge Luis Borges, "The Detective Story," in *Selected Non-Fictions*, Eliot Weinberger, ed. (New York: Penguin Classics, 1999), 498.

POEtry, Hamburg, 2000

POEtry, Hamburg, 2000

if they induce both attraction and repulsion. Satan, the most beautiful angel: Even Milton learned that the villain is always the most interesting character. Theater of the Grotesque refers to an anti-naturalistic school of Italian dramatists, writing in the early 20th century, who are often seen as precursors of the Theater of the Absurd. Grotesque implies the incongruous, from which is born its strangeness: the coming together of extremes: "On his stage the bliss of immersion and the horror of the void cohabitate," Nagel writes of Wilson.

The tension between beauty and loss, thus the grotesque. The giver of life is the agent of death: the exquisite figure of Sheryl Sutton moving slowly across a stage with a knife in her hand and the unimaginable silent murder of two children in Wilson's *Deafman Glance*. The double-edged blade once more: the mingling in one thing of both birth and death, wherein even water (like mother), necessary for life, can suddenly turn on life, become a danger, drown and swallow life, turn life into death. The tension is in the underlying current, the knowledge that the blade *is* double, and that in a fraction of a second it can switch sides. Wilson admires Richard Wagner, in whose works beauty and death often ride together. For much of his life Wagner dreamed of writing a Buddhist opera with the story of Prakriti and Ananda. He was never able to complete it. Perhaps he failed because in the Buddhist love story, there is no tragic meeting of the extremes of beauty and loss; there, loss instead leads to the greater beauty of illumination.

The meeting of extremes: Isn't this among the things that Wilson loves in Marlene Dietrich?

"I was 27 years old and having dinner with Marlene Dietrich," Wilson recounts, "and she was 71. I took her to a restaurant, and a man came to the table and said, 'Oh, Miss Dietrich, you're so cold when you perform,' and she said, 'But you didn't listen to my voice.' The difficulty, she said, is to place the voice with the face. She could be icy cold with her movements, but the voice could be [*Wilson's voice drops*] very hot. That was her power."

"Without time, there is no space," Wilson likes to remind us. Poe understood. Astronomer Edward Harrison in his book *Darkness at Night* credits Poe with being the first to come up with the correct answer to Obers's paradox. The paradox: If the universe is filled with stars, why is it dark at night? Because the stars are immensely distant, and their light has not yet reached us, Poe conjectured in 1848: space and time, inseparable.[9]

If for Poe, poetry is born of mathematics,[10] Wilson's exacting precision gives birth to such beauty as takes our breath away. In order to see the world, you have to stand it on its head and look through the other end of the kaleidoscope, Horacio Oliveira says. You make something to then destroy it, Wilson says. You have to kill something before it can be reborn, Oliveira says; all of Edgar Allan Poe's prose work is about making and unmaking, whether an alibi or a universe. Therein lies the tension, and the grotesque, and the perversity. The perversity of simultaneously doing and undoing, of constructing and undermining the foundations of the construction, a kind of positive perversity. And Wilson?

"Think about it," the wonderful Ruth Glöss's – the fool-jester in *Shakespeare's Sonnets* – impish smile might say.

•

Robert Wilson says: "Baudelaire said, 'Genius is childhood recovered at will.'"

Baudelaire translated into French the prose works of Edgar Allan Poe. Cortázar translated them into Spanish.

"And I think part of the genius of Balanchine," Wilson says, "is you always see the little boy in him, the curiosity."

9
Edward Harrison,
*Darkness at Night:
A Riddle of the Universe*
(Cambridge, Mass.:
Harvard University
Press, 1987), 148.

10
Edgar Allan Poe,
"The Philosophy of
Composition," in
Poe: Essays and Reviews
(New York: The Library
of America, 1984),
27–32.

Wilson, like Poe, can be funny, very funny. Cortázar can be funny. Like the kaleidoscope, it all depends from which end you're looking. In *Hopscotch* we meet the Uruguyan philosopher, Ceferino Pirez, a sort of Linnaeus of the New World, who classifies and reorganizes "reality" into corporations. The sole criterion: color. Thus under the auspices of the National Corporation of Commission Agents for Species Colored in Yellow, one could find a banana, a yellow Volkswagon, people of the "yellow" races, etc.[II] The way one looks at things, the criteria by which they are viewed, defines them, and those criteria are arbitrary. The base of 10 in mathematics corresponds to no material necessity. It is arbitrary. Why are words seen to form meaning rather than sound or music, or even visual pleasure?

•

Zeno's second paradox demonstrates the impossibility of motion via the fable of Achilles and the Tortoise. Against all expectation, Zeno posits, the swift Achilles can never reach the Tortoise, who has been given a head start to compensate for his slowness. Because before Achilles, starting at point A, can reach the Tortoise at point B, Achilles must first go half the distance between A and B; but before he can go half the distance, he must go one quarter the distance, and before he can go one quarter of the distance, he must go one eighth of the distance, and before...*ad infinitum.* The principle of infinite division theoretically makes movement in space impossible. All of Zeno's words are true, and his logic irreproachable. The paradox comes in the fact that these "truths" lead to an outcome that is utterly false when confronted with material reality of time and space: We can move forward, Achilles can reach, even pass the Tortoise.

Infinite division is what Wilson does with time and space. Wilson's "slow" motions are in fact made up of millions of instances of rapid movement, a kind of theoretical division of slow into fast using the concept of infinite division, consciously or not. It is as if Wilson sees every one of them (the instances) and also asks us to. This is one of the inhabitual "takes" on reality that he proposes. Another is light, wherein infinitesimal changes change everything. Even speech, its syllables and accents divided in unexpected ways, its running on and repetition, small alterations that transform intelligible speech into noise, chains of phonemes of which every now and then we catch an intelligible phrase, as in the books in Borges's Library of Babel; as in the genetic code of which we are made.

Laurie Anderson does not think that Heisenberg and fellow quantum physicists have anything to do with Wilson. I believe they have something to do with almost every avant-garde movement coming out of the interwar period, Dada, Surrealism, the interpretation of dreams, the liberation of the unconscious. Even Wilson's oft quoted "without time there is no space," is a reference to Einstein's relativity theories (1905 and 1915). Power to the observer (audience) – "meaning" is not in something, but is determined by the observer in his decision of how to measure it. It is possible to act both like a wave and a particle, which in theory are opposites. Classical Newtonian cause and effect is replaced by Heisenberg's probability. What we can know is limited, and these limitations are inherent in nature:

II
Cortázar, op. cit., 517.

Deafman Glance (video), New York City, 1981. Sheryl Sutton

DiaLog/Curious George, New York City, 1980. Robert Wilson and Christopher Knowles

St. John's Passion, Paris, 2007

Relative Light, Valencia, 2000

Overture to the Fourth Act of Deafman Glance, Hamburg, 1977. Robert Wilson

We can no longer calculate causality for the movement of any given particle, but only the probability of where it might be or go. These are concepts so radical that even the scientist Wilson names, Einstein, refused to accept them, and suffered that some of the theories rested on his very own. "God does not play dice," Einstein famously said, unable to accept the randomness and chance of the subatomic universe. But Einstein was wrong. Quantum theory changed the way we view the universe. It brought and demanded another way of seeing. It, like Wilson's theater, recognizes the invisible, the minute, the infinitely small particles of which the visible world – or movement – is made. This is not, of course, to suggest that Wilson is Wilson because he spent his childhood reading Niels Bohr and Werner Heinsenberg, which he certainly did not. But there is what the writer Severo Sarduy would call "residue," not cause and effect, but a kind of subterranean coincidence between two movements not related in time.

•

Wilson deconstructs in his refusal to assign meaning (Derridian deconstruction), or as Glass says, "The content is not in the work but is culled by the transaction between the work and the audience." Wilson also deconstructs in taking the parts out of the whole. Ears are ears and eyes are eyes and hands are hands. This is a variation on taking things out of their habitual context. Or rather, treating each part as a whole of its own. When Wilson tells lead singers that they are no more important a part of the opera than anyone singing in the chorus, it goes both ways: Anyone singing in the chorus is as important a part of the whole as the lead singer. For every part that Wilson frees, he never loses sight of the whole, and that whole is both exquisitely beautiful and holds on to something primitive in us: "My theater," Wilson has said, "is, in some ways, really closer to animal behavior. When a dog stalks a bird his whole body is listening....He's not listening with his ears, with his head; it's the whole body. The eyes are listening."[12] As Glass puts it, "It's a state of attention."

•

"You had to be there."

In Théophile Gautier's *Capitaine Fracasse*, about a roaming theatre company, the bedraggled, empty-stomached troupe of actors arrives at an inn, where the innkeeper, Maître Chirriguirri, lays before them with a flourish of adjectives and mouth-watering detail a description of his wild boar with smoked pistachios, venison paté, duck liver terrine, ham with croutons dipped in the finest goose fat, Ambrosion cabbage, suckling pig, new potatoes roasted to a golden brown....And the desserts! When his guests are in full salivation, the innkeeper announces that these gastronomic treasures are no more. "What a shame you weren't here yesterday!"[13]

Why does everyone end up writing a love letter to Robert Wilson? Why does everyone speak in the same superlatives? And when you ask them why a work is so great, why do they say,

12
Robert Wilson and Fred Newman, "A Dialogue on Politics and Therapy, Stillness and Vaudeville," The *Drama Review* 47, no. 3 (Fall, 2003), 120.

13
Théophile Gautier, *Le Capitaine Fracasse*, (Paris: Gallimard, Folio, 1972), 90–91. Translation MAS.

like Chirriguirri, "You had to be there"? And, of course, "there" was yesterday. I accept the answer: What irritated me at the start of this book – the inability of those who had been "there" to reconstruct "there" for me – I have become part of, and am resigned to my fate. It took not only the whole course of putting together this book, but also a new Wilson production for this to happen. Things have a life of their own, and they show themselves when *they* desire.

On July 25, 2010, I traveled to the Spoleto Festival to see Wilson's *Shakespeare's Sonnets*, played to music by Rufus Wainwright. In every way – conception, imagination, sets, costumes, staging, acting – the show was spectacular. It left one speechless. Until then, like many others, I agreed with Wilson, who considers *The Threepenny Opera* one of the most interesting pieces of work he has done in years. To the degree that Wilson's *Sonnets* are pure creation unbridled, they surpass even *Threepenny*. Brecht's text and Weill's songs give *Threepenny* a narrative, like it or not. But Shakespeare's sonnets give no narrative to this "plotless ballet." The sonnets are there, an element, one might argue a pretext, but not a narrative. A then-87-year-old woman, Inge Keller, was Shakespeare, Jürgen Holtz, who once worked with Brecht, was Queen Elizabeth I and II, Anke Engelsmann, a male Secretary, the then-82-year-old Ruth Glöss, the Fool, not to mention the chubby flying Cupid, Georgios Tsivanoglou. They looked like cartoon characters. At times, rather than being in Elizabethan England, one felt as if he were in some distant future, for instance when three identically dressed-in-white and white-faced pages stand beside three immense white "gasoline pumps" whose numbers start spinning as each respective page sings, almost like a pinball machine lighting up as the ball hits the pin (Sonnet XXIII). *Sonnets* makes clear why Wainwright insists that the French word "spectacle" suits Wilson's work more than "show."

And yet if you ask me to tell you about their *Shakespeare's Sonnets*, I will undoubtedly reply, as did those before me whom I pressed about *Deafman Glance* and *Einstein, the CIVIL warS* and *Stalin*, "You had to be there." It is, in fact, the only answer. Words, even in the most articulate of mouths, will not reproduce, or even communicate, the sheer wonder that was. The fairy godmother waved her wand and the pumpkin became a carriage; Tinker Bell sprinkled stardust on us, and we could all fly. The spectacle played on us, the audience: We were liberated by it, transported to another time in life when such flights of fancy were our dreams. Somewhere over the rainbow, Dorothy and Rufus. This was experienced deeply within each of us in a personal way. It is with resignation, then, but greater humility and tolerance towards those I had questioned about Wilson's early work, that I have accepted the inadequacy of language to transmit the experience.

The 16th-century mystical poets Saint Teresa of Avila, Fray Luis of Leon, and Saint John of the Cross wrote in Spain shortly before the time that Shakespeare composed his sonnets in England. Reaching mystical union with the divine, the mystics would return to those around them unable to communicate the experience. This was a great age for metaphors: To try to make their voyage understood, the poets were forced to invent metaphors and similes – "it was like, it was as if..." – that might translate a beyond-language experience into language, a battle by definition lost before the start.

Would I find El Mago?

To the degree that an absolute singularity cannot be apprehended or even accessed by the mere mortal, who inevitably comes face to face only with his own mirror image, human consciousness, this book is a failure. Had it been able to catch Robert Wilson in words, or even in still pictures, the creator would be just a man, as Cortázar put it: hopscotch, Heaven and Earth on the same dirty sidewalk. The measure in which this book fails is to the greater glory of its subject.

A daring in sharing whimsical visions and deep fantasies, a generosity in sharing a vision and a cleverness in not sharing all and keeping the mystery: ecstasy, beauty, made sharper by contrast, an undercurrent of peril, at the same time improvisation in the formal perfectionist, playfulness, the sudden break out of song and dance, or a Charlie Chaplin-Buster Keaton smile. What else can one do? Defeat, like triumph, must be accepted with dignity. And, joyfully, Wilson has defeated us all. Things have a life of their own.

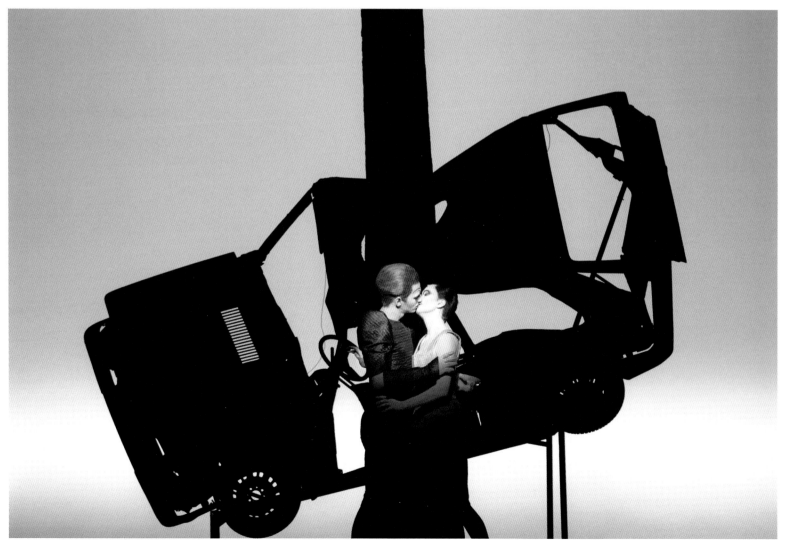

Shakespeare's Sonnets, Berlin, 2009

The Threepenny Opera, Berlin, 2007. Ruth Glöss and Stefan Kurt

Stefan Kurt

Shakespeare's Sonnets, Berlin, 2009. Jürgen Holtz

Robert Wilson from Within, points of entry

Wilson is not everyone's cup of tea, or even wild boar with smoked pistachios. His productions are boring, repetitive, beautiful but superficial, overly mannered, cold, and identical one to the next, we are told. But the contributors to this book are part of Wilson's aesthetic world, and nearly all have worked with him closely, thus *Robert Wilson from Within*.

There are those who have known Wilson "forever" from the downtown New York art scene of the 1970s: Bob before he was Robert Wilson. There are those, usually non-Americans, who had heard of Wilson through avant-garde theater circles and made determined efforts to see his work for themselves. And there are those who came to know Robert Wilson later, when he was a full-fledged international star, acclaimed just about everywhere for just about everything (art, drama, direction, design, etc.). There are two contributors who have yet to meet Wilson.

Ages range from 27 to 81: a Chinese dissident and an Italian living in Paris, a Swiss architect living in Oslo, Frenchmen in Milan or Paris, Germans living in Berlin or in New York, a German of Hungarian origin living in Hamburg, Americans living in New Haven, Paris, or Vancouver, a Canadian living in New York, two Dutchmen and a British citizen. They are filmmakers, a scenographer-architect, choreographers, artists, academics, fashion designers, costume designers, actors, producers, a patron of the arts, singers, musicians, and composers from contemporary classical to electro-acoustical to pop and rock. Some wrote essays; others I interviewed and introduce with a preface. Still others sent a short thought, a memory, or a story. Some say *Die Zauberflöte* and some say *The Magic Flute*. I have left the voice of each author in tune with him- or herself, with no attempt to impose a uniform "style."

Among all these differences, there is yet a deep structure. "Of course," one can say. "Robert Wilson is a common denominator among them." True, this is a self-selecting group. Still, in choosing at times to ask the same question of different people, I was not expecting to hear the same responses, and, in the end, what came to fascinate me was this abstract meeting ground wherein Robert Wilson becomes a kind of lingua franca. Wilson has surrounded himself with a variety of people of exceptional quality, each of whom has a profound sense of who Wilson is and what he does. They understand his language, while each still speaking his or her own.

Wilson on Balanchine: "In his formalism, his distancing presentation of works, he never got too close to interpreting works because in the formal theater there's a distance, so you have a place for reflection. And you don't interpret. You say, '*What* is the work?' and you don't say what a work *is*. A great artist says, 'What am I saying? What *is* this?,' and a bad artist will *tell* you what it is. A bad teacher would lecture you and tell you the meaning of something, and it doesn't work as well as if he asks you a question."

In order to give full aesthetic value to the photographs in this book, we have kept captions to a minimum: the title of the work, the place and date of performance, and where relevant to content, the names of actors. Photo credits and a catalogue raisonné with complete production information are found at the back of the book.

Rehearsal for *The Black Rider: The Casting of the Magic Bullets,* Hamburg, 1990. Robert Wilson

Rehearsal for *The Threepenny Opera*, Berlin, 2007. Robert Wilson

Yvonne Rainer

Earliest memory of a Robert Wilson production:
Picture a space like a corridor, wide enough to
accommodate three chairs in about eight rows.
We are looking straight ahead at a shade rolled
down over a window. Beside it is seated Robert
Wilson. The overhead lights are on. It is night.
Wilson reaches over to grasp the pull-string of the
shade, and to the bombastic strains of *Thus Spoke
Zarathustra*, he attempts to raise the shade. But
the shade has a faulty spring and will not cooperate.
He struggles, with only minor success, to raise
the shade. The music lumbers on. It is hilarious.
It must have been around 1970, possibly earlier.

DiaLog/Curious George, New York City, 1980

Madama Butterfly, Paris, 1992

Staging painterly visions

November 1992

> This essay was originally published in *The New York Times* on November 15, 1992,
> when Rockwell was the paper's European cultural correspondent. It is followed below
> by Rockwell's 2011 Post Scriptum.

"When I was young, I did a children's play," Robert Wilson recalled recently. "I had ten
10-year-old boys wrapped in Saran Wrap so tight they had only one finger free. After five
minutes, one of the mothers screamed, 'Mothers should take their children off the stage.'
Afterwards, my father said, 'Son, not only was that thing absurd, it was sick.'"

There are those who have the same reaction to Wilson's mammoth theater pieces today; at
every Wilson performance, some people can be counted on to walk out, huffily. Sometimes
half the audience does, especially in his native United States. But those who stay, stay to
cheer. Enough have cheered so that Wilson can be considered this country's – or even the
world's – foremost vanguard "theater artist," a term that almost seems to have been coined
for him.

Over his 25-year career in the theater, the 51-year-old Wilson has defined a new kind of hybrid
stage work, one that combines glacial movement, painterly visions, stylized articulation of
text or song and – especially when he isn't reinterpreting the classics and is creating new
work of his own – a bizarre, post-modern, neo-Surrealist world view. Within the universe
of avant-garde theater, at least, the term "Wilsonian" means something almost as distinct
and original as "Brechtian."

Wilson's astonishingly copious output is now produced mostly in Europe, with only occasional pieces seen here. Abroad, Wilson looks like the archetype of what Europeans prize in
American renegade movie actors, jazz loners, minimalist composers, and oddball authors:
a natural genius, an untutored eccentric who brings something fresh and uncompromised
to the jaded European palate. He even comes from a legendary American state, Texas,
to boot.

But his refusal to conform to mainstream conventions scares many Americans, unsure
of their high-art credentials. His own work – from the 12-hour *The Life and Times of Joseph
Stalin* in 1973 to the five-hour *Einstein on the Beach* in 1976 to the uncompleted day-long
the CIVIL warS: a tree is best measured when it is down of 1984 – is austere, stylized and,
usually, protracted. It clashes with the staid, loosely naturalistic conventions of Broadway,

films and television: A self-contained, more-than-three-hour act of *the CIVIL warS* was recommended for a Pulitzer Prize by the jury for drama, but rejected by the Pulitzer board. His interpretations of classics can seem willful and bizarre. His biggest, and hence best, works are enormously expensive to produce, both in terms of scenic requirements and especially in the huge amount of rehearsal time that Wilson demands.

Now, however, even in the teeth of the current recession, Wilson's American prospects may be improving. Houston is becoming one American base, with a well-regarded production at the Houston Grand Opera of Wagner's *Parsifal* in February (first seen in Hamburg, Germany) and a new association with the Alley Theater that this fall involves a Wilson production of Georg Büchner's play *Danton's Death*. Near New York, his official residence since 1962, he is building a museum, workshop, and residence in Water Mill, Long Island.

This summer, his staging of a Gertrude Stein play, *Doctor Faustus Lights the Lights*, acted by drama students from the eastern part of Berlin, was done at Alice Tully Hall in Manhattan as part of Lincoln Center's Serious Fun festival. And on Thursday, a second revival of *Einstein on the Beach*, his pioneering post-modernist collaboration with the composer Philip Glass that counts as his most famous work, will reappear at the Brooklyn Academy of Music.

"I don't want to be an expatriate," Wilson says plaintively in the coldly impersonal apartment he had taken for the Hamburg *Parsifal* rehearsals. "I'm an American, and I want to keep my American roots."

As a "theater artist," Wilson is a stage director and also (perhaps pre-eminently) a set and lighting designer. For the last decade, he has played those roles in the staging of dramatic and operatic classics and in modern repertory, including plays by Marguerite Duras of France and Tankred Dorst and Heiner Müller of Germany, an opera by the Italian Giacomo Manzoni and an *Orlando* monologue masterfully compressed from Virginia Woolf's novel by the European-based American novelist Darryl Pinckney.

He has also created his own work, but his way of creating and collaborating is most unusual. Wilson is not a writer (except for occasional neo-Dadaist scenes) or a composer or a chore-ographer, yet he remains the dominant force in any production.

"Collaboration is very personal," says Jennifer Tipton, the renowned lighting designer who has chosen to work regularly with Wilson – the set designer John Conklin has made the same choice – when she could be earning more elsewhere. "I've learned a lot from him, and I hope he's learned from me. But my work with him is in no way my work."

Even his "dead collaborators," as one could call Shakespeare, Mozart, and Wagner, are bent to his sensibility. Thus a Wilson staging of, say, *King Lear* is hardly the one *King Lear* you would like to pass on to your grandchildren (among other novelties, Wilson cast an

Danton's Death, Salzburg, 1998

Parsifal, Hamburg, 1991

Danton's Death, Salzburg, 1998

80-year-old German actress, Marianne Hoppe, in the title role). But as a statement in itself, a challenging clash of sensibilities across the centuries, it was fascinating.

Wilson blithely evokes canonical figures to justify his single-minded fixations: the dinosaurs, earthquake chasms, and elongated chairs that recur from production to production. "Proust said he was always writing the same novel," Wilson says. "Cézanne said he was always painting the same still life. It is one body, one statement. But laws are made to be broken, too. You build a vocabulary and then you destroy it, and out of this destruction you build a new vocabulary. The best thing is to try to contradict yourself, to find collaborators as different as, say, Tom Waits and Heiner Müller. Listening to other people helps you to find new ideas, new windows."

When left to his own devices, Wilson's projects often take on a Wagnerian grandiosity. For an artist who arose out of New York 1960s minimalism, Wilson is a true maximalist of ambition and scale: For him, more is more, so that his intimate or low-budget works, the ones usually seen in New York, seriously misrepresent his achievement. His blockbuster for the 1990s is to be a two-part operatic extravaganza with Glass. The first part, entitled *White Raven*, is scheduled for Bonn and Lisbon in 1994 and the second, *The Palace of the Arabian Nights*, is to follow a couple of years later, possibly in Paris, with the combined diptych also in Paris.

What has distinguished Wilson's theater from the very beginning, despite enormous differences of subject and collaborative participation, has been his visionary stage pictures. Even without texts, as in his early works from the mid-'60s to the early '70s, Wilson established a dream-like narrative logic through a succession of vivid images, some indebted to other artists but indisputably original in their three-dimensionality and cumulative impact. No one person could say definitively what the pictures "meant" or tell their "story," but every sympathetic observer felt sure they meant something, something personal and profound.

For example, the final tableau of his 1988 *Le Martyre de Saint Sébastien* in Paris was all in dazzling white, a heaven containing white animals and white trees against a brilliant white backdrop, with the dancer Sylvie Guillem poised ethereally at the center but with a blood-red medieval figure of Death, complete with blood-red scythe, creeping slowly across the lip of the stage. Or take an image from *Stalin*: a line of apes emerging from a dark and shadowy forest, scratching and picking at one another, then watching in dumb amazement as bright red apples rise from their paws and disappear upward, while a human couple in silver 18th-century formal dress appears from the left, the woman's parasol literally on fire as the curtain falls.

Such images stick in the memory with the force of an epiphany. Wilson himself is guarded about the religious implications of his work, and deliberately shied away from Christian trappings in his Hamburg-Houston *Parsifal*.

"For me, to work is a religious experience," he says. "But I hate the word 'religious' and I hate to see religion on stage. What bothers me about *Parsifal* is all this sacrilegious ritual when the music is religious. I tried to make the Grail scenes a private experience. Religion is inside. It's truth, in here, not some big gesture – that's just acting."

Wilson's real religion, his God, has always been light; hence his plays about Einstein and Edison, who shared that faith, and, perhaps, his initial interest in the Gertrude Stein title *Doctor Faustus Lights the Lights*. "Without light there is no space," he argues. "Light is the essential element in the theater, because it lets us see and hear. It's what produces color and emotion."

Robert Wilson is a 6-foot-4-inch man with a way of walking that oddly combines stiff reserve with sinuous, sensuous grace. His manner similarly blends grave introspection, weepy sentiment and giddy humor. He was born the son of a God-fearing lawyer and a homemaker; he has a younger sister who lives in Houston. Both his parents are dead. By all accounts, Wilson was a strange, self-possessed boy, marked for something different from what his parents might have wished for him.

Oceanflight, Berlin, 1998

A Letter for Queen Victoria, La Rochelle, 1974. Robert Wilson

The Life and Times of Sigmund Freud, New York City, 1969

At the age of 17 he was cured of childhood stuttering by a Waco dance teacher named Bird Hoffmann, who slowed down his speech and taught him to express himself through movement; in gratitude, he still calls his New York office the Byrd Hoffman Foundation (the spelling change perhaps reflects an early aspiration toward artiness). Although he spent three years at the University of Texas in Austin to appease his parents (his father was by then the city manager of Waco), his real interest was working with brain-damaged children and a children's theater group. In 1962, he quit Texas for New York to study design and the arts at the Pratt Institute in Brooklyn, where he graduated with a degree in fine arts in 1965. Although he acted in student plays and was exposed to the happenings and experimental theater of the time, Wilson thought of himself as a painter.

But something was lacking. In 1966 he suffered a nervous breakdown and spent several months as a patient in a mental institution. "I was very frustrated in the '60s," he recalls. "Then I realized I could do things on stage as a painter that I couldn't do on canvas. The stage brought together a lot of things; all the elements were there. Now I've gone back to painting, and I feel so much freer, so much more knowledgeable about myself."

His early theater, dance and performance works were both a refutation of prevailing conventions and an artistic expression of his continuing work with brain-damaged and autistic children and with chronically ill adults. In 1967 he created a slow-motion "dance" for patients in iron lungs. Important early collaborators included two teenagers, Raymond Andrews who was deaf and Christopher Knowles who was autistic.

Even though he frequently appeared as a kind of pioneer performance artist in New York in the late '60s, Wilson earned little money and had to teach and conduct workshops to support himself. His breakthrough, the work that established him as a hero with European intellectuals, was the production in Paris of *Deafman Glance* in 1971, first seen in New York earlier that year and later incorporated into *Stalin*.

"The French told me, 'You've had a phenomenal success,'" he says. "'You can work, if you want, for the rest of your life in the theater.' The offers came in. Before that, I really didn't know what to do with my life."

Proof of French enthusiasm was a $225,000 Government gift enabling him to present *Einstein on the Beach* at the Festival d'Avignon in the summer of 1976, then in Paris as part of a fall European tour and finally, in two performances arranged by Wilson, at the Metropolitan Opera House in New York in late November of that year. Its images of the scientist as innocent creator and inadvertent destroyer, of science and art on trial, of terrorism (Patty Hearst makes an appearance) and sentimental love transfixed audiences then and later in a popular recording: Glass's rippling minimalist music was also a landmark in his career. *Einstein* had a comparable success again in the slightly revised 1984 revival and again this summer and fall with the revival tour of the 1984 version due in Brooklyn this week.

"My father couldn't come to Paris in 1971," Wilson remembers. "Later, I invited him to *A Letter for Queen Victoria* in Paris in 1974. He said he'd think about it. It opened on his birthday. He arrived and left the next morning and didn't say anything about the performance and I didn't ask him. A week later, he wrote me a letter that said, 'Son, your play had great beauty and poetry.'" (Wilson's 90-year-old maternal grandmother played the title role.)

"In 1976, he came to *Einstein*. He said, 'Son, you must be making a lot of money.' I said, 'No, sir, it cost $1 million and I'm $125,000 in debt.' He said, 'Son, I didn't know you were smart enough to be able to lose $125,000.' I said, 'Dad, it was easy.' But that was one of the nicest things he ever said to me."

Over the years, for better and for worse, he has changed. For some of his early devotees, fearful that his style has hardened into mannerism, it sounds like a rationalization to hear him remark: "As you grow older, you realize that compromise is part of theater. At the time, it may seem very painful, but in the long run, you learn from it."

Beyond the move a decade ago to staging works by others, the major change in his working habits has been his switch from amateur, volunteer American actors, many of them overt disciples, to professionals, particularly an accomplished cadre of German and French actors. Another has been the decision not to produce his work himself, to avoid the endless fund raising and crippling financial obligations of the 1976 *Einstein*. There has been an increasing reliance on newly composed music and, more strikingly, a coming to terms with text.

A key to that development has been his collaboration with Heiner Müller, the (formerly East) Berlin playwright who looks and acts rather like Brecht and whose elliptical, densely

Rehearsal for *Alcestis*, Paris, 1986. Hans Peter Kuhn and Robert Wilson

layered works (notably *Hamletmachine*) enjoy a big reputation in Europe. Müller has learned from Wilson, too: Next summer he is scheduled to direct *Tristan und Isolde* at Bayreuth.

It would seem an open question just how much Wilson, who speaks only English, has really changed in his approach to words, or indeed to the craft of acting, and how intellectual he really is in his conceptualization of the classic pieces he directs. He prefers short texts, or he cuts theatrical classics radically and fills out the silences with gesture, movement, and images. And he is still a minimalist in that his designs and his philosophy of acting create a neutral backdrop against which actors simply declaim the words, avoiding traditional theatrical interpretation. Recently he has begun to employ a stiff, Japanese-style gestural language in place of naturalistic movement and articulation.

"He feels the less we inflect the line, the more impact the words and actions will have," says Annette Paulmann, a young actress whose leading role in *The Black Rider*, a popular Wilson collaboration with the rock composer Tom Waits in Hamburg, has propelled her to stardom in the German-speaking theatrical world ("She's my baby," the director remarks fondly).

Wilson is not above using psychology to elicit emotion. "An actor in *The Black Rider* was having trouble with a ballad," he says. "I asked him, 'Who do you love?' He said, 'I have my wife, but it's a mess. I do have my five-year-old daughter.' So I said, 'Sing it to her.'"

But mostly Wilson sets limits, suggests movements and then hopes the actor will fill in the blanks. As Dunja Vejzovic, a Croatian mezzo-soprano who sang Kundry in *Parsifal* in Hamburg and Houston and who is one of Wilson's more conscientious operatic actors, puts it: "Bob's language is pictures. He gives us the forms and we have to fill them with life."

Rehearsal for *Happy Days [Oh les beaux jours]*, Luxembourg, 2008. Robert Wilson

Jutta Lampe, the Berlin actress who played *Orlando* in the Wilson-Woolf monologue, says: "Bob doesn't actually direct the pieces per se. His school is his own school."

All his career, Wilson has had to contend with charges that his work is merely imagistic, merely "pretty pictures," as he once himself disparaged himself. In interviews, he would still rather sketch designs than describe intentions. Some critics see his obsession with scenery as little more than a pretentious version of the likes of Franco Zeffirelli and Andrew Lloyd Webber. But some of Wilson's actors think he is cleverer than a mere imagist. "Bob counts on the audience's knowledge of a classic," Vejzovic argues. "He uses that knowledge and plays against it."

Wilson's directorial technique is the same for all of his operas or plays. He videotapes workshops in which he answers questions from actors or singers by miming the roles on camera. As with any innovative choreographer, his own movements, spidery and intense, are almost always more riveting than any imitator's. Routine actors give rote reflections of his movements but miss his undercurrents of terror, surprise, and dark wit. The good ones build their own performances in a dialogue with his. The strongest ones, like Lampe and Guillem, blossom in the Wilson hothouse, finding in his devices liberation and inspiration rather than constraint.

It all comes down to the intuitive connection with Wilson that one performer may feel and another may not. "Look at her," Wilson says during a *Parsifal* rehearsal, pointing to one of two identically costumed Grail knights. "Look at her presence, the way the music is always inside her. That's what you need for Wagner." Or for Wilson, one might add. "The other girl, she looks like she's waiting for a bus. Dunja can be very still, and to do this kind of music, you have to start with stillness.

"Most actors are too text-oriented," Wilson complains. "The ones at the Schaubühne in Berlin are more into movement. Martha Graham said once that when you turn, the whole universe turns with you. I don't want interpretation. Pieces like *Parsifal* are so huge, so limitless, so full of ideas. As soon as you begin to narrow the interpretation, it's interesting but only that. Wagner has an inner logic. You don't need to interpret him psychologically; that only diminishes him. I look at it structurally. My idea is, If you don't know where you're going, you can't get there. For me, time is a horizontal line and space is vertical. So when Parsifal takes the lance and turns it vertically, that is time turning into space. The problem is when directors and actors think too much. Peter Sellars is too clever, too busy. I see Mozart, but I can't hear the music. In *Parsifal*, I wanted to make a space where you could hear the music. The trick is to keep it superficially simple. Theater has to be about one thing first, then it can be about a million things."

As he has matured, Wilson has developed a way of working that permits him to get an amazing number of complex new productions onto the stage every year: Four or more is normal. The system entails workshops involving either student stand-ins or the actual

Gerd Kunath

The Black Rider: The Casting of the Magic Bullets, Hamburg, 1990

Alice in Bed, Berlin, 1993

principals a year or more before the formal rehearsals begin, to help him refine his ideas. Thus, at any time as many as eight or nine productions are in various stages of development.

Alain Coblence, a French-American lawyer who is chairman of the board of Wilson's foundation, says Wilson has reduced by more than 50 percent the time he needs to achieve what he wants. Yet the director demanded and got 80 hours of rehearsals for lighting alone for the Hamburg *Parsifal*. There still wasn't enough time to light a starry backdrop he had built for the final scene and he had to play it against a blank cyclorama – an omission that was corrected by the time the production reached Houston.

Wilson's seemingly manic overachievement – dashing about the globe to meetings and workshops and productions, bowing stiffly at one premiere and then hurrying off to the next – has led to charges that he has greedily stretched himself too thin, particularly if compared to the mystical, contemplative, communal mode of working that defined his first theatrical ventures. Coblence answers the charge of greed by pointing out that Wilson negotiations involve demands for rehearsal time more than for money. Wilson receives a salary from his foundation – around $75,000 annually. He does have a sideline in his handcrafted chairs and other furniture, which are sold as art objects. But all his income from the theater, as well as the contributions of a few longtime patrons (including Pierre Bergé of the Paris Opéra and his business partner, Yves Saint Laurent), goes to the foundation and is spent on workshops and other developmental projects.

Those who admire him worry about his overextension. "He does too much, but he's a true workaholic," says Lampe. "He empties himself." Wilson believes his variety of work serves as inspiration. "When I was nine years old," he recalls, "somebody asked my mother on the telephone what I was doing and she said, 'I don't know, but he always has a lot of projects.' My father used to warn me to concentrate my energy on one thing. But it helps me to have many things going on at once; it makes things richer. It helped me to be working on *King Lear* and *The Black Rider* at the same time. It gave me different perspectives and let me contradict myself."

One problem all his wanderings have not solved is loneliness, which surely seems one reason for his longing for an American base. His closest collaborators become a source of emotional solace: Lampe remembers her initial fear of him turning into love and Wilson speaks of "the people I work with as a kind of family, even though they all have their own private lives." But that's not really enough, since Wilson, who avoids all public discussion of his private life, seems to have no steady intimate relationship and little immediate prospect of one, given his schedule.

In the meantime, the projects stretch into the future: a new *Don Juan* that has just opened in Madrid, a film with the dancer Trisha Brown, a second Hamburg collaboration with Tom Waits in December based on *Alice in Wonderland* and *Through the Looking Glass*, Mozart's *Idomeneo* in Budapest, a new play for the Comédie-Française in Paris, a Monteverdi madrigals evening produced by Milan's La Scala opera, a French version of *Orlando* with Isabelle Huppert that is then to be refashioned into Wilson's first feature film.

"Right now, I enjoy the work, I like the work, I'm in a very productive period," he says. "Ten days ago I was painting in Milan. A week ago I was talking to La Scala. Two days ago I spent the day with Phil Glass, and I just spoke with Marguerite Duras on the telephone. It's exciting for me. I know myself well enough that if I stay in one place too long, I have to move on. I think I know more people now in European cities than I know in New York. It's a very lonely life."

Post Scriptum, April 2011

Robert Wilson today is not much different from the Robert Wilson of nearly 20 years ago. He's a little older, a little grayer, a little paunchier (but so are we all), and he had (successful) back surgery not long ago.

By now, his yearly cycle is pretty set. He workshops new productions at his summer base in Water Mill, Long Island, which has blossomed into a truly lovely and workable arts center – spacious display rooms and work spaces and dormitories, gorgeous landscaping, a kind of minimalist masterpiece in its own right. The center is also the site of the annual Watermill July gala, which makes considerable money for Wilson and his foundation but also provides a lively good time for the attendees, some invited but most forking over considerable cash for admission and the chance to bid on pricey items in the auction. Wilson and his hardworking staff assemble a summer cadre of interns and artists who participate in the pre-production workshops, help prepare the gala, and pop out during the gala from behind every bush. For the rest of the year, the center is occupied by other international artists, who are chosen by a crack selection committee in the summer and who do their work in the relative calm (compared to the bustle of Wilson's own summer projects) of off-season eastern Long Island. Their performances and exhibitions crop up in the Hamptons, fulfilling one Watermill mandate, of community participation, but also increasingly in Manhattan and beyond. They also get their share of press attention – especially the sexy ones, like an opera in the Klingon language with Klingon music. It was noisy.

For the rest of the year, Wilson himself continues his restless worldwide rounds, staging as many as six new productions a year. These have included, since 1992, new original work, stagings of plays and operas, revivals, adaptations, installations, and adventures into new media.

An overview of the highlights of the new original work mostly involves collaborations, as with Tom Waits (*Alice, Woyzeck*) and Lou Reed (*Time Rocker, POEtry, Lulu*) and Philip Glass (*Monsters of Grace, White Raven*). Play stagings have included Georg Büchner's *Danton's Death, Leonce and Lena,* and *Woyzeck*; Susan Sontag's *Alice in Bed*; Marguerite Duras's *Malady of Death*; Brecht's *Oceanflight*; Ibsen and Sontag's *Lady from the Sea*; Strindberg's *Dream Play* and *Peer Gynt*; and Beckett's *Happy Days* and *Krapp's Last Tape*. His operatic productions since 1992 have ranged from Puccini's *Madama Butterfly* to Bartók's *Bluebeard's Castle* with

Schoenberg's *Erwartung* to Virgil Thomson and Gertrude Stein's *Four Saints in Three Acts* to Stravinsky's *Oedipus Rex* to Debussy's *Pelléas et Mélisande* to Gluck's *Orphée et Euridice* to Janáček's *Osud* to Weill and Brecht's *The Threepenny Opera* to Strauss's *Die Frau ohne Schatten* to Mozart's *Zauberflöte* to Verdi's *Aida* to Weber's *Der Freischütz* to Wagner's *Ring*. (He hasn't yet done Wagner's *Tristan und Isolde*, which seems an odd omission.) Yet to come, as of this writing, is an extravaganza for Taipei about the 1433 Chinese exploration of the known and then-unknown world, with more projects stretching far into the misty future.

There has been an increasing number of revivals and re-stagings of his particularly successful work, from originals and classics to adaptations (like Pinckney's ingenious transformation of Virginia Woolf's *Orlando* into a dramatic monologue for, so far, four great actresses in four languages, or Wilson's solo monologue version of *Hamlet*, acted by himself, or staged versions of Jean de La Fontaine's *Fables* for the Comédie-Française and Shakespeare's sonnets for the Berliner Ensemble). Still to come is the long-awaited revival of *Einstein on the Beach*, which hasn't been seen since 1992 and is now scheduled for a new world tour in 2012–13.

While Wilson has always thought of himself as a visual artist, his installations and explorations of new media have increased over the last two decades. *Monsters of Grace* was a not-too-successful animated film. But the *VOOM* video portraits were elaborate and compelling, each subject – usually famous or glamorous or both – posed in a theatrical setting. He's turned his hand to choreography, with *Snow on the Mesa* for the Martha Graham company and *2 Lips and Dancers and Space*, which toured Europe. Of his many installations, from department store windows to fashion shows to galleries and museums, the most striking was surely *14 Stations*, first seen at the Oberammergau Passion Play in 2000 – ostensibly about the Stations of the Cross but with a disturbing, hidden subtext linking Bavaria and its medieval ritual to Hitler and the Holocaust.

And all these account for a mere half of Wilson's projects in the last two decades alone. What does it all mean? Not much different from what I suggest in the article above. Wilson's work is still seen more often outside his native country. Central Europe remains his principal source of patronage, but increasingly countries not yet overly familiar with his trademark style have welcomed him: Spain, Greece, Portugal, Sweden, Denmark, Indonesia, Norway, Japan, Australia, Latvia, Taiwan. (Great Britain remains dubious.) Wilson has successfully anchored himself in Water Mill, but spends most of the year hastening from city to world city, fulfilling commissions and drawing creative and emotional sustenance from his family of collaborators and co-workers. It seems to satisfy him: He continues to be boldly productive, continues to come up with new ways of working, new ways of pouring his seemingly unceasing inspiration into the old flasks of classic texts and classic Wilsonian style.

Sometimes what results looks like a reiteration of the old Wilson mannerisms. But refreshingly often (I think of *14 Stations*, *White Raven*, the *VOOM Portraits*, *The Threepenny Opera* and much more), the old magic reasserts itself, sparked by new collaborators or a particularly congenial classic. There seems no reason to fear that as long as Wilson is still with us, new work of a similar quality and variety will not pour forth, unstoppably.

The Magic Flute, Paris, 1991

Unconditionally, from the start

I first met Pierre Bergé at a private reception that the French Minister of Culture, Frédéric Mitterrand, hosted in honor of Robert Wilson in the magnificent gilded apartments of Napoleon's brother Jérôme, overlooking the gardens of Paris's Palais Royal. The reception was to celebrate Wilson's production of *The Threepenny Opera*, which had just opened the 2009 Festival d'automne. Bergé was a long-time supporter of the festival, more so still of Wilson, and he, along with the festival, had produced this new work.

As President of the Opéra National de Paris from 1988–1994, appointed by President François Mitterrand, Bergé had continued a tradition of French support for Wilson's work that began with *Deafman Glance* and included the commission of *Einstein on the Beach* by Minister of Culture Michel Guy. As an institution, the Paris Opéra, of which Bergé retains the title of Honorary President, has favored Wilson's work, especially under the artistic direction of Gérard Mortier. Bergé is also a UNESCO Goodwill Ambassador and former head of the Athénée Théâtre Louis-Jouvet, where he founded its *Lundis musicaux*, which have included performances by artists such as Montserrat Caballé, Jessye Norman, and Jon Vickers. He has also produced concerts by Philip Glass and John Cage.

Together with Yves Saint Laurent, Bergé built the fashion empire under the late designer's name, and together they created, in 2002, the Fondation Pierre Bergé – Yves Saint Laurent: "I have always maintained that one must transform memories into a project," Bergé wrote, "and that is exactly what we have done with this Fondation. And so continues an adventure begun a long time ago, before we knew what destiny held in store for us."

Bergé sits on the Board of Wilson's Watermill Center, and speaks of Wilson with affection. On the 2001 Wilson production of Schubert's *Winterreise* song cycle, Bergé wrote, "This *Winterreise* has been more than ten years in the making….Those who committed themselves to this adventure are friends, accomplices: Jessye Norman, Robert Wilson, Yves Saint Laurent. They are part of my life."

A businessman who has been the director of a theater, a philanthropist and a patron of the arts who has lived at the center of a creative universe, Bergé was uniquely positioned to offer a range of insights on Wilson's work. I wanted to talk to him especially about a subject only whispered in public proclamations about the arts, but an inescapable reality: finance and funding. The website of the Fondation Pierre Bergé – Yves Saint Laurent proclaims, "Yves Saint Laurent and Pierre Bergé have supported the work of Robert Wilson since the early 1970s, unconditionally."

In his office at the Fondation, I began by asking him why, and above all, why "unconditionally"?

The Magic Flute, Paris, 1991

Because for me, Robert Wilson is if not *the* greatest contemporary theater director, certainly one of the two or three greatest contemporary theater directors. Because when Robert Wilson came to France with *Deafman Glance*, he completely changed the way that we looked at theater, that we did theater. As you know, France is a country of great theater directors. Of course, we're not alone in that: Russia has Stanislavsky, and there are foreigners like Edward Gordon Craig. In France, we've had the important theater of Jacques Copeau, a major world figure in the realm of stage direction. But Wilson's arrival made us completely rethink all of that. He brought a new reading to the theater, and particularly, I would say, to opera, where the direction of a character is now seen to be as important as his voice or the music. The character opens up; he doesn't *accompany* the music; he's not a singer who sings really well and opens his arms and says, "It's a beautiful day!" or "I love you!" It's not that. The rigor is such in Bob Wilson's direction that the singer becomes part of the work in the same way that the stage set, decor, costumes, music, and conductor are parts of the work; and that's a considerable accomplishment. It was never done before.

Before Bob Wilson, actors as well as singers were, of course, directed by directors, often brilliantly: Antoine Vitez was one of the last in France to make actors understand the text, to make them speak about it with intelligence and comprehension. Peter Brook has also been significant in that respect, but Bob Wilson has gone much farther. He has made the actor disappear, completely disappear, as a person who *plays* a text; the text is *ingrained* in him. It's remarkable, and it was completely new – it had *never* been done. We've had great set designers like Christian Bérard, great directors like Louis Jouvet, great actors at the Théâtre de Chaillot, it's true, but I think that Bob has gone beyond all other great directors to finally put actors in their place and tell them: "Get back in line; you're no more important a part of the opera than someone singing in the chorus." If you take Wilson's direction of actors alone, that's already considerable. But there is also an important aesthetic dimension to Bob Wilson's work, and there too, it's not at all an illustration, not an illustration of the particular subject at hand, nor an illustration of the play, but rather a full-fledged element in and of itself. I've had the good fortune to produce many, many things by Bob Wilson, and I have to say that, naturally, the work is new. I'm not saying that there are no other great directors who have staged Puccini's *Madama Butterfly* or Mozart's *The Magic Flute*; in fact, Peter Brook is going to stage a version at the Bouffes du Nord, as he did with *Pelléas et Mélisande* and *Carmen*, and obviously it will be very, very good. But after Bob Wilson does a piece, we have a version that remains definitive, by which I mean that we can no longer see that work with other eyes. We won't be able to. We'll never forget that work, and as good as other *Madama Butterfly*s or *Magic Flute*s that we'll be shown might be, Bob's vision will be the exceptional and definitive one.

You know, it's very simple. *Deafman Glance* was first produced in Nancy, and then came to Paris at the invitation of Pierre Cardin – it was like wildfire. The greatest French writer of the time, Louis Aragon, wrote a letter to André Breton to tell him that he had just seen the greatest show of his life. That, you know, is the truth: When the truth is there, it's there.

You did an exhibition of Jean de La Fontaine's *Fables*…

Of Bob's *Fables de La Fontaine*.

Yes, of course. What do you think attracted Wilson to this iconic French text?

It's obvious. *Les Fables de La Fontaine* speaks to children. All of La Fontaine is addressed to children – at least, it appears to be – even if it's actually an entirely different thing. In effect, it's talking heads, it's a dialogue between beasts, animals, a crow and a fox, etc. We're in the realm of childhood, where Bob is absolutely exceptional.

But it's not just *Les Fables*. Bob carries his childhood with him; it's always present in his works. Don't forget that Bob was an autistic child, and so it's quite obvious that *Deafman Glance* comes directly from his childhood. In *Butterfly*, there is a very important moment in the second act, a very long musical moment when no one sings, which is very rare in opera. It's normally a bit slow, a bit long, "a tunnel," as they say in theater jargon. Even so, Bob did something extraordinary. He took Madama Butterfly and Pinkerton's little son and had him walk around the stage and collect stones, which he put in his mouth, and all this with a great slowness, because time is very important in Bob's work, slowness is extremely

Les Fables de La Fontaine, Paris, 2004

Madama Butterfly, Paris, 1992

important. And all of a sudden, the story of *Butterfly* wasn't simply the story of a young Japanese woman, who thought she had gotten married and was called Mrs. Pinkerton, but also became the story of the little boy who is going to be taken away, who is going to lose his mother when she commits suicide. That's where Bob is at his best, because when he speaks about children, he knows what he's talking about.

> *Les Fables de La Fontaine*, the show and the exhibition, put Wilson face to face with one of the most French of all French writers. Did something emerge from the encounter? A new perspective on La Fontaine?

Yes, of course. It's all fine and well to put Bob Wilson in contact with Kurt Weill; after all, there isn't so much distance between them, nor, in an abstract sense, with Mozart, since we're talking about music there too. But with Jean de La Fontaine, one of the greatest French writers, a French writer from the 17th century – the century of Racine, Corneille, and the three unities – it's quite extraordinary to see. I don't like modern directors who do classics and decide they're going to shake things up, because in general, the work was better before. Bob, on the other hand, didn't shake things up just for the sake of it. He decided to illustrate La Fontaine's fables as a painter might. That's exactly what it was: He applied the usual Wilsonian procedures to theater, which were even more striking at the Comédie-Française. I don't have a great deal of admiration for the Comédie-Française, but no matter. For the Comédie-Française to do La Fontaine – you can't get more French than that – and to bring an American there, one who doesn't speak French, by the way – still doesn't – to treat that particular subject, that is wonderful.

> You did something similar in choosing Wilson to open the new Opéra Bastille.

Yes. I opened the Opéra National de Paris with Bob Wilson. It was only one night, and I wanted to open it exclusively with French music. All the heads of State from the world over would be there. But I didn't think that we had the time to put together an enormous production, and so I said to myself that rather than do more or less the usual thing, something fairly good, it would be better at least to come up with something of excellent quality. That turned out to be singers from all over the world, all singing French music, with Bob Wilson directing each.

> Did you encounter any resistance to that idea?

None at all.

> You've spoken of Wilson as the most modern of American directors. Is he also the most European of American directors?

He's certainly the most European American in the sense that he has immersed himself in European culture, whether it be Scandinavian, German, or French, Henrik Ibsen or Heiner Müller.

I have asked a number of people why Wilson's works are produced more often in Europe than in the United States. Marina Abramović answered me with one word. I'd like to know if your answer is the same as hers: "money."

Yes, that's my answer too. Clearly, it's the difference between a state that supports culture and private benefactors. I'm not a fanatic of state support, but, luckily, we have the state, because there are things that could never exist without it, and Bob Wilson is an example. Bob has been very fortunate in France because the state has supported him and he has also found private benefactors – it's not only me, there are others as well. But in the United States, unfortunately, as his work is radical, which is to say that it doesn't make concessions, it doesn't aim to please – let's say it as it is, which isn't hard to do: He is going to find less money than a weasel would from those elderly Park Avenue ladies. *Voilà*.

I have a great deal of admiration for Americans even considering what I just said, because I know many Americans, many who are friends of mine, whose primary motivation in being a patron of the arts is pride in their country, in their universities, in their museums, in their operas, in the cities where they live or where they were born. They are proud to leave a Poussin or a Picasso to their city's museum, and I have a lot of respect for that. Yes, American fiscal policy encourages this; it's true that it's tax deductible, but that isn't the primary motivation. In France, it is. The French are not used to being patrons. You can't appeal to people's pride in their city, or pride in the idea of art, which they don't believe in, but rather to the idea of tax-deductible. And what's more, in France, but also throughout Europe, we're used to the idea of a state budget, so the French say, "Well, I've already paid so many taxes, and there's a Minister of Culture who pays for everything, so why should I pay more?" But in the end, it doesn't matter if it's the state or a private patron. A creator is a creator, whether the money comes from here or from there, whether there is money or not, he's a creator.

You have participated enormously in the development of France's Festival d'automne, among other festivals. What role do you think festivals have today in the world of the performing arts?

Festivals today are absolutely not what they used to be or what they should be. In a different era, a festival, like the one in Salzburg directed by Mr. [Herbert von] Karajan, showed works created especially for it and had the best of the best, at least in terms of singers and music. That's not to speak of *mise en scène*; theater is a different subject. Today, the Salzburg Festival might show Richard Wagner's tetralogy [*The Ring Cycle*] in a production that was already presented in Aix-en-Provence, so they know in advance that it will be well accepted. But it's no longer the best of the best.

Real festivals, in my view, are really very rare, and that's what justifies their very high prices, because a festival like Salzburg costs a lot to produce. But as it exists today, in its current form, I simply don't agree that the Salzburg Festival should command such high prices.

I go to the Salzburg Festival as a tourist because it's so beautiful; I love Austria. And then there's the Festival de Pâques, of which I'm the creator, actually the co-inventor. Yves Saint Laurent and I have supported it since 1966, so I have to keep going. But if I didn't have that old connection to it and to Salzburg, I would not go. Even Glyndebourne, you understand, has the same problems. Everyone knows that the *Don Giovanni* done at Glyndebourne [in 1977] is an icon, a unique thing that is still sold on CD today. But now, it's the same thing as Salzburg: It's quite nice to go to Glyndebourne, to eat outside on the grass at intermission, to drink bottles of wine, but it's no longer the place where you say, "I have to go there because I won't see what they're presenting anywhere else."

> What is the difference for you, in terms of roles, in supporting a festival as opposed to supporting a specific production, such as you did with Wilson's *The Malady of Death* at the 1997 Festival d'automne, or in 2009 with *The Threepenny Opera*?

Well, I'm going to tell you: Today, I'm President of the Friends of the Festival d'automne, which is a very different role, calling for greater participation, and the Pierre Bergé – Yves Saint Laurent Foundation supports the Festival d'automne in a very major way. Before that, I financially supported the Festival d'automne *for* the production of a Bob Wilson work. Specifically for that. Not for anything else. *For* a Bob Wilson production.

> When you support a production, do you intervene in the creative…

Never! I don't have the right to do that. *Unconditionally.*

> Your personal life and your professional life have been shaped by your collaboration with Yves Saint Laurent, a master creator. Robert Wilson has collaborated often, and often with other great artists. What does it take for collaboration in the realm of creation to work?

In Bob's case, you have to "add up" creators. You can't make mistakes; he never does. When you set out to work with Philip Glass, one of the greatest contemporary musicians, you know you have paper and a match. Without a match, you wouldn't be able to start a fire, and without paper, you'd have nothing to light. You wouldn't have anything at all. So that's the true union of talent, and that's Bob.

> One would imagine that egos might get in the way and create problems.

Don't believe for a minute that everything is calm and peaceful. Of course egos create problems, but that doesn't matter at all. Eventually, it turns out wonderfully. You know, with artists, it's not at all important to know if they're going to climb up a step, then go down a step, then start down this little path or the other. The important thing is to know where they're ultimately going to go. That's the goal: Where do we go? And as of the moment they agree on that goal, they'll get there together.

Lohengrin, Zurich, 1991

Das Rheingold, Zurich, 2000

You are on the Board of Wilson's Watermill Center.

Yes. What do you want me to say about it? I think that Bob's project is fantastic, and I was the first on the Board to make a commitment to Bob for Watermill, so of course I'm deeply involved. But the creation of this kind of center is a very old concept. Stanislavsky did it, Copeau did it, Gordon Craig did it, which is to say pedagogy, surrounding oneself with people involved in the theater and making one's own kind of theater with them. And theater is, of course, concrete. It demands instruction in its totality, meaning the body, the costumes, the *mise en scène*, the acting and characterization, coordination with the musicians....Theater is monumental. It has a story all its own.

You handle the rights to Jean Cocteau's work, and, obviously, Yves Saint Laurent's. With any significant creator, there is inevitably a question of "afterwards." What happens to a great creator's work when the creator himself is no longer there?

In Bob's case, unfortunately, nothing much; very little will go on. In Cocteau's case, there was a written œuvre. In Saint Laurent's case, which is already something much more ephemeral, we still do exhibitions of his work; the clothes are there. But with theater, there is nothing, absolutely nothing, if the theatrical creator is absent or dead. You can try some things: I was very glad to hear that the Opéra Bastille was doing *The Marriage of Figaro* this year. You can, after the death of [Giorgio] Strehler, continue to produce *The Marriage of Figaro* because there are assistants who come to work on it, but it won't last for very long. Unfortunately, in theater we don't have anything. We don't have the firsthand accounts, the testimony of the people I'm talking about. We only have the accounts of their students and critics, which is very important, but it's not the same as having the artists there. The dead can't nourish or fuel anything; the only remaining thing will be a little scrap of film that people can watch, and, alas, it will be the same with Bob. The only thing that will remain is the influence he will have had in the sense that today there is a pianist who has had a teacher who was the student of the student of Liszt. So, that's what's left. Liszt is still a little present today in a different pianist. The same is true of Balanchine, people like that. Peter Martins is a lovely man, isn't he? But he isn't Balanchine. There's a moment when things fade. Of course, *Giselle* will always be produced, but it's no longer the same thing: We're no longer witness to the absolute rigor, the surgical precision, that is Balanchine's work, that is Bob's work. No. Alas, when these people are no longer around, these things vanish into thin air.

I asked Philip Glass, and later Joseph Melillo, if they thought audience reaction to *Einstein on the Beach* will be the same in 2012 as when it was first performed.

What was their response?

Yes. Glass said, "Absolutely," because today's public has grown up without having known any real creators of that quality.

I'm entirely of the same opinion, because, the more I think about it, after the death of creators like that it's finished, but while the creators are still alive, a production of *Einstein on the Beach* will not have aged, will not have a wrinkle. It will be perfectly ready for today's young audience.

Laurie Anderson said she was surprised, after having seen Bob's early work, that there wasn't a generation afterward that produced a lot of "little Bobs."

But so much the better that there aren't lots of little Bobs – there are already too many as it is and there mustn't be. Bob is a unique character. Saint Laurent is a unique character. There are plenty of people who try to model themselves after each, but none of that is relevant. That's life: Nothing else can exist around a great artist. There are other things of quality, other great directors in France who don't owe anything to Bob. There are other completely different paths. But there's absolutely no appeal in doing pseudo-Bob Wilson.

What do you see as the most important evolution in Wilson's work since you began supporting it in the early 1970s?

If you take *Deafman Glance*, as I said, you realize, "Ah, he wasn't an autistic child for nothing." He began, in a sense, as a director who addressed himself to himself, and who said to others: "If you like it, you like it, if you don't like it, you don't like it." And I think that bit by bit over the years, without making concessions, because there are no concessions to be made, Bob tamed himself and began to approach people. For me, that is Bob Wilson's evolution, because personal evolution is creation. Yes, it's true that he's moved towards classical opera, but that also has to do with what I'm saying here. If you take Schubert's *Winterreise*, for example, which he did with Jessye [Norman], you see that it's a path towards a discourse, words addressed to other people, to a group much bigger than himself. Today, Bob has begun to speak.

Translated from the French by Alexandra Schwartz.

The Malady of Death, Lausanne, 1996. Michel Piccoli and Lucinda Childs

The Malady of Death, Berlin, 1991. Libgart Schwarz and Peter Fitz

The time between fixity and motion

In July of 2010, I interviewed actress Isabelle Huppert at her home in Paris. Sixteen years earlier, on the occasion of the opening of *Une Femme douce* [*The Meek Girl*] at the Maison de la Culture de Bobigny, she had written a text about Robert Wilson, which she handed to me. Excerpts are reproduced here in translation.

The dreamer's voyage to the heart of the self, undertaken day after day in what he does, what he sees or what he hears, is what Bob Wilson has tirelessly brought to us for over 20 years.

Marvelous voyages, lengthy descents into the self, infinite crossings, miraculous dives.

With him, the theater becomes an exploration of one's self, a gamble of one's entire being, an affirmation of one's joys, pains, fears, dreams, unattainable and yet so close. An existential adventure....To undertake a journey with him is to clearly understand the mysterious connection between a director and his actor: an appreciation of each by the other and of each for the other, the feeling of knowing the other without telling him, the subtle dialectic between restraint and freedom.

....

Bob Wilson addresses each one of us with infinite attention and sensitivity, accomplishing this strange crossing through the looking glass where the watched becomes the watcher and the watcher the watched, gently lowering conventional barriers that were only erected to be lowered in the first place.

With Bob Wilson, theater becomes an inaugural gesture each night, a profound communication between elements of the unconscious that meet and begin to speak to one another. Then, sandman that he is, he gently slips away, leaving each person in the land of his own fantasies, his own dreams, at the gates to a strange world filled with shadows and light, sensual and childlike: a world all his own.

Quartett, Paris, 2006. Isabelle Huppert and Ariel Garcia Valdès

Overture to KA MOUNTAIN and GARDenia TERRACE, Shiraz, Iran, 1972

Bob and I met by chance through a common friend, Alain Coblence. Alain had invited me to a concert of some friends of his at the Paris Conservatory. I didn't really want to go, but finally I did. It was a rather unexpected way to meet someone, and even now, whenever I don't feel like going somewhere, I tell myself, "Ah, but maybe I should go because that's how I met Bob, and that was a pretty crucial meeting for me." After the concert, Pierre Bergé, Alain, Bob Wilson and I went to dinner, and Bob started doodling on the tablecloth as he often does, and he told me he was going to put on *Orlando* in Berlin with Jutta Lampe. He said that the production would most likely come to Paris. I'm almost certain he knew very well who I was, but we didn't speak about things he might have seen me in. I didn't get the impression he was meeting me as an actress; I really think he met me as a person, and that pleased me all the more. I think it was during that dinner that the idea came up that if the German production of *Orlando* didn't come to Paris, he could do it here again with me. He got in touch sometime later, and I spoke to René Gonzalez, who agreed to produce it, so we decided to put it on here. We gave ourselves the privilege of choosing the theater together, and in the end, the Théâtre de l'Odéon co-produced the show with René Gonzalez in 1993.

I knew Bob Wilson's work, naturally. I hadn't seen the great classics, the shows that revealed him to the world like *Deafman Glance*, but I had seen a remarkable piece of his that few people have seen. It was *KA MOUNTAIN* at the Shiraz festival in 1972. I myself participated in the festival with a quasi-amateur company in a show directed by Daniel Benoin, who later became a well-known theater director. We were putting on a play called *Le Champion de la faim*, based on a short story by Kafka melded with I can't remember what else – in any case, a pretty improbable piece; it was one of my first plays. We would go see *KA MOUNTAIN* every night after the show. It was seven days and seven nights long without interruption. It was cold at the top of the mountain, and we would doze off, then wake up, and the play would still be going on. It made you feel like you had suddenly fallen asleep, or that you were both awake and asleep, as in a daydream, and the impression was heightened by the unique experience of watching it at three o'clock in the morning as we did. So we would often stay through the night. We were in a kind of anesthetized state from the feeling of sleep coming on and from the dreamlike state the production itself induced, like being in suspended time or in memory.

Some time later, I saw a work of Bob's at the Opéra Comique with Madeleine Renaud, *A Letter for Queen Victoria*. Madeleine Renaud was on all fours. The performance lasted 24 hours, and we stayed there for all 24. And, of course, later when I began to work with Bob, I went out and watched everything of his. Well, actually, not everything – for that, you'd practically have to become a shareholder in an airline company! But I have seen a lot of his work, things that I just happened upon.

> People say you're Wilson's fetish actress. In your opinion, what is it about you that appeals to him?

I think that with the kind of intuition he has – Bob is quite the virtuoso magician – he reads through you. You get the impression that he really *sees* you. In any case, I think that's what happened with me. He accesses the secret language of others in a very short amount of time. In my case, he immediately sensed that I was entirely malleable, which is naturally ideal for working with him, meaning that he could ask me to do anything without needing to explain, and that I was also capable of being utterly precise, which is necessary to work with him. When working with Bob, you have to be able to listen and understand instantly what he's up to. It's more than understanding, actually. It's like entering a universe naked, without comprehending, without looking to grasp what he means. He never gives explanations.

We are obviously never dealing with the psychological realm, and even if one of the first steps in working with Bob is to extract the tone of the language and the text, the text is never envisaged literally, but rendered by way of its musicality: Meaning is constructed through rhythm and tone. It's close to the difference between abstract and figurative art, because he starts by taking the text as an abstract piece and then, by giving it different shades – not through words but through color – ends up re-endowing it with sense. I relate to that. It reminds me of a Mondrian painting, for example, which gets you to understand music or jazz solely through patches of color. Bob gets there by working the text as though it were a sound sculpture. Actors wear microphones in his performances. Sometimes we speak very loudly; sometimes the sound system stops so we have to project; sometimes we're translating a certain feeling; sometimes we're in an extremely intimate situation; sometimes we whisper, we shout, we speak slowly. But what's magical about Bob is that you get the feeling – maybe it's true, maybe it's not, I never tried to find out – that the choice of passages to whisper is completely arbitrary. It's not that he takes a pen and says, "Okay, here we'll translate literally, here we'll interiorize." It's an intuitive thing, as if he were accessing language. He's worked a lot with autistic people, as we know, and in the end you sort of feel like you're entering that world when you work with him. It's utterly mysterious.

What do you think made Wilson choose *Orlando* as a text or subject?

That I don't know, because he started working on it long before I came into the picture, using Darryl Pinckney's adaptation of Virginia Woolf's novel. But the answer's not hard to imagine. Clearly, it's a journey that deals with androgyny, a theme close to Bob's world. The story of a little boy growing up during the time of Elizabeth I in England who becomes a woman in the early 20th century. It spans the centuries. It's kind of like the story of humanity in a single trajectory.

You were alone on stage for two hours. What was that like?

I loved it. It's obviously a bit more daunting than being with others. You feel a little less secure if something happens. But in the end, you're not actually much more reassured with others around you. It's an absolutely extraordinary experience. I did it again with *4.48 Psychosis*;[1] I had a partner behind me, but he was more like a distant figure. *Orlando*

1
In 2005, Huppert starred in an acclaimed French version of Sara Kane's play *4.48 Psychosis* at BAM, directed by Claude Régy.

Orlando, Lausanne, 1994. Isabelle Huppert

was great, though, and as it turns out, I wasn't really alone: The stage was full of all the people I was meeting, or rather imagining. I was at the royal court, I was in an infinite world, and since it was minutely choreographed, everything hinged on the body language and the sound. Obviously, you're always afraid of forgetting your lines. You ask yourself, "What will happen if I don't know what to say?" But strangely, it's almost impossible to forget, as your body creates language memory: Every move my body made was associated with a word, so I never actually imagined the possibility of forgetting.

> Did it take a great deal of rehearsal time to get to that point?

We didn't rehearse that much, only for about three and a half weeks, plus a week or so of previews. Bob wanted us to play sooner than expected, and he was right. Some directors want the play to open only once it's completely ready: Claude Régy, for example, who would never allow the last step in the process of creation to take place before an audience. As for me, either way is fine, since I believe directors know what they're doing. But Bob believes that at some point, the more you play before an audience, the quicker the process will reach fruition, that a show radically transforms itself only onstage, in contact with an audience.

Bob also likes workshops a lot. They pave the way; it's largely about the body, about getting a sense of ease. For *Orlando*, we started off with a play that had already been performed. Even *Quartett* was the revival of a production he had put on 20 years earlier with Lucinda Childs.[2] Obviously, a number of things were altered for me in *Orlando* and for Ariel Garcia Valdès and me in *Quartett*, but in both cases, there was already a frame. For both plays, we did an initial workshop, and later two others before the start of rehearsals – one with Ann-Christin Rommen, who's a bit like Bob's memory – and several readings. Bob really enjoys the workshops and prefers them to arriving for rehearsals and getting to work at the last minute. It's almost like entering a very dark room and taking the time to get accustomed to the darkness: That's what the workshops are for.

2
During his profound collaboration with the German playwright Heiner Müller, Wilson created various productions of Müller's play *Quartett*, based on Choderlos de Laclos's *Les Liaisons dangereuses*. Actresses in the role of the Marquise de Merteuil have included Lucinda Childs, Miranda Richardson, Jutta Lampe, and Isabelle Huppert.

During the workshops for *Orlando*, Bob showed me three things that corresponded to the three parts of the show: in the beginning, when I'm a young page alone at court; next, in Turkey; and last, a woman during the Victorian age. For the first part, he showed me a video of Rudolf Nureyev to demonstrate the beauty of gesture, what it was to be a man who moved with that kind of grace. For the second part, he showed me a video of Tomisaburo [Wakayama], a well-known Japanese Kabuki actor and a good friend of Bob's, an androgynous performance where men play women. Several years later, I went to see a performance of his with Issey Miyake, and afterwards he took me to meet Tomisaburo. So this great Kabuki actor and I talked about Bob, because what Bob does is very influenced by Noh, by Kabuki, by all of Japanese theater. And finally, the third thing that Bob showed me during the workshop was Marlene Dietrich onstage – in one of those shows where she embodies the ultimate and perfect sophistication and femininity. It was brilliant, because nothing more needed to be said.

When you were alone onstage, did Wilson's lighting and scenery function as additional characters for you, in the sense of something playing with or against you?

In a way, yes. Still, even though it was sometimes dangerous – I had to climb to the top of this stair-like furniture with steps, then use a sword, things like that – I never felt they were playing against me. I remember *Orlando* as being more of a performance, one continuous movement. In *Quartett*, till the very end there were moments of extreme physical intensity. For example, the music by Michael Galasso was very, very loud, eerie and nerve-wracking. And I had to walk on this platform in high heels. I felt very unstable. The music was quite extraordinary and lively, but the night of the premiere, it was so loud that it ended up flooding your brain. And the lights: There was something raw about them until the end. There were moments in *Quartett* that I was happy to get through because it was stressful on the body. *Orlando* was less physically trying. It took place closer to the ground, except for that moment I had to climb up on that stair-like furniture.

Referring to your performance in *Orlando,* one critic wrote: "She brings in humor where you least expect it."

There's a great deal of humor in Bob's work, lots and lots of it, because it exists in an alternate universe, a childish and mischievous world. It's the kind of humor you'd find in the Surrealists when all of a sudden they get an idea in their heads. It's like Marcel Duchamp's bicycle wheel or like something out of Max Ernst. At *Quartett*, the audience laughed a lot, especially at the impersonation that takes place in the role-playing and gender switching between man and woman. There's a moment when I pretend to spit out chewing gum, imitating a man. After that, you can pretty much do whatever you want. In *Orlando*, we made funny faces. Bob loves doing that. All of a sudden, you distort your face; you stick your tongue out. And then, just as abruptly, an immense melancholy ensues. There is remarkable poetry going on, and in poetry there is inevitably some melancholy; it can seep through at any moment. Towards the end of *Orlando*, and also towards the end of *Quartett*, the atmosphere is saturated with melancholia and nostalgia, as if it were a lost soul who keeps recounting his story. It's like a dream about memory. At the end of *Orlando* I kept thinking back to my childhood in a very precise way, every night the same memories, always at the same moment in the play and with the same movements.

You've said that there's something close to animal behavior in what Wilson creates, something that touches the unconscious, perhaps the child, in us.

Bob's productions are like a bestiary. There's a frog, "Croaa! Croaa!" [*the French sound equivalent of "ribbit"*], dogs, a bear, the fish in *Quartett*, plenty of animals, or animal sounds, roars – which is why it was so great when he did *Les Fables de La Fontaine*. And, naturally, there's something childlike about the representation he gives of the world, which is something that Bob and I share: childlike because there's a way of moving, as children do, from one state to another, with no explanation. A child laughs and cries without transition, or the transition is an unarticulated, unconscious one, and that's what Bob does.

Do you find there is violence in Wilson's theater?

What defines Bob's theater is the magical exploration of theatricality and artifice; he has pushed this to the point of genius. But I don't see violence there. I'm sure I would feel it if it were there. Violence is present in a certain kind of realism, but with Bob, you're never dealing in realism, ever. You're always in an incredibly distanced and fabricated representation. However, there can be an immense emotional quality, for example that whole promenade passage with the little boy that Bob put in *Madama Butterfly*, which is incredibly moving. There are overwhelming moments, but they're closer to the notion of absolute beauty than to violence.

In *Quartett*, though, there's an intensity between the Marquise de Merteuil and the Vicomte de Valmont, two characters we know so well from *Les Liaisons dangereuses*, that suggests a kind of violence.

Yes, perhaps in *Quartett*, because we know a duel is taking place between a man and a woman. But the theme is Heiner Müller's. There's something animalistic about it, and the play on language is violent as well. But the violence is in the language; it's inherent to the subject matter.

What was it like to perform *Quartett* at BAM in front of an audience that didn't speak the language in which you were acting?

BAM is really like an island unto itself. There are places like that in every country. We were on tour a lot with *Quartett*; we performed in Brazil, where it was very well received. It's a bit like an opera audience that's used to seeing productions with subtitles. It had a very good showing in New York, which was very encouraging, and since I'm used to performing before foreign audiences, it wasn't all that different from performing before a German or Italian audience. And then, it's just as different performing before a Parisian public and an audience in Toulouse. All audiences are different.

That said, there are cultural differences. With *Psychosis*, where I was onstage immobile and teary, and later with *Quartett*, in the United States they said, "It's almost like performance art." In Paris they said it was theater. Bob gained recognition first in Europe, not in his own country. But it's no surprise that it should be that way. What he does is so sophisticated, so elaborate – you won't find that kind of thing on Broadway. Bob's theater is abstract; it doesn't fall under the criteria in vogue in the US, where the basic approach is much more conventional. It's all about entertainment, most of the time. And it's more realist. It still happens in the States that if I say, "I'm working with Bob Wilson," someone will ask, "Who's that?" It's unimaginable for us, because to us he's a genius. It's as though someone said they didn't know who Charlie Chaplin was.

Video portrait of Isabelle Huppert by Robert Wilson, 2006

> A reviewer of *Orlando*, after covering you with accolades – "stunning," "perfect," "exceptional," "admirable" – then asked: "Is something missing? A little tenderness perhaps, a bit of warmth, a touch of feeling…."

Well, Bob Wilson is the master of formalism. And formalism excludes a certain type of tenderness. It's as if you were asking a cat to resemble a dog. You can't ask this kind of formalist proposition to fall into what this reviewer means by "tenderness." It would be an antinomy: When you go see a Bob Wilson production, you know what to expect. That said, I do find that there's a lot of emotion in this kind of formalism, the play on lights. That tension is incredibly moving to me. Emotion is very subjective. Bob Wilson's work is never sentimental, but for me it is clearly emotional.

> *Orlando* and *Quartett* have two obvious things in common: the gender switch, and a unique way of approaching time. *Orlando* takes place over 350 years of the title character's life, and *Quartett* is set before the French Revolution and after World War III. Did you experience this "out of time" element in similar ways in both plays?

I didn't really draw that parallel between the two plays because, at least as concerns time, I do feel that the similarities result from Bob's approach. In theater, you're dealing with pure arbitrariness when it comes to temporality. Bob has a way of distorting time; he plays with this arbitrary temporality *ad infinitum* in a way that is inherent to the space of the theater. The stage is a limited space; the time of a production is arbitrary and limited itself. So instead of having a piece last two hours, you can decide it will last seven days, or bring you from one century to the next. This is exactly what Bob does. It's like he's trying to show what the constraints of the theatrical space open up to reveal. The stage, in its infinitely constrained smallness, allows for the infinitely large.

> Laurie Anderson wonders why Wilson has never made films, and you've said that he is the theater director who most closely resembles a film director. Maybe with film, where there are no constraints, Wilson could do whatever he wanted, and that is precisely why it doesn't interest him. Does it surprise you that he never made a film?

He acted in the Philippe Chemin film *The Death of Molière*, and of course he's shown a lot of interest in video work. I think he's made inroads towards film. Film is visible in his theater practice, and his use of light and sound recreate the idea of a close-up, a medium shot, a long shot. The intimate voice or whisper I spoke of earlier is an example; it's a way of giving the illusion of a close-up, as if he were getting into someone's interiority. He works with sensation, creating the sensation of a close-up or the sensation of a long shot, more than a direct use of film technique by actually putting video or screens or things like that in his productions. But he also does a lot of video, and video is also a way of questioning the intermediary point between fixity and mobility, like the magical moments in his theater when he makes people move very, very slowly. In his use of video, he undertakes the same exploration of the boundary between moments of stillness and movement.

In the *VOOM* video portrait that Wilson did of you, he pays tribute to Edward Steichen's 1928 portrait of Greta Garbo.[3] Was that his choice or yours?

No, that was his choice, as I suppose it was for all the other actors.

How did you feel about representing another actress? Was it fun, or strange?

It was fun, because the portrait is a tribute to a time when actresses fabricated their faces with a high degree of self-consciousness. Be it Marlene Dietrich or later Marilyn Monroe, it was a time when actresses created their own brand. I imagine that were Greta Garbo to be filmed in a realistic way like today, she would certainly look very different, even only by the use of color. Back then, faces were sculpted by the use of shadow and light – the shape of the eyebrows, the mouth – so it's not so difficult to enter into that picture. Of course, it also depends on your features: Mine are more angular than round, so it's easier for me to look like Greta Garbo than like Marilyn Monroe!

So for you, it was like playing another role?

Yes, although it wasn't exactly a role, and being directed by Bob on stage and for video is totally different. *VOOM* was more like a photo shoot, like taking a very long photo with a long exposure, nothing to do with the stage. But it was the same in terms of Bob's presence, something he exudes by his very nature. Bob's a very gentle person. That makes him unique compared to other directors. He never gets angry – in any case, never with the actors, sometimes with the technical staff, perhaps, because he's obsessive about the details of the production. With me, he had a kind of infinite gentleness. For the video, Bob worked on slowness. You had to lower your eyes. Then later, he slowed things down artificially even more, which makes the eye lashes fall very, very slowly over the eyes. And I stayed like that, completely immobile and slow for a long, long time, maybe 45 minutes. I know I could spend hours like that with him.

You've said on several occasions that you've never felt so free as when directed by Wilson. Can you explain what it is that makes you feel free?

Because Bob sets an infinite number of constraints, you really get the impression that you're caught in his net. But simultaneously, within all of that, you are free to tell your story as you please. I can do what I like. You get this feeling of freedom, much more so than with anyone else – I say "anyone else," because he doesn't intervene where most directors do. I can laugh when I want, whisper when I want. Bob only intervenes with technical things, with sound levels, for instance, but never with anything psychological. I can play as I choose to. At the same time, he doesn't care because he knows the constraints he's set will always rule over the rest. But within that space, the actor, I find, can exist fully and freely. He does something similar with bodies; the body becomes like rubber. You can do what you like with it.

3
Wilson's VOOM high-definition video portraits are a hybrid of still photography, moving pictures, and often, music; subjects range from celebrities to "ordinary" people, to animals. The portraits have been on world tour since 2006.

That's also noticeable in *Quartett*. You kept thrusting yourself forward while continually speaking the text, repeating the same words. That must have been difficult.

Yes, it wasn't all that easy. But you get used to it. You always have to overcome challenges. It must be even harder for opera singers. When Bob did *The Magic Flute* and he placed the Queen of the Night way up top – I love that – it's the highest voice in the repertoire, so he placed her on top of a three-meter-high column.

If you could choose to be in a production of any play directed by Wilson, which would you choose?

With Bob, it's about the work more than the play itself. *Orlando* wasn't really a play. *Quartett* – I like the play, but I wouldn't have thought of performing in it if he hadn't proposed it. Bob isn't a theater director in the sense of putting on plays written by others. That's something recent for him, and I think *Quartett* was one of the first times he did that. But it's interesting that he chose to take on [Müller's] more traditional language. I also loved *The Threepenny Opera*, to see Bob take on an already existing work. I heard that he was going to do *Lulu* with Angela Winkler. So I'm hoping he'll do it with me next. I would love that. But I'd love to do anything with him. Really, I dream of putting on *Orlando* again. I told Bob that we should revive it, and we may put it on again in Paris one day. I'd love to do it, because I'm sure it would be an immediate success again, and I'm sure I would once again think of the exact same things onstage at the same moments; that it would bring me back to the same childhood memories, the same feelings, every time.

Preface text translated from the French by Alexandra Schwartz, interview text translated by Lisa Damon.

Quartett, Paris, 2006. Isabelle Huppert and Ariel Garcia Valdès

Benoît Maréchal and Isabelle Huppert

Quartett, Paris, 2006.Isabelle Huppert and Ariel Garcia Valdès

Robert Wilson Solo, 147 Spring Street, New York City, 1974

The brain is a building[1]

147 Spring Street, New York City

In the 1960s, Robert Wilson's brain was a rundown building at 147 Spring Street in New York City that he rented for a legendary $100 per month: the "Byrd Loft," the de-facto home base for the Byrd Hoffman School of Byrds, a group of some 35 individuals who functioned as Wilson's ensemble during the early years of his career.

The Loft began on the second floor of the building that Wilson had taken over from the Open Theater group and shared with his partner, Andy de Groat. The living space was in the back, Wilson's desk and filing cabinets for the Byrd Hoffman Foundation's administrative work stashed under his bed; up front was the workspace where all of the costumes and props were made. The two spaces were hardly separated. Wilson always says that for the Japanese, the preparation is as important as the creation: Though he was constantly working on drawings, lighting plans, costume sketches, letters, and calls to potential supporters and theater critics, the space was always well organized.

All of Wilson's early work began between these walls, 25 × 75 feet, although in the Byrds's various recollections, its length ranges from 50 to 100. Rehearsals were staged between its cast iron columns, costumes and props thrown together with paper and scrap material. There was little on the walls, sometimes a production poster or something left over from a benefit auction. A photo of Sigmund Freud, the inspiration for *The Life and Times of Sigmund Freud* (often in Wilson's theater, objects serve as the basis for plays or characters) showed Freud in his study surrounded by objects from around the world. Wilson himself already owned the seeds of what would later become his huge collection of objects. The Byrd Loft had beautiful little chairs, African stools, stones from British Columbia, and an array of small objects, all carefully juxtaposed in unusual arrangements. Wilson was still too poor to collect seriously, but the interest was there.

In the early 1970s he added the first floor, building a spiral staircase to connect the two floors. A black door that he built himself opened on to the street, and the new space was like a telescope: A small room that acted as a sound and lighting booth opened onto a larger 10 × 10 foot room, which in turn opened onto the full space, complete with polished tin ceiling and wooden floors. Wilson built a mezzanine to house the office. Sixteen birch tree trunks were installed in a square in front of the door to the street, and he placed river rocks around the entrance as a welcoming gesture, the natural presence of the trees creating a weird connection between the outdoor and indoor spaces.

1

The *Mind is a Muscle,* the title of Yvonne Rainer's dance piece, has become in Wilson's mouth an iconic sentence that every actor or performer working with him has heard.

If the world is an organism, the New York of the 1960s was its pumping heart. An enormous intellectual and artistic transformation had taken place after the Second World War: Old patterns didn't work anymore, and artists came to New York to inject it with their blood. The art world seemed to be almost completely about the spaces where they met, concentrated between the Chelsea Hotel (probably the loneliest of these places) and the Clock Tower Building. Each place – the Judson Memorial Church, St. Mark's Church, the Factory – generated a certain kind of crowd and served as the epicenter of a social and artistic network of performance, poetry, literature, film, and glamour.

147 Spring Street was no different. From the Byrd Loft's earliest days, Wilson held movement workshops on Thursday evenings. Once he had rented the first floor, every Thursday night became an open house. People came from the Wooster Group and Richard Foreman's company, from St. Mark's Church, Judson Church, and the Factory. Artists such as Meredith Monk, Jeffrey Norwalk, Jack Smith, Bill Stewart, Jackie Curtis, and Gordon Matta-Clark came. None of it was planned. The door was just open. Anyone, including strangers, could walk in, and most everybody brought some food. People sat on the steps and on the street, or on chairs arranged like pews. You could watch the dancing happening on the first floor from a choir loft that doubled as a venue for musical performances. The performances and presentations Wilson happened to be working on were often featured, or he or Andy de Groat would start up some spontaneous performance or direct others. For the most part, the evenings were unstructured, artists spinning in their own orbs of freedom and creativity. No couple dancing or showing off, no walking arm-in-arm: Massages were as sexual as it would get. The music was eclectic – rock, folk, avant-garde, indigenous – and musicians from the Kitchen Center for Video and Music would drop by and perform. Other Byrds presented their individual work as well, and so did the new people who would constantly pop out of nowhere.

These open houses were vital to the development of Wilson's boundary-crossing stage movements. Wilson incorporated people like Raymond Andrews, deaf and mute, and Christopher Knowles, autistic, into his work by having the Byrds imitate their movements, and much of the dancing that went on was a spontaneous imitation of other people's way of moving. Wilson soaked up movements from these non-professionals and infused them with the more "educated" physical vocabulary of Merce Cunningham, George Balanchine, or a contemporary like Kenneth King, a member of the younger generation of Judson choreographers and one of the first to combine choreography and language.

World War II had destroyed the integrity of the family unit, and many children unable to identify with their parents' worlds left their homes and countries to create new "families," artistic ones. Most of New York's artistic epicenters were gathered around defining "parental" figures: Warhol, Foreman, and, of course, Wilson. At 147 Spring Street, Wilson set out to create the family he never had. People of all ages, interests, shapes and sizes lived and worked together, looking out for each other. The sense of a communal bond extended to the improvised sleeping quarters in the Loft's basement, separated off by curtains, which

2001

2011

The Watermill Center, Water Mill, Long Island, 2006

Robert Wilson at Watermill, 2001

would fill up when production work was particularly intense. (Jack Smith, for one, would come in the mornings to shave since his space had no hot water.) The basement also contained the kitchen and a single very long table where meals were served. On occasion, dinners were also held there for Wilson's uptown friends, the de Menils or Jerry [Jerome] Robbins, who were instrumental in raising funds to put on his shows. Everyone sat on benches and the cooking was communal, with a different person cooking every day and the others washing up. Lighting was rudimentary. "Comfort is a state of mind" is one of Wilson's chosen sentences. Watch for how many family scenes appear in his work, how many dining tables and chairs he has created for the stage.

Wilson has never differentiated between life and work, and at 147 Spring Street living and working were the same thing. Producing art was a part of life, a mentality reflected in Wilson and the Byrds's early extended-duration pieces like *KA MOUNTAIN and GUARDenia TERRACE: a story about a family and some people changing* – an ongoing performance of seven days and nights that required performers to sleep onstage. (While working on that show, the downstairs space at the Loft took on the aspect of an installation of its finished set pieces.) As Wilson's productions got bigger, the entire second floor had to be turned into a production office while he moved his personal living quarters to Vestry Street, where he occupied first the eighth, then the entire sixth floor.

Back in the late 1960s, Wilson had been offered the chance to buy 147 Spring Street for an alleged $9,000. He didn't, and he finally had to give it up after *Einstein on the Beach* was an artistic triumph and a financial disaster at the Metropolitan Opera. Downtown art had gone uptown and came back home broke.

When Wilson was forced to abandon the Byrd Loft and the Byrd Hoffman School of Byrds, the nest was emptied out and turned back into straw and dirt. While he had become a star in Europe, whose theaters must have appeared to him as California did to the American settlers, he now had no creative base in the United States. Over time, his loft on Vestry Street filled up with the objects he had made a point of collecting on his travels, and though he found temporary homes in theaters like the Schaubühne in Berlin or the Kammerspiele in Munich, he no longer had a space that could serve as his creative brain.

Watermill, Water Mill, Long Island

In the early 1990s, Wilson found something that reminded him of SoHo, a dilapidated and abandoned Western Union building in Water Mill, a hamlet of New York's Southampton: Shangri-La to the rich, but also to a generation of influential artists from de Kooning to Pollock and Warhol. He bought it with the help of (mainly European) friends, among whom Pierre Bergé played a key role, and named it "Watermill." Wilson carved out the summers from his hectic schedule and committed them to Watermill, where he brought his friends and collaborators to live and work together.

Robert Wilson at Watermill, 2001

In the early years, when only about 15 to 20 people spent their summers there – today, there are some 80 – the place did indeed resemble '60s SoHo: no fire codes, no emergency exits, no disability access. Wilson had not changed. He still did not differentiate between work and life, and work and living spaces at Watermill were no more marked off than they had been at the Byrd Loft. To cook together, a kitchen had to be built, and it was, by the artists living there; its cabinets were constructed according to the dimensions of Wilson's stage props, and its chairs frequently found their way out of the kitchen and into rehearsal and theater space. As on Spring Street, daily work was organized according to a rotating chore list, and meals were prepared and eaten together, today, often at huge outdoor tables built by resident artists and seating up to 150 people. A gallery in the principal room looks down upon the artistic activities below, and rather than "living quarters," there are cubicles separated by "open" walls that do not reach the ceiling, allowing noise to penetrate from one cubicle to the next. Interiors bleed into exteriors and are mirrored in the gardens, which, designed and planted by the artists, are arranged to move from chaos to order and back again. The building itself is like an epic two-act play, the main acts of the north and south wings joined by an empty "Knee Building" filled with river stones like those that marked the entrance to the Byrd Loft and open on both its horizontal and vertical axes, with a "floating" roof and slits for doors that let one's gaze glide right through the architecture without any resistance.

The collection of art, photography, and artifacts from all eras and cultures that Wilson had started in SoHo and housed at Vestry Street has grown to penetrate every crack of the Watermill building's 22,000 square feet. It arrived in 2007, when after more than 30 years Wilson lost Vestry Street, but it had long demanded such a space. His serious collecting had begun around the time that he lost the Byrd Loft. No longer responsible for the livelihoods of 35 companions or burdened with raising funds for his enormous projects, Wilson began to spend much of his time on tour in Europe. There, as a freelance director, he was given set, costume, and lighting budgets, as well as a creative team; his directing and designing fees for the first time gave him a real income that allowed him to collect significantly. From around the globe, he would send all sorts of items back to Vestry Street, and even while on tour, his collection – which Wilson calls a "History of Man" – became his home away from home, every office and hotel room "Wilsonified" with his latest acquisitions, reminding us daily that creativity does not start with a form but looks for its form, creates a form. An Eskimo mask can express the same duality between reason and fate as a Greek play. Art is the only global language that crosses cultural boundaries; it is what informs us about the past, teaches us about sunken and almost forgotten cultures, their architecture, their paintings, literature, music. Even today, when some art has become more like theater, over once the curtain closes, art is what remains.

The fruition of Wilson's vision from his time on Spring Street, Watermill is, aesthetically, the formalized expression of his creative mind and all-encompassing interests: furniture and objects carefully placed in space, attention to perspective, the interplay of scale and the communication of objects. At Watermill, the placement of a knife and fork on a table, the stacking of plates in a kitchen cabinet and the movement of grass are conceptualized and organized with the same care and attention devoted to the placement of actors and props on stage or to the setting of light cues. Like the Byrd Loft before it, Watermill reflects a balanced yet charged state of rest, beauty, and order that can burst into chaos and creativity before returning to its initial state; at the start and at the end of every work day, every object is to be found in its assigned place. Today, Wilson's "brain" is a building architecturally stunning and masterfully landscaped: The old Western Union telecommunication research lab has become a base for global communication through the arts, a building that puts one in awe.

Watermill, ultimately, is a utopian environment for a new generation of artists and thinkers: not a memorial for its founder, but a memorial for all future creators, a space where memory is preserved and new memories created, because it is through creation that we *can* remember. The offspring of an extraordinarily creative mind, it is a vacuum out of which innovation grows and finds its way into the world, a laboratory for performance, an incubator for ideas and a new take on the old style of communal living.

It is the place where Wilson has come home, and where he has created a home for others. The one space he has been able to hold on to, the space he himself created, it is the vantage point of a shared vision, the center of a web of like-minded artists, just as the Byrd Loft was a family for globally thinking (and traveling) artists in an area that was, for a few decades, the world in terms of art. To find open spaces nowadays that exist outside of a speculative market system is almost impossible, but Watermill tries to be a space that is free, that reverberates, that allows us to change it, that reminds us of where we came from and where we can go. Like the theater, the only space ultimately capable of producing constant change, Watermill is a stage that one can live and work in. It is Wilson's ultimate production, and, as such, eliminates the divide between stage and audience, making of every visitor a performer.

I want to thank the Byrds Mel Andringa, Robyn Brentano, Carol Mullins, John d'Arcangelo, Jessie Dunn-Gilbert, SK Dunn, and Sue Sheeny for opening their memories of the Byrd Loft times and opening my eyes to what this extraordinary place was like. JW

The Life and Death of Marina Abramović, Manchester, 2011. Carlos Soto

I have no education – not formally speaking.

I came into Bob's world by some strange circumstances. Around the age of 15, I went to see Bob's *Alice* at the Brooklyn Academy of Music (remembering a review of *The Black Rider* in an issue of *Interview* a few years prior) and found something that flipped my world upside-down in a profound way, which I hadn't consciously sought out, but the discovery seemed timely and very welcome. I was of the conviction that if something moved me to tears it was worth investigating. I wrote him a letter shortly after and corresponded briefly and found myself at Watermill just a few weeks after graduating from high school.

It was a wild sort of awakening, to be suddenly transplanted into a very intense atmosphere in what was then a muddy construction site in the Hamptons, living in trailers and following this charismatic man around, learning for the first time to stand still, to walk, to breathe. It sounds somewhat simplistic in retrospect, but it was this rigorous, extended lesson in discipline that I was most struck by. Everything was regimented, assigned a kind of value. I shared this meticulous attachment to all aspects of an action, to the conviction that everything making up the whole should be quantified, submitted to meticulous inspection.

I arrived with the self-appointed determination that I would be a director, and was made to perform. I abandoned the crippling shyness that I assumed since childhood and took part. I wanted to learn and take on every métier. There was an incessant need to work with others, but also a stubborn conviction to control all aspects of work – if you want things done right, you do them yourself: a gnawing need to collaborate, but a conviction that in order to properly communicate with others, one should have a certain knowledge of the craft involved.

I began to work with Bob as a performer on several projects while teaching myself to design costumes, to tailor, cut, sew, understand volume, line, silhouette. I continued to write, to make things, to conceive of impossible projects that I still try to somehow engender. I found early on while working with Bob that discipline applies to everything. The same tension that one adopts in movement is the same tension that enables one to draw a line, form a fold, speak a sentence, hold a note – all forms of mark-making.

Press conference, Avignon, 1976. Robert Wilson and Philip Glass

It's a state of attention

"I don't care about theories of music, I am interested in listening to music. I begin by hearing. Like images coming out of fog and becoming visible," Philip Glass says in Scott Hicks's film *Glass: A Portrait of Philip in Twelve Parts*.[1] I began by hearing Philip Glass, and not only his music. Unlike the other interviews for this book, his was conducted solely by telephone, from a hotel room in New York whose speakerphone, I was to learn later, was defective. My time with Glass was over, and even the sound I had recorded of him seemed to be coming out of a deep fog, not clearly enough. I had to go back to several documentaries about Glass to round out parts of our conversation. In one of them, he says that you can go along writing a piece without knowing where it's going, and suddenly one day, usually towards the end, it comes together: "Oh, that's it." It took adding the filmed image to the voice of Philip Glass for me to reach that point, to have everything he said to me over the telephone emerge out of the fog so I could listen to it, and hear it.

The Washington Post has called *Einstein on the Beach* one of the seminal artistic creations of the 20th century, and Robert Wilson and Philip Glass have since continued to collaborate regularly. Listening to each of them speak, I was struck by the number of shared values between them. These are deep structures, a coming-together on a profound level of sensitivity.

Wilson's work, some say, inhabits a space between dream and reality; Glass speaks of what we imagine and what is real, as the "conditions of our life." Neither man cares what people think; each simply does his art. Both can be very funny, and very serious. Rigorous. When Glass speaks about the structure of *Einstein on the Beach*, he is incredibly rapid in spitting out the 1, 2, 3, 4, A, B, C, D structure, as is Wilson; this language they both speak to try to show a structure to us only ends up confirming that they are speaking their own language: They see it, they hear it, they fire it off with machine-gun speed. Workaholics, both, each has a capacity to work on multiple projects at the same time, and for both, work and life are pretty much the same thing. Music is Glass's underlying passion. "My interest in music has been personal and obsessive," he says. "I am not thinking of bringing happiness to mankind. I just write a piece of music and I play it." One could imagine the words in Wilson's mouth, with only the word "music" changed. For each, written or spoken language is not the preferred mode of expression; for each, his art is his language, how he communicates everything he feels or is thinking.

We spoke about *Einstein on the Beach*, of course, and about the downtown art scene from which it emerged; we spoke about time and structures and "minimalism," a word both men have suffered; we spoke about East and West, and we spoke about culture then and now, and listening to Philip Glass speak of these things, "blind" to me and only a voice, what emerged out of the fog was a clear sense of how these two artists have been able to see and hear each other, and together create.

1
Glass's words set off by quotation marks here are paraphrased from *Glass: A Portrait of Philip in Twelve Parts*, directed and photographed by Scott Hicks and produced by Kino Films and Independent Media Inc., in association with Kojo Pictures, 2008. On the following two pages, in order to clarify the recorded material, an occasional anecdote recounted by Glass has been completed by reference to the film.

Einstein on the Beach, Paris, 1992. Lucinda Childs and Sheryl Sutton

The first staged work of Robert Wilson's I saw was *The Life and Times of Joseph Stalin*. I saw it at BAM in 1973. Bob and I both lived very much in the downtown world of the visual arts, and we were very attracted to people like Merce Cunningham, John Cage, Jasper Johns, and Richard Serra. All these people were people that we knew together and were part of the cultural environment that we lived in. We weren't, you know, kids from Des Moines who were finding out something new....

> Wilson is from Texas, and you were born in Baltimore.

Yes, he was born in Texas, but that's not his cultural reference. Our mutual cultural environment was the New York downtown art scene. It was high-end, abstract art. It was a world inhabited by extremely brilliant people. At one point, Chuck Close wanted to do a series of portraits of anonymous people, so we all participated; this was supposed to be an anonymous photograph, and within years, each of the "anonymous" people in the photo had become a famous artist. It was one of the great advanced art periods of any time. So there were dances and theater, there were actors and there were plays, theater productions, public theater. All kinds of things were going on. We were not isolated within the world of the arts that we were working in. We were in the performing arts, but we were very much in line with what people called "culture" in sculpture, in painting, in dance, and in psychology for that matter. You could do anything. We were all poor, very poor, and so we started living in what would eventually become SoHo, but then was the land of rags and rats. We performed in people's lofts or in art galleries, but never in a place where acoustics would figure – those places we weren't allowed in. So Bob and I were part of that art scene. We met in the fall of 1974. Bob was doing *A Letter for Queen Victoria*, on Broadway, I think, and Sue Weil, who was involved with Dance in America and White Oaks, was a mutual friend, and she introduced us. We met at Bob's loft on Spring Street and talked, and then Bob and I began meeting. Every Thursday that we were both in town, about twice a month, we met for lunch at a restaurant on Sullivan Street and we decided to do a piece and work together.

> It's said that when you first started discussing the opera project with Wilson, he wanted to do Charlie Chaplin or Adolph Hitler, and that you rejected Hitler and proposed Gandhi. Einstein was the compromise.

Einstein was never a compromise. He liked Einstein right away, and the original title of the piece was *Einstein on the Beach on Wall Street* and eventually it was cut down to *Einstein on the Beach*.

> Wilson has said that from the beginning, you both determined that *Einstein on the Beach* would be four to five hours, that each scene would be about 20 minutes long, and the scenes would be connected by what you both call "knee plays," the knee being the joint that links two similar elements. What does it mean to determine duration before content?

I'd done long pieces before, "extended time performances" we would call them. I was a founding member of Mabou Mines, which grew out of La MaMa and The Public Theater, and I wrote scores for their theater productions; I knew how theater worked. I've been in the theater since I was 20, and I was 37 when Bob and I met. Time in music is duration. This is one of the commonalities in our work: Both Bob and I have to work in real time. We share an awareness of time, of duration. Bob is extending theater into space and time, and I'm projecting music into space and time, and we use similar techniques, and use them for similar reasons, I think we'd agree. It's not really surprising that that should be so. I wouldn't say that Bob and I were that aware of it when we started working together, but it became evident as we looked at the finished piece.

> Wilson did a set of drawings for *Einstein*, and you set them to music. He says that you "built the opera the way an architect would build a building. The structure of the music was completely interwoven with the stage action and with the lighting." Would you describe the collaboration in the same way?

We divided the work. He made drawings of images: Landscapes, the train scenes, were the far distance; the dances were mid-distance; the trials were close. We took turns organizing. Trains and Spaceships 1 and 2; Trials, scene 2; Dances 3; Act I, 1 and 3, Train and Trial; Act II, Dance and Train; Act III, Trial and Dance; Act IV 1, 2, 3, 4 in a row. Bob made a book of drawings, and I wrote music to it. We rehearsed at his loft, and auditioned 120 people for twelve parts. They had to be both singers and dancers. Plus Sheryl Sutton, who speaks text in the piece, and Lucinda Childs, our choreographer. The show premiered in Avignon in July 1976 and went on to tour in Venice, Amsterdam, Hamburg, Paris, Belgrade, Brussels, and Rotterdam, and then had two performances at the Met.

> The progression from the Avignon premiere to the November performances at the Met was incredibly rapid – a few months.

Jane Hermann, who was working at the Met to produce some special events on the dark days – Sundays at the Met – came to Paris to see *Einstein*; she'd heard about it from Jerry Robbins, who had seen it in Paris at the Opéra Comique, where we were doing it. Afterwards, back at the hotel, we talked, and she asked if we wanted to do it. We told her we needed three days to set up the piece, which, of course, at the Met is impossible since they have a Saturday evening show that doesn't end until 11:30 p.m. Jane had the idea of starting at midnight and having a triple crew to set it up. She said they were the best crew in the world, and she was right. They did it in two shifts instead of three. But back in Paris, I never thought it was going to happen. We spoke to Jane and then we sort of forgot about it and did the rest of the tour.

We came back from our tour late in October or November, and a friend met us at the airport and said, "You're sold out," and we said, "What?" And that's how it happened. It was a special event at the Met. It looked like all of the downtown arts scene had decided to attend.

New York City, 1976

New York City, 1984

Einstein on the Beach, Venice, 1976

There was panic. You couldn't get a ticket. 3,500 seats, and then they even sold out all the standing room, so close to 4,000 people a night. My mother was there, and so were Bob's parents, and my mother turned around to Bob's mother and asked her, "Did you know this was going on in Bob's head? I certainly didn't know it was going on in Philip's head."

Of course for us, the most amazing night had come in Avignon. When we presented the piece there, no one had heard it. We'd been rehearsing for six to eight months, but I'm not even sure that we'd ever done the piece all the way through without stopping until that opening night. So by the time we played the Met, people in New York had heard about *Einstein*. It had become a myth, so everyone was prepared for something.

It all happened so quickly in 1976, but then there was a hiatus, and we didn't see *Einstein* presented again for nearly a decade. I've asked this question of others, but I'd like to know in your view: Why? What happened?

We lost a lot of money. Every opera loses money, and *Einstein* was no different. It's impossible to make money with high art, abstract art. And it was impossible to make money on this. We had no idea what we were doing. We had no idea we were going to lose money

Einstein on the Beach, Paris, 1976. Left, Lucinda Childs

every night. We had been sold out every night for the whole tour, and when it was over, we learned that we had lost over $100,000! This was a lot of money then, still is. Byrd Hoffman Foundation was the producer; I was involved in it, but legally the debt was incurred by Byrd Hoffman Foundation. Jane Hermann told us we could go on giving *Einstein* at the Met every Sunday, and they would go on selling it out every Sunday, but we said we couldn't afford it. Within two weeks of playing at the Met, I was back at my day job, driving a cab. Rich and famous don't necessarily go together.

We didn't have the money to do another production of *Einstein*. Bob had his organization and I had mine for fundraising, and we raised some money, but we didn't have the fundraising organization of the Metropolitan Opera House; it's not at all the same thing. We had to wait until we could organize a tour that would pay for the production. Ninon Karlweiss had pre-sold the show to those eight European theaters, and it was with that money that we made the piece. The debt was a burden on me, and I'm sure it was a burden on Bob, and it created some tension. We went from being collaborators to being debtors. So that's why we couldn't immediately make another production and tour. We couldn't even think about doing another production. And so that was the only *Einstein* that was made, and for four or five years there was no other production.

Einstein on the Beach, New York City, 1984. Robert Wilson

It was difficult, it was very difficult, despite selling out the Met. We had created this incredibly innovative work. We hadn't planned it. It just turned out that way. And it became more expensive to produce as time went on. Every time we did it again, we needed more things and more things. More lighting, more everything. In 1984, we did it at the Brooklyn Academy of Music. But it wasn't until 1992 that a producer came along and there was another big tour, and by then, we were more experienced theater people. Bob knew a lot more about what he wanted to do, and I knew a lot more about what I wanted to do. All the stagings had to be not reconceived exactly, but the way we did them before wasn't the way Bob wanted to do them. Both Bob and I had more sophisticated notions of exactly what we wanted. So we restaged the piece at the McCarter Theatre in Princeton, New Jersey, and took it to BAM again and abroad. But we could never have produced it on our own. This time it actually went to Japan, but never to the US West Coast or Midwest. To this day, *Einstein* has never been seen on the West Coast or Middle West of the United States.[2]

Do you consider *Einstein on the Beach* political?

I never did. We ran into a lot of trouble like that, especially when we were playing in Eastern Europe, in Belgrade, where people did think it was political, and also in Amsterdam. Young people were very interested in the political connections of the work. But Bob and I, at that point in our lives at least, were pretty innocent of politics. It took me time to move into it, and I think Bob also, when he started working with that German playwright [Heiner Müller]. Then Bob began living more in Europe, and I think that politics and theater are more easily married in Europe than in America. As for me, after *Einstein*, I wrote an opera about Gandhi [*Satyagraha*, 1980] and I did a lot of other more socially – and politically – oriented things, but *Einstein* would not have been one of them.

The 2012 revival of *Einstein* will bring in a new audience. How do you think an audience today – more than 35 years after *Einstein*'s creation – will react to it?

My experience is that each time we do *Einstein* with a new audience, they can't believe it. They just can't believe it. Because what's happened in the last 30 or so years is that theater has become more predictable, more conservative. Nobody's there. Nobody's doing the kind of abstract innovations that people did, people like Richard Foreman, Peter Brook, or Bob Wilson, especially in the big theaters. There's nothing like them anymore. The kinds of things that they did in the '70s and '80s, that no longer exists. It's very interesting, very interesting sociologically. Because now it's all coming out of entertainment, and the kind of idealism that we had – we didn't know it, we didn't think about it that way, but in retrospect we were very idealistic people, and we brought that to everything we did. We weren't thinking about making money or Broadway runs or advancing in the profession or anything like that. We just made art. We just did it. Today, everyone thinks about those things. It's everywhere. But when I first saw Bob's work in Brooklyn, there weren't 200 people in the audience, and then three years later, we went to the Met with *Einstein*, and there wasn't even standing room.

2
The 2012–13 world tour of *Einstein* will include a performance in Berkeley, California.

Paris, 1976

Einstein on the Beach, Venice, 1976

"Phil/Watercolor," 1977
Chuck Close portrait of Philip Glass
Watercolor and acrylic on paper, 147.3 × 101.6 cm
Photograph by Ellen Labenski, courtesy The Pace Gallery
© Chuck Close, courtesy The Pace Gallery

Essentially, *Einstein* is a non-narrative, artificial theater in which the function of narrative has shifted completely from telling a story to experiencing a story. We're talking about time itself. In that sense, I think that Bob and I were part of a general cultural shift. We happened to be at the forefront of it, but that's just the time and the circumstance in the way it happened.

People today are growing up looking at work that is a strange imitation of things that were done 20 years before, and then when they see the real thing, the actual production that was done, like *Einstein on the Beach*, they find it astonishing, absolutely astonishing. But that's happened to other people who are looked at long after what they've done. That's happened to Andy Warhol, happened to Meredith Monk. That happened to Peter Brook. People who are survivors of the '60s and '70s and '80s and are still working in the 21st century are seeing that their work is being given a new appreciation. And *Einstein*, every time we do it, will have the same effect, and probably more powerfully. I would say that the dominance of Hollywood storytelling in theater and opera has pretty much swept aside a lot of the best results of the kind of innovation that Bob and I were doing. So I would say that more than ever, *Einstein* will be a phenomenon. It will have a galvanizing effect on the audience.

But will a 21st century audience raised on that kind of Hollywood entertainment know how to react to *Einstein*?

I think they'll react the way they did when we did it in Avignon in 1976: When they saw it, they said, "What the hell is this?" By the way, we didn't know what it was, either. But people sat there for four and a half hours. It's autodidactic. You learn how to see it by seeing it. The piece teaches you how to watch it. The piece teaches you how to hear it. It's a state of attention. In that sense, it's a form of psychiatry. It is radically different from the way we look at logic. It doesn't need any course to be given on it – it's probably better not to have one. Don't forget that one of our writers, Christopher Knowles, was a brilliant young man who was autistic. No course could prepare you for his work. New audiences can't believe how new *Einstein* is.

That's interesting.

It's also depressing.

Your music repeats fragments beautifully, as if weaving. Robert Wilson often uses repeated gestures on stage. Does repetition as a shared motif or time-shaping technique serve a similar purpose for the two of you? Is it one of your connections or commonalities?

First of all, there's not repetition. Something is always going on. It's a very important point, and each time you use the word "repetition," it enforces an idea that's not true. It's a psychological way of listening where you think that you're in the same place exactly, but moving in order to stay in the same place – it's like treading water in a swimming pool. If you were actually not moving, you'd sink to the bottom. But in fact you're moving all the time. Repetition actually figures in the combination of acts that are constantly moving, constantly changing, even when they appear to be static. We're talking about a special kind of attention, which invites you to become focused on smaller changes in the midst of a rapid repetition.

If you look at Chuck Close's paintings, you'll see that he's working with dots and sets repeating over and over, but it's not that simple. It's a way of working where a thematic idea is stated and then constantly changed so that it is constantly morphing, constantly becoming something else. This is what John Cage did in *4'33''*. He opened your attention to the world around you. What these and other works do – whether it's Bob's work or Jasper Johns's work or Robert Rauschenberg's, any of these people – is enlighten; they create a heightened sense of attention which is radically different from the way that we attend to the world at large. That kind of attending – think about it – is the way that we personalize the work so that, for example, people can give any number of descriptions of what I actually think happened. The spectator completes the work. It doesn't exist independently of the person watching it. It's the way the spectator perceives the work that gives it the content. The content is not *in* the work itself. This is a very important point, and Bob is a master of this, of understanding exactly how people see his work, and I, on my side, of how people listen to my music in theater. We're talking about something that people rarely talk about, which is the actual psychological arrangement in the relationship and transaction that takes place between the work and the viewer. In that sense, Bob and I are true children of Marcel Duchamp and the 1930s Surrealists and John Cage.

> Wilson has described his work by saying, "What would maybe outwardly appear to be slow... is actually full of many, many different speeds."[3] The spectator has to do the work, first of observation and then of interpretation, to catch all the atoms displaced along the way.

Yes, I agree with that completely, absolutely. That idea that the work doesn't exist independently but is completed when the spectator views it is a crucial point. You can't even begin to talk about repetition or content without understanding that it's the transaction that culls the content, that there is no content in the work.

> Are Eastern cultures a meeting ground for you and Wilson?

Not as much as you might think. We both are very interested in the East. Bob had a big experience in Asia, and he did a big piece in Iran [*KA MOUNTAIN* and *GUARDenia TERRACE*] in the early 1970s, and he's very sensitive to the Japanese, and especially to the way they arrange objects, the arrangement of things on a shelf, which is very important to him. He told me that when he was a boy, he used to get up at night and go into his mother's kitchen and rearrange all the dishes on the shelf; he would spend the whole night doing that. And he had a number of Japanese choreographers. He was very attracted to that. I wasn't. I was more interested in the Himalayan cultures than the Japanese. But when we did *Einstein* in Japan, it was very successful.

> It's said that you don't like the word "minimalist," a word that is applied to both your work and Wilson's.

That I don't like the term? The point is that, unfortunately, when the word is used, it's used as a shorthand to describe a much more complicated process. It invites you not to understand what you're doing, what we're doing. They just say, "It's minimalism." It's sad. It's a word that was invented by journalists and used by people trying to make a complicated process more easily understandable. But making it more easily understandable misses a lot of what a piece is about. As Bob says, it's not about the big movements, it's about all the little movements that are happening, changing like sand. Saying "minimalist" trains your audience to look at a work in the wrong way. Better to say nothing. When people ask me what kind of composer I am, what kind of music I write, I tell them I write theater music. I'm a theater composer. They say, "Oh, I thought you were a minimalist." Well, you can call it what you like, but what I really do is write music for theater.

> And now, those ways of making art have been irrevocably changed by the entertainment industry and Hollywood?

3
"From a Distance," interview with Margery Arent Safir, in *Balanchine Then and Now*, Anne Hogan, ed. (Lewes: The Arts Arena and Sylph Editions, 2008), 113.

White Raven, Madrid, 1998

Persephone, East Hampton, N.Y., 1995. Marianna Kavallieratos

Oh, you know I've also worked in Hollywood. I've done quite a few scores for films. But apart from that, in terms of what I'm writing now, I'm in this interesting phase right now where many ideas that were important to me when I was in my 30s or 40s are re-emerging in a completely different context. So I find that in what I've worked on lately, an opera – *Kepler* – there are a lot of imprints of a structure and also of content of chamber music I did earlier, but it's also very different. In a way, I'm going back to my roots as a kind of way of going forward in my work. I think it happens often with artists. They go back and look at what they've done and rethink what can be accomplished and what techniques and materials can be used now. I write a lot of chamber music, sextet, quartet, violin, piano and things like that, and it's something like what I did ten years ago, and yet I don't actually think they sound like that; they are like that, but they don't sound like that. The difference is that the new pieces are more interesting pieces.

> *Einstein* was the beginning of your collaboration with Wilson, but certainly not the end. You were part of the international collaborative effort for *the CIVIL warS*, for instance.

About every seven or eight years, Bob and I seem to get around to working together – we did a piece called *White Raven*, we did the Rome and Cologne sections of *CIVIL warS*, we did *Monsters of Grace, Persephone* – and it's good. We come back with different ideas because we've been working apart for a while. It's turned out to be the best formula for us. We wait until something comes along and then we collaborate on it. One of the things that Bob and I have in common, and one of the best attributes of our collaboration, is that Bob has tremendous trust in the people he works with. He rarely tells anybody what to do. He invites them into his playground. I've done the same thing with my collaborative efforts. They're very comfortable. Trusting your collaborator is a big help; I invite them into the world that I inhabit. Once you trust them, you move forward. If you try to dictate what they do, you won't get anywhere.

> That sounds like wisdom itself, but when you put together two great artists, it doesn't always work that way.

It doesn't work that way in Hollywood or in commercial New York, but that's why live theater and opera are so important. Theater and opera have a lot in common. It's in the *process* that you work by. Opera by definition is cooperation. Collaboration is the lifeblood of theater. Bob has a great capacity for collaboration because with Bob, you feel respected, and it's a wonderful thing. It's a great spirit. When you work with Bob, you know that he believes in you, or you wouldn't be there.

Alcestis, Cambridge, Mass., 1986

I don't remember anything about it except his body

"I don't really consider myself an artist," says visual artist, composer, poet, photographer, performer, filmmaker, vocalist, and instrumentalist Laurie Anderson. "I think I'm more of a spy. That's really what I do. I look at the stuff in other people's lives."[1] Recognized worldwide as a groundbreaking leader in the use of technology in the arts, Anderson has collaborated with Interval Research Corporation, a research and development laboratory, and was NASA's first artist-in-residence, an experience that served as the basis for her solo performance *The End of the Moon*. Her work is shown in galleries and museums, and her performances have taken her from the streets of Sweden to Paris's Opéra Garnier, where her score for Trisha Brown's acclaimed piece *O Zlozony/O Composite* premiered in 2004.

Anderson and Wilson have known each other for decades. Part of the New York downtown scene that produced Wilson and Philip Glass (she even wrote the "New York" entry for the *Encyclopedia Britannica*), Anderson has worked with both men; like them, she went to Europe to work before returning to the United States, and like them, BAM has played a major role in her career, featuring her *Songs and Stories from Moby Dick* and her seven-hour, four-part multimedia work *United States*. Anderson was the female narrative counterpart to Wilson's voice in *Einstein on the Beach*, and acted as a narrator in *the CIVIL warS*. Wilson performed his solo piece *The Man in the Raincoat* to her music. In 1986, she wrote a 15-minute electronic score to accompany the *Kyogen* epilogue that was originally part of Wilson's *Alcestis*, his first major work to be developed in America in a decade and his first direction of actors in a classical dramatic text. *Kyogen*, literally "mad words" or "wild speech," is a form of traditional Japanese theater performed as comic relief between formal acts in Noh plays. The *Kyogen* for *Alcestis*, "The Birdcatcher in Hell," a 17th century farce added at Heiner Müller's suggestion, was true to the genre, described by one critic as "much closer to the Three Stooges than to the glacial style usually associated with [Wilson's] work."[2] "I think I do my work for some sadder version of myself, a woman who would be sitting in Row K," Anderson says. "I am trying to make her laugh."[3]

For Anderson, as for Wilson and for Glass, time is a deep concern. She mixes up media – "I try to make records that are cinematic, movies that are musical" – but the common denominator is "the sense of time that I'm trying to use. If I had to define my work, it would probably have something to do with time: how I try to stretch it, compress it, turn it into a couple of ice cubes, spread it all over the place, or turn it into air."[4]

The time is 9:00 a.m., Easter weekend. In Paris's 16th arrondissement, I sit down in the empty, dimly-lit breakfast room of a boutique hotel. At precisely the appointed hour, a short-haired woman walks in, comes up to my table, and sits down across from me.

"I'm Laurie," she says.

1
The Guardian, July 20, 2001.

2
Performing Arts Journal, Vol. 10, No. 1, 1986. The score does not seem to have entirely pleased either Anderson or Wilson, and the epilogue was later dropped from the piece.

3
The New York Times Magazine, January 30, 2005.

4
William Duckworth, *Talking Music: Conversations with John Cage, Philip Glass, Laurie Anderson, and Five Generations of American Experimental Composers* (New York: Schirmer Books, 1995), 368–85.

A Letter for Queen Victoria, Paris, 1974

One of the first things I saw by Bob was *A Letter for Queen Victoria*. It was an all-night event, and it was the first time I saw a very elongated argument, a visual argument. Was it an argument, or was it just a composed, very slow-mo conflict? I've never read about it, I just sort of remember it halfway in my dreams, like all Bob Wilson things. From one side of the stage there's a woman in a sari, and from the other a man in a bowler hat with an umbrella, who walk very, *very* arch, invariably, slowly towards each other, and as they pass, she falls. A very talented picture – ah, beautiful! Then they pass and go to the opposite side of the stage, then they turn and come back, and she falls again. He picks her up a second time and puts her on her feet, and off they go, they turn, they do it again, and she falls again, and he's like, *"Oof."* He picks her up briskly this time, and the same thing happens maybe ten, maybe 20 more times. Each time she falls, each time he pulls her up with more force, until he's yanking her up, until finally he's beating her with the umbrella as he picks her up. And I look at this as British colonialism: There it is, falling and being picked up, being rescued, something that turns an act of, if not kindliness, courtliness, into brutality and an endless loop of repression. Seeing it happen within a community made it even more intense. I felt for many years that I wasn't sure this scene was really in the play, or if I'd made part of it up. I still don't even know. I'd like to ask Bob what that scene was, because I thought it was one of the most interesting pieces of historical imaging I've ever seen.

Do you generally consider Wilson's work political?

I consider everything political, so I really don't know how to answer that.

You just gave a very political reading of *A Letter for Queen Victoria*.

I think that part was meant to be a very sharp comment. She's wearing a sari; he's wearing a bowler hat. There's no possible other way I can interpret that one – unless I dreamed their costumes. I think about that scene often, that and *The Man in the Raincoat*, and both seem mixed with my dreams. I feel that way about so much of Bob's work, that he does tap into a frequency that is the one in which we dream. I appreciate that more and more, especially now that I'm 62, which means that if I've slept an average number of hours per night, I've been asleep a little bit less than 20 years. What have I been doing all that time? How is that imagery affecting my waking life? My life as an artist? My image-making? My perception of who you are sitting across this table? You look behind you at the people that you've invented in your dreams and they're not quite finished, they're a little bit sketchy back there, and then they keep turning into other people....

That's what happens in dreams.

And in life. [*Laughs*] Do I know you? Or are you reminding me of someone else? And of course we're always imposing those associations, and Bob's always imposing them in his work, too. *The Man in the Raincoat* was one of the purest things I've ever seen, because it was a man caught in a windstorm, or, I don't know, life, dreams, whatever, and flailing and having a really good time. It's always in the back of my mind. The other person I love who can dance this kind of windstorm is Bill T. [Jones], and so when I was the director of the Meltdown, this big festival in London, I asked both Bob and Bill T. – in the Royal Festival Hall, without rehearsing it – to slowly come down, dance down these huge flights of stairs, while in the middle, Phil Glass played the organ. I told them, "I want you to join the festival. You don't have to rehearse, just show up; Phil's going to improvise on the organ, and you're going to move down those stairs over a period of four minutes, however way you want." Bob on one side, Bill on the other. Bob, Bill, and Phil. It gives you a chill. I was like, "My life's complete!" That was a really wonderful moment, one of my dreams come true, because there is something really deeply in common between Bill and Bob: their physicality. It's very controlled abandon; it's so impressive. I love what Bob does with wild-child Christopher [Knowles], but also I've listened to many of his long training sessions with actors and people who are moving and listening to how he's instructing them to move. It's very, very meditative. It's almost like doing walking meditation. I think it's about the closest to that we can come. The closest physical exercise I've seen is walking meditation. He's a Buddhist teacher.

> You and Wilson both started out with static forms of art, you in sculpture and he in architecture, which means that you both transitioned from forms of immobility to performance based in motion. What spurred that?

For Bob, I guess it was originally the body, and for me it was originally sound. I had made a sculpture in the early 1970s by putting boxes up on stilts, and my teachers, Sol LeWitt and Carl Andre, liked the idea of animating this thing with sound. And that really quickly led to my wanting to make something kind of portable, which of course turns out to be an instrument, which is a portable object. So I thought, "Why not invent an instrument?" I would imagine that for Bob, his route was moving through architecture more than language – certainly not language, although Bob understands text really well – and more than, let's say, music. For me, Bob's more about the body than about music. And when music is in his own work it's very, very secondary or tertiary. It's not that important.

> Did you attend Wilson's open houses at Spring Street when you were making your first pieces?

Yes, yes. I've known him for so long. I feel that I've known ten Bob Wilsons. Those were very interesting years, the 1970s. There was room for works that were interlocked. I just remember it as everybody always working on everybody else's work. Bob and I and Phil and William Burroughs and Trisha Brown were all part of the scene that was related to visual arts, because all of us were all engaging in visual arts, as well. There was also Meredith Monk and her multi-disciplinary works; that was the thing that tied a lot of famous artists together down there. And we were always doing things that were very borderless, and everybody seemed to be working on opera. "What are you working on?" "I'm working on the opera." It didn't mean traditional opera or anything particular; it was just a word, "opera," and I think that Bob took the word and ran with it, the first things he did especially; they were operas, but he took the word outside of its usual context, and people were saying, "Woah, look at this! What's this new multimedia opera?"

Isn't opera by definition a multimedia art form? There's music, there's text, there's acting, movement, all together. Is that why you were using the word? Or did you simply use it in the sense of "work," of "opus"?

Yes, work. We weren't doing opera in the sense of "opera house" and opera tradition. Even now, when people try to get young composers to make opera, the works that are made in that way are not adventurous; they follow tradition. Whereas opera 30 years ago was really open, really daring. It never followed the rules of opera in the sense that music is supreme, for example. That's not necessarily true of the work that Bob does now when he does

Rehearsal, *Alcestis*, Cambridge, Mass., 1986.
Laurie Anderson and Robert Wilson

Wagner, for instance. Then he puts himself in a different role. It's almost like composing music for a film. When I do music for a film, I know which thing is leading: The film is leading. When Bob directs an opera, he knows the music is leading. But when he does his own "operas," the motion of the body is leading and the music follows intuitively in a supporting role.

You were the first – and I believe the last – NASA artist in residence. Do you see science or scientific advances that have affected the way we experience the world as playing any role in Wilson's work?

I think no one ever assumed that *Einstein on the Beach* was going to be a portrait of Einstein or even a look at his ideas. It had nothing whatsoever to do with Einstein. It could have been called "Eisenstein on the Beach," you know what I mean? There were a couple of clocks in it and some extremely loose associations with his name. In a funny way though, it seemed to be somehow about Einstein, but that always struck me as kind of hilarious. But a lot of Phil's operas are based on a name; it's almost like a musical book. The connection is very slight in general, although maybe the work got a little bit more specific later. In Phil's work on Gandhi [*Satyagraha*, 1980], one got more the sense that it was about a person and that the opera related to some of Gandhi's ideas. But not so in *Einstein*. The performers spoke numbers and all, but it's not about *anything*, so I always felt that that kind of science connection was pretty strange. An homage is another way to think of it, but in no way is it a portrait of Einstein, and probably wasn't meant that way. [*Silence*] I'm just wondering what could the title possibly mean? I always feel uneasy about my own relationship to science, although one of the things I did learn at NASA was that artists and scientists have a lot more in common than appears on the surface. We both get a hunch and then make something, and then see what the outcome is and look at it. Scientists don't know what they're looking for either. You just sort of throw something up and see what happens. I often had conversations with nanotechnologists at NASA – these people were

ByrdwoMAN, New York City, 1968. Robert Wilson

working on tiny forms, and so were more willing to talk theoretically about things; there I was, wearing my artist's visitor badge, and there they were, the nanoscientists – and they would often cite Einstein, saying that he rejected many of his own major theories. Why? Because they weren't beautiful. What are they actually looking for? What are they talking about? Beauty. Symmetry, even, is valued differently by different cultures.

> You worked on two of Wilson's culturally and chronologically mixed projects, as a narrator in *the CIVIL warS* and as a musician for *Alcestis*, a 1986 adaptation of Euripides' play with additional text by Heiner Müller, an "audio environment" by Hans Peter Kuhn, and a traditional Japanese *Kyogen* farce, "Birdcatcher in Hell," for which you wrote the score. Can you talk about this later work you did together?

That "later work" was still a long time ago. I tried to make a work with MIDI triggers, although now, I look at it and say, "Why would I do something like that?" The score for "Birdcatcher in Hell" contained samples of all kinds of natural things, insect sounds and the like. But the music was a very, very, very small part of this production of *Alcestis*, so while it's fun to think of myself as working with Bob, we didn't really. He'd say, "Can you do something like that?" and I'd say, "How about if we do that?" and he'd say, "That sounds good," and so I did that, and that was that.

We did work together recently, though, just over a year ago, on an exhibition in Torino, *Egypt's Sunken Treasures*, and that was a lot of fun. Bob was designing the exhibition and wanted to have music between the rooms, and I loved the idea of trying to do that. It's something I'm trying to do in an exhibition I'm working on now. It's very, *very* tricky, because museums are not set up for that kind of situation, and Bob wanted to have speakers, not headphones.

So I made a number of pieces – maybe 12 or 14 – based on Bob's very minimal instructions: "far away, sad, and single," or "terrifying with some natural sounds." Now, those are great instructions, really wonderful. And then Bob would say the number of minutes. We worked perfectly like that. That was exactly like I would expect from a film director. Which brings me to another subject: I just don't understand – and I didn't understand it about Warhol either – why Bob doesn't make movies, like really spectacular major motion pictures. He has this grand mentality. I mean, I know he likes the stage, but I would love to see Bob's movie. That would be wonderful. It was the same thing about Warhol too, you know. Warhol did try to make Hollywood movies, actually, and it's just too bad that it didn't work out. Can you imagine what American cinema would be like if Warhol had actually done that, or if ten or 20 years ago Bob had said, "How about movies?" Of course his sense of time would be fascinating, that is, if he could imagine paring it down to about a three-hour movie. Maybe that's the limitation he just didn't want: "So short!" On the other hand, his video portraits are really exquisite. Really works. Really great. I've seen a lot of them together, and you can get a sense of how beautiful a film by Bob might be.

> What attraction did Europe initially hold for your group of downtown artists? Why did a number of you go there to work?

Well, I think that when Bob, like Phil, was starting out, all of the work was there. It was really simple. Americans weren't willing to fund or commission things at all. And I felt that way too. I was part of that expatriate surge. Off we went, because people in Berlin would say, "Hey! What would you like to do here? Would you like to work with an orchestra? Or can we get you some resources? Who would you like to meet here in Berlin?" And I practically started to cry when someone first asked me that there. They would never do that in New York or Chicago. Never! We just don't treasure our artists, period. We like them, I suppose, but they're more tolerated than liked. So we went where we were liked, and that was to other places.

> We've talked about the enormous creativity of that period and all the avant-garde art that came out of it. How do you make today's audiences feel the originality of that work decades later?

I don't know if that needs to be its most important purpose. That won't be its historical place. It's not necessarily what's going to excite anybody years later. I've always tried to remember that. It doesn't really matter if it's new; it matters if it's good. So works that were daring and broke a lot of ground sometimes are not all that interesting as works of art. They were really different, but they don't resonate. Looking at a work of art in its historical context can open up doors, but in terms of what it means as a work of art, no one will ever see it like that again. They won't feel that excitement, because, well, it's not exciting. Too many people went along that road afterward. It's like that with theme parks or with amusement parks: There's nothing sadder than something that used to be really cutting-edge and is now languishing away, unless, of course, it still has pizzazz. But a lot of avant-garde stuff doesn't survive.

> You often perform as a solo act, whereas Wilson, for the most part now, stays behind the scenes. Aside from the Meltdown Festival, what has it been like to see him on stage as a performer?

The Man in the Raincoat is one of my favorite things ever. So beautiful. I picture a man falling; it's so indelible, that image of Bob in his raincoat flailing around. I can't even remember what year it was. He played a man spinning and falling so elegantly, in such a terrifying and monotonous way. I'll never forget seeing that, even though I don't remember anything about it except his body. Did you see it?

> No. One of the great difficulties in researching Wilson's work is that a complete record of this sort of thing isn't available. Much of the work has never been filmed to commercial standards, and is found only in archives. You can read about a performance, but you can't see it in recording after the performance.[5]

5
There are exceptions. Wilson's re-engagement with *Alcestis* five years after the 1986 production is one. A DVD of his production of Gluck's *Alceste* at Paris's Théâtre du Châtelet was produced by the theater and is commercially available.

Well, I've been to some archives, where you sit in a miserable little carrel and look at a ratty little rectangle, and you're seeing the piece. So in a way, I'm relieved that there's no little carrel to see *The Man in the Raincoat* in. I can have it in my memory, where it's really, really beautiful.

> You're known as a performance artist, musician, and a visualist, but underneath it all, there seems to be a storyteller of the ancient kind: the bard who entertains and edifies us with stories. What's the story you would tell or invent about Wilson?

Well, that's funny, I was just thinking of a story, the play *bob*, about Bob Wilson, directed by Anne Bogart. Whenever I think of portraying Bob, I think of that play, because it was so beautifully done, really fascinating work. You know, 30 years ago, when I first saw Bob's work, I thought, "Wow, this is going to be the beginning of a new school, a whole new way of doing things," and certainly Bob's work has been really important and influential, but I don't see a school of Bob Wilson going on. Bob has done – he is – everything. He shows his actors how to walk, and though I don't know if that's codified in the way it would be for a choreographer, he really is a choreographer. Hopefully, there's someone who's noting how he focuses. But with a director's style, one of the things that makes it so wonderful is that it is unrepeatable. With a lot of live art, you realize that when the artist isn't there it isn't the same, and it's usually not as good. I appreciate the fact that Bob's doing Watermill, even though he doesn't have a "Robert Wilson School of Theater"; that is his school of theater, of course, and it's creating a huge amount of variety, so that's really exciting. I guess it would be pretty odd if there were lots of people doing Bob Wilson things. I kind of wish there were, and that there were more people trained in that way of doing theater. Maybe it would be creepy. The things he's done have so many similar elements in them. He develops a vocabulary that he sticks to. The way he spots people's faces, the way he does pretty elaborate scenes, the way there's one line of light that opens and closes. He has this vocabulary, and within that there's a world of room to move; it's amazing how much space he has within that language. Whatever he does always seems big, never small. His pieces open up another world, and also voids, really amazing negative space. That's definitely a trait of Bob's work. He's a visionary architect. I feel like it's a different world. He creates huge pieces, too. They're not little. There are walls of cities and time.

> "Visionary" is a word that's often used in terms of Wilson's art. Why do you think he's called a "visionary artist"?

Because he is able to see through things and work in different tempos, completely different time frames, he gives you this completely different way of seeing the world through time. I love falling into Bob's time, and it's been one of my experiences as an artist. Through the simple process of slowing things down, you literally see things differently. The work is visionary in the sense of affecting your vision of expectation and desire. Usually, you'll turn your gaze over to a part of the stage and watch for something to happen over there, and then you look over to the other side, but Bob doesn't do that. Your eyes just sort of relax and rest on this whole spectacle. I'm not looking just straight ahead; I'm looking around; I'm looking behind my head. He just has a different way of directing your vision. After seeing a Bob Wilson play, I realize, "Wow, I have a lot more peripheral vision!"

The Man in the Raincoat, Cologne, 1981. Robert Wilson

The Man in the Raincoat, Cologne, 1981. Robert Wilson

Einstein on the Beach, Venice, 1976

A day at the opera

Imagine you are a *New Yorker* drama critic, about to see *Einstein on the Beach* at Berlin's Staatsoper, riding the ICE Sprinter train from Cologne to Berlin, narrating into a high-end camcorder. A storm is brewing. The train is going 300 km/hr. A *Herald Tribune* science reporter, driving to see the same five-hour opera, is videotaping the train from a bridge near Hanover. You are describing Wilson's stunning lighting effects into the camcorder when there is a sharp, explosive boom, and you see two brilliant lightning flashes, one from each end of the train. That evening, before the opera, you compare notes with your colleague. Her camcorder shows two simultaneous lightning flashes, but yours shows the eastern flash happening just before the western flash. Who is correct?

The science reporter explains: Both are correct. Because of the relativistic effects of your speed, time was moving differently for you, so the flashes were not simultaneous in your frame of reference. Space was different too, being compressed in the direction of your travel, making the oncoming flash arrive sooner. Einstein himself used the train metaphor to explain the impossibility of measuring temporal simultaneity between systems moving at different speeds.

But this is precisely the problem: At our human scale, we cannot "see" the very large (relativistic) or very small (quantum and nuclear). We have learned to see at mid-scale. Yet the very large and very small have become very important. Ballistic missiles, nuclear power, satellites, computers, and the vertiginous possibility of nuclear annihilation – these involve the very large and very small, which most of our culture does not yet have the cognitive skills to see.

Einstein wrote his radical papers on special relativity, the photoelectric effect (quantum theory), and Brownian motion in 1905, a year after Thomas Edison's assistant and guinea-pig, Clarence Dally, died of radiation poisoning, four years after Queen Victoria's death, while Russia was losing its war with Japan. Six years prior, Freud's *The Interpretation of Dreams* proposed the unconscious mind, and the Second Boer War erupted. Shortly thereafter, Bismarck's balance of power system collapsed, China's revolution arrived in 1911, and World War I started in 1914. The Russian revolution came in 1917, and Stalin took power in 1924. Schrödinger's wave equations appeared in 1926, followed by Heisenberg's Uncertainty Principle in 1927. In short, in less than 30 years, the workings of the world were covered in shadows. Science and society seemed to be governed more by hidden forces, or what Frederick the Great called the "prince's mistress factor," than by common sense. How could we look through the shadows?

Einstein wrote his radical 1905 papers at the advent of Fauvism. Two years prior, Isadora Duncan gave her "Dance of the Future" lecture in Berlin. Picasso and Braque invented Cubism in 1907. Joyce started *Ulysses* in 1914, just as Kandinsky started painting abstract work, Gaudí completed Park Güell, and Expressionism began its dark phase. Bartók wrote *The Wooden Prince* in 1916. Dada arose after the war, and its smarter sibling, Surrealism, began in the early 1920s. Kafka's *The Trial* was published in 1925. *The Castle* came out the following year. These artists were responding to early 20th century turbulence. One thing art can do is to help us see through shadows.

Around this time, Viktor Shkolvsky and the Russian Formalists were proposing defamiliarization or "making strange" (*Ostranenie*) as a poetic method. Since the deeper mechanisms of the world are hidden by habit, common sense, convention, and familiarity, can we see them better by juxtaposing life against the unconventional and unfamiliar? Normal life can be invisible when we are submerged in it, but artists can make the normal strange and thus visible.

Robert Wilson uses this thesis to explain why he does not practice naturalistic theater: "If you place a baroque candelabra on a baroque table," he argues, "both get lost. You can't see either. If you place the candelabra on a rock in the ocean, you begin to see what it is."[1] Accordingly, like his formalist colleagues, Wilson's responses to unpredictable, dissonant, absurd, chaotic, contingent events have been unpredictable, dissonant, absurd, chaotic, and contingent.

How does this affect the old Romantic idea that artists have unique revelations, messages, or meanings to communicate to the audience? Do these ambiguous qualities not interfere with communication? "If I wanted to send the audience a message," Wilson says, "I'd use a fax."[2] So what, then, happens to meaning?

It is important here to distinguish between meaning and its production. As I have argued elsewhere, the effect of a work of art is not necessarily dependent on meaning. The aesthetic effect occurs during the passage between chaos and order, and order is not necessarily semantic meaning.[3] Otherwise, music and abstract painting would fail. Buddhists can appreciate Gaudí's Sagrada Família, and Bach's fugues are not identifiably Protestant as opposed to Catholic.

Even in works that use meaning, the audience may be responsible for constructing it. And this, in part, is how Wilson works. He presents multiple elements – text, image, sound, stage rhythms – then uses formalist methods to provoke you to construct whatever interpretations you can. Umberto Eco calls this "Open Work," and it is an essential feature of the Modernist repertoire.

Beyond that, the interpretations you arrive at may be less important than the process of constructing them. Perhaps what Wilson provokes in you is really a way of constructing,

1
Arthur Holmberg,
The Theatre of Robert Wilson (Cambridge: Cambridge University Press, 1996), 53.

2
Ibid., 48.

3
Roald Hoffmann, in *Accident by Design*, film directed by Daniel Conrad and produced by the National Film Board of Canada, 1998.

making sense, seeing. I suggest that he is, among other things, teaching you to see through the shadows, the mist, the looking glass. And in that case, given the challenges our culture faces in the new century, what he offers is more than just an evening's entertainment.

So when watching an opera like *Einstein on the Beach*, instead of asking what it means, might it be more interesting to ask what it does (to us), and then, perhaps, how it does it? To the first question, we can form individual answers, so let us look to the question of method. First, his stage is composed with painterly care: Textures and lines (particularly the diagonals) move the eye from layer to three-dimensional layer with a skill rarely seen on stage. Movement is composed with musicality: The elements move in unison, harmony, canon, counterpoint, and dissonance. The action follows a polyphonic structure, with independent actions – dialogue, music, blocking, text, choreography, painted backdrops, moving props, projected film, and lighting – often working independently, as individual voices with separate but interwoven motivations.

What effect does polyphony have? The poet Robert Bringhurst, who sometimes writes complex polyphonic poems (one of them has four voices, in Latin, Greek, English, and Cree) has studied the characteristics of polyphony in the arts. He describes the earliest known case of polyphonic painting, the Lion Panel in the Chauvet caves in the Ardèche: "Several dozen figures – lions, mammoths, bison, rhinoceros, horses – are rendered with great clarity in black, white and red on the undulating, tawny limestone wall. The figures are in clusters. Patterns form where the outlines overlap. The result is both emphatically pictorial and powerfully abstract." The last sentence applies well to *Einstein on the Beach*.

Bringhurst concludes: "We learn to think...by accumulating sensory experience of three-dimensional space. That experience is achieved by several means, including echolocation, binocular vision and voluntary motion....The mind, if this is right, consists of abstract patterns formed from multiple chains of concrete sensory perceptions. And works of polyphonic art – Josquin's motets, Bach's fugues and the Lion Panel for example – don't just express emotions or mental states; they are models and exemplars of the ground of mind itself."[4]

In my field, film, I often use superimposition, a form of visual polyphony. A more common filmic polyphony is montage (editing), though it is contrapuntal and antiphonal rather than simultaneous. One can make montage on stage with sudden shifts of light between parts of the stage, and Wilson sometimes does. More often, he uses more simultaneous methods, where different sides, layers, and levels of the stage display independently motivated, overlapping visions and voices. In both cases, he invokes the feel and methodology of montage.

If Wilson's polyphony can be viewed as a kind of montage, it is analogous in structure (if not in tone) to what Sergei Eisenstein, the Russian film genius, was doing in the early 20th century. Eisenstein studied engineering; Wilson studied architecture. Both artists initially worked designing stage sets, and both make complex, dynamic structures using forced "collisions" of conflicting images.

4
Robert Bringhurst, "Singing with the Frogs," in *Everywhere Being is Dancing* (Kentville, Nova Scotia: Gaspereau Press, 2007), 60–61.

For example, Act I, scene two of *Einstein on the Beach* opens on a courtroom with a giant white bed in the middle. A shaft of light hangs above it to echo its horizontal line. A numberless clock sits over the judge's bench. Philip Glass's music pulses. The chorus files into the jury box. Einstein sits downstage of the jurors with a violin. Two stenographers file their nails. Two judges, a child and an old man, robed and wigged, enter. An Einstein clone, Lucinda Childs, sits in a high witness chair made of steel pipes. The judges monotonously call the court to order six times. The chorus counts numbers on the beats of the music; the tempo and spare melody are constant, but the division of beats into measures seems to shift from 4/4 to 7/4, to 5/4, to 6/8. The counting raises associations to countdowns for missiles or atomic tests, or to time-dilations in Einstein's equations and Wilson's blocking. A lawyer, Sheryl Sutton, reads a monologue written by a child, Christopher Knowles. A giant test tube descends. Performers eat their lunches. The music halts. Everyone stares at their wristwatches and freezes for a few beats. A judge reads a romantic monologue.

These non-sequiturs are more surrealistic and less percussive than Eisenstein's "collisions," but the tactic of making polyphonic unity via dialectical conflict is similar. In Eisenstein's "Odessa Steps" sequence (in *Battleship Potemkin*, about the 1905 Odessa uprising), rhythmic "collision" of shots stems from kinetic and ideological conflict, not surrealistic incongruity. Each shot's movement within the frame conveys a screen direction, and the internal movements of adjoining shots collaborate with the movements of its neighbors to convey momentum or collision. Beyond kinetic conflict (the Cossacks move down and screen-right; the protesting citizens move up and screen-left), the two forces are antiphonal in an ideological way as well, which Eisenstein termed "dialectic" montage. But this is early Eisenstein; more convincing parallels with Wilson's work come later.

Shots, for Eisenstein, are not building-blocks but "cells." Their relationships are functionally complex, having a physiology as well as an anatomy. Together, they form an organism, which, like all nature, is in motion. "Art," said Eisenstein, "is always conflict...it is art's task to make manifest the contradictions of being...."[5] His "dialectic" montage created life out of conflict and contradiction.

In *Ivan the Terrible*, a film in which the brutal Tsar Ivan represents Stalin, Eisenstein's montage became far more elaborate. A key structural motif derives from haiku (which Eisenstein studied) and consists of a series of three "lines" (a shot represents a line), the last line of which "collides" with the first two, in an unexpected way, to deliver some surprising revelation. Here is a haiku:

> The piercing chill I feel:
> my dead wife's comb, in our bedroom,
> under my heel
> Taniguchi Buson

5
Sergei Eisenstein, *Film Form*, Jay Leda, trans. (San Diego: Harcourt Brace, 1949), 46.

Each line describes a sensation. The second line flows naturally from the first. The last line takes an unexpected change of direction, bringing all three lines into unity. The conceptual

Einstein on the Beach, New York City, 1984. Robert Wilson

New York City, 1971

Paris, 1971

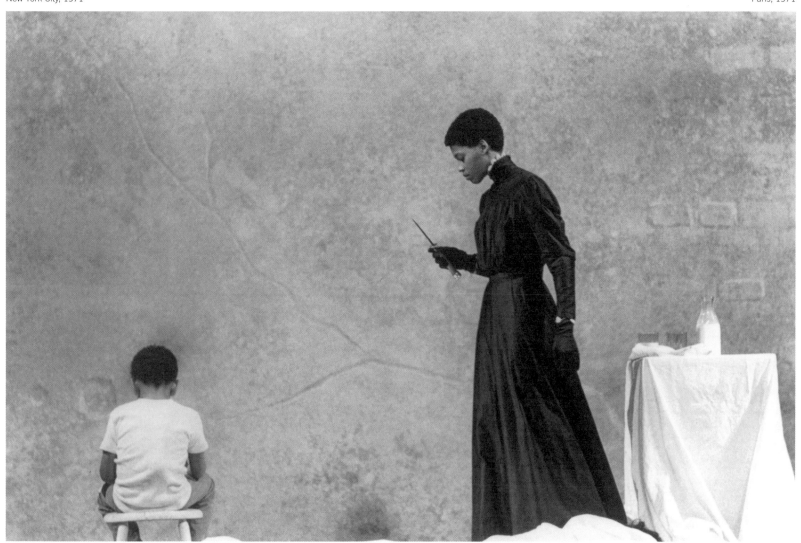

Deafman Glance, New York City, 1971. Sheryl Sutton

distance between the last line and the first is like a void, and the reader leaps over this void to feel the unity or epiphany. This unexpected leap and the sheer concision of structure evoke the special aesthetic effect. Wilson uses this in his surrealistic juxtapositions (although Wilson's unity is often much less direct and more intuitive).

Film scholar Gerald Mast calls this method "surprising inevitability."[6] In biology, when forms arise that make sense but which were not predictable from the known rules, we call them "emergent forms." We can use both terminologies in the arts. In Bach's fugues, for example, he generates emergent forms that were not predictable from the rules, but which make exquisite sense, producing an effect of surprising inevitability. And when Bach breaks his rules, particularly rules of canonic symmetry (which he does often), he reveals more complex rules and higher symmetries. By rewarding expectations in unexpected ways, he makes internal sense. We feel in this sense the same kind of higher purpose that we often feel in the work of Eisenstein and Wilson.

In his later work, Eisenstein played with what he called "Overtonal" montage, in which secondary emotional themes are overlaid against dominant themes by intercutting on multiple themes, such as sound, movement, music, and color. At its most complex, this three-ring circus bombards the senses with a wild excess of images, using non-matching-action and pseudo-matching-action cutting to overwhelm the normal sense of three-dimensional space, causing turbulence and aesthetic vertigo, creating what Eisenstein called "ecstasy." He was not referring to emotion; the root is "ex-stasis" (out from stillness), and to Eisenstein it meant an exiting of the frame provoked by all available methods of polyphonic montage. The audience leaps outside the frame to reach a transcendent rise in consciousness.

Kristin Thompson writes that Eisenstein wanted to tap the viewer's pre-logical "inner speech," which "accumulates through the repetition and combination of sensations from the outer world." He did this "...by orchestrating montage elements with repetitions and variations in a dense weave..." to "...touch off this pre-logical sensuous thought in the spectator. If correctly – that is intensely – done, the results for the spectator would be *ecstasy*, an irresistible carrying of the self completely over into the sensuous effect of the film."[7]

Certainly "...orchestrating montage elements with repetitions and variations in a dense weave..." well describes the structure of *Einstein on the Beach* and much of Wilson's other work. As we have mentioned, Wilson uses more surrealistic incongruity and non sequitur than Eisenstein. He also comes much closer to comic absurdity.

Consider the slow, frightening, absurd treatment of violence in the beginning of Wilson's *Deafman Glance*: On a white platform, a mother in a fancy black dress and red gloves puts black gloves over the red ones, slowly serves both of her children milk, and slowly, gently stabs them to death. A witness, the older brother, screams at each murder. A gray backdrop rises, revealing a forest with a backwards-walking pink angel and a group of women in white Victorian gowns with birds on their fingers. The "Moonlight Sonata" plays. A giant

6
Gerald Mast, *Howard Hawks, Storyteller* (Oxford: Oxford University Press, 1982), 30–31.

7
Kristin Thompson, *Eisenstein's Ivan the Terrible* (Princeton: Princeton University Press, 1981), 6–7.

frog in a smoking jacket drinks cocktails, and men with yellow fish on their backs drift on a red river. The older brother floats through the air on a bench suspended by wires. A giant bee and a giant rabbit dance to pop music. A giant ox swallows the sun which glows in his stomach as his head falls off. To the strains of Fauré's *Requiem*, a tribe of apes emerges and picks up apples as George Washington and Marie Antoinette walk by, her parasol catching fire, the apples floating away. Stars fall. A banjo plays.

The tones, images, tempos, and rhythms are completely different, but the polyphonic approach is similar and it has the same goals: to tap the audience's pre-logical inner speech "...by orchestrating montage elements with repetitions and variations in a dense weave..." to "...touch off this pre-logical sensuous thought in the spectator." That is, both directors are aiming for "ecstasy." They have something else in common also. In dealing with the deepest, most puzzling, most dissonant aspects of 20th century human experience, both directors use this "ecstasy" to invoke what some call "the sublime."

In Kant's usage, "sublime" refers to phenomena, which, through excess magnitude, force, or depth, overwhelm the aesthetic and cognitive faculties in a discordant but oddly pleasurable way. They expose the failure of our ability to perceive scale. Examples of the

Deafman Glance, New York City, 1971

sublime might include volcanic explosions, skydiving, or riding a train that is hit by lightning at the front and rear ends simultaneously. It can interact with the aesthetic faculties, but it differs from beauty. The two qualities can be hard to separate; e.g., some late paintings of Turner, organ fugues by Bach, or (for some) equations of Einstein can be both beautiful and sublime.

Going back to our initial question, if art can help us make sense (even non-rational sense) of the existential challenges of the early 20th century, how does invocation of the sublime help us make this sense? The sublime deals more with incongruity (things that don't fit) than with making sense. This incongruity applies to humor too, though it is often taken as the opposite of the sublime, as in the phrase, "from the sublime to the ridiculous." Comedy makes us laugh, but its subject matter is not usually pleasure. It deals mostly with misfortune. In a sense, it's worse than tragedy; at least in tragedy, the hero gets to die in the end.

Wilson can be quite comical, and he often uses incongruity to suspend us between the comic and the sublime. The sense that this makes is not any fixed interpretation or meaning. In the world as on stage, we humans are absurdly unprepared to deal with the pathologies we ourselves blindly create. Wilson plays with this as raw material. He gives no prescriptions,

Deafman Glance, Paris, 1971

Deafman Glance, Paris, 1971

Le Martyre de Saint Sébastien, Paris, 1988

or even a diagnosis. But his suspension between comic and sublime is a kind of "making strange" that allows us perhaps to see at least a fever rising through the mist.

Comedy uses incongruity by setting up expectations and paying them off with the inappropriate or disproportionate – something that doesn't fit. This is the device of surprising inevitability, only the effect is reversed. Your expectations are raised, but instead of getting more than you expect, you get less.

For Wilson, incongruity is often a case of surreal juxtaposition, in which we are provoked to make sense out of two or more ideas or images that initially display no rational connection. Sometimes it is a function of scale. The huge cat legs ambling across the stage in *The King of Spain*, the giant frog and dancing bunny rabbit in *Deafman Glance*, the enormous woman with a small head in *the CIVIL warS*; this strategy demands a strong sense of design, and in Wilson's hands, it works beautifully both as comedy and as a surreal invitation into the sublime.

In addition to surrealistic juxtaposition, incongruities of theme and scale, and the provocation of ecstasy through multiplication of ideas and images, Wilson's work is strikingly unique in its frequent use of extremely slow tempos. This is another way of making strange by playing with scale, but it is more than that: In his hands it is intensely lyrical. He is not being provocative by breaking rules just for the sake of breaking them, nor is he trying to bore or offend. His slow action is composed in a way that invites meditative, trancelike states not entirely foreign to Eisenstein's ecstasy.

In fact, Wilson's "slow" does not seem slow. There is so much compelling detail in the sets and lighting design, that the eye needs lots of time to process it. Even a static tableau can act as time-based art if it changes in the mind as you look at it (e.g., Picasso's early cubist work). And Wilson's tableaux are never completely static for very long. Even the relatively modest one-man-show *HAMLET: a monologue* used up to 350 lighting instruments and around 325 cues for lighting, sets, effects, and entrances (not including sound).

In *Einstein on the Beach*, time dilation plays a thematic role in addition to its formal one. To Einstein, as velocity approaches the speed of light, time slows down. Wilson, in response, often slows stage time, especially in the way a flat cutout of a locomotive (Einstein's train metaphor, but also a symbol of industrial progress) slowly ferments across the stage. By "making strange" the flow of time in this way, he calls attention to it. Often, time keeps busy, moving its arms but going nowhere, like a Hapsburg bureaucrat endlessly filing papers. And the actors flagrantly reinforce the theme by checking their watches.

Time dilation happens in other art forms also. In film, we use "slow motion." Kafka plays with it in *The Castle* (speaking of Hapsburg bureaucrats). And time typically slips its moorings in aboriginal mythological systems. In North American first-nations mythology, for example, mythical events take place in what Haida Carver and storyteller Bill Reid called "mythtime." This is a non-linear time-outside-of-time, which humans enter at their risk, in which the same events are always current. It has the temporal scale of tides, seasons, and the growth of trees. A human can get into a canoe and spend 30 years just paddling to the next village, half a mile away. They can leave as youths, arrive in time to meet grown grandchildren, and return, white-haired, to their own village just in time to take the stew-pot off the fire, where they left it.[8]

So after all these methods – ecstasy, time dilation, polyphony, making strange, suspension between comic and sublime, and a magic forest of rich associations without causal connection – after all this, what can this opera do to us or for us? Can it help us see through the shadows? The chemist and poet Roald Hoffmann, when discussing moments of aesthetic understanding, often mentions Rilke's poem "Archaic Torso of Apollo." Here Rilke contemplates the armless, legless, headless, strangely beautiful marble god. At the end of the poem, the poet, looking deeply at the torso as if it were looking back at him and using "du," the intimate form of "you," says, "...then there is no part of this that does not see you. You must change your life." The god, whom he cannot fully see, has looked at him intimately and fully seen him. Hoffmann asks why he must change his life.[9] The opera is perhaps like that torso we cannot fully see, but that fully sees and wants to change us.

Will watching this five-hour Wilson opera in Berlin change your life, or maybe just the way you think about trains? Here's what *New York Times* critic Bernard Holland wrote, concerning the same opera, in a different city, via a different train: "*Einstein on the Beach* changed my life. Everything I thought musical theater was, abruptly wasn't. St. Paul had his road to Damascus; mine was the Brooklyn-bound No. 4 train to Atlantic Avenue."

But how did watching this five-hour opera change him? What did it mean to him? "People smarter than I have expended a lot of brain power trying to figure out what *Einstein on the Beach* means," he writes. "I don't think it means anything. It is majestically two-dimensional. Its references to the atomic age, criminal justice, true love, air-conditioning, and Patty Hearst are merely art materials, like red paint or blue."[10]

Faced with the crises of modernity, particularly those of blindness and illusion, it may be useful to think of the universe as having no particular meaning or sense; then sense is something we have to construct out of our contradictory perceptions. Perhaps an opera that invites us (even in a lyrical, attractive way) to confront contradictions and paradoxes should not be expected to present us with fixed or pre-fabricated meanings. Perhaps Wilson's cognitively dissonant surrealism is more realistic than storybook operas with clear morals or messages. So Bernard Holland's way of watching the opera seems to work. He was able to change his life without extracting any meaning from the opera.

Measured by predictive value, there is likely no more objective mental pursuit than physics. But what do post-Einstein physicists say about meaning? Here is Steven Weinberg: "The laws of nature may dictate that there's something rather than nothing, but still, they leave

8
Robert Bringhurst, *A Story as Sharp as a Knife* (Vancouver: Douglas and McIntyre, 1999).

9
Roald Hoffmann, in *Accident by Design*, op.cit.

10
Bernard Holland, "Transformed by the Tonic of 'Einstein'," *The New York Times*, December 2, 2007.

you with the big 'why?' Why are the laws of nature? What has been revealed so far is that we live in a universe governed by mathematical, impersonal laws, in which we don't play a starring role. It doesn't mean that life is pointless, but it means we have to find a point for life. The purpose, therefore, has to come from ourselves."[11]

And here, again, is poet Robert Bringhurst: "Where mythology is openly important, the myths are healthy when they are told without morals. If a thing has real guts – if it has blood flowing in it – it's going to explain a whole range of phenomena, some of which we're going to take years to discover. The myth will have a life of its own. It isn't going to be tied to this rock or that tree. A real myth, like a real equation, or a real story, or a real melody, keeps reappearing, keeps explaining things you didn't even know needed to be explained."[12]

And maybe that is a fine way to look at Wilson's exquisite opera after a double lightning strike, or other exigencies that shake our modern equilibrium. He keeps explaining things we did not even know needed to be explained.

11
Steven Weinberg, in *Seducing the Guard*, film directed by Daniel Conrad and produced by Moving Images, 1999.

12
Robert Bringhurst, in *Accident by Design*, op.cit.

Einstein on the Beach,
New York City, 1992

Woyzeck, Copenhagen, 2000

Of Bob and BAM

"Brooklyn is outside the central core of the performing arts in New York City," Harvey Lichtenstein told one interviewer, looking back on his beginnings as he prepared to retire as Executive Producer of the Brooklyn Academy of Music (BAM), "so in order to develop our audience and our reputation, it was necessary to go outside the mainstream, do new work, take unconventional approaches." Under Lichtenstein's direction from 1967 to 1999, BAM systematically upended a traditional audience's expectations of what one might find in a venerable opera house. He installed all manner of genre-defying artists, including Robert Wilson, whose epic-sized visionary musical collaborations established BAM as an outpost for the avant-garde.

Over the following five decades, BAM would present Wilson's landmark works, including *The Life and Times of Sigmund Freud* (1969), *Einstein on the Beach* (1984 and 1992), *The Black Rider* (1993), *Alice* (1995), *Monsters of Grace* (1998), *Woyzeck* (2002), *The Temptation of St. Anthony* (2004), *Quartett* (2009), and, on Wilson's 70th birthday October 4, 2011, *The Threepenny Opera*. Such was BAM's commitment to Wilson's art that when funding for the 12-hour production of *the CIVIL warS* at the Olympic Arts Festival fell through in 1984, Lichtenstein briefly considered cancelling the entire 1985 Next Wave Festival in order to use the money to produce the work. It was at BAM that Philip Glass first became aware of Wilson's stage work, during an overnight performance of *The Life and Times of Joseph Stalin* (1973); shortly thereafter, the two would be collaborators. It is at BAM that the new production of *Einstein* will have its New York premiere in 2012.

From his office atop BAM, Lichtenstein's successor Joseph V. Melillo reigns over the country's oldest performing arts organization, widely considered its most important. Melillo came to BAM as founding director of the Next Wave Festival, and worked closely with Philip Glass and Robert Wilson on the 1984 revival of *Einstein on the Beach*. I had come to talk to him about Robert Wilson because BAM has presented more of Wilson's work than any other American theater.

The first work of art that I saw that Robert Wilson directed and designed was *A Letter for Queen Victoria* on Broadway, which predates my being hired to come to the Brooklyn Academy of Music in 1983 to produce the first Next Wave Festival. When I was hired, Harvey Lichtenstein had a list of names of individual artists and productions, and my first act was to make a file folder on each one to go about the process of structuring the festival. On that list was *Einstein on the Beach* by Robert Wilson and Philip Glass. It became readily apparent, both in my professional research and in discussions with the representatives of both of those artists, that we were not going to be able to produce or present *Einstein on the Beach* in the first Next Wave Festival. What we could do was work with the artists and their representatives to reconstruct *Einstein On The Beach*, which we did, and it ultimately premiered in the Howard Gilman Opera House in December of 1984.

BAM is always in the picture when one talks about *Einstein on the Beach*, which was originally commissioned by France in honor of the American bicentennial. After its premiere in July 1976 at the Festival d'Avignon and its European tour, followed by two performances at the Metropolitan Opera, it disappeared. We didn't see it until it was performed at BAM during the second Next Wave Festival in 1984, and then again in 1992. How do you explain that a work that had such impact then was not seen for many years, and will only be seen again now in 2012, 20 years after its last revival?

The question is: Why do we not have *Einstein on the Beach* in our lives the way that we have the works of Verdi, Puccini, et al., in terms of opera composers? Because *Einstein on the Beach* is a visionary work of two titans of the 20th century, and it's a meditation on the historic character Einstein and the implications of his history, his research for all of us as human beings, for our daily lives and our existence, as well as for our global communities. Because it does not have a linear narrative – it's an imagistic work – it's more of a challenge, I think, for opera companies to embrace this innovative, non-conventional, non-traditional form for their audiences. It is a work of a different vision, both musically and theatrically. There's nothing like it. In our society, that is an anomaly, because unless you see it and experience it, you don't know what it is. The Philip Glass score exists on a CD, but that is not the theatrical and the visual reality of the opera, of being bombarded by these extraordinary visual images and this movement by the Lucinda Childs Dance Company, which was commissioned to do the choreography for the 1984 production and remains the choreographer of choice for both Wilson and Glass. That is the reality: This work of art created by these two men out of their own passions and intellect sits by itself, and everyone has to wrestle with that fact.

But how can a work endure if new audiences can't see it? This is the larger question of how performance in general can be preserved. Is preserving performance something that BAM is concerned about? Or is BAM's role just to keep reproducing a work because, in the end, that's the only way to preserve it as a performance? Would you do a full video of *Einstein*, for instance?

That would be the responsibility of Robert Wilson and Philip Glass; they would have to see if they want to commit to doing a DVD of the work. That choice would not be up to us. BAM wouldn't have the resources to do that, and the artists are the owners of the work. We would be in the position only of enabling it to be restaged and then presenting it. We do have a digital video archive of our works that we present, but that is an archive of the work – it is not to be thought of as the actual work, so there's a cultural-historical imperative operating on BAM's part to record productions for posterity, versus the artists' imperative to originate and create the work and then decide how to present it in a different form to audiences outside of the theater, if at all.

To what extent is the question of reproducing a work also a question of funding?

Opera companies spend a lot of money producing opera, so I think the costs of producing *Einstein on the Beach* are relative. What is absolutely the gauntlet that is thrown down is that most audiences are not prepared to embrace this art. They have no relationship to the artistry of Robert Wilson and Philip Glass together. Yes, producers may do a Robert Wilson production, engage him as a freelance director or designer to do a project – Wagner's *Lohengrin* at the Metropolitan Opera – or they present Philip Glass's opera *Satyagraha*. But what those two artists agreed to do and accomplished together was something that simply changed our understanding of opera and music theater. It is just of itself. Audiences are less prepared for it because they don't have this art programmed within their daily lives, and they're unfamiliar with this particular aesthetic journey. I've referred to it as a non-linear libretto, but it's a visual libretto, and there's a musical score to support the visual libretto, and it's a kinetic experience because there are dance sequences in the piece. It is about all those forces coming together to render this particular experience.

I have done this project twice in my life so I have a kind of territorial affection for wanting to do it a third time, both for myself and for the audiences that come to BAM. I think it's been just a labor of intensity and love to support both those artists, and also the men and women who support them – the armature. God bless that there's a woman named Linda Brumbach at Pomegranate Arts who is going to produce *Einstein* for them again and make it happen now; and I'm there for her.

> Will an audience seeing the work today react very differently from the 1976 audience?

I think they won't radically be different. First-time viewers have heard about this project; it has a mythic quality, and it will have the element of surprise for many audiences. The audiences who have seen the previous incarnations will have a reverence for re-engaging with the material.

You can ask if there's a challenge in presenting avant-garde material decades after it was new and make it still feel new. I think the answer is to trust the material and its authenticity. Not to alter it, or try to contemporize it or take it out of its historical context, but to give the artists everything that they require in order to do their work, and I believe that that kind of authenticity communicates from the stage.

> You have said that the production of *Einstein on the Beach* at BAM was one of the highlights of your career. Why?

My answer, personally, is I've never seen the stage used in this way, so it was a discovery for me. But also, I had my own emotional and psychological journey through the art of this particular work, which is very gratifying and nurturing for me, and so I long for the next experience because I feel it very physically. It's certainly an intellectual experience, but it's also a very sensual, physical one for me. The operative word is "journey," and that is what I viscerally felt at the multiple performances – and remember, I've seen many, many performances of *Einstein on the Beach*.

New York City, 1969

The King of Spain/The Life and Times of Sigmund Freud, New York City, 1969[1]

> Do you consider *Einstein* a political work?

No, no, far from it, not at all. As I characterize it, it is really a meditation on Einstein and the implications of who he was, what he developed, what he discovered and revealed to us in science.

> BAM has presented other Robert Wilson works. In 2009, you put on his version of Heiner Müller's *Quartett*, with Isabelle Huppert in the leading role of the Marquise de Merteuil. You put the play on in French, in Brooklyn: a German play spoken in French before an anglophone audience. Who made that decision?

I did. The production originated at the Théâtre de l'Odéon in Paris, and we took that production and brought it to BAM. And that production was in French. We added an English translation in overhead. Despite what might have been language barriers, this was a very successful production for BAM.

> What makes for a successful production at BAM? You said that you can look at different theater pieces and tell what will work for BAM's audiences. How do you know?

There was a great artistic director who, when asked about his art – and I'll quote him – said, "You feel it in your hips." I am nearing my 30th year of working here at BAM; I have been trained professionally to be the curator of this institution. And that's the answer. I've made more successful decisions than failures, which means I still have my job. But I can do it here. I would not say that I could replicate my artistic career at another institution.

> Has BAM "trained" its audiences to be receptive to a certain kind of avant-garde work, such as Wilson's?

I would never use that language. I would say that New York City has been exceptionally responsive to the art that Harvey Lichtenstein programmed, and that Joe Melillo currently programs here at BAM, where we seek to find new and innovative, progressive ideas in all the performing arts and make that a reality for New Yorkers. New Yorkers are fundamentally curious about art, and contemporary art is what they're curious about here, in the venues that we operate. There's a certain trust that exists in the audiences that come to BAM. They know fundamentally that they will be challenged. They may be completely unknowledgeable and unfamiliar with the artist, the name of the production or the company, but they are just instinctively curious about a discovery.

> Do you consider that BAM and the Berliner Ensemble have privileged relationships with Wilson? He seems to work repeatedly with both of you.

Well, the direct answer is yes. BAM has put on numerous works by Bob Wilson since 1969, and you know that Harvey Lichtenstein even considered cancelling the entire Next Wave

1
The King of Spain was incorporated into and became Act I of *The Life and Times of Sigmund Freud*, and both were performed in New York City in 1969. In the Robert Wilson archives, these photographs appear under the titles of both plays.

Festival to do *the CIVIL warS*. It's obviously different with the Berliner Ensemble because they have an acting company. With BAM, Robert Wilson has a commitment, previously from Harvey Lichtenstein and currently myself as Executive Producers of BAM, that we want to ensure the consistent deliverance of his art in various, different forms. And secondly, with BAM, Wilson has the confidence to know that the stagehands at this theater understand the precision, the preciseness that he desires for his art.

> Robert Wilson has created an enormous body of work, and is criticized by some for repeating himself in an almost formulaic way. Can an artist who has such a distinctive, identifiable language avoid accusations of repetition?

I don't think he can escape that criticism, except that the truth is he is never repeating himself, that in each work, he knows exactly what story he wants to tell and how he wants to tell it. He has a vocabulary. He has this particular color blue that he can create through lighting instruments on the stage. He paints the stage with his light, and he has given audiences in the theater and opera the beauty of what the saturation of light can provide. On some autumn nights when I'm crossing the Brooklyn Bridge or the Manhattan Bridge to go home to Manhattan in the evening, I recognize the blue in the natural sky and I go, "Oh! It's a Robert Wilson sky!" And it's how he *uses* his vocabulary that is unique and distinct to each production.

the CIVIL warS – Rome Section, New York City, 1986

Take *The Golden Windows*, a piece Bob created in Germany in 1982 and at BAM years later. It shows a different side of Robert Wilson. There is only distant background music. The central image is a black house that moves to three different locations on the horizon. There is an earthquake in which the set pulls apart and rocks fall from the sky. Central to the piece is Hans Peter Kuhn's "audio environment," which diffuses the voices of the four characters around the theater. Some of the lines are spoken from the stage, others are pre-recorded, and others amplified by radio microphones attached to speakers that are strategically placed throughout the theater. The effect is of sounds literally zooming at the audience from every direction.

Are there playwrights that you see as having a special affinity with Wilson?

I've been educated by his interest in playwriting, and I've had two surprises: one, August Strindberg, and the second, Bertolt Brecht. I think that it's magical how a playwright and Wilson coming together reveals itself in unique, distinct ways. When Wilson put on Strindberg's *Dream Play*, which we did here with a Stockholm-based acting company, the surprise was that you found yourself saying, "Oh, yeah! He's made sense of this obtuse play." With Brecht's *Threepenny Opera*, it is as though, when you see Wilson's rendition and interpretation, you think, "Okay, yes! You know, this is what Brecht exactly wanted!"

When you produce Robert Wilson's work, do you stay out of the production entirely? Do you come in with ideas?

I try to see a lot of work before I curatorially decide which is the right work. Therefore, I don't editorialize Wilson's work as a presenter. I go, I see a fully staged production, and I decide: "Is this the right Robert Wilson work to bring to either the Opera House or the BAM Harvey Theater?" And that has to do with the intrinsic values and scale operating in the work that he's created and crafted, and with whether or not it can fit into one of those venues. In translating a work of art to one of our venues, you're intimately involved in the transference; it's ultimately what producers do. But I govern a staff that then deals with the details and delineations of it. So no, I don't intrude.

So there are no conflicts?

Conflict with Robert Wilson is a different kind of conflict. It's about how much preparatory time is required, which means tech time, lighting time, and because time equals money, there's never enough time. He has to come to some resolution, and he does, but it's always about engaging him and his representatives and trying to be practical about the amount of stage time.

Inevitably, this brings up the question about the difference between Europe and the United States in the reception and production of Wilson's work. Why is Robert Wilson produced more in Europe than in the US? Is it because state funding of culture in Europe allows

The Golden Windows, New York City, 1985

Dream Play, Stockholm, 1998

Dream Play, Stockholm, 1998

for his productions? Is it a question of money alone, or are there other reasons? Cultural differences?

I do think that the money question is important. Bob's works are very expensive to produce, in part because he's such a perfectionist. As I just said, he wants more rehearsal time, and that costs money. That's easier to do when you have state funding for the arts than when you have to look at raising money for a production. But I think there are cultural differences as well. European audiences are more sophisticated in their taste; it was Europe that first recognized Bob's work. I can't put my finger on exactly what the difference is, but I do think that a European audience brings with it an ease with culture – and with avant-garde work in particular – that favors the work of someone like Bob Wilson.

> You refer to yourself as "curator" of BAM, which is usually a term associated with museums and the visual rather than the performing arts. It recalls something Wilson has said about *Monsters of Grace*: "You go to our opera like you go to a museum."[2]

It's a title of a practice that's based on aesthetics and analysis, judgments, research, and I relate to that because I travel a lot for our artistic programming. I see a lot of work here in New York City and other places, and research and experience all the possible choices for BAM myself. It's very Aristotelian: Selectivity is the first prerequisite for art. I make a selection. In other words, I make a curatorial choice. My title is Executive Producer, and yes, I know how to originate work; but on the whole, I'm much more comfortable characterizing it as curatorial judgment.

> When you spoke earlier about seeing Wilson's *A Letter for Queen Victoria* on Broadway, you characterized it as a show "directed and designed" by Robert Wilson. What do you call Wilson? What is Wilson? Is he a director? Is he a designer? Is he a curator? A producer?

That's a very provocative question, and the answer is: He's an artist, and his art flows into the world of theater, opera, and music theater, into the performative world and into the visual art world; lighting design, the design of the sets, the physical environment of the theater also are part of his art. And that's the wonderful discovery about working with him and becoming familiar with his aesthetic.

> If you could produce any work by Wilson from any moment in this career – not necessarily at BAM or for BAM's audiences, but in the abstract – what would it be?

Exactly what I've done.

2
Quoted in Seth Rogovoy, "Concert Review Glass/ Wilson's *Monsters of Grace*, heralds new perspectives in performance at Mass MoCa," 17 July, 1999, published in *Berkshire Eagle*, 20 July, 1999.

Silent frog

Frogs usually talk a lot, right? They talk and talk, and it never makes any sense. Superficial creatures, one would say. But not the frog in this story. He hated to talk. He loathed the sound of his own croak.

Only in the middle of the night, when the water lilies were asleep and if he really couldn't help himself, would he utter the occasional *ribbit*.

During the day he would sit motionless at the edge of a pond, looking silently at the two water lilies inside swaying in the breeze. But his frog-thoughts ran deep. "Why am I green? Why is there still sound when it's silent? How can the sun disappear and then reappear the next morning?" he would muse. But he kept his mouth shut and his thoughts to himself.

When the sun set, the water lilies would become silhouettes against the sky. The frog imagined them to start dancing, but of course they never did. They would just fade into black, and he'd fall asleep. The next day everything would be just the same.

But in his dreams it was all very different. The sun would go up and down by his command. He would sing the frog anthem, and the water lilies would dance. The pond would turn into hundreds of fountains, making music that sounded like harps and violins playing. The sun would kiss his cheek and the water would feel like a warm coat.

But then he'd wake up with the mystery gone, and he would sit again and watch. It started to make him blue.

The water lilies had been in the pond for as long as they could remember. They loved to chat all day long, but had never learned how to quack. So they only had each other to talk to. Their shy whispering sounded like the water and would mix with the breeze. They had been around the frog forever and noticed his change. "He sits differently," they murmured. "And his eyes are distant." They started to worry about their neighbor.

"Maybe we should dance a bit for our frog," they said to themselves. "He looks so sad, especially around sunset." Slowly, they started swaying their stems to a sudden gust of wind. The setting sun colored their leaves bright orange and they shivered rhythmically to the sound of a sudden rain shower.

The frog smiled. How could they have guessed his thoughts?

Sometimes a wish is as real as a spoken thought.

Try it!

Der Freischütz, Baden-Baden, 2009. Costume by Viktor & Rolf

156

Rehearsal for *The Forest*, Berlin, 1988. Robert Wilson and Heiner Müller

Death, Destruction & Detroit, Berlin, 1979

The child as magician: sketches for a portrait[1]

Word

September 1976: A young giant with a perplexing baby face, out of which gaze, with uncomfortable directness, two very light blue eyes. Not a "hard" gaze: merely not lined with the ordinary velvet of appeal or participation. The gaze that looks but does not speak (does not advertise, ask, feign comprehension) – it makes one feel insecure.

•

When I met Robert Wilson, he could not yet speak. His answers were dragging and somehow beside the point – as if they stemmed from a core that could not be expressed or brought forth in everyday logic. Many of the strangely clipped sentences came out with such difficulty that communication seemed already coercion to betrayal. Wilson was 34 when I brought his and Philip Glass's *Einstein on the Beach* to Hamburg. Like an obstinate kid of three or four, he could not, he would not, speak.

Six years earlier, 1970, his great piece of theater was called: *Deafman Glance*. Louis Aragon wrote (in an open letter to the dead André Breton): "The world of a deaf child opens itself to us like a mute mouth. We live in this world for more than four hours, there, where in the absence of words, 60 people have no speech other than movement. Listen, André, to what I say to those that have the ears for things unheard: Never have I, as long as I have lived, seen anything more beautiful."[2]

•

In ancient Greece, one would lay large pebbles upon his tongue in order to learn to speak "pleasingly" and to gain communicative flexibility. Wilson appears to have filled his mouth with heavy, staggering words in order to prevent himself from speaking lies.

Today in his rehearsals he works all day on language (Gertrude Stein's, Heiner Müller's). He has no aim of making the intonations pregnant with content, nor does he bend them to the expression of a thought or feeling. He helps the word back to its materiality and repose.

The word: no snake this time, to coil through all and everything; but a thing. A stone perhaps (only there is no light within a stone).

•

1
The original German version of this essay was published in Ivan Nagel, *Liebe! Liebe! Liebe! ist die Seele des Genies* (Munich: Hanser, 1996), 202–13. Nagel made minor changes for this publication, the first to appear in English.

2
Louis Aragon, "An Open Letter to André Breton on Robert Wilson's *Deafman Glance*" (June 2, 1971).

Often his actors are gripped by untamable fits of rage against the ordering, orderly impositions of speech. Their members sharpened in spastic pushing and stabbing gestures, out of their gorges flow bellowing, squeaking sounds that have escaped from all sociability and discursive utility. Against Wilson's other stage time of extreme slowdown – the fury of a convulsive "no."

A recollection of Wilson/Müller's *Hamletmachine*, Thalia Theater, Hamburg 1986. Taunting and alluring bird calls burst forth from a half-grown drama student, then whole monologues of hers in cold-blooded possessed chirping and twittering: a brainless ecstasy. Are birds crazy? (In the program I read: "Annette Paulmann.")

Image

February 1982: Müller's texts could be blind; nowhere are depicted landscapes, animals, or men. Out of perfidious curiosity I bring together Wilson and Müller. What shall one who turns himself blind and one who turns himself deaf have to say to each other?

Müller's laconism (leaps in syntax, holes in rhythm) hinders the creation of a "style." The lumpy hard word cannot embrace images, it cannot be enfolded by an image. Such was Müller's *challenge*; and Wilson's *response*?

A vacuum inserts itself between word and image: Voided by fear, the splintering shards of speech might chafe and tear colors, figures, forms. But in this luminous void (which is Wilson's stage) an immense happiness also may spread. Composure arises, where eyes and ears are liberated from the slavish eagerness of serving one another.

•

Since primordial times human praxis has commanded that the senses cooperate: Without unity of vision and hearing, the hand could neither work nor kill well. Wilson's theater frees the eye and ear from the compulsion of being mere tools (for us, and for one another). It gives them with one parting blow inutility and autonomy. In technical terms, the specificity of Wilson's theater can thus be defined: Image and word never mix or double one another.

One could say: Wilson protects the word, the gesture, the image, from their profitable pragmatic misuse by separating them into alien useless things. His time erases our chronometrically-driven time of producing, buying, and consuming. The repose of the action, the patient concentration of the actors, the freely choosing, wandering, tarrying gaze of the spectators, all brace themselves against a hurried rationalized world. But is Wilson not then hawking the jargon of cultural criticism?

The force of his artistic vision lies precisely in the fact that it neither attaches itself to imitating nor to complaining about the routines of everyday life. (It is neither "mimetic" nor "critical.") He invents no better world; but, every time, another world. The words speak themselves; the images appear – as if both came from innermost depths and extraterrestrial distances. This doubled abyss dizzies us. Again: On his stage the bliss of immersion and the horror of the void cohabitate.

Even the weak moments follow from this with distressing consequence. His art of non-instrumentality uses itself pragmatically: The artist supplies his public with happiness.

•

Until today, he has explained his plans almost without words. He draws what will happen on the stage on a piece of notebook paper, on a paper napkin. He says, while he places it at a right angle: "Scene 1. A locomotive. It comes from behind." A new, still empty rectangular plane: "Scene 2. It is nearer; the sky is now...five rash strokes: black."

A painted locomotive in two framed boxes, clad in prisms of light. He shows them; he says no more. (Wilson's projects have, as art often does, something dictatorial about them: One can contradict words, but not images.) Above all, one never receives directions like:

DiaLog/Sundance Kid, New York City, 1975. Christopher Knowles and Robert Wilson
In audience, Miguel Algarín, William Burroughs, Alan Ginsberg, Jackson Mac Low, Yoko Ono, Steven Taylor of the Fugs, et. al.

"A young man travels by train from Boston to Baltimore, in order to kill his father, in order to found a factory, in order to stop a bank robbery." No. A locomotive. A black sky.

On the paper rags now stand seven little caskets: the first act of a new piece. Patricide, the founding of factories, bank robbery, these were exchangeable movie-stuff decisions, therefore none at all. That it will be seven images, however – not six or nine – that is unalterable. The name of the law is: *structure*. It defines the individual works not imma-nently/ unconsciously/ organically, but as a lucid (light-like) positing, deciding.

Wilson admires only artists who create structure: Barnett Newman. Above all Balanchine: explorer of the stellar orbits of human bodies – not of picturesque little scenes.

Number

September 1987: The "comportmentally disturbed" youth, Christopher Knowles (Wilson's performance partner, now his astonishing Parsifal), can repeat endless series of numbers after having heard them but once. If he walks into a theater, he can say at a glance that it contains 1,930 seats. He is never wrong.

Death, Destruction & Detroit, Berlin, 1979

The mathematical genius of children is misunderstood, whenever one speaks of abstractions. Certainly, in a pure, almost objectless brain, logic is more translucent than in a post-pubescent, feverishly driven one overcrowded with things. But for such a child numbers and proportions are like things. "Thing" for their brain does not mean: an object for a measuring ego, that is, an object for a distance – creating subject. "Thing" means: something that is magically near, present through its own power.

.

That proportions grew out of number mysticism was self-evident to the great architect-engineers of the Renaissance. Not before our era (one full of the junk of misused subjectivity grown helpless) did art critics presume, as soon as they come upon numbers or proportions, that these arc cunning new marketing discoveries enhancing individual earning. "Minimalism" is to them a patented procedure, "Minimalists" are its professional exploiters. Wilson does not belong to this crowd.

If Wilson's work has something to do with minimal art, then it is with the childish unity of things and transparency. Not the drive towards irreducible form (radical or derivative European abstraction) stamps Wilson's figures and props, but regression into the seclusion of a child with his toy. In the twilight cave of the infantile, the child is a mathematician

Death, Destruction & Detroit, Berlin, 1987

Hamletmachine, New York City, 1986

only insofar as he is a magician. Robert (called Bob) Wilson the stage cave builder, the light inventor is a technician only insofar as he is an illusionist. He devised dozens of toys, magic rattraps, for himself giggling fun, for us literal wonder.

Well-paid, hard-trained extras hid under the skins of the dinosaurs in *KA MOUNTAIN* and *Death, Destruction & Detroit*. No extras, however, in the minuscule closet-palace of *Orlando*, whose doors inexplicably open and close until the tiny construction begins to wander by itself. No extras behind the columns of light in *Parsifal* and *Bluebeard* which, swinging free, change color and measure and place according to their own whims. The celebrated illusionist of today's opera houses from Milan to Tokyo hearkens obediently to the magician in a playpen from Waco, Texas. Robert (Bob) Wilson is the child of the child that he was.

That means also: The monstrous dimensions of his space, the post-subjective power of his light, the archaism of his gestures and steps far beyond particular expression – they do not form a completely constructed monument of beauty. Instead, they change the scene into dream-as-reality, craved for and frightening. The expanse and purity of this universe are packed with invisible traps, wrapped loopholes out of which bursts forth smart and defiant, immature and cruel rebellion. Wilson's technical aesthetic perfection often lets us ignore his appetite for disturbance and destruction. If the stage is a gigantic toy – it like all toys attracts attempts to break it.

•

The horror of the uncouth child has been painted by Goya, Picasso. (It haunts even those *Biedermeier* idealizations of childhood from Runge to Waldmüller, who unwittingly combine innocence and idiocy in puzzling images of sweet horror.) Wilson's minimal art ventures into the ghost night of hebephrenia, of infantine stupor, in order to search and preserve there the minimal essence of human being. The student of painting from Waco, Texas encountered these images of gentle horror in his first years in New York: not as an artist-and-exploiter, but (at O. D. Heck School for the Disabled) as a therapist and helper.

Help there does not mean normalization, adaptation to the working world. In the middle of that black knot of ego and viscera, that hiding place of tortured souls, an undamaged seed must be tracked down, protected, and nourished. Whoever wants to help must somehow feel and know for certain that there is a shelter where (in fear of the razor sharp self-certainty of the grown up world) the remainder of thought and feeling of one incomparable being has fled: amongst the brooding apathy, the raging anger of the abandoned child.

Wilson's rehearsal work (often with the very young and the very old) is so to speak therapeutic: full of curiosity for bizarre, unexpected observations – and full of an absurdly patient trust.

Body

The laughter that suddenly breaks forth from him has something violent about it – like the foolishness of some jokes with which he (in his best work) mercilessly interrupts that majestically vain triumph of beauty.

Foolishness is not blank simplicity, but refusal. European high art walked the way of reason (that is part of its radiance). How reason moves from things to concepts, from concepts to ideas, so art climbs from body to representation, from representation to ideal beauty. Wilson's art refuses to crawl after the mediation of the ratio: It despises how reason, fluctuating between arrogance and skepticism, goes about its business of disempowering things and bodies in an attempt to completely think the matter of the world. Wilson's foolishness (like William Blake's) proclaims the arbitrary sovereignty of the "I" against all respectable role-playing of pride and humility. His laugh is the gesture of the naughty brat toppling a meticulously constructed house of cards.

Can the monadic absorption, out of which stems the violence of the laugh, be taken seriously? In Wilson's theater teaching and actor training, the counterpoint to foolishness is dignity. Let's admit: Dignity of even the most refined kind in its tactics of domination in our endless world history, has had not friendship, but enmity at its core. When rolled up in a human body, dignity conquers space: It acts against. Wilson does not teach his actors meek self-denial. The first thing they learn is to occupy the stage instead of obeying the parquet. They do not play for the spectator, but for themselves – which in truth means that they play against the spectator. Wilson cites no phrase more devoutly than Maria Nicklich's principle (out of a rehearsal for *The Golden Windows*): "We must hate them." – Wilson's art succumbs straight away to ingratiation (admittedly of the highest and most luxurious kind) as soon as he forgets this sentence.

Dignity he brings to those whom everyday life denies it. With immense tenderness he cares for the fallen. What his laughter and contempt brutally wrench from our hierarchy of reason and beauty, he gives to beings who are left out of that system: the very old as well as children. The dance of the elders in *Death, Destruction & Detroit* and the entry of a sclerotic 80-year-old as comforting messenger of death in *Alcestis* belong to the most sublime moments in his oeuvre – no less so than the Medea-like child murder in *Deafman Glance*, and the border crossings of the 12-year-old Christopher Knowles in *A Letter for Queen Victoria*. Children and old people are nonprofessionals in the theater: Their presence on stage would be betrayal and exposure, if the play did not first rid them from the curse of spasticity or dementia. They "play no role" – in life. On the stage that means: They are permitted, in the end, to play no role but themselves. They are, each of them, incomparable.

•

It is said that Wilson sighed with relief in the middle of rehearsing his first piece of theater, *The King of Spain*: "The piece will come together, because the actors are so different." He helps even professional actors to achieve their greatest possible difference (being themselves). Many of the best were better than ever with Wilson: Maria Nicklich, Isabelle Huppert, Otto Sander, Martin Wuttke. Others appear as great actors for four hours or four minutes.

•

Theater of images? One probably ought to discuss that with his (German, Flemish, Japanese) emulators. They try hard to heave their actors from one pre-fabricated image into the next. Wilson's curiosity and knowledge, however, aim at movement: the mental and physical conditions, which the actor must generate in himself so as to fill every gesture, every step with continuous inner poise and outward suggestion.

I told him: In the mid-'50s, *Tannhäuser* ran in the Prinzregent Theater. In the second act, right after the "Hallenaria," Tannhäuser is led by Wolfram to Elisabeth. All three came together right on the first plane at the middle axis. Then Wolfram (Fischer-Dieskau) turned and retreated in steady slow pace to the back wall of the empty scene. In the front, two capable singers (Cunitz, Aldenhoff) sang a duet in ever-brighter ecstasies. Only: The gaze could not pull itself away from the back of the superfluous third – not even while he finally stood motionless at the greatest distance. Wolfram's comment on his unwanted, defeated love (*So flieht von diesem Leben/Mir jeder Hoffnung Schein*): It was pathetic as ever to hear – but for 12 minutes of majestic intensity impossible to overlook.

Wilson replied with another story: For six hours he regarded a famous Japanese actor in a Kabuki romance. Then he was led into his dressing room. He asked the star of the evening whether he would tell him how he had taken the one, incomparable pace into the depth of the stage: the pace with his back to the public. The secret:.Now he had his gaze directed towards a suburb of Tokyo, now towards New York. On many evenings it sufficed to follow two straight train tracks retreating into the distance until the horizon (a piece back, a piece forward again). Wilson did it for me. One could guess every vertebra of his back through his thin black jacket; but nevertheless he seemed to be cloaked in a king's mantle from his shoulders to the soles of his feet. Dignity and animation are usually mortal enemies; now they were one.

Light

January 1987: His large coal and chalk drawings are still stage images. His stage images (this time for *Alcestis*) are light images. They create non-measurable space. The beam of light defeats measurable space as well as measurable time. The fact that light has the greatest possible velocity (when it lights up, it has already arrived) makes it into a force of stasis.

Now the light on Wilson's stage changes incessantly; some pieces have 800 to 900 "effects" (permutations of several hundred light units, steered by two computers). They change with the smallest movements of the players, of their chins, of the tips of their fingers. But the light does not become temporalized through that movement. Rather, the light detemporalizes each movement, because it goes with it, that is, is virtually always there before it.

The deception that is treated in the fairy tale of the Hedgehog and the Hare is the deception of light in time: "Here I am already." The more secret moral of the fairy tale, however, is valid for all of Wilson's theater: There is no use in hurrying. The most extreme possible velocity in the universe teaches slowdown until a standstill: *Ick bün all hier.*

•

Robert Wilson being the master of the standstill, his fans and enemies make it hard for him to develop. Whenever he continues with his own (*Death, Destruction & Detroit II*), he is supposed to repeat himself. Whenever he renews, and suddenly perfects a guiding genre of contemporary theater (*The Black Rider*), he is supposed to have betrayed himself. Critics reproach him for knowing everything; still more, for trying not to.

•

Wilson's most intense, most exact interest is technology: lighting technique as well as acting technique. To the former, he dedicated, thirteen years apart, two somewhat tautological mystery plays, *Edison* and *Doctor Faustus Lights the Lights*. To the second, he keeps dedicating all of his plays, operas, dances, and solo work.

When God said, "Let there be light" – perhaps he also had in mind Newton and Huygens and Maxwell and Einstein. But did he imagine, and moreover would he have permitted, that Edison should repeat his phrase every time he turned on an ordinary light switch, producing said effect? Technology (not physics) appears to revoke the primordial act of creation by virtue of its imitation.

What then is art? Since the Renaissance, or more perceptibly since the Age of Genius, the artist appears as creator. If Wilson now imitates technology instead of creation, Edison instead of God – does he then revoke that first, modernist revocation of 1400–1800 by force of imitating it?

Does the illusionist of light follow some return path: out of maturity into childhood – from technology back to creation? While other producers put pieces on stage, Wilson has invented a universe, created a theater.

•

Acting technique, says Wilson, seeks the point where consciousness and the unconscious intersect within the body. Ought we to name this concealed intersection the soul (even though it has neither to do with moral principles nor with immortality)? It is better to seek, and not to name.

Translated from the German by Samuel Tabas and the author.

Edison, Paris, 1979

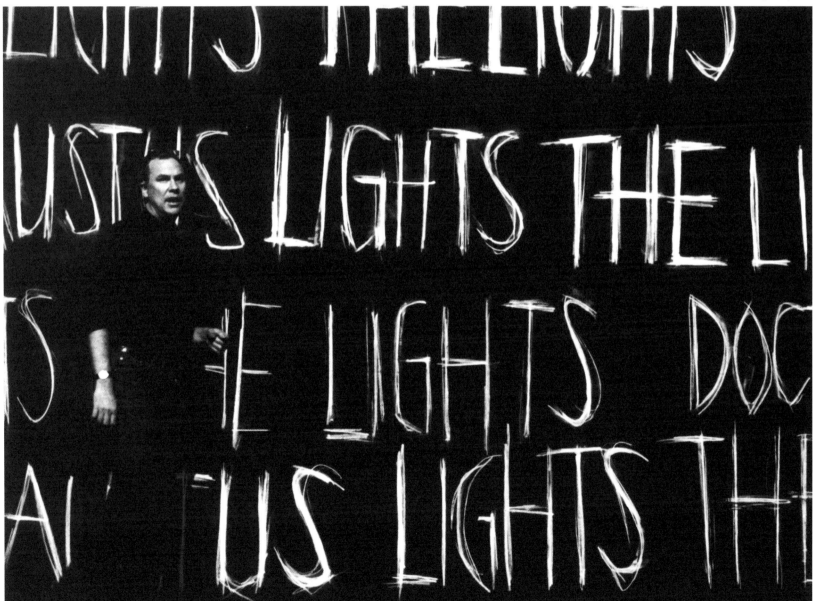
Rehearsal for *Doctor Faustus Lights the Lights,* Berlin, 1992. Robert Wilson

I was sitting on my patio this man came along I thought I was hallucinating (press release), Ypsilanti, Mich., 1977. Robert Wilson and Lucinda Childs

Looking in the mirror at the younger

When I think about Bob Wilson, I think about a new way of looking, sensitive, without preconceived notions. It's a state of perception that passes through the skin as well as through the ears, where the inexpressible rules, where coldness mingles naturally with voluptuous pleasure. It's a window into an eminently poetic world of signs that offers infinite possibilities. Bob doesn't try to understand what a human being or flower consists of, or to explicate a given story or myth. He doesn't try to know what the actor has in mind when he walks onstage. He fixes his gaze, smiles and sees, listens, dreams. Things don't have to have strict meanings; people don't need definitions. He hates categories, and prefers to look at discrepancies, or offer them up for observation, to pursue the meaning of things rather than attempt to possess them.

His view of the world is closely linked to the events of his life. Bob is not a militant. He doesn't want to change the world; he doesn't care. He hates therapy and religion. His actions have no salutary intention. He is led, above all, by curiosity, by the desire to preserve difference. When, in 1970, he prevented the police from harming Raymond Andrews, he prevented the established order – white, dominant, homogenous – from hurting a young black boy, deaf-mute and poor. He refused to allow the boy's particular brand of difference to be repressed, to wither. A few years later, when Bob cared for the young, autistic Christopher Knowles, he wasn't motivated by charity or notions of social work, but acted because he cherished Chris's connection to the world, so different from his own. It was the reflection of a certain curiosity, of a tenderness that informed his point of view. Even today, driving from cocktails to a celebrity dinner, where he probably won't meet anyone deserving of his attention, Bob might see a destitute person on the side of the road and take an interest in him, begin to wonder about his personal history. In that moment, Bob would have a voyeuristic smile in his eyes, a smile that has nothing to do with pity or the urge to adopt someone else's cause as his own. He looks at a person for the sake of his individuality.

What is true of his life is true of his work onstage. He likes approaching performers through an examination of their complexities, and thus their differences. Old people, children, even animals fascinate him because they exist in another reality. The most beautiful aspect of his oeuvre is the way that he works with each person, whatever his past or present, whether or not his distinctiveness is externally visible. It might be someone picked up in the street, or it might be a world-famous star, an art or theater student or a professional actor. Bob's motivation is the fact that anyone is able to get on stage without hiding behind his social or intellectual identity. Anyone can give up the codes of his everyday life, and in doing so reveal the particular thing that differentiates him from other human beings.

As I've known Robert Wilson since I was born, I have been influenced by theater rooted in abstraction and interiority since my earliest years. Bob arranges his actors in what could be considered flesh tones, abstract movements as a way of getting them to expose their own emotions. In seeking their point of disconnection from the reality of life, and even (or especially) the reality of theater, he plays with the interiority of each. Theater tends to be far too exterior; emotion is imposed on the viewer by vulgar means. Bob has often said that the best actors are those who ultimately don't know what they're saying. This might seem provocative, but it's a way of treating the stage as a tribunal, where the actor's responsibility lies in asking questions rather than answering them before they've been fully formulated, in preserving his doubts rather than sacrificing all other possibilities for the sake of a single interpretation. The actor knows what he's saying in broad strokes, of course, but this kind of theater intentionally avoids effacing mystery. Bob is convinced that no director, choreographer, or composer can tell someone what to feel. Everyone feels something specific. For each actor, every performance will be something different. Even within a method that is generally executed according to a set of specific criteria, there exists a certain freedom in its application, which is improvised at every performance. You know in your mind how to go from A to B, technically. But when you do it, you never know exactly how you happen to get there. It's always a mystery.

My father, Philippe Chemin, a movie and stage actor and director who had studied with Maurice Garrel and Daniel Mesguich, went to Rome in the 1970s to join other actors who were working in the emerging German cinema of Fassbinder, Schmidt, and Schroeter. They were there to audition for the latest work being staged in Germany by an American theater director. In 1977, on a café terrace, my father met Robert Wilson, and accompanied him to a cab. "Wilson was carrying an impressive number of empty shoeboxes," he recounts. A few months later, my father went to the premiere of *I was sitting on my patio this guy appeared I thought I was hallucinating* at Théâtre de la Renaissance in Paris. Wilson performed the first half, Lucinda Childs the second. "It was a magical moment. I went to other performances of the show, and a world opened before me, a world of emotion, contemplation, and depth."

My father narrates: "I showed Bob Biette's *Le Théâtre des matières*, in which I play a theater actor, and he asked me to perform in *Video 50*, a series of 30-second spots shot at the Centre Georges Pompidou in Paris. From there, I went to Berlin, and after an audition in front of Peter Stein and members of the Schaubühne company – for which I learned a German text phonetically – I was chosen for Bob's *Death, Destruction & Detroit*, and settled in Berlin for a year. From this play involving a young couple during the Nazi period, Robert Wilson created a waking nightmare that won the 1979 Berlin critics' prize. Bob was writing a lot of his own texts then, and they often consisted of pieces of everyday speech. He would write them while watching TV, constantly changing the channel, and then he would arrange them so that the sentences would repeat in different scenes without ever having the text illustrate the action. When beginning to rehearse, Bob would explain his way of working, starting with the body. 'The body moves faster than the mind, and releases complex emotions at a normal speed,' he would say. He was interested in the fractions of a second, and the complexity of feelings expressed in a body, short lapses that can only be perceived in theater by re-scaling time and using a form of acting that de-emphasizes psychology and refuses emotions 'assigned' by the director. Thus began an 18-year collaboration, one of the last pieces of which was the 1994 film *The Death of Molière*, which I developed at Watermill, and Bob directed and starred in, playing Molière."

I didn't meet Bob, as I've said; born in 1983, I've always known him. Even today, Bob likes to recount how he would phone me when I was a little boy: My parents would put me on the line, and he would bark into the receiver. We would converse in a language that, though it had no meaning, was full of impressions, feelings, and the unpredictable. Barking is something that Bob often uses in his plays, precisely in order to communicate something aside from rigidly defined ideas. He was always very tender with me, and always cared about what I was thinking, which was a striking attitude considering how little importance is generally attributed to children's ideas and opinions. He didn't make distinctions based on age. He was dealing with a human being, one younger than he was, but with its own experience and view of the world. It was the same with Raymond Andrews and Christopher Knowles. Bob was collecting the stories of a part of humanity that remained largely untold in theater.

Video 50, Paris, 1978. Philippe Chemin

When I was six years old, I began acting in the first plays that my father directed, including one that Bob lit, *Paysage*. Soon after that, I worked with Claude-Alice Peyrottes on *Un fils de notre temps* by Ödön von Horváth. Bob came to see the show, and had the idea to make a play about three generations of narrators: Bob, around 50 years old; a 25-year-old German actor; and me, age 11. This led to an adaptation of *The Meek Girl*, based on a story by Dostoevsky, which Bob developed between 1993 and 1994.[1] All three actors had the same text, divided into sections that were placed in a different order for each. It made us listen to ourselves and to each other as we recounted the same events, like echoes. What came at the beginning of one person's story came at the end of another's, as if we were the same man at different stages of life. The notion of "otherness" is very important to Bob's work. It implies a break in conventional time, as well as in the realism inherent in a person's uniqueness, a split where time could be free. Like a flashback, it allows for things to be re-lived from different points of view, giving a person total mobility. Bob would tell interviewers that he was working with a young person who, onstage, became an old man.

In *The Death of Molière*, still 11 years old, I appear as a young Jesuit reciting a lesson in Latin in a flashback of Molière's youth. There again, the parallel drawn between two generations created a contrasting effect of the human being as never complete, always in the act of becoming something else, even when close to death, as Molière is in the film. Not only Molière's character, but also the actor who embodies him, is revealed in his composition. The actors' beings are not hidden behind their characters; they always push through to the surface. In the Jesuit scene, we can see Bob Wilson scrutinizing himself through the lens of another generation.

He has always sought to confront himself with generations other than his own. Since the beginning, his work has almost always included an elderly person. It's a way of seeing the human being as infinite, without any given borders. It also allows him to place himself outside a perspective focused on final outputs, to distance himself from an efficiency-based outlook that considers a person to have reached his full potential only as an adult. Above all, life in his work becomes a circle where real time no longer exists, where a childhood can follow old age, and where the viewer, no matter his age, can recognize something of himself in any of the generations onstage.

The Watermill Center was founded in this spirit, a place where Bob could work with students in theater and the arts, young people of all nationalities, with or without arts training, who above all brought with them their singularity, their accents, their experience. He loves it. He has always shown a strong desire to transmit whatever he can, something open, where meanings are not closed off to interpretation, where one can think that it's possible to make theater and art without following prescribed pedagogical or analytical paths but simply by following one's dreams and sense of aesthetics. He teaches that explanations and certitudes are superfluous. What matters is not to know, but to always be new, simultaneously old and young. At the same time, Bob cherishes technique. The point of departure in his pedagogy is always the body, not in the sense of the European mind-body divide, but as a full entity

[1]
Adapted from
Dostoevsky's
The Possessed by Wilson
and Wolgang Wiens,
the piece premiered
as *Une Femme douce*
at the 1994 Festival
d'automne in Paris.

of perception that can apprehend textures, sounds, images and reproduce what it feels, or go against and even transcend ambivalence to find its own way, becoming, at last, a creator of perceptions. But Wilson doesn't teach technique as a professor teaches a method. He acts as a guide, plunging his students into real, concrete work with a structure. He challenges them as he would any professional actor, without imposing any hierarchy. A lot of the works he has done with students have become full-fledged shows, some of which are important pieces of his oeuvre, like Heiner Müller's *Hamletmachine*, first performed in 1986–87.

At age 20, I went to the Comédie-Française to perform in Wilson's *Fables de La Fontaine*. This is an eminent company, with its own traditions, but that didn't prevent Bob from employing there the same simple elements that have come to form his theatrical vocabulary. The stage is a special place; you have to behave differently, to hear, gesture, and move differently. It commands respect. It's a forum where the most important thing is to pose a question, even if only by the fact of one's presence. And it's the particular structure of a given piece that determines whether its constituent elements, its text or its music, reinforce or contradict one another. The actors of the Comédie-Française opened themselves up to confront those theatrical values, which are a far cry from the traditional manner of speaking a text or employing a naturalistic or exaggerated physicality. They learned to live in this other kind of time, and Bob used what each was made of in order to get him to evolve onstage. As Bob often teaches his technique by showing how it's done, I served as a medium for demonstration to help the company become familiar with his approach. La Fontaine's *Fables* is a monument of French culture, and so I was struck by the respect that the actors showed for Bob's direction, a formal view of *Les Fables*, where the stories would appear as illustrative images onstage and then expand until one could see more in them than simply the strict moral of a given tale.

After *Les Fables*, I went back to Watermill only to discover that it had changed a great deal. The building had been knocked down and rebuilt again. The gardens had become their own art space. There was no longer the same spirit of a small team working on a few projects, as there had been 12 years earlier. Many more people had come, and now every artistic discipline is represented. Now, there is a shared, ordered life in which everyone participates, helping out not only with chores but also with the projects that germinate at Watermill before going elsewhere, or with those created expressly for Watermill by Bob or other artists. There's a kind of passivity and obedience to the rules of communal existence, which can also act as a wonderful encouragement to do and create things oneself. One can follow a given rule, then consider its structure and go beyond it. To that end, Bob regularly invites artists who differ substantially from his aesthetic world to come and help shape Watermill.

What kind of a relationship can a young artist have to Bob's artistic heritage? At Watermill, I met another young artist, Carlos Soto, with whom I have now been working for several years. We have both have been immersed in the transformation that Bob's initiated in the arts, but we'll take our own artistic paths, paved with our own fascinations and anxieties, our own fragments. We draw inspiration from different sources, visual, aural, textual,

The Meek Girl [*Une Femme douce*], Paris, 1994. Top left and bottom right, Robert Wilson

The Meek Girl [*Une Femme douce*], Paris, 1994. Top left, Robert Wilson;
top right, Thomas Lehman; bottom right, Marianna Kavallieratos

that we cut, distort and then rearrange in order to create vivid material that corresponds to ourselves. Of course, structure plays a big part in this. We think about it before, in terms of length, repetition, rhythms, and we arrive at certain sections. Of course, we are concerned with time; and, of course, we try to approach a narration of form, first working to achieve a continuity of gestures that doesn't illustrate the foundational material but is inspired by it. We are children of Watermill, and there's no denying or getting away from that. But, like my father before me who went from collaborating with Bob to devoting himself to his own *mises en scène*, both Carlos and I are of Watermill, and of ourselves.

The latest stage in my relationship (and stage relationship) with Bob began in 2008, when I began working with him on *Krapp's Last Tape* by Samuel Beckett. We developed the piece at Watermill and later in Spoleto, Italy, with Sue Jane Stoker collaborating on direction. At first, Bob had asked the dramaturge Ellen Hammer and myself to think about the piece and to improvise a reading, since his original idea was to stage a reading with himself as sole performer. He realized, though, that the work would have more power if it were put together as a full show with light, sound, and scenery. The monologue is a form that he has often worked with. When there are several actors onstage, he treats each individually, superimposing each person's piece to create interacting monologues. If several actors are alone onstage, their presence enters into a dialogue with the other theatrical elements present, like the sound or lighting. With the Beckett play, Bob's task was to direct himself, as he had already done in *HAMLET: a monologue*. But to do that, he needed to establish a dialogue with another actor (in *HAMLET*, with Keith McDermott) in order to direct himself as if he were a separate person, and so in addition to assisting with the direction, I acted onstage during rehearsals for *Krapp's Last Tape*, though I was much younger than the title character.

Krapp, almost 70 years old – like Bob – listens for nearly the whole piece to a tape that he had recorded about 30 years earlier. As he listens to this earlier version of himself, much younger, full of aspirations, his dreams as yet unrealized, he reconsiders his hopes with the hindsight he has gained since.

Bob drew inspiration from the concrete circumstance of directing me in this role, a younger actor necessarily influenced by him, by his rhythms and gestures, but with a diction belonging to a different generation. When Bob came onstage, I would go to the other side and try to communicate my experience of being directed by him. Thus, not only was he undertaking his own inner journey living his role from within himself, but he was also receiving what he had himself transmitted to others by passing through my much younger voice and body, connecting with Beckett's play in a very vivid and tangible way. On tour, we performed *Krapp's Last Tape* in many and varied theaters, and I helped prepare it to come to life in each new place, assuming the role again, so that Bob could see what it looked like, and improve the visuals, sound, and rhythms according to the space where we were performing. In the end, he could get back onstage, buoyed by the experience of looking at the other, younger man.

HAMLET: a monologue, Berlin, 1996. Robert Wilson

Krapp's Last Tape, Rome, 2009. Robert Wilson

Robert Wilson Solo/A Letter for Queen Victoria, New York City, 1975[1]

The quest for proto-language

The quest for a language that came before the languages we now speak is a quest for a sort of authenticity or purity of speech. It fascinated several composers in the postwar years, as well as, at about the same time, Robert Wilson. Indeed, it was profoundly formative for all his later work. In a 1970 interview, he describes how Bird Hoffman provided him with the decisive experience:

> I had a speech impediment until I was 17 and I couldn't talk – hah, hah, it was like that. I couldn't get it haaaa, ssssssstutter, also my – I was tongue-tied too, my tongue has been clipped I think it was tied to the bottom of my mouth. Most of it was just fear, not being able to talk. When I was 17 uh my my parents had taken me as an infant to people hum professional people to help me with speech and I I still hadn't learned to talk – and I met a woman who was a dancer (you actually couldn't talk) I could but it was like thaaat, it took me a long time to it was very very difficult. Yes, and uh and it even got worse as I got older cause I couldn't I became self-conscious of it and just it became an enormous problem. And teachers – I got to school and teachers would say, ask me to read aloud and-and then say, no there's more, you have to have a longer pause between the words but there is even a little longer, if there's a comma, but it's even longer if there's a semicolon, but the longest is when there's a period and suddenly it became so complex it it was just so difficult for me to do and this woman was a dancer – she was a ballet dancer – she was in her 70s when I met her. She taught the dance – she understood the body in a remarkable way, she she said – oh, you can learn to speak I know you can and uh in about three months of working with her I did, by somehow relaxing and taking my time uh finally I learned to say, I learned to talk. She uh, she pointed out, she noticed I was, that I was very, very tense all through the shoulders and through here and she talked to me about the energy in my body, about relaxing, letting energy flow through so, so that it wasn't blocked and she worked also...she, she would play the piano and-and I would, I would just move my body.[2]

In another interview given three years later, Wilson describes how he took this idea further, into the domain of art. "I worked with an anthropologist in New York," he recounts, "and we made 300 films of a mother picking up baby."[3] By slowing the playback, one clearly sees that the mother lunges aggressively at the baby, who responds with fearful noise. The mother denied it totally, and was shocked. Wilson often cites this as a formative discovery in his life.

The notion is that the surface (speech, normally) is problematic, and even when achieved is mendacious and not true to the basic realm of expression it is meant to serve. This notion

[1]
Robert Wilson's *Solo* included material from *A Letter for Queen Victoria*.

[2]
Stefan Brecht, *The Theatre of Visions: Robert Wilson* (London: Methuen Drama, 1994), 14.

[3]
Ibid., 32.

Cynthia Lubar and Sheryl Sutton

A Letter for Queen Victoria, Paris, 1974. Stefan Brecht, Kathryn Cation, Christopher Knowles, Robert Wilson

found powerful expression in his stage work of 1975, *A Letter for Queen Victoria*. Here, Wilson was using speech in a big way for the first time. He created many long texts for the actors and had them speak expressively and dramatically, but the words are, as a rule, rather commonplace and banal and have no connection with the expressivity that the actors are required to give them. What we normally look for in drama are words that communicate interesting meanings. Here, and this is Wilson's originality, the opposite is true: The words themselves are meaningful but the meanings are totally uninteresting. The point of interest lies in something underneath the words, portrayed by "musical" prosody, movement, and gesture. Here, Wilson is hinting at the possibilities of a proto-language.

A brief example of Wilson's text will give an idea of what is being spoken. Two actors share these lines alternately:

> Seem what
> Seemed what
> Seem
> Seems the same
> Seemed the same
> Seems
> Simultaneously o'city o'verst
> Wheel what when now how
> An alligator's span
> Seem what
> Seemed why
> Seemed
> Seemed
> Seems
> Screen tell a vision
> Screened told a visions
> Screen
> Scream
> A million dances,
> a bit
> a little bit
> the pilot tilting
> a slanting pilot tiltings
> a round a little bit
> the angle of the thing anglig.
> *a scream.*[4]

In musical circles surely unknown to Wilson, people like Karlheinz Stockhausen were moving in the same direction. In works like *Momente* of 1964 or *Mikrophonie 2* of 1965, Stockhausen drew on his studies with Werner Meyer-Eppler of Bonn University, a professor

4
Ibid., 306.

of phonetics and information theory. These studies had an important effect on Stockhausen's application of such modes of analysis to music. In *Mikrophonie 2*, for example, he instructs one of the singers to talk "like a confused, toothless old crone enraged." The text given is "talking intersects talking and there is there is none none." It is taken from the "nonsense" poem "Einfache Grammatische Meditationen" by Helmut Heissenbüttel. That phrase is repeated several times in the mode requested by the composer using the "old crone's" expressive filter. The text assaults normal grammatical structure, and what meaning comes out of it results entirely from the emotional carpet on which the text is laid. Moreover, a further transformation is added by electronic ring-modulation, which adds many strange and unworldly pitches to the "old crone's" sonorities. Much of Stockhausen's later work, in the seven operas entitled *Licht*, for example, is composed on nonsense texts or texts that have meaning but are delivered in a way completely contrary to their evident semantic properties. György Ligeti, in his classic works *Aventures* and *Nouvelles Aventures*, of 1962 and 1965 respectively, was probably influenced by and also influenced Stockhausen around this time. These works are for three singers/speakers/shouters who deliver extraordinary and powerful non-semantic phonemes and emotive exclamations.

The Hungarian composer György Kurtág echoed something of Wilson's evolution. As Gabriel Josipovici has movingly described, Kurtág's crisis came in the years following the war when he underwent a sort of breakdown; he could not compose any longer, so

Snow on the Mesa (dance), New York City, 1995

he sought the advice of a therapist called Marianne Stein.[5] She advised him to go back to basics, just to put one note down and then perhaps one more – already a composition. Very gradually Kurtág began to compose again, but nearly always with miniatures, some of which he strung together to make longer pieces. At the same time, he had become fascinated by Samuel Beckett and his famous linguistic crisis, as well as by Beckett's similar discovery of a new way to be creative: The search becomes the work. The most poignant part of the story is how Kurtág came to compose a work for Ildiko Monyok, a famous pop singer in Hungary. She had suffered a car accident that tragically left her unable to speak. Kurtág wanted to help her, clearly seeing a broader aesthetic issue, too, and wrote a work for her in which he turned to the Beckett poem "What is the Word" to find the appropriate psychological equivalent. The singer hardly sings, but she "finds her voice," syllables and odd words; she makes a kind of agonizing ritual of the coming into speech, which we witness when we hear her perform. There is something very moving, very rounding when we hear this singer heroically find her voice and discover that it is expressive of a mysterious and perhaps archetypically authentic, transformative movement.

Proto-language, then, has been seen as a kind of critique of normal language. In its negative form, the critique attacks the triviality of language, its mendaciousness, its misleading powers, and its frequent banality. But there is a positive function to proto-language, too. This might be characterized as a move to purify speech.

Two and a half millennia ago the Buddha recommended "right speech" as one of the paths in the Fourfold Path to enlightenment. What did he mean by "right speech"? Quite simply, it is speech that is rid of negative clutter and concentrates on essentials, particularly on words directed towards alleviating suffering in others, pointing them towards the most positive direction possible in our lives, that which leads towards enlightenment.

Steven Mithen, an archaeologist who draws much on cognitive science, has written persuasively on the proto-language of early hominids.[6] He argues it to be holistic, which means that utterances cannot be broken up and reassembled syntactically to convey different meanings. Such proto-language is "multimedia" and probably utilized, for instance, in gesture and touch; it might also be manipulative, which is to say that very often it would be concerned with greeting, warning, commanding, threatening, requesting, appeasing, etc. It would be mimetic of the actions or objects being referred to. Finally, Mithen conjectures, it would be musical. Pitch and the contours of pitch-shaping would be important, as would the expressive support of rhythm. All these suppositions are arrived at by analyzing the vestiges of proto-language audible today, in animals and people. At a certain point in evolution, Mithen says, proto-language forked into speech on the one hand and music on the other, and amidst enormous gains in cognition, the original unity – expressive richness – was lost. The singing Neanderthals from whom Mithen's book takes its title used a language that encompassed many facets of personality, and was presumably much more forcefully expressive than our language. It might reasonably be said that we still have a proto-language in what we call "song," whether art song or vernacular, though in general, song is too

5
Gabriel Josipovici, "Eén noot en daarna nog een," in *Nexus* 55 (Tilburg: Nexus Publishers, 2010).

6
Steven Mithen, *The Singing Neanderthals* (London: Weidenfeld and Nicholson, 2005).

formalized by the highly organized constructs of the music, line, and rhythm to be very suggestive of unifying proto-language; even early Baroque opera, imitating the supposed raw expressive style of classical Greek theater, lacks much of the holism of Mithen's Neanderthals. It is only when something that breaks much more wildly out of musical conventions – such as Ligeti, Stockhausen, and Kurtág conjured up – that music gives a glimpse of what might once have been.

In my work *Speakings* (2008)[7] for orchestra with electronics, I wanted to go right back to the basis of what we hear more than any other sound – speech – and combine it with an orchestra, so the two bifurcating voices in their highly developed modern forms are brought to collide together and hark back to something which is before and behind both of them.

The orchestra speaks in three main ways. First, it imitates speech, going up and down in the rhythms of odd conventional phrases which I chose more or less at random. Women, men, tranquil, angry, banal, poetic: all these tones of voice and many more. This is not particularly new in music, as listening to Modest Mussorgsky or Leoš Janáček will testify.

Second, it uses speech literally transcribed into music; this means elaborate computer analysis of recorded speech and the notation of it onto music paper. Notation cannot easily cope with all the fluctuations and slides present in the act of speech, which makes it very different from song. There are also the fluctuations of spectrum, and of timbre, which define the vowels and the color of the consonants. These form a notated tower of higher notes sounding softly above the basic fundamental tone when we speak; with a fast talker they change extremely quickly, sometimes ten times per second, far faster than music normally changes color. But a lot of time was spent rendering exactly these sorts of transcriptions and writing them out for the orchestra to play. Another method was to have the notations played by the computer itself using sampled sounds from its memory. These simulated orchestral passages were also used, played from the loudspeakers. Of course, string instruments and trombones and instruments that can make sliding sounds are favored above those that cannot make such rapid transitions between pitches.

The third, and possibly the most interesting, simulation of speech was to marry inside the computer the input of a recorded speech passage, such as an actor reading *The Waste Land*, with the input of the orchestra as it plays at the moment. The marriage is then put out through the loudspeakers, a little louder than the orchestra, so that one hears the rapidly changing conjunction of the two inputs above the sounds of the actual orchestra on the stage. A very sophisticated program was developed to capture the timbral qualities of the passage of speech being used as a model and to use those qualities as a window through which orchestral sound could be pushed. So, only those bits of the orchestral spectrum that fitted that frequency window would be permitted to sound through, and, of course, the window itself would fluctuate rapidly. Thus a very curious sensation emerges of the orchestra playing speech-like music with speech-like color fluctuations. No one in the audience could, or should, understand what words are being spoken. It is probably like an

7
Jonathan Harvey,
Speakings, Aeon AECD
1090 (2010).

observation of real speech in a dog or higher ape that is fascinated by speech without being able to understand a single word of it. We have something approaching this sensation when we hear a foreign language we do not understand. We pick up the speed, the emotion, the type of person speaking, the poetic quality or even the banal quality of what is being said, but not the normally dominant surface meaning.

In *Speakings*, I concentrate on baby sounds in the first movement, which are quite often a literal transcription of recorded babies' utterances: screaming, cooing, and babbling. Like Wilson in *A Letter for Queen Victoria*, I start with a scream, the first sound we make. And from that moment of incarnation, the evolution of language gets gradually more speech-like, up to the babbling stage. The big second movement is a sort of picture of the negative side of speech, the effect being of incomprehensible chattering, arguing, pomposity, timidity, and all the other facets of social intercourse. It reaches a climax of theatrical clamor, and then some silence. This is followed by the transcription of a Buddhist mantra, a mantra that the Buddhists maintain to be the origin of speech itself. In whatever sense this may or may not be true, I have chanted this mantra many times and find it powerful and suggestive. When the orchestra with its computer manipulation "chants" this mantra, that in its turn becomes very loud and climactic and finishes the second movement in a sort of cleaning sweep. The third movement is a purification on a further level. It approaches song, or a purified type of song: musically speaking, Gregorian chant. These chant-like sounds are grandly reverberated to simulate the acoustic of a vast temple or "sacred space," wherein the separation of audience and sound is dissolved in a primal unity. The audience listens *in* the sound, not *to* the sound. In Buddhist terms this would be called "a notion of a pure land." There is a unity about such "plain-chant" lines, a holism, which eliminates the sense of separateness between sound and semantic meaning.

Speakings itself is part of a trilogy concerned with Buddhist purification rites: rites that I witnessed at a Tibetan Buddhist temple and that are centered on the annual New Year purification of body, speech, and mind. Obviously, the movement I've just described is the central one, concerned with the purification of speech. Whether the journey I have described is that from speech through music to a sense of proto-language, or from speech through proto-language to music, is an ambiguity I leave for audiences to ponder.

As for Robert Wilson, in conclusion, I must with great admiration acknowledge the extraordinary vision he has contributed through his dealings in this area of artistic research, which continues to prove so resonant.

The Life and Times of Joseph Stalin, New York City, 1973

Eating the giants

At first we stand in the shadows of giants, possibly in awe, then we attempt to knock them down and perhaps even kill them. As time passes, we recognize their role in our lives and we finally offer them the heartfelt thanks that they deserve for being so present for us. It is in this spirit that I am writing about Bob Wilson. I seem to have passed through all of these stages in the proximity to his example. He stands steadily before me as a mountain or as what Virginia Woolf describes in *Moments of Being* as a "rod":

> If I were painting myself I should have to find some – rod, shall I say – something that would stand for the conception. It proves that one's life is not confined to one's body and what one says or does; one is living all the time in relation to certain background rods or conceptions.[1]

As a director, I define myself in relation to other theater artists who have thrown down the gauntlet via their productions. Bob Wilson is one of the figures in the world that stands as a rod, an orientation, a marker, or a buoy in the ocean defining the parameters of recently crossed boundaries and newly explored waters.

Before I experienced any of Bob's productions directly, I was already in a certain thrall to his legend. Even in the days before the Internet, news traveled fast, and I was captivated by countless stories about Bob's monolithic vision and the adventures that his productions engendered both in audiences and in those who worked with him. The stories piqued a vicious curiosity in me. I regretted missing his early seminal works in New York, including *The Life and Times of Sigmund Freud* and *The Life and Times of Joseph Stalin*, the sprawling creations that stretched out through entire nights at Brooklyn Academy of Music. I knew about the avalanche of fascination that his *Deafman Glance* triggered in what seemed like the entire country of France. In Iran, his seven-day spectacle *KA MOUNTAIN AND GUARDenia TERRACE* unfolded across a mountain range and was renowned in theater circles. Bob's conscious effort to slow down time in his productions had impacted upon the theater world, doing nothing less than widening the available time signatures in perform-ance. Film, via its technology, is able to look at the infinitesimal; he figured out a way to translate exactly that to the stage, and in the process he changed an audience's experience of theater. By the time I arrived in New York City in 1974, fresh out of college and ready to begin a career as a theater director, Bob Wilson already cast a long and definite shadow.

My own direct experience with Bob's work began with *A Letter to Queen Victoria* and soon afterwards *The $ Value of Man* and *Emily Likes the TV*. The rare ecospheres and atmospheres produced by these productions felt novel, strange, and fascinating and I could not figure

[1]
Virginia Woolf,
Moments of Being,
Jeanne Schulkind, ed.
(New York: Harcourt
Brace, 1985), 73.

out what arrangement of sensibilities could create such enchantments. Around that time, in the mid-to-late 1970s, Bob's loft on Spring Street, the Byrd Hoffman School for Byrds, attracted artists every Thursday evening when the doors opened and the world was invited in to join the "Byrds" in what seemed like elaborate rites and rituals. In 1976 at New York's Westbeth Center I sat in on a rehearsal showing of *Einstein on the Beach* during its gestation period. All of these occasions provoked my curiosity even further. But Bob the man remained an enigma. I went so far as to secretly follow him on the streets of New York City to try to figure out who he could possibly be, looking to see if he would cross some boundary that would reveal something about him that had not been evident to my eyes before.

Since those heady New York days, I have kept track of the ups and downs of Bob's career throughout Europe, Asia, and the United States. I saw many segments of *the CIVIL warS: a tree is best measured when it is down,* Bob's sprawling, multi-national project before it was tragically shut/cut down as hundreds of theater artists from around the world were preparing to gather in Los Angeles to perform it in full piece for the Cultural Olympics of 1984.

Occasionally his work infuriated me. After seeing a production that felt overly formal or too cool, in despair I would think, "Oh, Bob has finally lost his Midas touch. He directs too many plays in too many places and now the passion, the life force is nowhere to be found."

In the spring of 1987, during one of my periods of impatience with Bob's work, I was directing a play in West Berlin and attended Bob's production of *Death, Destruction & Detroit II* at the Schaubühne. Though I was ready to reject his work, I was also inextricably pulled towards it, but I went with no expectation of the delight and surprise that awaited me. I walked into the lavish theater building on the Kurfürstendamm in which I had seen many productions and knew well, and I was immediately utterly disoriented by the spatial arrangement. Bob had changed everything. He placed the audience upon swivel stools. Four stages filled all four sides of the theater. You could spin yourself around on the stools by holding on to metal railings designed specifically for that purpose. And the performances were wonderful: funny, vaudevillian, tragic, and with a distinct glow of mischief from each actor.

Afterwards, I went for a drink with the wonderful Schaubühne actor Gerd Wameling who had played a large role in *Death, Destruction & Detroit II*. "How did that miracle happen?" I asked him. "What an amazing production!" Gerd explained that the production came together over a rather long period of time. Bob would fly in from La Scala or from Japan, or from wherever in the world he was making plays, and he was usually quite exhausted. The actors pushed him. He pushed back. Somehow, what they created together seemed to me to thrust theater, as I knew it, out of the 20th century and into the 21st. Here I was, ready to dismiss him. Again and again he proved me wrong. Again and again he rocked my world when I least expected it.

Death, Destruction & Detroit II, Berlin, 1987

the CIVIL warS – Rotterdam Section, Rotterdam, 1983

Exhaustion

Until then, I had assumed that when you reach a state of exhaustion, you must take a break until the creative life and force returns. Gerd's story and my experience of *Death, Destruction & Detroit II* provoked a new insight into the whole issue of exhaustion and its role in creative development. Bob's example showed me that through exhaustion, it is possible to be catapulted into the next octave, to catch the next wave.

When exhausted, our guard is down. We are not able to control the events around us with our own assumptions and preconceptions; rather, things start to happen that are larger than the perimeters that we have predetermined. Within the exhaustion, we have to be patient and to get out of our own way. And despite the exhaustion, we have to stand vigilant, watch out for our preconceptions and assumptions and be ready to let them go. We have to make careful plans, create a schedule, and then just "show up." Show up and be present. Tell the truth. Do not hold on to expectations of the outcome. Stuff happens. We just have to be patient, stay present, and remain open to the unexpected.

The lesson about the role of exhaustion in the creative act is only one of the many insights that Bob's work and example has provided me over the years. Some other insights are detailed here in no particular order of hierarchical importance.

Violence

I had the opportunity to watch Bob rehearse with undergraduate actors at New York University in 1986 where he directed Heiner Müller's *Hamletmachine*. As I watched, I realized that I had never before had the opportunity to observe another director rehearse with actors and I also recognized, perhaps more profoundly, the necessity for violence in the creative act.

The rehearsal was scheduled to begin at 7:00 p.m. I arrived early to find a buoyant atmosphere. In the back row of the theater, Ph.D. students and scholars waited expectantly, pens poised, for Wilson's entrance, while on the stage young actors warmed up. A stage management team sat behind a battalion of long tables at the edge of the stage. Bob arrived at 7:15. He sat down in the middle of the audience risers amidst the bustle and noise and proceeded to gaze intently at the stage. Gradually, everyone in the theater calmed down until there was a penetrating silence. After about five excruciating minutes of utter stillness, Wilson stood up, walked towards a chair on the stage and stared at it. After what felt to me an eternity, he reached down, touched the chair, and moved it less than an inch. As he stepped back to look at the chair again, I noticed that I was having trouble breathing. The tension in the room was palpable, almost unbearable. Next, Wilson beckoned an actress to come towards him in order to show her what he wanted her to do. He demonstrated by sitting on the chair, tilting his torso forward, and moving his fingers slightly. Then she took his place and precisely copied his tilt and hand gestures. I realized that I was straining forward on my own chair. Never having experienced another director at work, I felt as though I was watching other people in a private, intimate act. And I recognized that night the necessary cruelty of decision. The decisive act of setting an object on a precise angle on the stage, or an actor's hand gesture, seemed to me almost an act of violation. And I found this upsetting and distressing; yet, deep down, I knew that this violent act is a necessary condition for all artists.

Art is violent. To be decisive is violent. Antonin Artaud defined cruelty as "unrelenting decisiveness, diligence, strictness." To place a chair at a particular angle on the stage destroys every other possible choice, every other option. When an actor achieves a spontaneous, intuitive, or passionate moment in rehearsal, the director utters the fateful words: "keep it," eliminating all other potential solutions. These two cruel words, "keep it," plunge a knife into the heart of the actor who knows that the next attempt to re-create that result will be false, affected, and lifeless. But, deep down, the actor also knows that improvisation is not yet art. Only when something has been decided can the work really begin. The decisiveness, the cruelty, which has extinguished the spontaneity of the moment, demands that the actor begin an extraordinary work: to resurrect the dead. The actor must now find a new, deeper spontaneity within this set form. And this, to me, is why actors are heroes. They accept this violence and work with it, bringing skill and imagination to the art of repetition.

The Surface and the Submerged

I often make plays about people I admire, people who have been a "rod" for me. I feel that my work on these plays is a way to eat the gods: I ingest their lives and they become part of me. I have made plays about Orson Welles, Virginia Woolf, Gertrude Stein, Marshall McLuhan, Leonard Bernstein, and, yes, I made a play about Bob entitled *bob*.

I did not intend to make a biographical portrait. Rather, I wanted to enter into Bob's sensibilities and to look at the world by embracing his view of theater. The script for *bob* was developed from hundreds of interviews with Bob, out of which I put together about 100 pages of his words and sent them off to the Irish writer/dramaturge Jocelyn Clarke. She returned volley with a razor-sharp 32-page script. The actor Will Bond did not attempt to imitate Bob; he found some essence that felt true.

Since its premiere in 1997, we have performed *bob* in scores of cities throughout the United States and in many venues internationally. The play is a love letter to the art of theater. Through Bob's example, it celebrates the deeply attractive qualities of the art form, and is full of philosophical and anecdotal illustrations. But submerged beneath the surface of the subject matter, *bob* is ultimately not so much about Bob himself as about my own fascination with the art form of theater. I found my own expression via Bob's vision. I ate him and digested him and something new was engendered from that action.

Hamletmachine, Hamburg, 1986

In the creation of *bob*, I gained a deep appreciation of a central principal in Bob's work. He has often repeated, in various iterations, the following:

> On the surface there has to be something accessible. The mystery is on the surface. Underneath it can be complicated, about a million things. The surface has to be about one thing first.

In rehearsal, I often call the narrative of the play, the opera, the dance-theater piece, or the devised work, "the stupid story." I do not mean to be derogatory. The "stupid story" is the magic carpet ride that allows the journey to occur. The creators are responsible for the integrity and forward momentum of the "stupid story," and I often stop a rehearsal to ask, "Where are we in the stupid story?" Everyone needs to be on board in the telling. Ultimately though, as director, I am the first audience and an audience's primary conscious access to the experience is "the stupid story." I must sense its forward momentum and be able to identify when it stops. The filmmaker Alfred Hitchcock nicknamed the object of all the characters' pursuit in a film the "MacGuffin." The microfilm that the characters in *North by Northwest* are chasing is the film's "MacGuffin." The pursuit gives the narrative an opportunity to include a love story, a chase scene, and all of the other thrilling essentials: The "MacGuffin" can provide force and suspense to the storytelling, but ultimately, who really cares about the actual microfilm?

The "stupid story" remains on the surface. But what lies submerged beneath its facade is key to creating unforgettable moments of artistic experience. There, one finds what James Joyce in *A Portrait of the Artist as a Young Man* describes as "the secret cause," and it is that which bestows complexity and rich ambiguity to an event. Joyce writes:

> The instant wherein that supreme quality of beauty, the dear radiance of the esthetic image, is apprehended luminously by the mind which has been arrested by its wholeness and fascinated by its harmony is the luminous silent stasis of esthetic pleasure, a spiritual state very like to that cardiac condition which the Italian physiologist, Luigi Galvani, using a phrase almost as beautiful as Shelley's, called the enchantment of the heart.[2]

But a play's surface is made up of a great deal more than its narrative or "stupid story." A play is also a kinesthetic event. It is rhythmic in time and colorful in tone and space. It moves as music moves. And ultimately, the experience of the narrative is derived from the way moments in time are arranged in time and space. As a director, I must first attend to these animalistic ways of perceiving. Logic and narrative devices can be woven into this fabric and sensation later. The surface must be comprehensive and seductive as the audience receives it. The narrative helps to deliver the physical and emotional experiences, the associative leaps, the neural re-patterning and visceral information processed below the conscious awareness of the brain. The complexity of the submerged demands a concomitant simplicity of surface. This I learned from Bob.

2
James Joyce, *A Portrait of the Artist as a Young Man*, (Ware: Wordsworth Editions, 1992), 164–5.

Actors, too, are responsible for the interrelationship of the surface and the submerged. The audience sees a clear and expressive gesture or hears a beautifully spoken sentence, but how an actor handles what lies beneath the surface and how that interacts with the visible and audible surface is key to the integrity of the audience's experience.

Generally I feel that German actors are better in Bob's shows than American actors. It is not that I think that German actors are better than American actors, but that I find that in Bob's productions, German actors seem freer and more irreverent, unafraid to challenge and disagree with the director whereas American actors tend to accept more quickly whatever idea is proffered. Bob asks an actor to raise his arm while counting to 100. An American actor by and large does exactly that, raises his or her arm while counting to 100: The submerged agrees with the surface. A German actor, in contrast, generally raises his or her arm while counting but carries on internally a vehement disagreement, one that I feel bestows more presence and magnetism to the actor onstage.

There are, of course, some Americans who perform Bob's work marvelously. The first time I saw *Einstein on the Beach*, I was utterly captivated by the performance of the choreographer Lucinda Childs in a solo dance that took place about halfway through the five-hour production. The dance lasted for what was probably about 20 minutes and consisted of Childs repeating identical moves as she moved swiftly back and forth on a diagonal line from upstage left to downstage right and back again and again. I returned to see *Einstein on the Beach* many times over the years since its premiere, mostly to see if Childs could repeat the mysterious and magnetic solo performance. And she did, every single time. I wondered what she did to make this repetitive dance so fascinating. Finally, a journalist interviewing Childs asked her the very question I wanted to ask: "What were you thinking during the dance?" Her answer was complicated and ultimately unintelligible. And this is when I realized that the submerged, the actor's "secret cause," is a necessary but private process that takes place within the performer; no one else needs to know about it.

Postcards

I have never had a cup of coffee with Bob or really ever even engaged in a sustained conversation with him, but we do enjoy some semblance of a relationship. At least I like to think so. I received a fax from him once in 1994 wishing me well for the premiere of my play *Small Lives/Big Dreams*. Perhaps I had invited him to the show, I do not remember, but the fax meant a great deal to me. It is remarkable how small gestures of generosity, even sending a fax, can make a huge difference in the lives of others.

Apparently, Bob writes postcards to his friends. I do not know if he still does this in the age of email, but it is clear by that action that he makes an effort to communicate and maintain relationships over time. The fact that he writes or wrote these postcards so regularly feels significant to me. I imagine Bob waiting in an airport while making some connection or

Rehearsal for *The Threepenny Opera*, Berlin, 2007.
Robert Wilson directing Georgios Tsivanoglou

other. He is between rehearsals of multiple productions in different parts of the world, winging from one city to the next. I imagine him writing the cards in an airport bar before getting onto the next plane, and then tossing the cards into a mailbox, like flinging seed out onto a barren landscape, across space and time. I see this action as a beautiful metaphor for the kinds of networks that he has created between himself and others that often escalate into sustaining long-term creative relationships that in turn produce creative endeavors crossing disciplines and boundaries. To me, the image of these postcards, winging in various directions, sent out to friends and acquaintances across the planet, tells a story. Bob's allegiances and links with others in this manner have born tangible fruit in the form of a 21st century version of global cultural exchange.

Perhaps it is a stretch to relate the sending of postcards to the wide menagerie of collaborators that Bob has accumulated over the years. But examine just a few of the artists with whom he has collaborated: Philip Glass, Heiner Müller, Tom Waits, Jessye Norman, Rufus Wainwright, Lou Reed, Ryuichi Sakamoto, William Burroughs, Marina Abramović. The list goes on and on. And it is possible to chart the development of Bob's aesthetic in tandem with the talents and proclivities of his collaborators. Bob, too, seems to be ingesting the giants in order to digest and be transformed by them.

In the years since my first exposure to Bob and his theater, I continue to be endlessly moved and fascinated by his personal trajectory, his ideas, and his creations. He is a masterful poet of the stage. He loves and murders the art form simultaneously. He kills it with love and brings it back to life with a sustaining breath. He speaks the currency of exactitude and courage. He offers up dynamic, expressive, and surprising ways to listen and to see. If it is true that we define ourselves in relation to other people and that the giants in our lives serve as the very best measuring stick against which to gauge our own achievements, I turn squarely towards Bob.

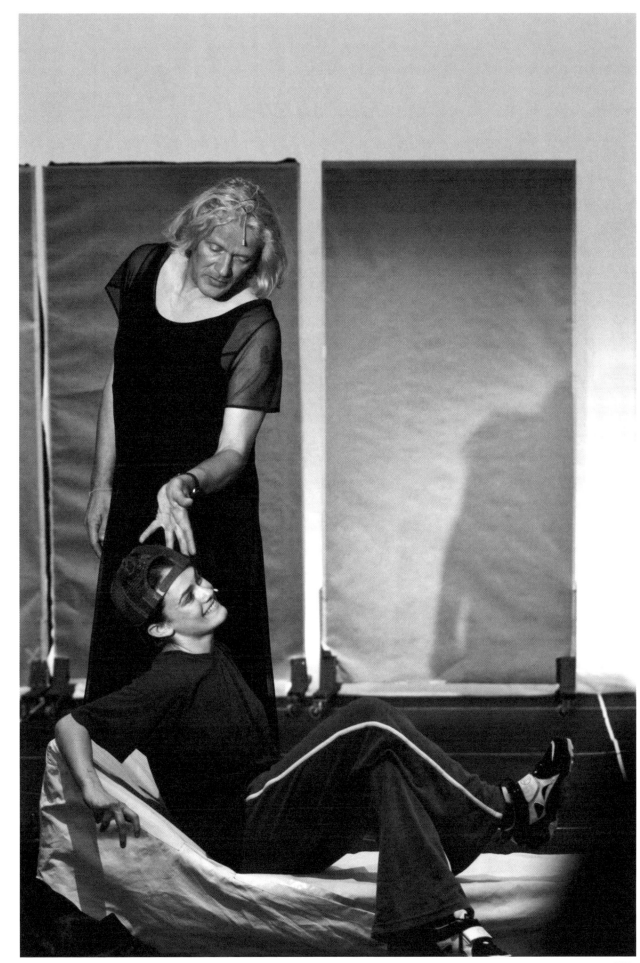

Rehearsal for *Shakespeare's Sonnets*, Berlin, 2009.
Georgette Dee (standing) and Anna Graenzer

Jessye Norman

It is not possible to describe in few words the experience of bringing Schubert's *Die Winterreise* to a Paris stage, the Théâtre du Châtelet, directed by Bob Wilson, supported by Pierre Bergé, and with costumes by Yves Saint Laurent, all dear friends. These wonderful songs, often erroneously associated with the male voice, were not written originally for the male voice, but for the "voice." It happens that over the decades, for the most part, this cycle has indeed been performed by men. As is known widely, most poetry was written by men, and the view of the world thereby expressed was indeed the male point of view. Countless songs speak of life, love, and all its adventures from this perspective. But the wonderful Lotte Lehmann and the marvellous Christa Ludwig, among other female singers, made these songs a regular part of their repertoire. The distance that one travels in life figuratively, emotionally, and in actual fact, can only be viewed from the place at which one finds oneself at any given moment. This is true and brought into stark relief in the songs of *Winterreise*. The journey and the heartbreak expressed in these songs are not those necessarily of a man, but indeed, of a person, a character too young and inexperienced to even imagine that yes, life will go on; this particular distress need not spell the end. This is a universal sentiment, not one that is male or female.

L'Orfeo, Milan, 2009

L'Orfeo, Milan, 2009

Stop making sense

To paraphrase David Byrne, I take my title from a Talking Heads album that to me is emblematic of what Robert Wilson represents: *Stop Making Sense*. This is also an appeal to Wilson's critics and historians: Stop making sense. During the many years I've worked with Bob Wilson in opera, since 1988, one constantly experiences this frustration and misunderstanding about "sense."

Opera is an art of artifice. You don't go to the opera to follow a story in the traditional sense of the term; you go to the theater for that. Opera is not theater put to a soundtrack. It's a different sensory experience, one in which sound and image are short-circuited, where the immediate perception of sight and the mnemonic perception of hearing collide. The listening brain and the seeing brain don't function at the same speed: Music is constructed in the memory, which is, in turn, constructed moment by moment by the listener, and so the perception of an opera entails the continuous shifting of individual perceptions; the meaning of each note is contained in the previous one.

How can we bring to opera, an art so encoded with the dictates of a weighty and conservative tradition – not to mention burdened with the linear, obsolete narratives of its librettos – a new approach that can give space and attention to isolated sound and emphasize the experience of the moment? How can we listen with our eyes and watch with our ears? How can we create the visual and perceptive conditions that can allow spectators to truly hear the music?

Rock opera perhaps comes closest to Wilson's early work for the simple reason that the form of the songs and the flexible spacing of time allow him to manage time, perception, and dramaturgy in a much freer manner than classical opera permits. Rock operas, and in particular the operas that Wilson made with Tom Waits, whose human and artistic availability were an enormous advantage in the collaboration, are also similar to the *singspiel* form in which it is possible to manipulate time between arias or even recitatives, and to infuse the work with disruptive elements, shortenings, ellipses, or sometimes total detours. That was the case as well in one of the first *mises en scène* that I worked on with Bob, *The Magic Flute*, which in some ways resembles *The Black Rider* (also from that period) but which also resembles the schizophrenic, fragmented style of a piece of work in which certain elements are arranged hierarchically in a manner aside from chronology. At the opposite pole, there is all the Wagnerian work that Bob has done, a sort of synesthetic fusion with the music that one comes across in working on Wagner but also Debussy. Wilson's work is comprised of these two poles: the fragmented and centrifugal.

The discrepancy between an image that can be perceived in its entirety, in its immediacy, and one that is assimilated into a temporal, musical structure is at the heart of Wilson's work in opera. Because music is constructed in memory, it demands an effort of concentration that has very little to do with the kind of visual impact that functions through *gestalt*, the kind of immediate images that traditional opera employs. There is a gap between an image that can be understood in a universal sense and the temporal space in the perception of a musical structure. This gap is central to Wilson's work, and he has tried to create it from the beginning in terms of the perception of sound and words in relation to a non-linear hierarchical structuring of sound and image. He is simply continuing the same work that he began with *Deafman Glance* and *Einstein on the Beach*, but obviously applied to conventional librettos.

In contrast with this linearity imposed by traditional operatic dramaturgy, Wilson instead imposes his own intuitions, his own aesthetic vision of the world. One sees this in *The Magic Flute:* the clicking and clacking that comes straight from Japanese theater and greatly disturbed music lovers, and also the ellipses constructed in the text. There is here a certain freedom that Bob had trouble finding in other systems far more coercive than traditional opera.

The force of Wilson's work lies in the dissociation of a gesture from its meaning, and in the continuous fluidity of shifting signifiers, which recalls the psychoanalytical science of associations between images and iconography rather than clear or clichéd concepts. The traditional operatic form constitutes, at first glance, a major handicap to his vision, particularly where the Romantic repertory, characterized as it is by sentimentality and pathos, is concerned. Wilson's work deals with this problem by accomplishing a progressive purification of the sentimental pathos of librettos so that the music's own dramatic force can flourish. The stage, set, and physical gestures of the performers become framing spaces that allow the music to resonate beyond all parasitic, superimposed, and gratuitous sentiment.

A case in point is *Madama Butterfly,* an opera that Bob had refused repeatedly to do, and that, paradoxically, has become perhaps his major operatic success to date. This opera is saturated with sentimentality, but also with incredible richness, it has to be said. It has a certain quality that it shares with Debussy, with Mahler, with certain pieces by Strauss, which are not as terrible as one is often led to believe; there is, in this music, a truly sentimental quality, a passion and sentimentality imposed by a defunct tradition. And Wilson's purging of its pathos is, I think, expressed in the final part of the opera in the memorable scene of Butterfly's death. In Wilson's production, this was perhaps one of the most beautiful moments, with the child's dream, and Bob put it there to accomplish the fusion that he was after, when we taste the drama of the music expressed in all its evocative force, and, at the same time, experience a visual landscape that resonates like an amplifying chamber without all the rhetoric and vulgar sentimentality of a rote device like cherry blossoms onstage. It's a moment that Bob prizes enormously in his *mise en scène.*

L'Orfeo, Milan, 2009

Part of the goal is to find the exact moments at which musical tension demands to be filled-out through rich visuals or, on the other hand, a rarefaction that allows the music to express itself best. This combinatorial game of placing gestures independently of the text but on key moments in the music is more or less the work I do.

Working with singers often poses a problem of frustration for Bob. It's for that reason that he often delegates direct work: not out of contempt, but rather out of reservation and frustration. Take as an example *L'Orfeo*, most of which I personally have trouble watching, not because of the memories but because beyond the splendid singing – it's an extremely beautiful opera – is the point where people most misunderstand Wilson's work. Generally, by forcing a certain *pathétique* onto the interpretation, traditional *mises en scène* try to create more than what the music itself contains. This is the typical example of what not to do with Wilson: to adapt a more or less schematic position in the arms with pathos or some way of compensating in the face, a pathos that the singers cannot manage to express differently. In trying to establish a certain formal rigor with absolutely un-lifelike gestures, Wilson, on the other hand, often gets into trouble with his performers as well as his audience, because the spirit of the singer is distracted, or rather occupied (to put it more nicely), by other things – by a piece of singing, a rhythm that doesn't allow the singer to go beyond a certain orthodox, rhythmic rigor. This is where all the mistakes and misunderstandings about Bob's productions occur. When people say, "It's like singing robots," I think of Michael Shamberg's phrase: "It's because my music is played wrong."

If Wilson's work highlights the sensibility of the performer and his or her re-appropriation of an imposed, formal code of gestures, it does so precisely in order to go beyond false expressive spontaneity, burdened as it is with stereotypes and tics inherited from legendary

Pelléas et Mélisande, Salzburg, 1997

performances. It entails a physical attention and tension and a concentration that often conflict with the preoccupations of a singer who is in the process of following a dramatic script. This is one of the first stumbling blocks that presents itself. Another is the dissociation between a gesture and its meaning. The force of Wilson's work comes from this shifting of signifiers. Wilson's power lies precisely in these continuous shifts and fluxes that again recall a psychoanalytical science of associations between images and ideas, or rather images and icons, because they are absolutely not concepts. Wilson's work is about re-animating a repertoire linked to the traditional preliminary element of a story or narrative, a re-animation that consists of watching sound and listening to images. The dynamic is affected by the performer's attention to what happens in experience itself; such a state of attention and tension is at once a physical and mental entity that passes through the performer and disentangles his or her gestures from all their functional and referential purpose to savor their essence, the vectorality of their internal force and emotional resonance.

This direct contact with the potential of the performer's lived experience, his tactile and sensory reactions, his attention to what goes on in his body and in his imagination, are far more important as elements than any dramaturgical prospective conception of a character. The character is simply the performer himself (with all his characteristics, potential, and limits) confronted with a formal proposition. The performer's qualities complete the form: The performer doesn't *represent*, but *presents* himself in frictional confrontation with the scenic apparatus and the character. The individuality of the performer therefore expresses itself in the fact of its existence when confronted with a pre-established form. The extreme rigor of choreographic instructions and the constraints imposed by the director often lead to a phenomenon of paradoxically liberating mechanization, a trance, even, where singularity can flourish in spite of all apparent formality.

Pelléas et Mélisande, Salzburg, 1997

The trouble that Wilson has with singers is often due to their lack of physical training and the difficulty that they have in dissociating a given gesture from its meaning in the score's literary context. This lack of training, as well as the reduced time of apprenticeships (the time given over to production is constantly growing shorter and shorter) do not permit the performer to appropriate gesture as experience, thus often reducing gesture to serve as a simple symbol of characteristic traits. Certain performers' stiffness arises from this lack of sensorial experience.

Often, people tell me that singers ask, "Why do I have to do this?" I respond: "Listen to the music that you're making, and you'll find your answer." And there is often this aspect of resistance vis-à-vis an experience that crops up through the music itself and that a dancer, perhaps, could convey differently. There are exceptions. Jessye Norman is truly an example of one of the artists whom Bob values the most because she has a nobility, an extraordinary lyrical grace. Or Dawn Upshaw in *Pelléas et Mélisande*, an extraordinary Mélisande, or José van Dam, who is one of the best, and who does the minimum when it comes to Wilson's direction. He reduced Wilson's suggestions for gestures, and yet we were proud to have him, because, through his presence, he was the perfect embodiment of Wilson's work: a presence that spread through the duration, through the sensation of time as one experiences it.

•

Wilson's work is often called a "theater of images." But it's necessary, rather, to speak of it as a "theater of perceptive strategies," perception being the reading of the real. Wilson's

Der Freischütz, Baden-Baden, 2009

conduct vis-à-vis traditional opera is at once complex and critical, in that he applies, as he can, all of his intuition, perceptions, and personal relationship with the world to opera. However, what could be hastily mistaken for the representation of an imaginary world or dreamlike landscape is actually the transposition of perceptive states, the re-appropriation and reinvention of the reality by the subject, audience member, and performer alike. This is the very thing that *creates* the subject: this elaboration upon the basic inputs that represent our vision of the world. The process for the actor is the same as for the spectator: Each encounters a unique experience through the production that sends them back into their own memory and existence.

Ultimately, Wilson doesn't have a message to transmit. I, too, staunchly oppose all imposition of ideology in opera. It's not by pushing the laws of the theater as far as possible onstage, or by superimposing a narrative, even the most intelligent, sophisticated, elaborate, and profound narrative, that opera will be saved. The basic principle must always be to create the perceptive conditions that will allow the audience, through the opera's staging, to hear, even read, the music from a visual point of view. Wilson often says, "I'd like the audience to be able to hear my staging and envision the music." He is always trying to create the visual conditions that allow the spectator to truly listen, and doing so shows an enormous respect for the music above all. Wilson's work achieves its greatest results with performers capable of great intellectual openness and sincere receptiveness to the experience of reinventing the relationship between words and sounds, and that between vocal and physical presence onstage. It's all, quite simply, in the hearing.

Der Freischütz, Baden-Baden, 2009

The scenographer as architect

The following observations and statements are the result of thousands of hours spent working together with Robert Wilson, combined with my background in architecture, my experience of urban environments, performances, and exhibitions, and my other projects in the performing and visual arts. It seems impossible and also inadequate to separate my experience and knowledge of scenography from Robert Wilson; they are too much connected to my collaboration with Bob over the last 12 years. Initially coming from architecture to the theater as a guest, I found myself at the convergence of both fields. The lack of the performative in today's architecture became apparent to me when working with Wilson the theater artist, and as I gradually became a professional in the theater, my collaboration with Wilson the architect revealed to me how little space there is in today's theater. Working with Bob is always an act of architecture, whether onstage, in a museum or in a public environment. It is the same driving spirit that results in a performance, a video-portrait, or an exhibition. Being an architect, I never intended to change my profession. Rather, I strove to expand my horizon. And with Bob, I immediately found myself at the core of my questions with a long journey ahead of me. I felt deeply at home as we were two architectural minds in the realm of theater.

From the beginning, there was and still is a deep communication between us, though with few words. We would sit in a room, work silently, and converse with drawings. When I met Bob for the first time in Paris and presented my portfolio to him, he asked me who my favorite architects were. How to answer that question! I mentioned the names shooting through my head: Scarpa, Barragán, and Kahn. Bob did not say a word. Our talk lasted for about three minutes. The next time I saw him was at Watermill. Before the table workshop began, we started our research. Next to the table I was sitting at was a cabinet containing three books: one about Carlo Scarpa, one on Luis Barragán, and the third on Louis Kahn. I knew this was the right place for me!

It all began in architecture: the somatic experience of our physical environment. Prior to the will to create a work of art, architecture fulfilled human necessities as they exist in a shape. These are the most distinct shapes of mankind's creation. And there is an intrinsic need for these shapes. Later on, the notion of the functional came to distinguish the two. But when the ancient Greeks built temples of stone, with triglyphs and metopes imitating previous constructions in wood, an act of cultural transcendence took place. With this act of conscious artistic creation, a new spirit emerged in the temple. The inner structure was still the same, but the shapes began to have their own life. These inherently classical relationships and proportions are what all architecture, as well as Wilson's visual language, is about.

Shakespeare's Sonnets, Berlin, 2007

On Visual Languages and Abstraction

Scenography is the art of writing space; it is narrative architecture. A scenographer tells a story through visual means. In verbal language, the arrangement and composition of words follow certain rules, defined as grammar, and can convey meaning or be abstract, evolving as intrinsic, compositional elements, as in Dada poetry. Although a purely visual aspect becomes apparent in the context of these abstract poems, the way the words are composed and relate to each other also contributes to the fields of linguistics and semiotics. Words alter their meanings by the way they are used throughout time. Nevertheless, this is a slow and rather technical development. While the words are simply the bricks or elements of construction, the relationships between them are the essential part of the creation. *The Sun* uses the same words as *The International Herald Tribune*; it is the way in which they are put into relationships that matters.

The same pertains to visual languages, where proportions regulate the relationships between components. An ancient Greek temple and Caesar's Palace are built from very similar basic geometrical elements, and yet we sense the difference in their architectural quality. Colin Rowe showed us in his *Mathematics of the Ideal Villa*[1] how the complex interdependence of proportions is very much the same in Le Corbusier's and Andrea Palladio's villas though their outer appearances could not be more different. And in the same way that an abstract text can make use of concrete words, scenography operates with concrete and distinct images to give shape to an abstract environment.

Abstraction in its original sense of "withdrawing something" requires some pre-existing, seminal thing. This act of withdrawal is an essential artistic tool, as it allows for individual reading and perception; I can either perform this process of withdrawing in an artistic creation or merely evoke it, while it is the spectator who actually completes the act of withdrawal in his or her mind.

Robert Wilson's scenographical work is fundamentally abstract. This dependence of the work of art on the spectator's perception plays a crucial role, especially in the performing arts field where the dialogue between artist and audience is a prerequisite condition: The work of art is not complete without acknowledgment. In Wilson's visual world, we encounter an ongoing dialogue between the artist and his spectators that takes place by dint of the work of art itself. The spectator's reading of the work, his or her awareness of this dialogue and hence essential contribution to it, may be one of the reasons for Wilson's widespread recognition, also particularly outside the art world. The audience can never be separated from the performance; it is a distinct part of it. A performance of Robert Wilson's is not a monologue but always a conversation with the audience, even if it happens in silence.

1
Colin Rowe, *The Mathematics of the Ideal Villa and Other Essays* (Cambridge, Ma.: MIT Press, 1976).

Dream Play, Stockholm, 1998

Perception of Space

In the theater, we witness a performance taking place on a stage, inside a real space. Since we (usually) sit in the same spot, we have an unchanging perspective on a spatial event, a "two-dimensional perception" of a three-dimensional action. In the cinema, we watch a two-dimensional motion picture from a changing point of view. (The contemporary attempt to experience the motion picture in three dimensions so far tricks our brains with the impression of depth rather than indulges us with a true special experience.) The changing viewpoint is the deliberate and precise definition of the movement, the iris, and the zoom of the camera as specified by the director, the cinematographer, and the set designer. It creates "three-dimensional perception." (I am aware that our two eyes are made to see things, even in full immobility, as three-dimensional volumes. However, this is a technical observation. In terms of our instincts, as well as phenomenologically, the continuous change of position of our eyes and the according perception of our surroundings is a precondition of human survival.) In architecture, we perceive a three-dimensional setting "three-dimensionally" and though we have the freedom to change our perspective intentionally at whatever speed we choose, there often are more directives than we are aware of. We usually are given but a small choice of possibilities more or less clearly defined by the architect. It is a dialogue in space between the architect and the spectator, visitor, or user of a site that should be, but not necessarily always is, unbiased. The spectator's conscious or unconscious decisions must play a crucial role in the perception of architecture. The unfolding "performance" is a combination of the architect's composition of space and the spectator's interaction in it. There is a balance between free will and spatial stipulations.

This duality within architecture must be present in all scenography. In an exhibition or a site-specific venue, similar principles apply. What distinguishes scenography from mere buildings is an emphasis on the element of narrative implemented through spatial dramaturgy.

In the theater, the scenography can anticipate the changing perspective that eventually evolves in the spectator's imagination. For example, the direction, the amount, and the focus of light onstage can accomplish the effect of a changing perspective, as we see it very often in Wilson's work. His distinct use of silhouettes against a strong counter-light, usually the *cyc*, turns the mental perspective by 180 degrees, causing the viewer to look from the back of the stage towards the audience. (The *cyc* is an ever-changing, color-flooded back wall that opens into an endless abstract space instead of closing the stage in the back. Wilson uses it in most of his stage productions.) The very accurate use of a single light, which could fall only on an actor's fingertip, functions like a zoom: We are pulled onto the stage. And a very low light spreading over huge slates, as Wilson and I used them for Monteverdi's *L'Orfeo* at the Teatro alla Scala, makes us feel lost in a vast space. When Orpheus begins his journey into Hades, the relationships between the different light cues are an integral part of the composition of light and space on the timeline. We are a part of an endless continuity in which everything relates to what occurred before and builds towards what will happen

Three Sisters, Stockholm, 2001

Der Freischütz, Baden-Baden, 2009

in an instant. I experience pitch darkness differently if the lights slowly fade out than if they are turned off abruptly. When the house curtain opens, the performance is different depending on whether I have come to the theater from rush hour in New York City or from a meadow in the French countryside. Wilson says, "Theater should never start or stop. It is one continuous line." An actor's movement never does stop but continues in space: The lines an actor speaks are but a moment in time. And of the points of view mentioned above, the way a spatial setting is lit throughout time alone can fulfill the requirement of the changing perspective. But it is not only the condition of light that is always a fundamental part of a scenography; the arrangement of elements in a space can also invoke varying viewpoints.

This change of perspective can also be understood metaphorically in the sense of bringing something into a different context. This establishment of an unfamiliar or unknown relationship between two existing things alone can be a scenography. One work of Wilson's in which the changing inner perspective of one thing to another strove also to attract a different audience was the exhibition *Imágenes del Cuerpo* in the Museu Barbier-Mueller for Pre-Columbian Art in Barcelona in 2004. We placed the 15 pre-Columbian works of art into the contexts of 15 still lifes of contemporary consumer goods – a skyscraper, a crashing B-52, floating planets, the shoulders of a deer, etc. – wrenching the pre-Columbian works from their temporality by casting a present-day light on them.

Scenography should never show how things are, but rather stir the imagination by hinting at something that is not directly visible. Scenography's duty also consists in keeping the ongoing dialogue between the spectator and the scenography (and the whole performance) alive. In the case of the moving camera or the eyes of the observer of architecture, it is the relationship between the moving subject and its spatial objective that is continuously being established and redefined while the scenography gradually evolves in our minds. A lack of this inherent architectural prerequisite results unavoidably in a flat, two-dimensional setting.

Scenography and Physicality

In his multifaceted works, Bob Wilson permanently inquires into the relationship between perception and the perceived. His process of composing a stage and everything occurring on it is strictly holistic. The changing relationship between objects, persons, materials, lights, and sound constitutes a performance's inner spatial dialogue. In his exhibition or installation projects, Bob poses in their essence the same key questions that he poses in the theater. By not changing a point of view physically but rather by fictively abstracting it (as described above), he frees himself in the working process and us as spectators from the physical constraints that bind the cinematographer. Thus, in comparison to film, basically everything you can think of is possible in the theater. Our and the performance's physical presence frees us from the naturalism to which film usually is bound. Because we are in reality, everything we experience with our senses is immediate and true, and does not have to be processed by our brains to be put into a comprehensible format (although very often this still is the case when we go to the theater.) With the cinema and more so with television, our brains translate the fraction of images our eyes capture into information we understand, mostly by comparison with our own empirical knowledge. (The television reduces reality to a standard resolution of 640×480 points. Although today's technology grants us a considerably higher resolution, it is still far from our eye's capacity to grasp space. The reality-trained brain brings this information into conjunction with experience to make sense. There is growing concern as to younger brains, which derive reality from an accordingly mediatized assemblage of images.)

By using a visual language to further abstract the spatial reality on a stage, a freedom similar to the changing of perspectives arises for the objects, the performers, etc. In order that the audience not be excluded from the resulting abstraction, Bob's visual language often operates with very common visual references, almost visual archetypes. It is an essential aspect of any scenography to allow the spectator, visitor, or audience to gain access to the work. It is like an open door that invites entrance. Once inside, we can be guided or left alone to explore and discover on our own. The visual (and musical) world that we enter must stir something. I need to find things – spaces, objects, materials, lights, sounds, smells – that are familiar in one way or another, that allow me to connect. The very archetypes mentioned above guarantee this admittance by definition. The profoundly architectural and hence scenographical in Bob's work lies in his compositions not only of the directly apparent elements of a performance, but of the inner relationships connecting them within space and time. True scenography is defined by the fact of its inner dialogue establishing a space; what is inside, behind, and in between things is more relevant than their immediate appearance. But while the first three elements are hidden, it is the latter that reveals them.

Scenography is but the starting point of an avalanche in the spectators' imagination. Seeing a work of Wilson's or experiencing one of his exhibitions is an abstract mental journey. Although I have very clear or even explicit images in front of me, be they abstract, concrete, or even tangible, the real event takes place on my inner stage. This may be the reason why it is so difficult to talk about Wilson's work. It almost seems contradictory to write about it, as it is a profound individual and personal experience.

The role of scenography lies in *the creation of a potential with a face*. It is potential that has to keep a sound balance between those parts that are accurately defined and those that are fundamentally open. It is a potential for the occurrences onstage, for the actors, dancers, singers, and performers, and hence for the director. In Wilson's case, this may sound contradictory due to the fact that he acts as both the director and the scenographer of his productions. A closer look at his artistic working process should make this clearer and throw some light on my role as his scenography collaborator over the last 12 years. All productions I have worked on begin with a workshop where Wilson's collaborators sit around a table with him and discuss the results of their previous project-related research. The result of the workshop is a visual book drawn by Wilson, similar to a storyboard, which already considers all aspects of the production. Very quickly, first thoughts are evaluated in real scale.

"I have to see to know!" are among Bob's most frequent words during the working process. He uses them in the practical sense of making final decisions, but they are also the deeply philosophical and phenomenological key to his work. Bob is like a conductor: He controls and defines every detail of his production while composing and arranging the direction, scenography, and light with input from his collaborators. Although Wilson has a very sharp and clear idea of what he wants, he is open-minded. And his works finally arise from the contributions of diverse minds. The notion of clearly distinguishable parts of a collaborative work of art becomes obsolete. Rather, the collaboration is like exchanging ideas and opinions, speaking Wilson's visual language together. Things keep changing up to the opening night until all components of a performance, exhibition, or installation are soundly balanced.

Doors

The architect's responsibility regards not only the direction of our movement and view, but also the mental condition that unavoidably results from our immersion in architecture. The way I enter a courthouse, the head office of a big corporate building, or the gate to an entire city very often has a strong psychological impact. Because of the holistic physical experience of architecture, the architect acts as the mental founder of society. The architect who contributes with built structures to the physical environment where our everyday life takes place must fulfill his according responsibility to society. The scenographer, on the other hand, can make use of every possibility inherent in these mentally active aspects of architecture. Scenography in this sense is not so much a laboratory for architecture as one of its components. The incessant mutation of architecture and the transmogrification of scenography mutually depend upon and influence each other. The aspect of narrative plays a crucial role in this context: Scenography always stands in relation to *something*, whether it be a text, piece of music, person, or topic. This reciprocity is of a neutral, not necessarily narrative, kind in regard to raw architecture. But it is the scenographical component in many great works of architecture that constitutes their spirit, if we think of Le Corbusier's *promenade architecturale* or Scarpa's architecture with its significant itinerant scenography as paradigmatic cases.

Wilson often operates in the same field from a theatrical perspective. He often says that "architecture is about doors." The experience of a space depends to a great extent on how I enter it. The notion of "entering" is the starting point of the three-dimensional experience of a space, and thus a significant element of any performance. This produces an obvious dichotomy in that entering one space means leaving a previous one. This crucial aspect of any spatial transition emphasizes the continuity of space and time as described above. I always have to leave one space to enter another, and whether this passage is precipitate or gradual represents a distinct aspect of the particular architectural creation in question.

DiaLog/A Mad Man A Mad Giant A Mad Dog A Mad Urge A Mad Face, Shiraz, Iran, 1974.
Christopher Knowles and Robert Wilson

What appears obvious in architecture is crucial in theater and scenography, too. From where, and how, does an actor enter a stage, and what does he mentally bring with him? The audience here is merely observing how an imaginative space is being created by this actor, the space in his head (which can differ from the actual space of the stage set). While the case of architecture is about the duality of the spectator and the space, theater is about the relationship between the spectator, the space, and the performer (or performing agent). The scenographer's task consists in creating a potential, not in anticipating, so that the constructed space, the space that the performer imagines, and the space that the audience perceives are not necessarily the same. There is an imminent tension between these three spaces. If they are identical, the result is redundancy and the audience will be left out.

The spatial experience of a door or the act of entering a room is a highly performative aspect of architecture. Because entering a room implies temporality, it is a clear architectural statement that converges with space. This is the point at which theater and architecture are akin and become scenography. Bob's work continuously explores these points where architecture and performance meet and merge, where they exchange roles and enter into dialogue. In the 2009 Berliner Ensemble's production of *Shakespeare's Sonnets*, Bob and I further explored the concept of the door in theater. The stage was a white wooden box. A variety of different vertical and horizontal openings and doors in the back and side walls were the essential elements of the different spaces where Shakespeare's 15 sonnets were recited. The back wall opened by two horizontally sliding sides, leaving a tall and narrow gap for the king's entrance. Later, this entire back wall would fly up, leaving only a low horizontal gap with a view to the *cyc*. For Wilson, time is a vertical line going to the center of the earth, space a horizontal line. They depend on each other; the one does not exist without the other. This is the basis of everything. Any play of Bob's could be identified and analyzed solely by its concise use of the vertical and the horizontal and how this relationship evolves throughout the performance. In *Sonnets*, the side walls mainly consisted of eight panels at full height that could be opened towards the center of the stage. During the first part of the production these panels open individually like doors, serving as entrances through the white-varnished walls; actors walk or are "flown" onstage. Towards the middle of the play, the panels open one by one until finally, fully turned, their black velvet backs become visible, the white space metamorphosing into an empty black void. The walls slowly dissolve as they become mere arrays of doors. At some point in *Sonnets*, each wall with all its panels flush is rotated towards the audience, turning the concept of the door as a moveable part of a wall upside down again as the entire side wall appears as a single door. The importance of doors for Wilson may also reside in this meeting between theater and architecture: A door is simply a performative piece of wall.

Robert Wilson is an architect, maybe one of the most profound. He explores the essence of architecture, its almost naked, fragile, vulnerable inner core: its very philosophy. He strips away all of the protective layers and skins of a given thing, subsequently reshaping its raw substance. The resulting forms are holistic temporal compositions in space. Structures, objects, materials, bodies brought together in light, a meticulous narrative mapping in continuous movement balanced with every space's particular music, crystallize from the long process of project development and rehearsal work with collaborating artists. The visual language Wilson has developed and is constantly refining further allows access to everyone from any background and culture. He opens a door, welcoming any audience to enter and perceive. All you need is to open your mind and trust your eyes and ears: There are no prerequisites you were not born with.

Shakespeare's Sonnets, Berlin, 2009

Preparatory drawings by Robert Wilson for *the CIVIL warS – Marseilles Workshop,* 1984

Preparatory drawings for *Doctor Faustus Lights the Lights,* Berlin, 1992. Robert Wilson

The drawings of Robert Wilson

A scene of Robert Wilson drawing, from a 1987 documentary, distills to a single kinetic sequence the purposefully unresolved tension between making and unmaking in all his art. The film shows Wilson late at night, bent over a table sketching scenes from what looks like the Cologne section of *the CIVIL warS*. In long, vigorous strokes, he draws the cross-hatching lines of a grid that fills the entire page. The grid's promise of rationalism and order is seemingly threatened by Wilson's haste and by his unconcern for the straightness of any given line. The same division is visible in his body. His left arm and hand are pumping and restless, grinding coal into the page. The right arm, meanwhile, lies flat and rigid against Wilson's thigh, as if he'd strapped it down in fear of its disruptive potential. This arm, in its discipline and poise, models the actorly restraint we remember from Wilson's productions. Yet juxtaposed with the aggressive other half of Wilson's body, it also complicates our impression of that elegance. The close kinship between chaos and order here, over the drawing table, suggests a similarly uneasy detente on the stage. There, as here, poise remains aware of everything that could unsteady it.

And so it is with the sketch as a whole. At the end of the filmed episode, Wilson tacks the page to a wall and takes a cold eye to marks drained of the erotic heat of their making. Wielding an eraser, he rubs out images, or smears once sharp or bold lines, turning borders into haze. (One may remember a comment by Adolphe Appia, in many ways Wilson's most important ancestor: "I design with my eraser."[1]) The unsentimental briskness with which Wilson effaces the source of earlier visual pleasure demands that we again adjust our thinking about his theater, qualifying conclusions we may have held about the value of seeing. This theater of images (as we commonly classify it) depends for its pathos on our awareness of the image's vulnerability, of the ease with which Wilson can dissolve or renounce a beautiful tableau. Walter Benjamin describes exactly this in a passage written on the eve of World War II: "That which one knows one will soon no longer have in front of one's eyes becomes an image."[2] Drawings bearing a history of erasure train us to look upon his stage with an eye less covetous – to be more the anticipatory mourner than the complacent connoisseur of the world he lets us see.

If, when we enter Wilson's theater, we remain haunted by the drawings, each production will begin to seem less a singular work than the second half of a diptych, or the second act of a two-part spectacle. The first part, enacted alone over Wilson's drawing table for an audience of one, isn't merely preparatory, nor should its products be approached as mere records of the more fully realized theater. If anything, the reverse could be true. The productions can be treated as the memories of the drawings, recalling us to a period when the cool, idealized shapes onstage churned with unpredictable energy, each mark retaining

[1]
Adolphe Appia, quoted in Walther R. Volbach, *Adolphe Appia, Prophet of the Modern Theater: A Profile* (Middletown: Wesleyan University Press, 1968), 126.

[2]
Walter Benjamin, "The Paris of the Second Empire in Baudelaire," (1938), quoted in Wolfgang Schivelbusch, *The Railway Journey: The Industrialization of Time and Space in the Nineteenth Century* (Berkeley: University of California Press, 1986), 184–85 n, 21.

something of the motion that made it. It's possible to view all of Wilson's productions, regardless of their ostensible subject or narrative, as being "about" drawing. One need only note the frequency with which Wilson shines isolating light upon an actor's hand to recognize how every gesture on Wilson's stage summons the memory of his own hand moving the pencil across the page. It's a process that the drawings themselves memorialize. On many sheets, Wilson leaves a dirty handprint, or smudged, smeared fingerprints – evidence allowing us to trace the image back to its fugitive source.

The proliferating hands point to other scenes of drawing on Wilson's stage. Some are explicit, as in the presence of Wilson's own, enlarged drawings in *The Malady of Death*, allowing actors to be *in* drawing, and of drawings by others, as in *Einstein on the Beach*. *Einstein* is also full of characters typing, chalking figures on blackboards, filing their nails, and counting on their fingers. They ensure that we'll see the pipe Lucinda Childs holds in her first dance and the flashlights that Wilson holds in his last as surrogates for the graphite pencil.

There are other, less overt signs that Wilson's theater is preoccupied with drawing even as it traces other narratives. The receding columns in his production of *Alceste* will recall the perspective studies familiar from any drawing class, just as the many cubes, spheres, and pyramids in *Pelléas et Mélisande* (among other works) imply the presence of a conscientious student affirming the rules of geometry before he renders the scenes they comprise. When one sees the perfect circles of light in *Pelléas*, or in *The Threepenny Opera*, one may think of the famously perfect "O" by Giotto, the form by which the painter's virtuoso hand most clearly announced itself. A painter's hand is also apparent in the many grids that anchor Wilson's scene and articulate the stage landscape, as we saw in the drawing from *the CIVIL warS*. That grid, and those in *Doktor Faustus* (Manzoni), *Einstein*, *the CIVIL warS – Knee Plays*, and *I was sitting on my patio...*, are versions of the grid with which a painter discovers and then fixes the relationship among parts of his composition – an aid to transferring the drawing to canvas. When those structures turn up in Wilson's theater, they suggest that what we see onstage is itself but a preparatory composition preceding the creation of a later, fully realized work – something that we never get to see.

Still another allusion to drawing is subtle and perhaps unintentional. Eluding the strict orthodoxy of a grid's horizontals and verticals are the sinuous S-curves that Wilson allows to weave through his compositions. Their presence is more than merely decorative; they argue a point about refined drawing technique. Those who remember William Hogarth's definitions of the "line of grace" and the "line of beauty" from his 1753 treatise *Analysis of Beauty* may think they've spotted illustrations of them throughout Wilson's oeuvre.[3] One wants to imagine Wilson silently agreeing with the Hogarth who prized the "serpentine" and "waving" lines above all others whenever the director releases a serpentine line into an otherwise regimented scene, as he does in *Madama Butterfly* (a stone pathway), *Le Martyre de Saint Sébastien* (a riverbed), and the installation *Portrait, Still Life, Landscape* (a vacuum-cleaner tube) – or even more aggressively (if less visibly) when he shapes a production's

3
William Hogarth, *The Analysis of Beauty* (1753), Ronald Paulson, ed. (New Haven: Yale University Press, 1997), 41–42. The original title page, reproduced in this edition, includes an image of the line of beauty, as does a Hogarth self-portrait, *The Painter and His Pug* (1745).

"Danton's Death"

Robert Wilson, "Danton's Death," charcoal on paper, 1992

DOCTOR FAUSTUS LIGHTS THE LIGHTS

Drawings by Robert Wilson here and on the following pages, courtesy Paula Cooper Gallery.
Robert Wilson, "Doctor Faustus Lights the Lights,"charcoal, oil-based pastel, and graphite on paper, 1992

overall dramatic structure to a Hogarthian S-curve, the line of beauty, as he does when sketching the narratives of *The Life and Times of Joseph Stalin* and *The Forest*.[4] In these pieces, the entire production draws a line over the course of its many hours, even if we can't see it.

If the grids and primary shapes refer us to an unseen future in the life of Wilson's images, other elements on his stage refer us to an unseen past. The rectangular panels that often form the background to the knee-plays look like sheets of unmarked white paper. (Wilson has said as much, describing each knee-play as "a blank canvas."[5]) They return us to Wilson alone in his studio, before he made a single mark. The panels of decor or squares of light are among the most charged spaces in his compositions – cool, yet also producing heat from how completely they exclude the mark. Wilson teaches us how to see them in the many drawings in which he preserves one white island in a churning black sea, assailed on all sides by slashing charcoal marks. In such a context, the square's purity hardly seems transcendent; rather, it is defiant, a declaration of neutrality as militant as the strokes that would violate it. Several of these spaces sit in the lower corner of his compositions, each like a memento of the larger, no longer empty sheet. In their positioning on the page, the white squares recall the famous title page to Goya's *Caprichos* – an echo that is more than merely formal. Goya's white square is an artist's desk, from which spring the marvelous, terrifying images that populate all the other drawings – the "monsters" born of the "sleep of reason." So, too, in Wilson does reason remain in ambivalent kinship with his own dreamlike, occasionally nightmarish imagery. With his classicizing method, he animates, shapes, and reins in the "monsters," yet, beyond that, he also preserves a space apart. The "blank canvases" within each work offer relief from the surfeit of visual pleasure.

These drawings help us value the many others in which Wilson vigorously inscribes the borders of the entire page. He asserts and then reasserts the rectangularity of the sheet, as if wanting to confirm its dimensions before proceeding further. Of course, one could say he is merely defining the proscenium, but in his obsessiveness that stage begins to seem an ever more porous, uncertain container. Norman Bryson and Avis Newman, in separate statements, suggest that every artist must contend with what Newman calls the "dreadful… boundlessness" of the page, and so too, here, as the sheer expanse of the space for drawing causes vertigo or even terror – conditions that can be ameliorated only when the artist confines himself to an ever tighter frame.[6]

In certain Wilson drawings, prosceniums nest within prosceniums, while beyond their borders rages a storm of lines or an equally dizzying emptiness. A drawing by William Blake, *Elisha in the Chamber on the Wall*, may help clarify the motivation behind these pictures. In Blake's frankly theatrical work, the prophet Elisha sits at a table in a room set within a room, a stage at the end of a house: six different frames enclose the seer. And seeing is Blake's subject: "I suppose it to be a vision," reads a line below the picture. Elisha has envisioned his host's future child, but his local act of prophecy is customarily taken as a metaphor for Blake's own creation. It is as if the artist – drawing at Elisha's table? – feels

4

See the sketches for *Stalin* in *Robert Wilson: Lecture*, Jan Linders, ed. (Berlin: Alexander Verlag Berlin, 2007), 61, and for *The Forest* in the program book published by the Theater der Freien Volksbühne, Berlin (1988), 77. An S-curve also provides the structure for a scene in Wilson's *King Lear*. See the sketch reproduced in Arthur Holmberg, *The Theatre of Robert Wilson* (Cambridge: Cambridge University Press, 1996), 140.

5

Robert Wilson, quoted in Theater der Freien Volksbühne program book for *The Forest*, 84.

6

Norman Bryson, "A Walk for a Walk's Sake," and Avis Newman, "Conversation: Avis Newman and Catherine de Zegher," in *The Stage of Drawing: Gesture and Act: Selected from the Tate Collection*, Catherine de Zegher, ed. (New York: Tate Publishing and The Drawing Center, 2003), 150–51, 233. The drawing by William Blake, described below, was part of this exhibition.

he must lodge himself in a close-fitting space if his mind's imagery is to surface in forms legible to his audience. (It's telling, in this regard, that Wilson's art has been termed a "theater of visions.")

Seen another way, the many boxes and prosceniums in Wilson's drawings can resemble apertures – routes of escape rather than instruments of containment. The drawings help us gauge the pressure that builds inexorably within even the most placid Wilson composition. Space that is empty in a Wilson production is, in the drawings, alive with activity. Pencil strokes fill the space, tracking electric currents invisible to the naked eye. Leonardo da Vinci described this very phenomenon, proleptically helping to explain why Wilson, for his part, rarely leaves empty space truly empty. "The air is full of infinite lines, straight and radiating, intersected and interwoven, without their displacing one another; and they represent for every object the true form of their cause."[7] Yet a vision of cause and effect that Leonardo finds fluid is, in Wilson, chaotic and often treacherous. The scrum of lines in Wilson's drawings is typically fervid, distracted, impatient – seeming, in some cases, like absent-minded scribbling, or mere plenitude, or even waste. In others, the marks are more rhythmically purposeful, the pencil strokes accelerating, intensifying to an almost intolerable level. The membrane does tear; the volcano does erupt. The many windows, doorways, and arches that perforate his drawings function as valves, letting off steam that can (or should) no longer be repressed by the pictures' larger frames. Light gushes from doorways in numerous drawings (in one for *The Golden Windows*, it's like the visible sound from an open mouth) or spills through other apertures – events that, when drawn thus, help us register the true cataclysmic power in light that seems effortlessly (and innocuously) to illuminate the stage. The apertures in other drawings seem forcibly to discharge or expel the light, or to fail at stanching a wound that hemorrhages anew. In one drawing of a scene from *Lohengrin*, a beautifully positioned box indecorously evacuates itself of light – a purging of a toxin.

What causes the pressure to build? A passage from a text that Wilson knows well – Osip Mandelstam's *A Conversation on Dante*, for which Wilson created a series of extraordinary lithographs – speaks for many of them. Writing of the *Inferno*, Mandelstam argues that its "compositional basis...is the movement of a thunderstorm...and all questions and answers essentially turn around one single fact: Will the thunderstorm break or not?"[8] Other natural phenomena are equally appealing points of reference for Wilson's manner of marking. Lines look windswept, or like so much particulate matter in the air, or like scratches on ice. Some clusters recall a bird's nest, a beaver's dam, a swarm of flies, or (moving indoors) a tray of metal filaments awaiting a magnet to organize them. Other drawings, thick and muddy, exploit the properties of charcoal to suggest the smouldering remains of a scorched forest. There's a related posthumous quality to drawings far lighter and sparer. Two, from *Madama Butterfly*, suggest stains left in the aftermath of a trauma; others, linked to the knee-plays in *Time Rocker*, are so terse as to invite all manner of projected scenarios. Are they the tracks left by a tire skidding just before an accident? The trail of an oil slick? Was a body dragged across this surface? Whatever the lurid narrative, this imagery insists *something*

7
Leonardo da Vinci, quoted in David Rosand, *Drawing Acts: Studies in Graphic Expression and Representation* (Cambridge: Cambridge University Press, 2002), 104.

8
Osip Mandelstam, *A Conversation on Dante* (1933), trans. Paul Schmidt (Paris: Picaron Editions, 1993), unpaginated.

MEDEA ACT TWO

Robert Wilson, "Medea, Act Two," charcoal on paper, 1983

Robert Wilson, "Time Rocker,"charcoal on paper, 1996

happened here less innocuous than marking. The drawings convert their audiences from mere viewers into witnesses, and even into interrogators – detectives scrutinizing evidence.

Despite the ease with which we refer Wilson's drawings to worlds beyond the page – whether it be to his stage, or to larger landscapes and more melodramatic narratives – all the drawings inevitably return us to Wilson himself. Here he is least guarded and most exposed. The Wilson who leaves us the traces of his presence (*he* is what happened here) purposefully chooses not to assume the aloof persona we imagine presiding over the productions. As we've seen, his fingerprints are literally all over these works. Such art has nothing to do with the disclosures of confessional artists, but rather goes deeper and is more daring. We see the accidental, uncomposed, or dirty self, the surplus self, everything that even confessional artists can't accommodate, or transform into something shapely. The drawings allow us to see a Wilson in process, going *toward* the image rather than presenting it as already won. In one series of sketches, the *Parsifal* circle remains a distant ideal as Wilson draws one approximate loop over another. He lingers in frustration and even welcomes failure – at least he can be imagined doing so, if we read certain marks as acts of crossing out as much as sketching in. Such is one way to regard a drawing for Gluck's *Alceste*. A cube first seen in the distance in that production is, in the drawing, rendered as only a few hatch marks. It sits on the page like an error. In many drawings, a series of legible second or third thoughts suggests that Wilson finds the page a hospitable arena to confront self-doubt, and to exercise the drive to overcome it – activities that have no place on his stage. Wilson uses the pencil to harrow the depths of consciousness otherwise unreachable, and to scrape off the layers of affect encrusted by habit.

As such, they are documents that record a particular degree of attention. The best description of this state of engagement can be found in Paul Valéry's writings about Degas's sketches. "He is like a writer striving to attain the utmost precision of form...never admitting that his work has reached its *final* stage."[9] The link to writing is explicit in Wilson's famous series of drawings depicting the word "there" from *A Letter for Queen Victoria*. Each drawing is progressively more urgent; the lines shaping the letters are ever more forceful – these are the neurotic symptoms of an artist worried, perhaps, that there is no *there* there. Lest we think such a process is without risk, Valéry later writes in a well-known passage of a "violent, self-devouring activity," the artist "attack[ing], invad[ing]" the "empty space" of the page, hoping to vanquish "the indeterminacy of the mind" and "possess...what one wants to *see*."[10] It was this same desperation that Antonin Artaud recognized when he spoke of his own drawings: "the piteous awkwardness of forms crumbling around an idea after having for so many eternities labored to join it" – drawings in which "the anguish and exhaustion of the consciousness of the seeker [is] in the centre."[11]

Artaud's drawings come to mind when one sees certain Wilson sketches for *The Golden Windows*: Their surfaces are scarred and punctured by the pencil, leaving stigmata that attest to a long struggle. In many drawings, Wilson seems to test the paper's durability and pliancy, hoping to learn how much activity a single surface (page or stage) can handle.

9
Paul Valéry, "Degas, Dance, Drawing," (1935), in *Degas Manet Morisot*, David Paul, trans. (Princeton: Princeton University Press, 1989), 39.

10
Ibid., 67.

11
Antonin Artaud, "Commentary on *Dessin à regarder de traviole*" (c. 1946), quoted in Paule Thévenin, "The Search for a Lost World," in Jacques Derrida and Paule Thévenin, *The Secret Art of Antonin Artaud*, trans. Mary Ann Caws (Cambridge: MIT Press, 1998), 26.

The violence in that ambition rises to the surface in many other ways. A drawing for *Salomé* sums up the ambivalence at the heart of so much Wilson. On this landscape, a monolith that conforms to a classically elegant triangle shape has been scratched out with almost maniacal fervor. In the gesture of defacement (more candid about its motivating emotion than the erasures and smears we see in other drawings), we can read a deeper rage against any image and a broader prohibition on seeing. Here, away from the visual splendor of his productions, Wilson declares himself an artist concerned as much with touch as with seeing. Indeed, one of the many drawings that show Wilson's hand most literally – from *King Lear*, with Wilson's palmprint visible in the middle of the page – is captioned "Bless thy sweet eyes, they bleed." The play's narrative of blindness can be read as contesting, if not rescinding, the performance's (and the drawing's) invitation to see it. Jacques Derrida's recognition of the close kinship between drawing and blindness is pertinent here. "It is as if seeing were forbidden in order to draw, as if one drew only on the condition of not seeing," he writes of the daughter of Butades, who (we're told) turned away from her lover to draw his shadow.[12] This narrative of art's origins refers Derrida to Medusa, whom he imagines presiding over all drawing. It may not be far-fetched to see her hovering over Wilson's theater, too. The Hogarthian S-curves that, as we've seen, are so common in his work now have an additional meaning. In their serpentine form, they stand in for Medusa's snakes, and therefore may warn us against looking too trustingly upon Wilson's beguiling spectacles. (The enlarged drawing that serves as a backdrop for *The Magic Flute*, dominated by a snake and an eye, would suggest that Wilson is at least aware of the linkage.)

The embattled state of vision in Wilson should be apparent even if one doesn't pursue these allusions. The purposeful austerity of the drawings – few deviate from a black-and-white palette – disabuse those expecting the theater's lavish sensuality. In that agon between black and white (the drama of the drawings), one expects one side to prevail – a denouement that, whichever the victor, makes definitive the end of seeing. Some of Wilson's most memorable drawings arrive at this ultimate state. In drawings for *De Materie* and *Swan Song*, the mark thins to the point of imperceptibility, or dissolves into the ether, until absence becomes a substance – an opacity, a cataract. In others, such as the exquisite drawings for *Dream Play*, vision suffers a more conventional fate. Darkness falls almost completely, as if Wilson, the master of light, reserves his ultimate mastery for extinguishing it. The most enduring beauty in Wilson, here and in his always-ephemeral theater, points to its certain loss.

12
Jacques Derrida, *Memoirs of the Blind: The Self-Portrait and Other Ruins*, Pascale-Anne Brault and Michael Naas, trans. (Chicago: University of Chicago Press, 1993), 49.

Robert Wilson, "Salomé," graphite and crayon on paper, 1986

Robert Wilson, "Dream Play," charcoal on paper, 1998

RUMI – in the Blink of the Eye, Warsaw, 2008

Shakespeare's Sonnets, Berlin, 2009

The Forest, Berlin,1988

The Forest, Berlin, 1988

The Life and Times of Joseph Stalin, New York City, 1973

The Forest, Berlin, 1988. Geno Lechner

Doktor Faustus (Manzoni), Milan, 1989. Robert Wilson

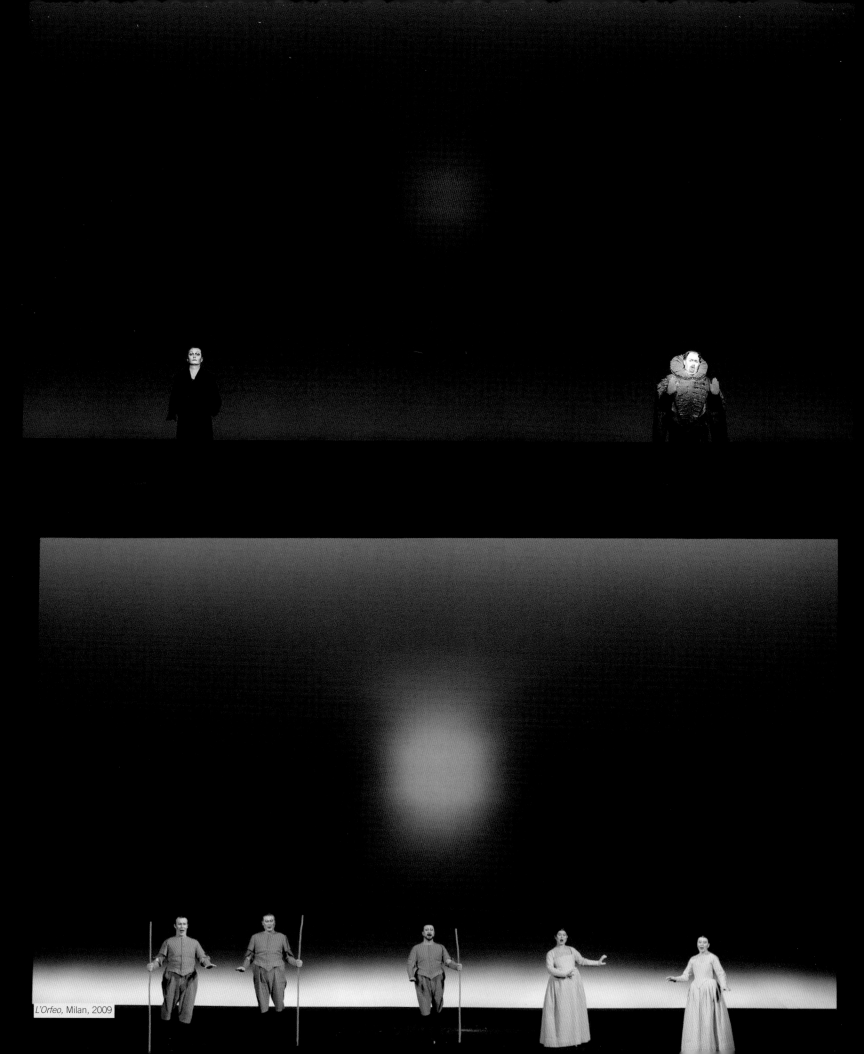

L'Orfeo, Milan, 2009

Three Sisters, Stockholm, 2001

The Threepenny Opera, Berlin, 2007

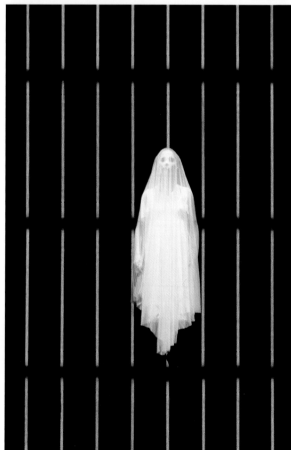

The Threepenny Opera, Berlin, 2007

Doctor Caligari, Berlin, 2002

A costume is an actor

I met Jacques Reynaud at the same time that I met Robert Wilson, who introduced Reynaud with high praise for his fabulous costume design; it was obvious that the two men were very comfortable with each other, and that this was born of a long collaboration and real understanding. Reynaud is part of the Wilson "family." An internationalist par excellence, the Franco-Italian Reynaud, who was born in Milan and studied in New York, works constantly on both sides of the Atlantic, traveling nearly as much as Wilson himself. His collaborations with Wilson include all of his productions with the Berliner Ensemble, among them *Woyzeck*, *Leonce and Lena*, *Wintermärchen*, *The Threepenny Opera*, *Shakespeare's Sonnets*, and *Lulu*. Elsewhere, Reynaud has designed the award-winning costumes for Wilson's *Peer Gynt*, *L'Orfeo*, *The Life and Death of Marina Abramović*, and, once again at the venerable opera house where the two men first met, Monteverdi's *Il ritorno d'Ulisse in patria* (2011).

Bob and I met at La Scala in 1987. He was directing Strauss's *Salomé*, and at the time I was working as Assistant Director of the opera house. Working closely with Bob, we became good friends, so many years later, when the German costume designer Moidele Bickel needed an assistant on a show Bob was doing in Munich, Bob suggested that she call me. She did, and we worked together a couple of times, and I realized that I was much more interested in designing costumes than in directing. Moidele asked me to be her assistant in Salzburg, where she was designing costumes for the Italian director Luca Ronconi. Ronconi and I got along well, and in Rome he asked me to design the costumes for a production of *Peer Gynt*. That was my first collaboration as a costume designer. A few months later, Bob called and asked me to design costumes for a Brecht play at the Berliner Ensemble, which, of course, I did. Bob liked my work very much, and ever since then I've designed the costumes for most Wilson productions.

One of the reasons for the success of our collaboration, I think, is that Bob and I never quite talk about the play we are going to do. As long as I respect the necessity for Bob's stage to show clear shape and line in space and monochrome fabrics, I am totally free. Those are the criteria. We work independently. Of course, in Stage A of the rehearsal, I am always aware of Bob's suggestions on costume, and if they make sense within the overall line I'm impressing on the show, I certainly follow them. Nevertheless, the collaboration is based on freedom, and I have never felt forced to do something very specific by Bob. He might make a sketch, show me a picture and so on, but only as a mere suggestion, as a "take it or leave it." In the end, it is up to me to decide.

> There is a drawing by Wilson for *Shakespeare's Sonnets* that has directions such as "maybe a dark lady" or "Anna in white in bed," and another with three dark triangles with "heads" and the note: "3 dark ladies." How does this translate into the final costume design?

Designing for Bob is very, very different than designing for other directors. In general, directors fill your mind with concepts and ideas that are never visual. Personally, I get very confused by all their abstractions. Bob, in contrast, doesn't speak, but his visual language speaks very clearly. I get more ideas looking at one of his sketches than I do in an hour of costume discussions with any other director.

When there are historical elements, I research historical costumes very carefully, studying the shapes of each element of a garment in order to stylize it or change it into something different, but I've never copied a painting or a photograph, for instance. As I've said, I must respect the necessity of Bob's stage for clear lines and shapes, and Bob's idiosyncrasy regarding patterned fabric.

Costume design enters at the beginning of the Stage A rehearsal period. So I knew from the very beginning in *Shakespeare's Sonnets* that the then-86-year-old actress [Inge] Keller was playing Shakespeare and the actor [Jürgen] Holtz Elizabeth I, but I didn't allow this to influence my designs at all. What was very important for me was to not turn the entire show into a drag show because of this reversal of gender, a woman playing a man and a man a woman. I tried to think of Keller as a man and of Holtz as a woman. And it worked: The show doesn't have any vulgarity or the exaggeration that a drag show could have.

Leonce and Lena, Berlin, 2003

To what degree do the show's other stylistic elements – lighting, make-up, etc. – impact your designs?

Lighting, staging, make-up, all of those factor into the costume design. As well as respecting Bob's need for clear shape and line in space, I also have to respect his original ideas regarding make-up, which means strong, heavy make-up. The make-up is as important as the costumes. It is a key element of Bob's idea of theater as a formal theater, and, I would add, an anthropological one. The strong make-up you see is not done just for the sake of it. It's functional. It's so that you can better see the lines of a face, and especially the eyes of an actor. When people say, "Oh, I am so tired of seeing that make-up!" I get upset, because they don't understand that this kind of "painting the face" is part of a more general aesthetic, which I like to think of as part of that anthropological idea of theater. The face turns into a mask; it is transformed through elaborate make-up. This is what every kind of Eastern theater does. The characters on Bob's stage are larger than life. They live in a supernatural world of light.

I said that costume design enters at the beginning of Stage A rehearsal, but in fact, at that stage, we use rehearsal costumes that come from the theater's stock of costumes. It happens sometimes that a rehearsal costume can influence the eventual design of the original costume, but it doesn't happen very often.

Leonce and Lena, Berlin, 2003

Peer Gynt, Oslo, 2005

One peculiarity with Wilson is that the original costumes have to be ready by the beginning of light rehearsal. It often happens that Wilson lights a single costume or several in order to pull them out from the overall look of the stage in a single moment. But when he does that, it is always to stress a narrative moment or more generally to bring attention to something he is interested in. This is really important, because while I know a rough version of the staging from Stage A, the light will be a surprise, even though Wilson generally likes cold light. I have to keep that element in mind when I'm considering the choice of color for fabrics. I tend to remain within a cold scale of colors or to use clear strong color like white, red, deep purple. To be honest, I don't know if a bright yellow or orange would make Bob happy.

Costumes are never recycled. Never. Each production keeps its full set of costumes. Ideas, alas, are sometime recycled.

> Is costume in a Wilson production a "player" in and of itself, or is it there to support other elements: movement, text, music?

I have to take into account all the elements you mention and make them fit into a purely aesthetic vision. The role of costume design in a Wilson production is equal to all the other elements. There is a brief, beautiful page by Heiner Müller that says the "being American" of Wilson, the essence of Wilson's "Americanness," is that for him a stone is the equal of an actor and a tree the equal of a light. It is the American landscape. If you don't already know that Müller text, look for it – it is very beautiful and a truthful insight into Bob's genius.

Is there a "look," an identifiable signature, to the costumes used in Wilson productions?

I do not think there is a look for the *costume* of a Wilson piece. The look is given not by the costumes themselves – Bob has worked with many designers other than me – but by the *light* that Bob puts on a costume. After all, as with everything else in Bob's theater – space, narrative, etc. – the costumes also come alive under Bob's lights, and that can give the impression of the same look, even if the work of the designer is not the same at all.

Is it unusual for a costume designer to be so identified with a director, as you are with Wilson?

No, it's not. Think of [German director Peter] Stein and Bickel or [Italian director Luchino] Visconti and [Piero] Tosi, etc. Nonetheless, it's also true that it's more frequent in theater collaborations that a director is identified with a stage designer. In my collaboration with Wilson, I think he likes my design because it has simple lines within the costume itself and because there is a single line that runs throughout each piece. So it doesn't matter what kind of production it is, and Bob and I have worked, and continue to work, together on both plays and operas. And, of course, over the years our collaboration has evolved, and today there is a stronger mutual trust, respect, and friendship.

Wintermärchen, Berlin, 2005

In all the productions you have designed with Wilson, which costumes are the most interesting in your view?

I am very fond of *Woyzeck, Three Sisters,* and *Doctor Caligari,* all done in the early 2000s. I like them because they push the idea that I had at the beginning all the way through, and even far beyond.

What is different about designing for the stage as opposed to normal dress design?

I have never designed fashion. Fashion seems to have an extreme need to exist and at the same time its existence is rooted in a very aleatory ground; it is an extremely interesting and important facet of our society. A costume is an actor, a character, a play in a context like theater that seems more and more outdated. Costume lasts even less than fashion: the length of an evening. It is its melancholic and magic side.

Woyzeck, Copenhagen, 2000

Peer Gynt, Oslo, 2005

If I were to relate Robert Wilson to the movie *The Wizard of Oz*, an exercise I often practice with regard to the various people and elements of my life – me being Dorothy, show business being black-and-white and "real life" color, my boyfriend a slightly more butch version of Glenda the Good Witch, and so on and so forth – Bob would of course be the Wizard.

But there's a twist! Instead of the brutal discovery at the end of the MGM film of a little fat man behind a red curtain, nervously grasping at switches and microphones in order to control the staged colossus of a powerful magician, Bob would in fact be that immense sorcerer, that huge giant head projecting fire and sound in all directions; no smoke and mirrors, no tricks of light or false perspectives (though, ironically, these are some of the elements he uses daily in his creative process), but a tempest masking a god.

When I say "a god," I speak of his tireless work in the theater (though I'm always struck by how fantastic he looks with such a constantly hectic schedule). It is his unearthly power to both destroy and create onstage in that reversed order, smashing to bits and then building up again, that I think sets him apart from most artists throughout history.

Artists are mainly concerned with capturing the human condition. Artistically, Bob has no interest whatsoever in the human condition. He wants us all to be Wizards.

Speaking of the human condition, as a person, Bob is one of the kindest and most generous gentlemen you will ever meet. In working with him, one eventually realizes through the toil and turmoil that he puts personal relationships above and beyond everything else: a true prince. But in terms of work, the first thing to go is what's expected of the mortal body, and like the creation of a refined instrument, the actor's gangly arms and legs slowly change through hard labor and concentration, transforming into strings and pedals in order to project the physics of light and harmony. In the end, a group of players, writers, musicians, and technicians becomes one big great orchestra, or actually something even bigger than that: another planet, somewhat like our own but definitely much better dressed, where every element is intimately related and the loss of a piece makes the puzzle worthless. Essentially, the play builds itself: the goal, I believe, of every great director no matter what style or genre. As a musician, this is an amazing experience to be part of. In this type of democratic system where whatever's offered is instinctively judged and one knows immediately what works and what doesn't, the piece as a whole chooses its accompaniment, and like any attempt at great art, the message transferred through the vessel of the artist is much easier to identify without a cloud of insecure questions related to "the self." Whatever it takes to run the vehicle of the play is eaten up by all and enjoyed like apples of the sun. It's a great privilege to have one's music swimming in the ether of such a moving spectacle.

And do let us use the French term for "show" – such a better way of putting it – since it emphasizes both beauty and accessibility, two elements so very important to Bob. When Robert Wilson puts on *un spectacle*, he creates a true, palpable form of magic. And there's no going back to Kansas after that.

254

Die Frau ohne Schatten, Paris, 2002

A whole world in an instant

Robert Wilson's world is like one of his little houses lost in the wood, artwork made, like a drawing of a child, without a door. Impossible to get in, impossible to get out. The house of being, Heidegger would say. The being of Wilson. When I first met Wilson 40 years ago, the aspect that struck me about him (and there are many) is the consistency with which his art is linked to his personality, and, even more so, to his childhood. One might wonder whether his construction of total-art systems results from a fervent search for his lost childhood, a childhood that never happened, a childhood that remained eternal. I listened to him speak of the dreamscape he came from, a place he, as it turns out, never left. And so, as the years went by, my initial fascination grew with my understanding that nothing, absolutely nothing new happens in his opus, that he draws everything from what was already there a long time ago, a very long time ago – well before knowing that a newborn spends more than 80 percent of total sleep time in REM, well before he began pondering the question: What does an infant dream about anyway?

Wilson recalls the creative force of sameness, of reviving things of yore, with an anecdote about Albert Einstein who, interrupted during a press conference by a journalist asking him to repeat what he had just said, replied: "What's the point of repeating myself when I've only been talking about the same thought my whole life?"

To understand Robert Wilson's singular creative power, we can draw on the remarkable posture he assumes when one of his creations is presented before him. His peculiar gaze takes in everything, eyes wide open, eyes wide shut; a gaze that speaks a child's surprise and the wonder of someone seeing the play for the very first time. His is the singular transformation of any man caught in the sudden grip of theater and its magic. Nothing else exists around him; wide-eyed, mouth agape, he takes in the stage like a kid utterly bewitched.

In *The Aesthetics of Disappearance*, Paul Virilio designates these moments of absence by the term "picnolepsy": a *petit mal*, a daydream.[1] The consciousness of those who are subject to it seems to be put in parentheses, their senses active but nevertheless closed to external impressions. Children taken by their games often also – and without any pathology involved – experience such moments of relinquishing reality. And then, just as suddenly, they resume their activity where they had left it, as if nothing had happened. Maybe when he immerses himself in his own universe, Wilson experiences a similar kind of abduction from any spatial-temporal context. Maybe the power of a given moment releases him from time. No here-and-now, but only "here" and only "now"; and, aside from the moment of creation, no presence whatsoever. In this way, he is the first to succumb to the force of his own creative impulse.

[1] Paul Virilio, *The Aesthetics of Disappearance* (New York: Semiotext(e) Books, 1991), 9–10.

The necessity of immediacy is omnipresent in a child's behavior. It happens, in a moment of weakness, that we give in to a child's demands and before we know it, the little solicitor ups the ante with a final: now! And so it goes with all acts of creation. The moment of inspiration exacts this now, along with its counterpart coordinate: here. To corroborate the hypothesis of immediacy, I remember that during the 2004 premiere of *Les Fables de La Fontaine* at the Comédie-Française, when a journalist asked Wilson what his favorite fable was, the banality of the question gave way to the spontaneous, disarming truth of his answer, "the one I'm watching right now." Forever in the present, intensely in the moment. NOW.

The artist is often bewitched by the landscape of his childhood, that HERE that frames all acts of creative inspiration. When I visited Wilson's hometown, Waco, Texas, I dropped by his childhood home. Knowing well how a ten-year-old Wilson used to put on plays in the garage, I went out back behind the house, and there (what a surprise) stood a definitely Wilsonian shape, an elongated and wide-open structure built with minimalist simplicity. Its shape immediately reminded me of Wilson's drawings, their elongated frames, often purged of all content leaving but a framed void. I wondered what kind of pull this memory had of a small backyard garage in a little country town, a childhood home lost at age 11 when Wilson's family moved away. Did this memory pursue him the way Rosebud pursued Citizen Kane? Or the magic words sung by Fellini as a child after bedtime, the words supposed to have the power to bring to life shadows projected on the wall: "Asa-nisi-masa." I later told Bob Wilson the story of my visit to Waco and my fascination with his "primal theater," its elongated shape recalled in his drawings, his *mise en scène*, the screens on which his magic happens. While eyeing the snapshots I had taken of his childhood garage, Wilson, disappeared in his thoughts with his characteristic "hmm...hmm" and then slowly re-emerged with a hint of a smile: "Well, that form can be vertical too." And he pointed to the high narrow doors of the Watermill building that he had conceived.

In *Speech and Phenomena*, commenting on Edmund Husserl's *On the Phenomenology of the Consciousness of Internal Time*, Jacques Derrida explains, in a way that could perfectly well apply to Wilsonian "picnolepsy," that there is no discontinuity between a source-moment A and the following moment B. A part of the intensity of the creation-moment A always takes refuge in moment B. The source-moment is therefore always already carried beyond itself, ready to be reactivated, re-presented. Derrida concludes: "As soon as one allows for this continuity between the now and the not now...one accommodates non-presence into the blink of an instant. Blinking takes time; and it shuts the eye. This otherness is the very condition of presence." Wilson analyzes his own creative process in much the same way: "I think that everything I've created comes from a subjective internal screen on which I see differently what I see when I blink. I look at something and my gaze is interrupted by blinking, and then I see the thing again, differently, on the black screen of my eyelids."

Wilson thus demonstrates an exceptional acuity of mind that compels him to embrace each representation of his creations as already, infinitely multiplied – hence his moments

Video portrait of Jeanne Moreau by Robert Wilson, 2005

of exaltation. It is not surprising that he went looking for Shakespeare in the work he did in 2009 with the Berliner Ensemble:

> When most I wink, then do mine eyes best see,
> For all the day they view things unrespected;
> But when I sleep, in dreams they look on thee,
> And darkly bright, are bright in dark directed.
> Then thou, whose shadow shadows doth make bright –
> How would thy shadow's form form happy show
> To the clear day with thy much clearer light,
> When to unseeing eyes thy shade shines so!
> How would, I say, mine eyes be blessed made
> By looking on thee in the living day,
> When in dead night thy fair imperfect shade,
> Through heavy sleep on sightless eyes doth stay!
>   All days are nights to see till I see thee,
>   And nights bright days when dreams do show thee me.
> (Sonnet 43)

Fascinated by such a marked sense of instantaneity in Wilson's work, I showed him the phenomenon of the Polaroid in 1984 during rehearsals for *the CIVIL warS* in Rotterdam. He took the camera like a child takes a toy. Seizing the moment as it surfaces, capturing it like an object of prey in a single click, avoiding the endless hunt – developing, calibrating, reframing, reprinting – couldn't but fascinate him. So Wilson kept the camera and began a series of Polaroids taken from airplanes during the trips in preparation for *the CIVIL warS* between Tokyo, Los Angeles, Paris, and elsewhere. Sheets of clouds stretching across the sky, overhanging the terrestrial orb, the moment caught, suspended in time and in space. At the bottom of the little Polaroid, in its white margin, Wilson would write a few lines inevitably inspired by the absolute intensity of the moment.

At the turn of the century, in 1999, I brought Wilson a gigantic Polaroid to be used in a production that we were working on. He created around 100 one-off photos with it in his studio at Watermill, each about 50 × 76 cm (20 × 30 in). Taking picture after picture, Wilson finally reached the last one, nearly entirely black with flat tints: a striking self-portrait, almost invisible, like a shadow projected onto the wall of childhood, and a soul gradually taking it over, Fellini's childhood anima – asa-nisi-masa, asa-nisi-masa.

Yet it's always and ever about seizing the grace – impalpable, unreal – of the magic of the moment; that moment when the world dissolves though there be no apocalypse in sight, when life stops without losing its momentum in the slightest. To step out of one's self and into Wilson's Polaroids as he does in his self-portrait is to feel what Maurice Blanchot calls "the ever-pending moment of my death."

Translated from the French by Lisa Damon.

"Watermill Dolmains," Polaroid photograph by Robert Wilson, 1999.
Courtesy Sacha Goldman Collection

Video portrait of Gao Xingjian by Robert Wilson, Rome, 2009

Jo Kondo & Robert Wilson, New York City, 2007

Portraits for an absurd world

Writer, translator, dramatist, director, critic, and visual artist Gao Xingjian met Robert Wilson in 2005 in Paris, where the Nobel Laureate in Literature (2000) has resided since he arrived in 1987 as a political refugee from his native China. The two had a lot to talk about: Gao, like Wilson, is a visual artist with dozens of international exhibitions to his name, and an experimental dramatist and theater director.

During the Cultural Revolution, Gao had been sent to a re-education camp and felt it necessary to burn a suitcase full of manuscripts; until 1979, he was prohibited from publishing his work or travelling abroad. Still, his pioneering plays, in part inspired by Brecht, Artaud, and Beckett, whom he has translated, were produced at the Theater of Popular Art in Beijing, and his theatrical debut in 1982 with *Signal Alarm* was wildly successful. *Bus Stop*, his 1983 absurdist drama, sealed his reputation and brought him official condemnation during the campaign against "intellectual pollution." Following the publication of *Escape*, written in France but set against the background of the 1989 Tiananmen Square massacre, Gao was declared persona non grata by the Chinese regime, and all of his works were banned. His novel *Soul Mountain* enacts, by means of an odyssey in time and space through the Chinese countryside, an individual's search for roots, inner peace, and liberty.

Guggenheim Museum Works & Process, New York City, 2007. Robert Wilson and Jo Kondo

In 2007, Wilson asked Gao to sit for one of his *VOOM Portraits*. Wilson also made a short video, *Gao*, which would end up pitting the two artists – both vocal defenders of human rights – against the United Nations Office of the High Commissioner for Human Rights. In the spring of 2010, Gao came to speak at The American University of Paris upon publication of his latest play, *Ballade Nocturne*, which he describes as a "libretto for a dance performance." Shortly thereafter, I met with Gao in his home, surrounded by the framed black, white, and grey originals of his elegant ink paintings.

I had heard about Bob long before I saw any of his productions with my own eyes, and long before I met him in person. I'd heard a lot said about his *mise en scène*, and about the opera he had created with Philip Glass. *Einstein on the Beach* truly left its mark on contemporary theater; it was famous in the theater world, which is why I knew of it. Then I saw it, and I also saw some of his other productions when I had the good fortune to be in Paris when they were playing. Much later, when I actually knew Bob, he invited me to see his productions. That's why I know his work fairly well; not all of his plays, of course, because he has produced a huge amount all over the world.

What made the strongest impact on me as well as others were primarily his images, and his manner of direction. It's not really the play, the text, or the author that strikes you at first, but the direction and staging as a whole. You are immediately taken by his vision, the image, and the impression of his performance, so particular. All of a sudden, you know it: It's Bob Wilson.

Then some five years ago or so when Bob was working in Paris, we were finally introduced. We spent an evening together and we understood one another right away. He was also interested in my plays and knew exactly what I had been working on; that's why we immediately had lots of things to discuss. He was thinking about staging one of my plays, *Snow in August*, which is a big piece that I've directed myself. I think that was the one that interested him. He'd seen a video of it. I was thrilled. With Bob directing, it would have been an entirely new version of the play, and why not? In the end, though, we weren't able to stage it because the production was too big. It was much too costly.

Can you imagine Wilson directing your very short play *Ballade Nocturne*?

Yes. Why not, it's a much simpler play to produce because it doesn't need much money. It would be enough to have an actress and two dancers, a musician. It's an excellent idea – if he happened to read the text, it would be very desirable, absolutely. Everything he does fascinates me.

You and Wilson are both what could be called "total artists." Wilson works with the visual arts, fine arts, theater, and choreography, and you, with the fine arts, literature, drama, and theater direction. Is this commonality between you a place where you come together?

It's true, there aren't many artists who work in multiple disciplines, and Bob, too, is a complete artist. He's a director, he dances himself, he draws, he paints, often even his own stage sets. All of that made a big impression on me. There are very few directors who conceive their sets themselves, but he takes a pen and draws. One of the first works of his that I saw before we met in person was a production in which his painting really struck me: It was *HAMLET: a monologue* in Paris, and he had done the sets himself. There was this gigantic projection on a screen, and, onstage, Bob by himself. You see, that showed his side as a painter. It was remarkable.

Of course, he also has a very special and innovative rapport with lighting. He was among the first to use such sophisticated, elaborate, ultra-modern lighting, with a specialized team of technicians, a computer, and changing colors. Now, we've introduced lighting technology into the theater; but he was one of the earliest in theater to suggest the possibility of working with *light* beyond simply *lighting*. Light, for him, is the set, is the space. It plays a major role.

You speak Chinese and French; how do you and Wilson communicate?

He speaks a little French, but we still have difficulty understanding one another. [*Laughs*] Sometimes we use a translator.

Even if he doesn't speak much French, France has played a very important role in Wilson's career, as it has in yours. Do you think there is a particular reason for the French to experience an affinity with your work?

La Femme à la cafetière (video), Paris, 1989. Suzushi Hanayagi

I think, first of all, that it's because France is open to the outside world. She welcomes artists from the entire world. It's long been a tradition, especially in Paris. It's part of its allure. And Bob Wilson also has this particular quality: He's one of the rare American directors who is, in fact, very European, one of the rare directors to work so much in Europe. I read somewhere, I think in an interview he gave in Germany, about his frequent visits to Europe, and the difficulties of directing in the United States. And he's someone who doesn't limit himself – he is, a bit like me, a universal artist, perhaps one of the first. In his case, it's obvious. He has made masterpieces all over the world, like his production at the Comédie-Française of *Les Fables de La Fontaine*, which I was lucky enough to see. He's also done a production that I haven't seen, but that my Taiwanese friends speak about, in which he worked with a famous actress from the Beijing Opera,[1] and, of course, he's paid homage to Suzushi Hanayagi, the Japanese choreographer. The Asian influence on his work is noticeable. I've seen a play of his where he introduced Kabuki actors into his stagin.

It's also evident in his manner of eliciting performances from actors, his manner of directing them. He makes singers work like actors, which is fairly rare because often singers don't act in traditional Western opera. The singer stands and sings. That's all. But I think that Wilson was one of the first directors to get singers to act. It's rare, because it's not easy. It's not easy to get singers to act because that's not their profession, but he had that vision and that desire to establish a particular relationship with singers.

Your theatrical work as a dramatist and director generally takes place behind the scenes. When Wilson made your *VOOM Portrait,* did you find yourself adopting the role of an actor?

[1]
Wei Hai-ming, whom Wilson directed in the 2009 Chinese version of his adaptation of *Orlando.*

the CIVIL warS – Tokyo Workshop, Tokyo, 1984

Yes, exactly. I was acting. I was his actor. It was very entertaining. A beautiful adventure. Bob had suggested taking some photos of me, but I had no idea how he was going to do it. He had found a cinema studio for rent. It was gigantic. A whole crew was there. There were two big cameras, as well as make-up artists, hairdressers, assistants, and even full-scale, three-dimensional models of sets! And I found myself there, discussing the *mise en scène*. It was also quite entertaining to act. He asked me what approach I was going to take, so I said, "I am you." At the beginning, I thought that it would be a simple sequence of photos, but in fact we worked the whole day.

Bob asked me, "What do you want for makeup?" I told him that I wanted white. And he asked me, "Can we write a sentence on your face?" "Well," I said, "why not?" and I chose a sentence.

It's a very beautiful sentence: "Solitude is a necessary condition of freedom." Did it come from one of your works, or did you invent it on the spot?

On the spot. It was spontaneous, though the sentence came from a speech I had made when I won a prize, the Golden Plate Award, given by the Academy of Achievement, an American institution, on the occasion of its international summit. It was in Dublin. There was a big awards ceremony: Gorbachev was there, along with the Irish Prime Minister, the President of South Korea, and a Nobel Prize-winning American physicist. Clinton was also there, though he wasn't President anymore. Each of these people also received a prize, and I gave a short thank-you speech entitled "The Necessity of Solitude." With Bob in that cinema studio, I suddenly thought of that phrase. He liked it and so we kept it.

It's since caused you and Wilson problems, no?

[*Laughs*] Ah, yes! That's the consequence of adventure. To commemorate the 60th anniversary of the Universal Declaration of Human Rights, the United Nations High Commissioner for Human Rights decided to make a film with short pieces done by filmmakers and video artists. Bob was one of the invited artists, and he made a three-minute film that consists of a close-up of my face. After some time, the text "Solitude is a necessary condition of freedom" appears on my face, and then disappears. The UN film was shown in September, 2008. The next month, the Office of the High Commissioner for Human Rights, OHCHR, sent a letter saying that it was not appropriate to have Bob's video of me in the film because the sentence I chose was incompatible with human rights. For them, "human rights" implied solidarity, and they claimed that the spirit of the sentence was opposed to this aspect of human rights. What an unbelievable interpretation.

They cut the segment, the OHCHR. Bob was furious. "By silencing Gao Xingjian's voice, the OHCHR promotes the very cause the project was set up to denounce," he wrote. He also wrote to me, and I responded that I shared his sentiment. We were both livid. He asked me to write something about it to be published in the American press, and I sent him the English translation of a short text I had written. Nothing happened....There were difficulties.

> Can support for the arts come from the state or an official international institution without any form of censorship, in China or in the West?

For the moment, it's nothing more than a wish. Power is always allied with certain interests, and it's the opposite with artists. Artists are beyond interests. That's why it's difficult to establish a dialogue with politicians, with power. Politicians always want artists to fit in with their politics and not really to encourage artistic creation. That's the problem of censorship. But then, sometimes governments give their support in order to put their political mark on artwork, and artists can't accept that.

> Regardless of the OHCHR's interpretation, do you consider solitude, as opposed to collectivity, to be a necessary condition of individuality?

I think so. Solitude is necessary for a man to become a real adult, to achieve a maturity of reflection. I think that Bob really understood that, and so he appreciated the sentence. I believe that he lived the same thing. That's clear in the film that was made about him.[2] He didn't speak much as a youth; he even felt handicapped in terms of speech. Perhaps it's for that reason that he later worked with mutes. He understood that solitude allows the spirit to ripen, awakens reflection, and so if one wants to begin to think, one must first have the experience of solitude. He's a great artist, and I think that all artists know this experience of solitude, which is a condition of creation.

And in Bob's case, solitude is reflected in his work. Certainly. Now that we speak of it, an image comes to my mind from one of his plays – the CIVIL warS, perhaps – that was very touching. There's a child on the stage who doesn't speak, who crosses back and forth, and at his side is a bear, I think. It's an extremely striking image of solitude. It's an expression of the individual consciousness that is very profound and very poetic.

> Your plays tend to be quite short, at least in comparison to Wilson's work. How does the length of a performance affect the piece itself, as well as the audience watching it?

We don't feel the length of such pieces, even if they are very long. Take the music of Philip Glass, for example. It seems repetitive, but it creates a sustained tension so that we don't feel its length; we feel the tension building. This is also a very special side of Bob's work. He really knows how to work with time. I just finished writing a book in Chinese. I was reading the proofs just before you arrived. It's an essay on my theater in which I speak about a process that I consider my own, although today, it's generally acknowledged that dramatic theater is a process that takes place in the dimension of time. Before, in antiquity and in Shakespeare's plays, theater was action: a dramatic action that happened on the stage. But if we look at things more closely, that action is lengthened by miniscule changes,

2
Absolute Wilson, produced and directed by Katharina Otto-Bernstein, Film Manufacturers Inc., 2006.

the CIVIL warS – Rotterdam Section, Rotterdam, 1983

variations. And if it's in the process, we see then that it's dramaturgy, the process in time. Bob understands very well how to show this notion in his work, this new theatricality. The *process* can also become dramatic, and that's entirely contemporary. It's an innovation that creates a truly powerful tension.

> How does writing for a Chinese audience, or an audience that is familiar with the traditions of the East, differ from writing for a Western audience? You do both.

Actually, I've never done really traditional theatrical pieces. Even for a Chinese audience, it's always something very new. But of course there are audiences that understand very well, and bureaucrats who don't understand anything at all. When I had problems in China, it was for that reason: They didn't understand anything at all, and, what's more, they found it improper. But Chinese and Western are two completely different genres of theater, and I conceive of the two audiences as totally separate, so I don't try to make a bridge between the two. Bridges can work if you want to and can understand the other; however, the "other" is not only national or cultural. A man can come to understand, for example, the woman who lives in him.

Rehearsal for *Orlando*, Taipei, 2009. Wei Hai-min and Robert Wilson

Precisely in Wilson's production of Heiner Müller's *Quartett*, there are moments when Valmont's thoughts are spoken by Mme de Merteuil; that is to say, there is an inversion of gender between the mental – thought – and its physical incarnation, which results in a gripping tension. Are you trying to accomplish something similar in your plays when you mix pronouns?

This comes from an idea that is very important for me. If you designate a subject, a person, in any language, you don't find more than three pronouns, and it's with these three pronouns that we create, that we put human consciousness in space. First, there is an "I" that expresses itself; the "I" that expresses itself in front of life. If, in addition, there's a "you," which is the projection of oneself upon the other, that's where violence begins and it becomes dramatic. If you take the same subject created in "he," it's in that person that reflection begins. I think that human consciousness, in fact, can't be expressed *except* through language. Language, with its triple subject, creates in us this interior mental or psychological space where consciousness fulfills itself. To introduce these three different pronouns into novels or even theater or an actor's performance is enriching. In my essays on the theater I speak precisely of this, of the actor's work. If the actor can base his performance on three persons, if, mentally, interiorly, there's an effort like that, it's magnificent.

Rehearsal for *Orlando*, Taipei, 2009. Robert Wilson and Wei Hai-min

Are you saying that our brain is structured on the basis of these three pronouns? What happens in the case of someone who doesn't know outwardly expressed language in any form? How do those three persons manifest themselves, or can they?

That we don't know...and the question is very interesting. Nothing in my experience would allow me to answer it, or feel it. But Bob, I think, through his experience, is very close to that sensation.

Your paintings and drawings seem to share a sensitivity with Wilson's work in that they are very purified, refined, uncluttered. Wilson has said that his work always leaves a great deal of space for meditation, for reflection, for thought, and I find this also while reading your *Ballade Nocturne* or looking at your pictures. You also leave yourself that space.

Yes. For pictures, there's an interior space that you have to know not to fill. I call it a "false perspective," a false perspective that isn't the geometric perspective of classic painting. It's another depth, mental, ephemeral, and it evolves at every moment, difficult to define, so subtle, but so profound and rich.

What were you thinking about while Wilson was making your video portrait?

Pleasure. The pleasure of seeing this little spectacle that he was producing.

The *VOOM Portraits* have been called "provocative." Do you think they are?

No. I think they're funny. [*Laughs*] Because all artistic creation is a challenge. It's a personal challenge. A personal challenge to an absurd world.

Translated from the French by Alexandra Schwartz.

Video portrait of Steve Buscemi by Robert Wilson, 2004

In praise of emptiness [and Buster Keaton]

I first saw Stefan Kurt perform at the Theater am Schiffbauerdamm, home to the Berliner Ensemble, where Robert Wilson created his production of Kurt Weill and Bertolt Brecht's *The Threepenny Opera* in 2007. It had been commissioned by Stefan Brecht, the playwright's son, for the same stage inaugurated by the play's August 31, 1928 premiere under his father's aegis. Like Brecht's, Wilson's new production was a sensation, and, with the Berliner Ensemble, it went on to open Paris's 2009 Festival d'automne at the Théâtre de la Ville. Every seat was sold well in advance, and Wilson, together with both a former and the present French Minister of Culture, was in the audience. When the production returned to Paris in April 2010, it was the same story: Robert Wilson was in the audience, and there was not a ticket to be had. On Wilson's 70th birthday, October 4, 2011, *Threepenny* makes its New York premiere at BAM, with Robert Wilson in the audience and Kurt in the leading role.

The curtain rises on one of the most breathtaking sets and stagings Wilson has concocted in recent times. Prostitutes and low-lives, among them Angela Winkler as Jenny and Ruth Glöss as an aged lady of the night (*une vieille putain*, the French program reads) – both sporting Wilson-red hair – parade slowly across the stage, gigantic, carnival-like circles of lights intersecting like mechanized clockworks, blinking in the background. Stefan Kurt appears. He is the unquestionable star, Mackie Messer. In tuxedo, he strides and struts across the stage, holding forth with "Mack the Knife." Towards the end of the number, Kurt turns his back to the audience, his head coyly cocked over his right shoulder to look out at us in a coquettish 1930s-style pose, and lets his tux jacket slip off a bare shoulder to reveal the shoulder-length black gloves and the Black Widow corset concealed underneath.

Wintermärchen, Berlin, 2005. Stefan Kurt

Rehearsal for *The Threepenny Opera*, Berlin, 2007.
Robert Wilson directing Stefan Kurt

Time Rocker, Paris, 1997

We had arranged to meet backstage after the show. Although I had been watching Kurt onstage for the second time and for several hours, he was totally unrecognizable to me when we met, and had to come up to me and introduce himself. It was not only that he was no longer a lacquered platinum blond with heavy black eye make-up and red, red lipstick as he had been 20 minutes earlier playing an androgynous Mackie Messer: His entire physical being had changed. Even his body, long and slender onstage, was not visible in the broader muscular man in front of me, and he did not move in the same way. I looked at him as if I had never seen him in my life. "This," I thought, "is a testimony to a great actor."

Kurt had been an actor, but not a singer and dancer, before he met Robert Wilson. Wilson, he says, was the director who brought that out in him: "Once in a lifetime you meet a director who is your director. Whoever, whatever brought me onstage, he knows it and can make it bloom. It's a love story."

You are reputed to be Robert Wilson's favorite actor in the world.

In the universe! Look at this.

[*He takes out an A4 size sheet of paper, on which Robert Wilson's unmistakable handwriting declares, "You are my favorite actor in the entire* ~~world~~ *UNIVERSE."*]

Time Rocker, Paris, 1997

Well, I'd like to know why you think that's the case. What is it about you as an actor that interests Wilson?

When I first saw Bob's work I was fascinated by it, by the movement he did, by his way of thinking, and my approach to his work was to copy him. Because I was so fascinated with his way of moving and it was so different from everything I knew, it was so much fun to copy him, to get into his world; and only by copying him could I connect to his way of thinking or to his way of being. Maybe he saw that, and he saw that we somehow have the same sense of humor. He very much likes Buster Keaton, and I like him too. Also, Bob understands understatement; maybe he sees that in me onstage and likes it.

What was the first thing of his you ever saw?

It was *the CIVIL warS: a tree is best measured when it's down*. I saw it in a French production. I went there especially, six hours by car, to see that production in France because I had heard about Bob's work. I was fascinated. I had never seen that kind of theater. It was so simple, and it didn't want to explain *the thing*. All good German theater is always about: "We want to tell the people a story, so how do we tell that? Where is the main line?" Bob said, "Oh don't think, just leave it very simple and don't push the people to think what they have to think. Just lean back and let the audience come to you." It was so new for me, because being onstage was always: "Love me, love me, look at me!" Bob is right: The opposite of "love me" is not to hate the audience, but rather just to let them come to you. You're here. So you have the freedom as a spectator to go into the piece or not, or to have your own fantasies, and it was just something quite new for me.

> This seems like Brecht's distancing effect, wherein there is no attempt to have the spectator emotionally identify with a character. How did Stefan Brecht come to choose Wilson to do the production of *The Threepenny Opera* with the Berliner Ensemble?

I don't know, but I think they are quite similar, Brecht and Bob. They create a distance between what you're saying and what you're seeing. Well, of course Brecht is more intellectual and he really wants to send a message. [*Laughs*]

> Whereas Wilson says, "If I have a message for you, I'll send a fax!"

That's right, and he refuses to put any of these things into the *The Threepenny Opera*.

> The Berliner Ensemble, like the Brooklyn Academy of Music, seems to have a special affinity with Wilson. Why is he so appreciated in Germany?

It's difficult to say, but it may be because he's really so different and so exotic coming into that strong environment of theater for ensembles. Bob is also very fascinated by *it*; he'll say, "That's so amazing, you play in my play this evening and tomorrow you're playing Shakespeare, and the next day you are playing a tragedy. That's so amazing, that you are able to switch and to perform." He is so happy that there are these ensembles. And I think that the German theaters are so happy to have a person like him, coming from the States with another sense of time and of feeling and of telling stories, because we in Germany normally are very much in our heads.

> How did you and Robert Wilson begin working together?

After *the CIVIL warS* I lost him a little bit, and in the meantime I went to acting school, and then to Hamburg, where I started my theater career. Then I received an invitation from Bob, who was doing *Hamletmachine*. I couldn't be in it because I was in another production. I was really pissed, and I told the director, "If I'm not in Bob's next production, I'm going to quit." Then he did *The Black Rider*, and I was in it. It was lucky.

The way Bob worked was quite new for me, just to have this separation of Stage A and Stage B. Normally when I go to rehearsal, I try to have figured out my character, to know what he likes, what he doesn't like, and I did that here. I had my opinion about this character, and Bob didn't care about it. He has a structure in his mind – first he needs a structure to make his thinking flow fluidly – and then he just directs us. "Just come in, stop, pause, do that," without any text, so I'm treated like a dancer.

the CIVIL warS – Cologne Section, Cologne, 1984

The Black Rider: The Casting of the Magic Bullets, Hamburg, 1990. Top left, Stefan Kurt; bottom, Stefan Kurt and Dominique Horwitz

Or like a puppet.

If you want to say it positively, it's like a dancer. If you want to say it negatively, it's like a puppet. Many people say, "Oh, you're working with Bob Wilson, you're like a computer!" But you say, "No, that's not true, you have no idea." At that time, Bob was doing movements, and they were recorded by video, or he directed us and said, "Okay, stop, go forward, stop, turn, make this, open your mouth, scream, big eyes, open your mouth, shut your mouth," and you had to learn it by looking at the video and then repeat it 1,000 times. And then he added the movement or gestures, and after some time, there came Stage C, when he put some text to it, to his movements. So he really separated movement from talking, from the text, and that is very different from the way other directors work: They want it all together, whereas Bob takes it apart. We didn't understand at first. It was, "Why does he do that?"

Normally, if you really want to express something, you have to combine – you *want* to combine – your thoughts with your movements. If actors hear music, we always try to illustrate the music. But Bob doesn't like that. He's always watchful that you don't see what you hear and you don't hear what you see: Every time, there must be a counterpoint. If I want to show the public that my character is an angry person, I [*roar!*] and it's so obvious. But if you separate movement from talking, it gets interesting. The final character may be the same as it would otherwise have been, but you go from a different approach to reach that point, and that's what makes Bob's work so special. He doesn't care about the *résultat*, it's not his first impulse. He goes to these questions from another side. Maybe this is linked to his biography. He had to learn to take the time to simplify things, to be very quiet, to think about what you're saying, so there are no "umms," no "uhhs." And that gives you space. It also is very *künstlich,* artificial, if you slow down and talk in this way. The work performed onstage has to be simple, very, very simple. It has to be seen in focus and in the light, but then what you do as an actor is really free.

In the early days, I really tried to copy him, as I told you, and I did it very exactly, but after some years of working together, he really let me do something too, and I had my free space to do any style. It was very nice for me to see him letting me do his things but in my style.

Where exactly does an actor find that freedom in such a system?

Freedom is emptiness. When I first worked with Bob, I didn't really get that; it took time to know what he means when he speaks about the emptiness of the movement. If you are repeating a gesture, whatever it is, 1,000 times, and it really gets to be like a computer or like a puppet and you don't have to think about what you're doing, the moment you're on-stage you have your freedom to express it in any way you want, to express it with whatever feelings you have in the moment. And that's really great, and I think that Bob wants that. The secret of every great actor is to live in the moment. Bob's work gives me that freedom. I have the pattern, I feel secure, I know what I have to do, but it's not fixed. When movement has become automatic, ingrained, when you don't have to focus on it, you are truly here, onstage, in that moment, in that second. And that counts.

If the movement is really empty, it can be everything. I can tell a very good dancer by just concentrating on his walk coming from the back of the stage to the center, which Bob says is the strongest line. That is so beautiful, for me, just to work on a walk, and if that works, I can concentrate on the text and other things. That makes his work so special for the audience and also for me as an actor, because I'm not only an actor. I'm some sort of a dancer, I'm some sort of a singer, I'm some sort of a text-machine, I'm all of that.

> Wilson's early work, like *Deafman Glance* or *Einstein on the Beach*, used little or no text. What is the role of text and language in a Wilson production, as opposed to movement and visuals?

Well, it's very strange, because he always says he doesn't know German – he does meanwhile, I think – but his approach to languages is another thing. He knows precisely when a text is spoken right or not for him. I don't know how, but he's very musical. He's *very* musical! If he doesn't know the meaning of the text, even if it's in Korean or Spanish, he knows when it's right or he knows when it's not right, and he can work that very, very, very precisely. In *The Threepenny Opera,* he was very concerned about the songs; he said, "Everybody knows these songs, and after two minutes I get bored!" So he tried to design it by his heart, or by his feelings. It's very structural, very simple in a way. If you have a black scene that is very slow, the next scene has to be light and quick. Or if you have a high note, it's good to have a lower note to have a balance. He's very good at listening. I don't think he is really interested in the text, but he knows what's right and what's wrong.

The Threepenny Opera, Berlin, 2007. Center, Stefan Kurt

And he'll go to great lengths to achieve the right effect. I remember being at the Paris dress rehearsal of *Die Frau ohne Schatten*, Wilson was sitting in the audience taking notes, and I mentioned to him that in one scene, something was a little odd in the placement of a bench in the back and to the right, as seen from the audience. When the opera opened the next night, it wasn't there anymore. As you say, he sees everything and takes care of all the details.

And he keeps taking care of them. After the premier night of *The Black Rider,* Bob was there the next night, giving us notes. He doesn't go away. One time he came to my dressing room during intermission and said, "Okay, that's great. Maybe there you should change that...." But he's always very, very nice. Normally, he doesn't give corrections during the show. He gives the notes, and then his assistant comes to me and says, "Try this, or do that, or there you're not in the light...."

How does it feel playing with the light as your leading lady? Did you have to learn to see light almost as a character onstage?

Yes, yes, we hated Bob, you know. We *hated* Bob. Because we were late in the rehearsals for *The Black Rider* and we wanted to rehearse our scenes, to go through the text, the movements, and Bob didn't care. He was lighting. He said, "Please stand." And not only for hours, for *days*. We had no chance to rehearse the scenes, we just had to go up and stand there, stop, go forward, stop, and then half an hour later, the next step. We were standing for hours onstage. But we had to learn that we were in the light, in the focus.

The Threepenny Opera, Berlin, 2007. Ruth Glöss, Stefan Kurt, and Angela Winkler

Then there was the premiere of *The Black Rider* at BAM. A big thing: BAM! Tom Waits! At a quarter to eight on opening night, Bob was still lighting, so BAM's Executive Producer Mr. Harvey Lichtenstein said, "We really have to let the people in." Bob didn't care. It was five minutes to eight, and he was still lighting. Eight. They were shouting at each other! Bob was really angry; he took another 15 minutes, and only then was the audience allowed in. I admire that, Bob's confidence and ability to say, "Well, I don't care, it has to be like this, I like it like this."

> You've seen Wilson work with, among others, Susan Sontag, Tom Waits, and Lou Reed. What is the nature of his collaboration?

Bob needs strong counterparts, and Tom was a strong counterpart. He was very, very sensual, singing smooth but also dirty, and Bob was very formal, very strict, so that fit well together. Also with Lou Reed, who was also very straight in a way – his music has to be sung, and he has his rock-'n-'roll thing. They like each other's work, and so they're all very respectful: "I'll let you do your work, and you let me do my work, and let's see what happens."

> German playwright Heiner Müller was one of Wilson's significant collaborators. Did you ever know him?

Yes, yes, yes. My first production was in the Bochum Theater, and he was doing his *Anatomy Titus Fall of Rome: A Shakespeare Commentary*. I met him there for the first time. And then of course I met him when he was doing *Hamletmachine*, too. But I never worked with him in a production of Bob's, unfortunately.

> What do you think there is in Müller that attracts Wilson?

Müller leaves space around everything: the text, the lighting. Everything must be organized, everything very clear, very simple. Some say it's too simple, but I think that's the way to have freedom, to have space between even the words. Bob respected Müller's words, but he wasn't much interested in their sense. It was their sound, which with Müller was quite different from other German playwrights. And maybe it was an attraction on both sides. Heiner Müller loved Bob's way of acting because there was no meaning. There were just images, but filled with some mystery, and I think there was a good connection between these two very extreme personalities and very extreme ways of making art.

> Müller was political, and some say that Wilson's work became more political after he started working with Müller.

Well, it may be. It's political in the way that he really lets the audience think what it wants, in that he doesn't push the audience too much in a direction.

Alice, Hamburg, 1992. Stefan Kurt

One of the first people to praise Wilson was Louis Aragon, the Surrealist. Do you see a connection between Wilson's work and Surrealism?

Yes, of course. In Bob's case, though, I don't know where this different way of thinking, of being, of seeing comes from, maybe from childhood, or from working with disabled people. I never uncovered the mystery. I just was fascinated by this way of thinking and of being. I saw this wonderful documentary film about Bob's work, Howard Brookner's *Robert Wilson and the Civil Wars* (1987). There is a scene in it where Bob works with Christopher [Knowles] onstage, doing "Emily Likes the TV." And it's so touching! Because there is such interaction between these two people, and there are words but they are not very important, but there is such an energy and such love between Bob and Christopher Knowles. That was also a very strong key for me to really love Bob, to say, "Wow, I want to be an actor of this star, this artist." And it's beyond words, really.

Earlier, you mentioned Robert Wilson's humor, which is something many people don't talk about, or even see, in his work: the winks, the irony, the sly smile or gesture. In *The Threepenny Opera*, there are some rather dramatic moments, but they're also funny. What would be other examples of that?

Ah, it's difficult to speak about humor. [*Laughs*]

How about "comedy"? Any better?

Well, Bob showed us one of his favorite DVDs, Marlene Dietrich's last concert, which he's seen maybe 20 times. He went to the concert and he met Dietrich and had dinner with her. That's very special in him: When he loves someone, he's very focused on that person and really gets to know her, which is not easy. When he talks about Dietrich and about her performance, there's always a great deal of humor in the way she performs: "Well, everything is very severe, very dramatic...but, on the other hand...." She doesn't play it 100 or 120 percent. It's a way of playing and of being onstage, saying, "Oh, I'm a *very* dark person, I'm very mean...and on the other hand...." He likes that very much.

Of course, in Bob's work there's no intention of things being natural. With Bob, it is very much: "This is theater, this is artificial, it shouldn't look real." And thank God!

Playing *The Threepenny Opera* in a realistic way would be – yuck. It would be awful. I have the same feeling as Bob: For me, too, the stage is a sacred space. It's not common, it's not like sitting here. It must be a different space. Walking onstage is very different than walking on the street; your behavior must be different, and must be artificial, too.

> One of the ways that Wilson gets the audience to notice things is to put them in odd settings. This goes back to the Surrealists and the classic image of a sewing machine on an operating table: Extracting an object from its usual context makes it visible in a different way. It might be the same with movements. When performers onstage walk according to Wilson's direction, it spurs the audience to mediate on the motion that goes into what is otherwise such an instinctive action.

That's great, that when people see someone walking, they think about it: "Oh, that is so strange that we, as human beings, have two things like this [*points to his legs*], and they are made like this, and they *walk*."

> If you had to choose among the productions of Wilson's that you've been involved in – and that might be like choosing between children – which is the most important to you?

That's very difficult to say. Of course, the first one, *The Black Rider*, is like an initial fire. It was the first work, the point of first contact. Now, to play this leading role in *The Threepenny Opera* and to have the confidence of Bob looking at me and saying, "That's good," helping me in a friendly, adult way – that is quite moving for me.

> What would you call Wilson? What would you call his function?

Well, it's a universe. You work with a universe. [*Laughs*] For me, Bob is really an artist, an artist, artist, artist, because his whole life is art, and not an art that I don't understand or is only for very rich people. It comes from inside. Bob's soul is so curious, and you can feel, if you work with him, that it's not an attitude and it's not to make money. It's really *passion*, a deep desire to create things, to make them happen. He's also very charismatic, a person who can inflate other people. Even in the early times I've read about, he always had some disciples around him, people who loved him, who believed in him and his way of theatrical work. When I first met him, he had such an easy time getting all the people in the theater on his side. They were doing everything for him, even the technicians. He was attentive to everyone's work, even the wardrobe woman's, and she was so happy and delighted when he thanked her. He could work 24 hours a day and people would not say, "Okay, I have to go," because they knew that he *saw* their work. He was very smart, very smart.

What do you consider the essence of Wilson's theater to be?

He likes to watch. To see something onstage, to create a space. To create tension between human bodies. Tension, light, space, time. To listen, to be aware of that moment, of people moving and speaking, of the way the light is changing. It's very simple, but in the best way; it's a meditation on celebrating the here-and-now, a way of saying: "Okay, I'm here!" This is a convention: that there's a theater, there's a curtain, there are people who are pretending to do something and people who paid something to sit here and celebrate that with others, like a holy mass of celebrating humanity.

Bob always does Bob's work. Of course, there are also other directors who try to copy it, but I think that it's unique, it's close to Bob. It's very linked to the person. In 100 years, his work will still be *Bob's* work.

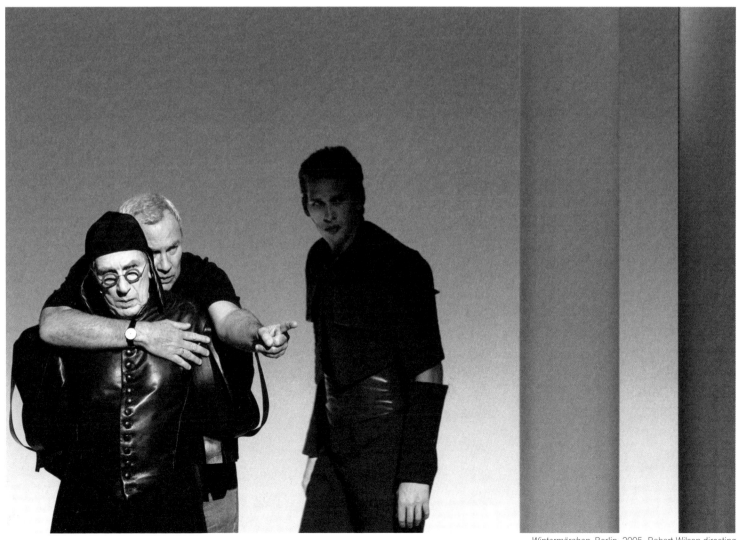

Wintermärchen, Berlin, 2005. Robert Wilson directing

The artist's presence

"Come in," Marina Abramović said to me. "Come in, be comfortable. Where would you like to sit? Take off your shoes. Put your feet up. I want you to be perfectly comfortable." I looked at my watch, since we had agreed in advance that this conversation would last one hour. "Forget about the time," she said.

I first met Abramović at the Venice Biennale in 1997, when she was awarded the Golden Lion for Best Artist for her video installation/performance *Balkan Baroque*. Now, nearly 13 years later, she had not visibly changed. Whatever adjective may be used to describe Abramović's work, the noun is always "body," and Abramović rigorously takes superb care of her *instrument de travail*.

We were in her SoHo loft on the eve of her departure for India, where she would begin in-depth preparation for her show at MoMA, *The Artist is Present*, the museum's first retrospective on performance, as well as the longest performance in duration that Abramović had ever done. For 700 hours over a period that stretched from March 11 until May 31, 2010, she would sit in a long red gown, motionless, at a small table, where anyone at all could come up and sit across from her and return her gaze.

Abramović is a presence onstage or in a room, and perhaps that and questions of time and duration alone would have prompted me to come to talk to her about Robert Wilson. But Abramović was also about to begin her first work with Wilson, a collaboration for a staged piece with music to premiere in 2011: *The Life and Death of Marina Abramović*. Abramović had attended a few funerals of late, notably that of her friend Susan Sontag, and she had been disturbed that the funeral had nothing to do with Sontag's amazing energy and purpose and determination.

"And when I saw that, I said, 'No, no, no!' I was going to rehearse my funeral, because I can, you know. This is the only thing that an artist can control – his own funeral. After this, you can't.' I told Bob, 'This is the title I want to do. So please, can you direct my life with this title?' And then I said, 'So why don't we make the funeral?' "

The Life and Death of Marina Abramović, Manchester, 2011. Marina Abramović

It's a really funny story, how I met Bob for the first time. I was in Yugoslavia, and very young; it was the early 1970s, after the big 1968 demonstrations. In Belgrade, like everywhere else in the world, there were huge student demonstrations, and we made demands on Yugoslav President Tito. We especially had 13 points – health care for students, better food and education systems, and so on – and we also asked for the building of the former secret police in the center of Belgrade, which was actually used on the weekends by the secret police to play chess and their wives to gossip and do their needlework, to be our student cultural center. Tito agreed to only three of our demands, and one of these was the center.

That really started the most important moment in my life because there was a group of six of us – I was the only woman and there were five guys – called the "Youngsters of the '70s" that entered the center and started making what became avant-garde art in Yugoslavia. We stopped painting and doing sculpture or anything figurative, and were really looking for new ways of expression: We did performance and installations and film experiments. Prior to this, Atelier 212, the avant-garde theater festival going on since the 1960s, would invite important artists, so if someone was invited in the theater context, very often he would also perform in the student cultural center.

One day, it was announced in the newspaper that the "genius from Iowa" was coming, which is very funny because Bob Wilson is not from Iowa – he's from Texas – but he directed one of his first pieces in Iowa.[1] Of course, all of us were interested in what he was doing. There was a little space in the basement of the student cultural center and that's what he used, not the large auditorium. He actually wanted the smaller space. Bob was

1
Deafman Glance premiered in 1970 at University Theater in Iowa City, Iowa.

Doctor Faustus Lights the Lights, Berlin, 1992

making his monologue at that time, which was kind of an improvisation of a text and demonstration, and it was fascinating. It went on close to midnight and the center closed at 11:00 pm, so the night porter entered several times, very loud, to interrupt the whole thing, saying that they were closing, but none of us reacted. We were all mesmerized by Bob. Finally, the guard entered with a pistol and said, "I'm shooting everyone if you don't leave," and so we literally ran out, and the piece was interrupted.

For me, the most interesting thing was his presence. Later on, I saw his *HAMLET* and other things where he had an actual presence onstage, but even then it was like he owned the space. You couldn't focus on anything but him. That kind of complete presence was striking and was essential for me later on to learn in my own performances. Not what he was saying, not what he was doing, but that total presence. Even if you just sit or stand there in silence.

> Wilson says that he once gave instructions to an actress in *Medea* to stand absolutely still, and she complained that nobody would notice her. He told her, "If you stand there truly still, absolutely like a statue, like a goddess who's been there for 1,000 years, they will notice nothing but you."

It's taken me a long time to understand that actually the minimum is the best, and when you are really just there, present with you and the audience, whatever is happening is happening. When you are insecure, especially when you are a young artist, you need props, you need elements, you need the different lighting, different stories, you need so many different things. But when you are really *there* in your mind, in your body, in that space

Doctor Faustus Lights the Lights, Berlin, 1992

in front of the public, then you have to take the public into that space with you and then become this whole thing with this performance about the here-and-now. There is no past, there is no future. Past already happened, future hasn't yet. It's only what is left: present, and that's the essence of performance. It is timeless.

That's why what you said about Bob – about the goddess – is really what happens: It is a complete involvement with your mind and your body. There are so many times that you can stand in front of an audience but your mind can be in Honolulu or who knows where. The idea is how to put the mind and body of the audience and the mind and body of the actor, or the performance person, in the same time and place. When this happens, then it is magic. Then everything happens.

For both Bob and me, time is very important. From my point of view, I need more and more time for my pieces. I always see that life is getting shorter and shorter. Bob is like me: We don't have any time for life, we're just running, running, running from one place to another. There's so much infrastructure to organize in order to be able to do what we do, but once the performance starts, time is somewhere else. That's why I'm going to perform in the MoMA for nearly three months, literally every day – but it's so hard to come to that point where performance starts and everything stops: no longer any kind of machine or computers or talking to people. I just enter into the performance. And then, for its duration, that performance becomes life itself. When you become life itself, like what Bob's doing on the stage and what I'm doing in performance, then that is everything. Then we are there. Where we always want to be.

With my students, I do these exercises called "clean the house." You write your own name on paper very slowly, for one hour, always moving the pen, so that actually your name is existing as hundreds of thousands of little dots with your place in time. Bob understands this. It is such an enormously difficult exercise because today everything in life is always fast, and everything is information – we are constantly scattered and everything is in pieces. So the moment when you take one hour to write your own name, if you really succeed, then you understand that actually this is the *universe*. When you sort of let time happen, then you forget about time. I'm always saying to my audience, "I don't want you to spend time with me looking at my performance. I want you to forget about time." Time stops existing.

Which of Wilson's pieces particularly interest you?

One I especially like is *Doctor Faustus Lights the Lights*, which you don't see very much. I'm always interested when Bob actually goes somewhere else and experiments, you know. Because Bob creates a certain language, and that language in every play is very visible, but sometimes he kind of goes off somewhere else. He worked with second-year students from the drama school in East Berlin who never knew English. He gave them English text to memorize without explaining to them what it meant. In this way, language becomes invented. They were saying flat things, "How are you, I don't know, blah blah," but they

Robert Wilson Solo, Rennes, 1976

didn't understand what they were saying, so they would not have the right pronunciation or put the accent on the right things. That made the whole play incredible. This was in the beginning of the 1990s, when I saw it in the Hebbel Theater in Berlin. They had a huge success – and then when they were touring, the students learned English, and the play was lost. They could not play anymore. It was amazing. Really. This is something I enjoy very much.

> What do you and Wilson have in mind for your autobiography, *The Life and Death of Marina Abramović*?

Working with Bob on that now, I really think I want to introduce some trashy elements, mess things up a bit. This is the danger of Bob's productions: It's so pleasing to the eye how he uses each element, how the props become a part of the set, how everything is in perfection and harmony. I want to attack him with some contemporary things that are just not perfect, to go a different way and to have some reality, because performance is about reality. If you hold a knife in a theater, this knife can't kill. If I hold a knife in performance, that knife can kill and the blood is real. I need that kind of reality.

I've been staging my "biographies" since 1989, with the first one directed by Charles Atlas. I always ask different directors to stage them, always with the same condition: I give them all my material, and they have to remix it the way they want without me giving any veto, so that every time I see it staged, my own life will look different to me. In *The Biography Remix* with Michael Laub, which I played in Avignon, my entire Slavic origin was completely taken away because he was not interested in that part of my life. And now with Bob doing the biography, I'm bombarded with these Slavic elements, the kind of darkness, the black humor, the men with oversized erections, the women who are holding their breasts and looking to the sky or crying over the dead.

We start the whole thing with a funeral, a black funeral, very dark, and then we go through four stages of life, and then we end with a white funeral, and the white funeral is dissolving light as the spirit is going transcendent, somewhere else. So from earth to spirit, life contained by two funerals, one physical, one transcendental. During the play I am three Marinas. I play only one, but visually you will always see three. I want to have three bodies, one real, and two fake, and then we bury them in the three different places where I have lived the longest: Belgrade, Amsterdam, and New York.

In the beginning, Bob was thinking that I should not perform at all, that someone else should perform me, but the producers went crazy. There will be other performance people as well. I want to see the performance people who can really do things, who really can run the world, who really can slap and do physically demanding things that actors are not supposed to do. Bob is also thinking of having Willem Dafoe narrate the piece to make it abstract; it's a female story, but being narrated by Dafoe gives it another perspective. We take the personal life, transform it, and make it universal. And in that process, funeral

Rehearsal for *The Life and Death of Marina Abramović* (press release), Madrid, 2010. Above, Robert Wilson, Wolgang Wiens, Marina Abramović, Willem Dafoe; below, Willem Dafoe, Marina Abramović, Antony Hegarty, Robert Wilson

to funeral, especially working with the music of Antony and the Johnsons – who have this ethereal voice, incredibly emotional – the cruel reality of my stories and Bob's need to abstract, it's going to be really like I'm attacking him with reality.

> You and Wilson are both used to collaborative work, but you also both have strong personalities and theatrical presences.

It's very difficult working with people who don't have a strong reputation because there is always this ego thing. But Bob doesn't have this problem at all. He always asks, "What do you think about this, what do you think about that?" If I have a good idea that is not what he was thinking, he really accepts it. He has this ability to collaborate, to accept good ideas and throw away the bad ones, and to rethink. And that's why it's great to work with him, and why this collaboration is so interesting, because I have to make compromises getting into his space, but he has to make compromises getting to mine. There's this real, true equality. Even in age, you know. I think he's three years older – how old is Bob, 66?

> He'll be 70 in 2011.

He looks fantastic. He spends his life in hotels or on airplanes. He doesn't even have a place here, he just squats somewhere. He's moving ten times more than I am. I'm really impressed.

> What brought you to choose Wilson as a director?

One of the big connections between me and Bob, as I mentioned, is time. Nobody else works in such extremes of time at the moment. But duration is one thing, and another interesting thing is the opposite: how Bob abstracts. He takes a life and makes it completely an abstraction in an abstract space, and I take the performance and make it completely a reality. So how are we going to combine this abstract space and real space? That will be the interesting thing. The theater is about abstract space, and he's going to the extreme in that direction, and performance is about the real, and I'm going extremely real. How are we going to meet the two extremes?

> Your biography, as well as your work, invokes violence. Do you see any underlying dark sides and violence in Wilson's work?

Oh yes, very much, yes; but it's completely psychological. Look at *Quartett*: what is it that she says? "The whore is dead, we're alone"? It's amazing this sentence she says, and then she just disappears into nothingness. The danger in Bob's piece is the mind going mad. In mine, it's that the body can be hurt.

> For 12 days in 2002, 186 hours to be exact, you stood on a raised platform, a kind of "house" cubicle, in Sean Kelly's New York gallery with people looking at you the entire time: a performance called *The House with the Ocean View*. To do such a long-duration piece, does your mind retreat into abstraction, or do you find your own internal privacy?

The Life and Death of Marina Abramović, Manchester, 2011

The Life and Death of Marina Abramović, Manchester, 2011. Marina Abramović and Antony Hegarty

No, no, no, it's something completely different. It's a very spiritual state of mind that you achieve by not eating, by drinking only water. You purify yourself and you actually become empty – you become receiver and sender of the energy – and as you become like a shell of mind and body, at the same time you are totally in the present and you reach something that I can call a "luminous state of being." Every ascetic tradition from Saint Teresa of Avila on – Catholic, Orthodox, Protestant, Eastern, Western – talks about this. Done in front of the audience, in the gallery, it's something you transform to another space, which is unbelievable. It's like bliss.

This is why I'm so attracted by time. Working with time, I feel this is the only manner that the performer and the audience can go through a spiritual transformation. We need time to get there. I can't do it in 15 minutes. But if I have days, I get to that space that I could never get to otherwise, and when I get to that luminous state, the space changes, the molecules of air change. With *The House with the Ocean View*, I had 12,000 people coming and going, and coming back and going, and spending an hour and then three hours in the gallery, which is unthinkable in America. Why? Because something changed. Because that kind of state is real.

This was a very important piece for me, because I found it was closest to my purpose. And while it was happening there, I had to just gaze. I was just looking at people, everybody who came close enough that we could have this eye contact without words, without anything. This was all, but it was so incredibly strong what happened in this eye contact: It was just this enormous unconditional love that came out completely to total strangers, but that love was so overwhelming, and I could see them in a kind of true light. I could see their pain, see everything – it was like there'd been a transplant in front of me – and sometimes there was such pain there that my heart nearly burst into crying. And then they would cry in front of me. And then they would come back and cry again. It was amazing. I've never had such a thing.

I realized during this piece that I had done something wrong, but I couldn't change anymore because I was in the piece. I wanted to create this picture where you have three elements of the wall, and the public looking at me is like a painting in a way, but it's a living element. But I understood that the public standing there looking up creates some kind of altar and it becomes like worship, which I didn't want. I want it completely democratic. I want the same level, so now when I'm at MoMA it's going to be on the same level. There will be no difference. It will be direct and simple, nothing where the artist is up and the audience down.

Wilson quotes Martha Graham as saying, "The body doesn't lie." He thinks that's true. Do you think the body can lie?

A body can lie, but for very short times. That's why in the long-durational works, it's impossible to sustain lies for so long; so they just crack, become truth. I think in short terms the body can pretend, but even in pretending it actually becomes maybe true. It doesn't lie. You see it's fake, so you know it's wrong. I always think that when someone performs, the audience is like a dog: They can smell insecurity, they can smell when something is not true and when the body lies, and they just leave or lose attention. Martha Graham also said: "Wherever a dancer stands is holy ground." I have a different version. So many artists say that they don't care about the audience when they're in the zone, when they are performing, but I care very much. I'm thinking my sentence will be: "Wherever the audience is, is holy ground." For me, the audience is extremely important because performance is a dialogue. The moment that that kind of interaction is broken, it's gone.

> You make me think of ritual in traditional societies, as with a spiritual leader or shaman who guides the lives of his followers.

Joseph Beuys talks about the artist as shaman, and I don't know about having or not having that quality, but one thing I have as an artist is a very strong sense of purpose as to why I am here in the first place. I've sacrificed my entire life: I'm private, no children, I don't have a husband because it was too much and he left, and I'm just by myself. It's really possible only this way.

> That makes you like a transmitter.

Yes, and more and more so as I get into this last stage of life. The third act always starts out very well with everybody happy, but it always finishes tragically because the main actor dies. So I'm in the third act! And this is what I feel more and more. It's the end of November, 2009, and I'm 63. You don't know if you're going to live another five years or 20 more, but you know that this is the last part of the unit of your living and that you really have to make sense of it all, what your life was about and what you want to do. And one of my main purposes is to make performance art into mainstream art, because up to now it has always been alternative. This retrospective at the MoMA isn't important just because it's mine. It's important for every single performance artist coming after me that performance will be recognized as a real, mainstream art, somehow leveled with everything else. I've spent all my life to do that, to arrive there.

> One issue that concerns you, and which is also of concern for Wilson, is the preservation of performance. Do you think there is a way to recreate a live performance that once took place?

This is exactly what I am trying to do. In the 1970s, I wrote with Ulay the statement saying, "No rehearsal, no repetition, and no predicted end."[2] Then, in *Seven Easy Pieces* at the Guggenheim in 2005, I re-enacted the past performances of very important artists like Bruce Nauman, Vito Acconci, Valie Export, Joseph Beuys, Gina Pane, because now I really believe – I didn't know this in the 1970s – that performance is dead as a video documentation, is dead as slides or as the image in a book. The only way it can work is if it's live. And even if it's loose, even if the new interpretation will change – like you're performing Bach, and

2
The German artist known as Ulay was Abramović's life and performance partner from 1976 to 1989.

someone says, "Okay, I want to make techno Bach" – still you have to let it happen. The future is re-performance, but performance has to be performed not by dancers, not by theater, but by performance artists, because it's a different type of body, a different attitude, completely another type of reality.

> This brings up questions of training and pedagogy for performance artists. Wilson has his laboratory for performance at Watermill, and in 2012, you will have The Marina Abramović Institute.

Bob's idea for Watermill is different than mine for my institute. Watermill is really the place where Bob tries out and practices new works; of course, he has a relation to the young artists there, but at the same time their activity is limited. It's more about Bob than them. You enter into Bob's space, there are rules, and that's how everything functions. In my foundation, I want everyone to create his *own* space and not be overwhelmed by my presence, apart from the name of the institute. So I will withdraw. I will not have my works there. I want it to have only my name. My name is like a legacy, like a jeans brand, or Coca Cola: I am the brand for performance art. But my institute is not going to be run by me. It's going to have curators and directors, and it's going to address all performance art. I really want people to teach about performance, and I want to have young artists creating new works, and I want to have education for the public. Because the public doesn't know how to look at performance art. It doesn't have the key of how to look at something when nothing is happening. In performance, the audience and the performer are the body, they become unified, and that kind of unit is so fragile, so important. It's not just the audience or just the performance: One would fall down without the other.

The difference between this and any other kind of performance center in the world is that mine is based only on long-durational work, minimum of six hours. Our life is going at such a frenzy that we have to have art be longer and longer, we have to really spend time in the piece. So I'm creating seats that are going to be convertible beds with a little blanket. In the middle of a piece ten hours long when you maybe are falling asleep, you put on the blanket and you are sleeping inside the piece. When you wake up, there's going to be, on the left arm of the chair, a cool drink, and on the right side, hot milk. You can put it on a table and you eat and you look and you are still in the piece. I haven't figured how we are going to do the toilet so you don't ever leave – that's impossible – but the rest is going to be there.

So this is something that doesn't exist in the world. I would like to commission different artists – young artists, of course, but also very important artists – to make this kind of work. I will commission Bob – we will never find the budget for Bob, but never mind – to do something long-durational. He will do it in a second. *Einstein on the Beach* was first eight hours, then five hours. It's the piece, it doesn't matter: People go to eat and come back, and the piece continues, even if you're not there the entire eight hours or five hours, the piece continues in your head because you know at every point of time in that frame, it's there, and this is what makes it of such incredible quality.

In a recent interview, you said that you've made three groups of works: artist/body works (your performances), public/body (your sculpture and interactive public installations), and student/body (your teaching young artists to perform).[3] Obviously, there is a common denominator there: body, body, body. Wilson is enormously polyvalent in his artistic production. Do you see a common denominator in his works, the way we can in yours?

I don't know, it's so different. He takes so many different things, but he makes them his and reduces them to his language, so it doesn't matter what he's taking on: He's reducing to this abstract light, space, sound. Everything becomes Bob Wilson. He creates his own mix. It's like in cooking. You can have 300 soups, but you can try one and you know it's exactly the Bob Wilson soup, where another one may be the Pina Bausch soup, and another soup is maybe my soup, but there are many soups that you don't know what they are, and that means it's not good work.

Yet Wilson has been criticized for being a recognizable "taste," in that some people say that it's always the same "soup," the style so imposing that whatever the subject, what you see is Wilson.

His work is his life, and he's constantly working. If you make ten productions a year, you just can't not repeat. My old professor told me once that in your life you have one idea, and if you're a genius you maybe have two, and this is it. So you know, it's not easy. That idea, you have to be careful. Also, when you get older, it's more difficult to take risks and more difficult to give up things that you have already learned, and that's why I think that Bob's and my collaboration is so important for me. I know that in this collaboration I have to give up something, but I also know that he has to learn, because for him it will not be easy. But I always like to see new territories, and for Bob, I think that it is a great chance that at this point in our lives, we are both going to unknown territories. Both of us have to go somewhere that we have never been yet.

3
David Ebony, "Marina Abramović: An Interview," *Art in America*, May 2009.

The Life and Death of Marina Abramović, Manchester, 2011

From Within

I asked Robert Wilson to select a series of images outside of his own productions that hold particular personal significance for him. His response begins with a picture of Lucinda Childs. A transcription of a video in which Wilson lays out the classic version of his origin stories follows on page 316. Together, they form a portrait of the artist from within.

Robert Wilson directing, 1995

This is a portrait by Robert Mapplethorpe of Lucinda Childs.
It was taken in 1977, the year after *Einstein on the Beach*
premiered. Lucinda is wearing the white silk robe that she wore
in the play I wrote for the two of us called, *I was sitting on my
patio this guy appeared I thought I was hallucinating.* Lucinda is
at once icy cold and hot. In the glance of her eye, she knows
the power of stillness and the movement within.

This photograph is by Robert Mapplethorpe of Christopher Knowles when he was about 15 years old. It was taken soon after we finished our world tour in which we performed in Europe, Latin America, and Persia. The last performance of the tour was in a 17th century house in Shiraz. For this occasion, Chris added an epilogue. It was the end of the tour and Farah Diba, Shabanu of Iran, was in the audience. The epilogue was Christopher repeating the word "tape recorder" for ten minutes. He repeated the word in a very light, delicate, joyous tone of voice. A bit like the music of Satie. Because of the beauty of the delivery, after three or four minutes I had tears in my eyes, and the audience was crying in the opposite way. "How long is this kid going to say the word "tape recorder?!!" As we were leaving the stage, Chris turned to me and said, without anger or defiance, "Bob, who cares to have your mind be so smooth."

I went to Pratt Institute with Robert Mapplethorpe.

Terracotta figure of a Han dancer. The form in proportion of the
figure. The dancer is caught in mid-action of quickly throwing
her sleeves in the air. The serene interior beauty of the figure –
the eye is almost in back of the head – shows the depth of
emotion and the power of the movement.

Photograph of Marlene Dietrich. In 1968 I briefly met Marlene
Dietrich in New York. A few years later I got to know her when
she was performing at the Espace Cardin, the same time my play
Deafman Glance was performed. I saw her performance there
17 times and got to know her. Some years later I visited Marlene
at her apartment and asked what her favorite photograph of hers
was. She said with her deep, husky voice, "I don't know. I have
been photographed to death." I said, "What are some of your
favorites?" And she said, "1941, Horst," where she is leaning on
the arms of a chair. "With this photograph, I finally learned to look
at the camera." Photographers used to say to her, "Ms. Dietrich,
open your eyes!" And she said with her seductive voice, "They
are open." She often used that sleepy, camel-long eyelash glance.

Photograph of Edwin Denby, classical poet and dance critic. Edwin was the finest writer on dance that America ever produced. His great gift was that he could simply describe – in a very few well-chosen words. He is someone who actually saw what was onstage, and not what was in his mind. I have never met anyone in over 40 years of working in the theater who could talk about my work better than he. He talked about the proportion of space, could describe the quality of light. With questions, and never answers. This photograph by his friend Rudy Burckhardt was taken on the rooftop of the building where he lived for many years, in the West of Manhattan. Willem de Kooning, who dedicated his first retrospective at MoMA to Denby, at one time lived in the same neighborhood.

Some years ago I was asked to place a sculpture in a park surrounding a castle in the southern part of Sweden, in Wanås. I designed this little wood-framed shingled house that one does not enter. It was a house for Edwin Denby. One hears high in the trees surrounding the house an ethereal piece of music by Michael Galasso. As one cannot enter the house, one looks through the windows to the interior. The walls are light grayish blue. The floor and ceiling are pinewood. Suspended overhead in the room from front to back are blue exposed light bulbs emitting a cool, Nordic-like light. Towards the back of the room is a small wooden table with an open book. In back of the table is a chair placed slightly at an angle to the table. Inside the room we hear Denby's suicide note: a letter written to Dante about flying over the North Pole.

A shoe. For a number of years I have collected shoes. I have
shoes of Rudolph Nureyev when he danced with Margot Fonteyn.
Soon after he defected. The shoes of George Balanchine, of
Jerome Robbins, of Marlene Dietrich, of a Russian princess.
Minnie Mouse shoes. This sharkskin single shoe I found many
years ago in the flea market in Paris. I paid close to $1000 for it.
A lot of money for a single shoe, but for some reason I was
attracted to it.

This photograph is by Lee Miller. It was taken in Germany in 1945 at the end of the war. Pictured is a dead Nazi, lying on his back with his clinched right fist held in the air. To his side is a painted portrait of Hitler with his face punched out. Out of the window of the room one sees the stone figure of justice with her left arm in the air holding scales of balance.

In 1976 I created an opera with Philip Glass called *Einstein on the Beach*. I began with this photo of Einstein in his study in Princeton. All of the performers were dressed in the same way: baggy grey pants, starched white t-shirts and suspenders. They wore tennis shoes and a wristwatch. I looked at many photos of Einstein. Photos of him when he was two years old, 20 years old, 40, 60, 70 years old. In all standing portraits of him, he held his hands in the same position as in this photo. The little space between his thumb and the next finger is always the same. I started the opera with this gesture. And continued. I thought about this space: Between his two fingers he held his chalk with which he made his calculations. He held the bow for the violin that he loved to play. And he pulled the ropes of the sailboat that was his favorite pastime.

When I was about 12 years old I went to Natchitoches, Louisiana to visit the Melrose Plantation, where I met Clementine Hunter. The Melrose Plantation was owned by the Metoyer family, and after its slaves were emancipated, they stayed on the property and continued to work the land. The family had a very good relationship with the slaves. They had houses built of mud with thatched roofs like they had in Africa. Later, the Henry family purchased the plantation.

Clementine Hunter was a painter with no formal education. She could not read or write. She mixed paints from natural pigments and began to paint plantation life: washing clothes, funerals, baptisms, harvests, etc. She painted on the interior walls of some of the houses. At that time, I acquired this painting. It was the first painting I ever collected. In the following years, I acquired four other, larger works, which, when I was 22, I donated to the American Museum in Bath, England. Clementine Hunter was shown how to sign her name. She did not like for the "C" to be facing the "H" because she said it looked as if the arms were closed. She preferred the arms of the "C" to be opened outward.

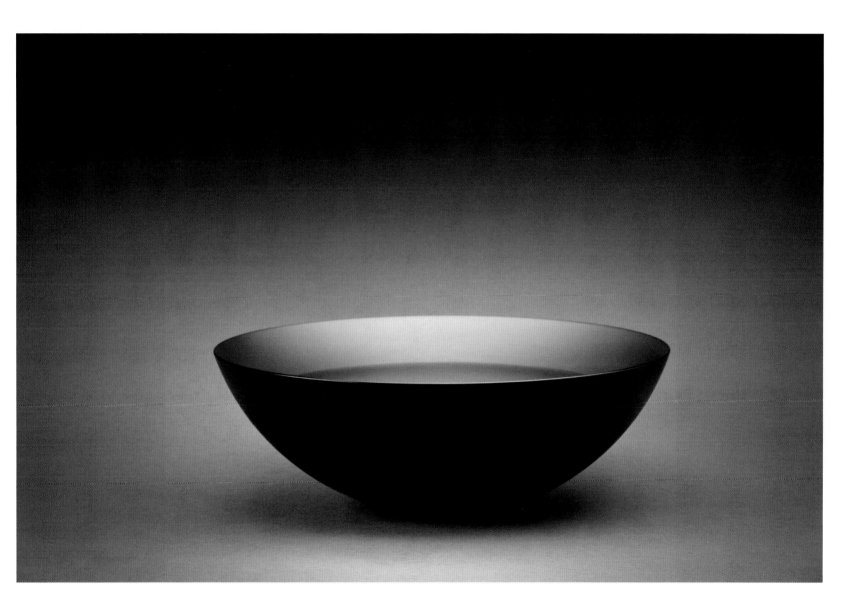

This piece of glass is by František Vizner; he made it especially for me. He is my favorite glassmaker. It is in two parts. The inner part is highly polished and the interior of the larger piece is slightly polished. The outer surface of the larger piece is slightly frosted. The texture of the outer surface breaks up the transmitted light in a very interesting way to the interior surface. The highly polished second piece looks like liquid. The whole piece has a great power in its simplicity of form and surfaces. It is a very meditative work.

DiaLog/A Mad Man A Mad Giant A Mad Dog A Mad Urge A Mad Face, Washington, D.C., 1974. Christopher Knowles and Robert Wilson

Rehearsal for *Danton's Death*, Houston, 1992. Robert Wilson directing

I'd like to talk to you a little bit about my work[1]. The reason I work as an artist is to ask questions, that is, to say, "What is it?" and not to say what something *is*, for if we know what it is that we're doing, there's no reason to do it. The reason to work is to say, "What is it?"

[*Suddenly, a loud scream comes out of Wilson. A screech or roar, an indescribable sound, more animal than human, a sound accompanied by radical facial contortions. Just as it came on, in a flash it is gone, as if it had never been, and we see Wilson "normal," as he had been before in both vocal tone and facial expression, calm and articulate.*]

What am I saying?

> How all occasions do inform against me,
> And spur my dull revenge!
>
> Examples gross as earth exhort me:
> Witness this army of such mass and charge
> Led by a delicate and tender prince,
> Whose divine ambition puff'd
> Makes mouths at the invisible event....

That's *Hamlet*. I learned it when I was 12, and I'm 68 and I'm still saying it, and each time I say it I can think about it in a completely different way. That's not to say that it doesn't have meaning. Of course it has meaning, it's full of meanings. But to attach an interpretation to it would deny all the other ideas of what it's about. The reason I work is to say, "What is it?" – and not to say what something is.

I grew up in a rather small town in Texas and didn't have the opportunity to go to a theater or to go to art museums. It was not until my early 20s that I first got to go to the theater. As probably most of you know, my work is best known as for someone who works in the theater. I went to Broadway plays and I didn't like them and still don't for the most part, and I went to the opera and I didn't like that either, and I still don't for the most part. But then I saw the work of George Balanchine and the New York City Ballet and I liked that very much, and I still like it. I liked it because it was classically constructed. It was formal in its presentation. And in particular, I was very interested in the abstract ballets of Balanchine. There was so much space, mental space, virtual space. Soon after seeing the work of Balanchine, I saw the work of Merce Cunningham and John Cage, and I liked that and I liked it for the same reasons. It was formally constructed and formally presented, and it was *all* abstract. And it's very curious that often the music was put with the dance only on the first night. So what I was hearing was one thing and what I was seeing was another. And it was curious how these two, when thought about separately, when put together, could reinforce one another through their oppositions, through their dualism, through their parallelism. And that was very different from what I heard and saw on Broadway or what I heard and saw in the theater. I guess if I had gone to school and had studied theater, if I'd gone to Harvard and

[1] Robert Wilson made the video that is transcribed on the occasion of receiving an honorary doctorate from The American University of Paris, May 22, 2010.

studied theater, if I'd gone to Yale or Northwestern, which are major theatrical schools, and studied theater, I would not be making the kind of theater I'm making today. I basically learned about theater through life experience, and I think the first major influence on the work I'm doing today was looking at the dance and especially at the work of Merce Cunningham and John Cage, and of course George Balanchine.

In 1967, I was walking down the street in Summit, New Jersey, and I saw a policeman about to hit an Afro-American boy over the head with a club [*in silence, Wilson raises his left arm in a fist, with a motion that could imitate the policeman about to strike, or the black power salute*], and I stopped the policeman, I said, "Why do you hit this boy?" And the policeman said, "It's none of your business," and I said, "But it is. I'm a responsible citizen. [*Slight amused smile crosses Wilson's face.*] Why do you hit the boy?" And after much to-do I left with the policeman and the boy and started walking to a police station and on the way, I heard the sounds coming from the boy and recognized them as those of a deaf person. And after some time at the police station, the boy was released, and I went to a two-room apartment where he was living with 13 people, an Afro-American family. And I had learned that recently he had been sent to New Jersey, where I had met him. And before that time he had been living in Alabama and Louisiana in rural communities. And the people with whom he lived didn't understand that his problem was one of not hearing. He'd never been to school. As far as I could tell, he knew no words. I thought he was intelligent, perhaps highly intelligent, and it became apparent after a short period of time that he thought in terms of visual signs and signals. He had no legal guardian, and he was going to be institutionalized. It was thought that he couldn't learn. And to make a long story short, at age 27 as a single man I went to court to adopt him, so that he would have a legal guardian and I could prevent him from being institutionalized. I had a 27-year-old lawyer. I said to the lawyer, "Do you think I'll get this boy?" and he said, "No, I don't think so." [*Wilson smiles, knowingly.*] The judge said, "Mr. Wilson, what makes you think this child's intelligent? [*Wilson in a seriously adult voice*] I said, "Your honor, Judge, he has a sense of humor, and that's a sign of intelligence." Towards the end of the proceedings, I asked once again the lawyer, I said, "Do you think I'll get the boy? What can I say to the judge to convince him to give me the boy?" He said, "I don't know." So in the final moments of the trial, I said to the judge, "You know, Judge, if you don't give me this boy, it's going to cost the State of New Jersey a hell of a lot of money to lock him up." And the judge said, "Mr. Wilson, you've got a very good point," and they gave me the boy, [*big smile*] and he came to live with me. And my first work in the theater was written with this 13-year-old deaf-mute boy who had never been to school and knew no words. It was based on observations of the boy, dreams he had, drawings he made. It's how he heard and saw the world.

And about that time I met a man who was head of the Department of Psychology at Columbia University, Daniel Stern. And Stern was making films of mothers and babies. The baby would cry, and the mother would reach for the baby, pick up the baby and comfort the baby. [*Wilson raises his arms and hands in an abstract, Wilsonian suggestion of a mother about to put a baby on her shoulder.*] Stern did a very curious thing. He took the film and slowed it down so that you could see the 24 frames in a second, $1/24^{th}$ of a second, and in eight out of ten cases, the initial reaction to the mother in the first frame, the first $1/24^{th}$ of a second, is that the mother is [*Wilson contorts his face, his hands reach out as it they want to strangle someone*] lunging at the child, and the child's – [*Wilson makes a face of fear, hands held up, as if to protect himself from a danger coming toward him full-front.*] The next two or three frames, the mother – [*Wilson makes grimaces and gestures with hands*], something different. And the child once again – [*makes face of horror*], something different. The next two or three frames, the mother – [*again, Wilson demonstrates in mime – or silent movie – fashion the horror*], something else, again different. So that in one second of time it's very complex what's happening between the mother and the child. Now, the mother, when she sees the film, is shocked and terrified. She says, "But I love my child." [*Wilson repeats the facial and hand and arm gestures of the threatening angry mother ready to strangle the child.*] So perhaps the body is moving faster than we think. But there is a language there, and it was this language, almost imperceptible, that Raymond Andrews, this 13-year-old deaf-mute boy, was more readily, more easily reading.

There are several things that are important with Raymond. One night he was at my loft in lower Manhattan, a factory space, and he was at one end of the loft and I was at the other end of the loft, that's about 25 meters long, and I cried out to him, "RAYMOND," and he didn't hear me. I knew that if I were to stamp my foot on the floor he'd feel the vibration and turn around. But I did a very curious thing: "*EHAH*," [*Wilson shouts, almost a croaking sound, like someone who cannot speak "normally"*] "*MAN,*" the sound of a deaf person, and he turned around and started laughing, and went, "EH Man...OW R U?" He started walking towards me, like, "Hey, man, you're talking my language." And I started to think about it. His body was more familiar with those vibrations of sound than the sounds of the hearing world. And the more I thought about it, the more I began to realize that in a sense his *body* was hearing. As far as we could measure his hearing in decibels, up to 110 decibels he heard nothing; but the body was feeling the vibrations. So I think the second most important influence on my work today was the meeting of Raymond Andrews, this deaf-mute boy, and how he could hear, and how he saw the world.

Soon after that, one day a former professor of mine gave me an audio tape and said, "I think you might be interested in this tape," and I played it, and it went something like this: "Imp [*Wilson changes to a high, shrill mechanical or computer-generated voice*] imp, edt, edt, imp, imp, imp, imp imp imp butad imp imp imp n in imp eh en imp ah imp ah ide imp imp et adda imp in imp imp imp AGHH, imp imp anda limpand an af af af af a n AGHH, AGHH a imp, dada la imp, imp, imp, ADDA rrrrh [*makes facial and hand gestures*] limp ad de air lip in AND iradede *EMILY LIKES THE TV BECAUSE A!* Because she likes Mickey Mouse. *BECAUSE B!* Because she likes Minnie Mouse. *BECAUSE A!* Because she likes Donald Duck. *BECAUSE BEEEE!* [*Wilson swipes a hand in front of his face like a windshield wipe*] Emily likes the TV because she watches it." So I called the professor and I said to him, "Who made this tape?" He said, "It's a 13-year-old boy and he's in Schenectady, New York. He's in an institution for brain-damaged children." And I said that I'd like to meet him. And I got to know him. I went to the institution where he was living and saw that they were correcting all of his audio tapes, and I began to take note of them, and what seemed very arbitrary – "imp imp nnn mm" [*Wilson's voice again somewhere between Mickey Mouse and a computerized voice*] – was not arbitrary at all, that it was mathematically phenomenal. There would be patterns of sounds, sometimes words, and they would repeat in geometric patterns – eight, then four, then eight, then four, then two, then six, then two, then six, then eight and four, and eight and four, and two and six, then eight and four. The numerical counts were absolutely perfect. And he could speak very rapidly and extemporaneously. Chris could open a page of a book and say, "There are 68 words on the page" – in one second. The amazing thing about him is that he can see large patterns quickly. And after some time, he left the institution and came and collaborated with me at this early age. And my first play that had text was written with Christopher Knowles, where the text was arranged musically and mathematically, and the structure of the work was arranged architecturally in terms of math and geometry so that he could readily see the whole. So I think that the third most important influence on the work I'm doing today was the meeting of Christopher Knowles, a 13-year-old boy who was institutionalized in the O.D. Heck school since age two. Chris taught me how to think quickly on a large scale, how to see big pictures quickly.

The best class I ever had in school was taught by Sibyl Moholy-Nagy. She taught the history of architecture. It was a five-year course and in the middle of the third year, she said, "Students, you have three minutes to design a city. Ready. Go." [*Wilson smiles.*] And I've never forgotten what I did. I drew an apple and inside of the apple I put a crystal cube. She said, "What are you thinking about?" I said, "I'm thinking about our communities, about a plan for a city, that our communities need something like a crystal cube at the core of the apple that can reflect the universe, the world, like a medieval village with a cathedral as the highest point in the village, a place where people congregated, came for an exchange of ideas and for enlightenment."

We learn to walk by walking. You can read all the books about it you want, but you learn by doing. I've learned theater by making theater. Several years ago I was in London, and I was with my friend, American opera singer, soprano Jessye Norman, and she was on a talk show, and they asked her, "Miss Norman, what is your favorite recording?" [*Wilson speaks in a gently mocking imitation of a mass journalism interview voice.*] And she said without hesitation, "Martin Luther King, 'I've got a DREAM.'" [*Wilson raises hand and fist in similar posture to when he was speaking of the policeman about to hit Raymond Andrews, or a black power salute.*] Yes, we can.

Robert Wilson

Catalogue raisonné

ALPHABETICAL LIST OF WORKS

Works are listed by title, followed by the section and year under which they appear in the catalogue below: Theater Works, Film and Video Works, Audio Recordings, Solo Exhibitions and Installations, Selected Group Exhibitions. Only exhibitions with distinct titles are identified, not those entitled simply "Robert Wilson." Dates normally designate premieres or openings and follow strictly those given in Robert Wilson's official Resumé.

Robert Wilson's texts and preparatory drawings published to coincide with productions; published interviews and public lectures; eulogies, conversations, and short commentaries in collective works, while all being the work of Robert Wilson, are not strictly speaking artworks and therefore do not figure in the catalogue raisonné.

As throughout the book, titles are given as set out in the Robert Wilson Chronology 1965–2010 provided by the Robert Wilson archives. Exceptions are made only in cases where clarity or consistency makes them necessary: **Aïda** in the archives is listed here as **Aida**; **Die Zauberflöte** as **The Magic Flute**; **Doctor Faustus (Manzoni)** as **Doktor Faustus** to distinguish it from **Doctor Faustus Lights the Lights**; **Fables** as **Les Fables de La Fontaine**; **Mozart's Geburtshaus** as **A Space for Mozart (Mozarts Geburtshaus)**; **Saint John's Passion** as **St. John's Passion**; **Sonnets** as **Shakespeare's Sonnets**.

2 Lips and Dancers and Space (Theater Works, 2004, 2005)
14 Stations (Solo Exhibitions and Installations, 2000)
30th Anniversary of Solidarność (Theater Works, 2010)
70 ANGELS ON THE FAÇADE: Domus 1928–1998 (Theater Works, 1998)
1433 – The Grand Voyage (Theater Works, 2010)
Aichi World Expo: In the Evening at Koi Pond (Solo Exhibitions and Installations, 2005)
Aida (Theater Works, 2002, 2003, 2004, 2006)
Alceste [Gluck] (Theater Works, 1986, 1990, 1999, 2004)
Alcestis [Euripides] (Theater Works, 1986, 1987)
Alice (Theater Works, 1992, 1995)
Alice in Bed (Theater Works, 1993)
Alley Cats [Meredith Monk's *Co-op*] (Theater Works, 1968)
America Hurrah [van Itallie] (Theater Works, 1965)
Anna's Room [Stanze e Segreti] (Solo Exhibitions and Installations, 2000)
Baby Blood (Theater Works, 1967)
Binnenalster Door (Solo Exhibitions and Installations, 1992)
The Black Rider: The Casting of The Magic Bullets (Theater Works, 1990, 2004, 2005, 2006)
Bluebeard's Castle (Theater Works, 1995)
Bob Wilson Solo (Theater Works, 1976)
Byrd Hoffman School of Byrds Spring Student Concerts (Theater Works, 1973)
ByrdwoMAN (Theater Works, 1968)
Carpets for a magical garden [*Vorwerk* installation] (Solo Exhibitions and Installations, 1998)
Chair Air (Solo Exhibitions and Installations, 2003)
Chair Chairs (Solo Exhibitions and Installations, 2003)
Choreographie des Designs (Solo Exhibitions and Installations, 1990)
the CIVIL warS: a tree is best measured when it is down – Cologne Section (Theater Works, 1984)
the CIVIL warS – Freiburg [second] Workshop (Theater Works, 1982)
the CIVIL warS – Knee Plays (Theater Works, 1984)
the CIVIL warS – Marseille Workshop (Theater Works, 1984)
the CIVIL warS – Munich [first] Workshop (Theater Works, 1981)
the CIVIL warS – Rome Section (Theater Works, 1984)
the CIVIL warS – Rotterdam Section (Theater Works, 1983)
the CIVIL warS – Tokyo Workshop (Theater Works, 1984)
Clorox (Theater Works, 1966)
Come in and go out (Solo Exhibitions and Installations, 2003)
Connecting Collections – Four Perspectives (Group Exhibitions, 2004)
Contemporary Magic: A Tarot Deck Art Project (Group Exhibitions, 2011)
Convidados de piedra (Solo Exhibitions and Installations, 1992)
Cosmopolitan Greetings (Theater Works, 1988)
Creative Arts Workshops for Kids [mural] (Group Exhibitions, 1995)
[Dance Event at New York World's Fair] (Theater Works, 1964)
[Dance Pieces at Peerless Movie House] (Theater Works, 1964)
Danton's Death (Theater Works, 1992, 1998)
THE DAYS BEFORE: death, destruction & detroit III (Theater Works, 1999)
Deafman Glance (Theater Works, 1970)
Deafman Glance (Film and Video Works, 1981)
Deafman Glance: Video Installation (Solo Exhibitions and Installations, 2010)
Death, Destruction & Detroit (Theater Works, 1979)
Death, Destruction & Detroit II (Theater Works, 1987)
The Death of King Lear (Film and Video Works, 1989)
The Death of Molière [La Mort de Molière] (Film and Video Works, 1994)
[Demonstration/Lecture/Press Conference] [Belgrade] (Theater Works, 1971)
DiaLog [2] (Theater Works, 1975)
DiaLog [3] (Theater Works, 1976)
DiaLog/A Mad Man A Mad Giant A Mad Dog A Mad Urge A Mad Face (Theater Works, 1974)
DiaLog/Curious George (Theater Works, 1980)
DiaLog/Network (Theater Works, 1977)
DiaLog/Sundance Kid (Theater Works, 1975)
Disegni di Gibellina (Solo Exhibitions and Installations, 1994)
Doktor Faustus [Manzoni] (Theater Works, 1989)
Doctor Faustus Lights the Lights (Theater Works, 1992)
Doctor Caligari (Theater Works, 2002)
The $ Value of Man (Theater Works, 1975)
Don Juan Último (Theater Works, 1992)
Don Juan Último (Film and Video Works, 1992)
Dragons and Silk From the Forbidden City (Solo Exhibitions and Installations, 1995)
Dream Play (Theater Works, 1998)
Dreams and Images: The Theatre of Robert Wilson (Solo Exhibitions and Installations, 1988)
Duricglte & Tomorrow (Theater Works, 1965)
Edison (Theater Works, 1979)
Einstein on the Beach (Theater Works, 1976, 1984, 1988, 1992, 2001, 2012–13)
Erinnerung an eine Revolution [Remembrance of a Revolution] (Solo Exhibitions and Installations, 1987, 1989)
Erwartung (Theater Works, 1995)
Erwartung: oeuvres sur papier (Solo Exhibitions and Installations, 1995)
Exhibition: Wilson/La Fontaine (Solo Exhibitions and Installations, 2005)
La Femme à la cafetière (Film and Video Works, 1989)
Les Fables de La Fontaine (Theater Works, 2004, 2005)
The Forest (Theater Works, 1988)
Four Saints in Three Acts (Theater Works, 1996)
Die Frau ohne Schatten (Theater Works, 2003)
Der Freischütz (Theater Works, 2009)
From a Theatre of Images (Solo Exhibitions and Installations, 1980)
G.A. Story (Theater Works, 1996)
Galeries Lafayette Installation (Solo Exhibitions and Installations, 1996)
George School Activity (Lecture/demonstration, Theater Works, 1970)
Götterdämmerung (Theater Works, 2002, 2006)
Giorgio Armani (Solo Exhibitions and Installations, 2000, 2003)
Giorgio Armani: A Retrospective (Solo Exhibitions and Installations, 2003, 2004)
The Golden Windows (Theater Works, 1982, 1985, 1988, 1995)
Grace for Grace (Theater Works, 1991)
Great Day in the Morning (Theater Works, 1982)
Hagoromo (Theater Works, 1994)
HAMLET: a monologue (Theater Works, 1995)
Hamletmachine (Theater Works, 1986, 1994)
Handbill (Theater Works, 1970)
Hanjo (Theater Works, 1994)
Happy Days [Oh les beaux jours] (Theater Works, 2008, 2010)
H.G. (Solo Exhibitions and Installations, 1995)
Hot Water (Theater Works, 2000)
The House (Film and Video Works, 1965)
Huaco – 1941 (Theater Works, 1969)
I La Galigo (Theater Works, 2004, 2005, 2006)
Imágines del Cuerpo (Solo Exhibitions and Installations, 2004)
Immaginado Prometeo (Solo Exhibitions and Installations, 2003)
The International Festival of Films on Art (Group Exhibitions, 2004)
I was sitting on my patio this guy appeared I thought I was hallucinating (Theater Works, 1977)
Isamu Noguchi (Solo Exhibitions and Installations, 2003, 2004)
Isamu Noguchi: Sculptural Design (Solo Exhibitions and Installations, 2001)
Jessye Norman Sings for the Healing of AIDS (Theater Works, 1996)
Jo Kondo & Robert Wilson (Theater Works, 2007)
Junk Dances [Louis] (Theater Works, 1964)
KA MOUNTAIN AND GUARDenia TERRACE: a story about a family and some people changing (Theater Works, 1972)
Katya Kabanova (Theater Works, 2010)
King Lear (Theater Works, 1985, 1990)
King Lyre and Lady in the Wasteland (Theater Works, 1973)
The King of Spain (Theater Works, 1969)
The Knee Plays [from *the CIVIL warS*] (Theater Works, 1984)
Knee Plays and Other Acts (Benefit for The Kitchen, Theater Works, 1995)
KOOL – Dancing in my Mind (Theater Works, 2009, 2010)
Krapp's Last Tape (Theater Works, 2009, 2010)
Lady from the Sea (Theater Works, 1998, 2006)
Landscapes [Louis] (Theater Works, 1964)
Leonce and Lena (Theater Works, 2004, 2005)
A Letter for Queen Victoria (Theater Works, 1974)
The Life and Death of Marina Abramović (Theater Works, 2011)
The Life and Times of Joseph Stalin (Theater Works, 1973)
The Life and Times of Sigmund Freud (Theater Works, 1969)
Lohengrin (Theater Works, 1991, 1998, 2006)
Lulu (Theater Works, 2011)
Macbeth (Theater Works, scheduled 2012)
Madama Butterfly (Theater Works, 1993, 2003, 2004, 2005, 2006, 2007, 2008, 2009, 2011)
The Magic Flute (Theater Works, 1991, 2004)
Makropulos Case (Theater Works, 2010)
The Malady of Death (Theater Works, 1991, 1996)
The Man in the Raincoat (Theater Works, 1981, 1987)
Le Martyre de Saint Sébastien (Theater Works, 1988)
De Materie (Theater Works, 1989)
Medea [Wilson/Bryars] (Theater Works, 1981, 1984)
Medée [Charpentier] (Theater Works, 1984)
The Meek Girl [Une Femme douce] (Theater Works, 1994)
Memorie della Terra Desolata (Solo Exhibitions and Installations, 1993)
Memory/Loss (Solo Exhibitions and Installations, 1993)
Mind Gap (Solo Exhibitions and Installations, 2011)
Modern Dance (Theater Works, 1965)
Moveable Seats (Solo Exhibitions and Installations, 2003)
Der Mond im Gras: einmal keinmal immer (Theater Works, 1994)
Monsters of Grace (Solo Exhibitions and Installations, 1993)
Monsters of Grace (Theater Works, 1998)
Monuments (Solo Exhibitions and Installations, 1992)
Mr. Bojangles' Memory (Film and Video Works, 1991)
Mr. Bojangles' Memory: og son of fire (Pompidou exhibition, Solo Exhibitions and Installations, 1992)
Never doubt I love (Solo Exhibitions and Installations, 2002)
Norma (Theater Works, 2011)
Notes for a Conversation on Dante (Selected Publications, 1993)
La Nuit d'Avant le Jour (Theater Works, 1989)
Oceanflight (Theater Works, 1998)
Oedipus Rex (Theater Works, 1996)
Opus 2 (Theater Works, 1966)
L'Orfeo (Theater Works, 2009)
Orlando (Theater Works, 1989, 1993, 1996, 2009)
Orphée et Euridice (Theater Works, 1999)
Osud (Theater Works, 2002, 2003)
Other Rooms, Other Voices (Audio Recordings, 1999)
Overture [KA MOUNTAIN AND GUARDenia TERRACE] (Theater Works, 1972, 1973)
Overture for a Deafman (Film and Video Works, 1971)
Overture to the Fourth Act of Deafman Glance (Theater Works, 1980, 1982, 1986, 1987)
Paris de Nuit (Catalogue), 1998
Parsifal (Theater Works, 1991, 2004, 2005)
Parzival [Dorst] (Theater Works, 1987)
Paul Landowski: le temple de l'homme (Solo Exhibitions and Installations, 1999)
Peer Gynt (Theater Works, 2005, 2006)
Pelléas et Mélisande (Theater Works, 1997, 2004)
Persephone (Theater Works, 1995)
POEtry (Theater Works, 2000)
Poles (Solo Exhibitions and Installations, 1967)
Portrait, Still Life, Landscape (Solo Exhibitions and Installations, 1993)
Program Prologue Now: Overture for a Deafman (Theater Works, 1971)
Prologue to a Letter for Queen Victoria (Gallery presentation, Theater Works, 1974)
Prologue to Deafman Glance (Theater Works, 1978)
Prometeo (Theater Works, 1997)
Prometheus (Theater Works, 2001)
Quartett [Müller] (Theater Works, 1987, 1988, 2006, 2009)
Reading/Performance 1969–1984 (Theater Works, 1985)
Relative Calm [Childs] (Theater Works, 1981)
Relative Light (Solo Exhibitions and Installations, 1998)
Relative Light (Performance, Theater Works, 2000)
Rescue [Laurie Anderson's *Meltdown*] (Theater Works, 1997)
Reservations (Reconfirmaton of) (Theater Works, 1976)
Das Rheingold (Theater Works, 2000, 2005, 2006)
Il ritorno d'Ulisse in patria (Theater Works, 2011)
Robert Wilson on Video (Solo Exhibitions and Installations, 2000)
Robert Wilson's Vision (Solo Exhibitions and Installations, 1991)
The Rooms of Seven Women (Solo Exhibitions and Installations, 1995)
Royaumont Residency (Selected Workshops, 1972)
RUMI – in the Blink of the Eye (Theater Works, 2007, 2008, 2009)
Saints and Singing (Theater Works, 1997)
Salomé (Theater Works, 1987)
Scourge of Hyacinths (Theater Works, 1999)
Shakespeare's Sonnets (Theater Works, 2009)
Shirley, Keep Off (Theater Works, 1981)
Siegfried (Theater Works, 2001, 2006)
Silent Play (Theater Works, 1965)
Skin, Meat, Bones: The Wesleyan Project (Theater Works, 1994)
Slant (Film and Video Works, 1963)
Snow on the Mesa (Theater Works, 1995, 2011)
A Solo Reading (Theater Works, 1975)
The Spaceman (Film and Video Works, 1976, 1984)
Stations (Film and Video Works, 1982)
Swan Song (Theater Works, 1989)
The Temptation of St. Anthony (Theater Works, 2003, 2004, 2005)
The Tempatation of St. Anthony (Solo Exhibitions and Installations, 2003)
Theater Activity (1, 2, Theater Works, 1968)
The Threepenny Opera (Theater Works, 2007)
Three Rooms (Solo Exhibitions and Installations, 1994)
Three Sisters (Theater Works, 2001)
Time Rocker (Theater Works, 1996)
To Street: One Man Show (Theater Works, 1975)
Le Tombeau de Suger (Solo Exhibitions and Installations, 2000)
The Tragedy of Hamlet, Prince of Denmark (Film and Video Works, 1994)
Transmutation of Archetypes: Medea & Parsifal (Solo Exhibitions and Installations, 1986)
T.S.E.: come under the shadow of this red rock (Theater Works, 1994)
Video 50 (Film and Video Works, 1978)
Video Portraits (Solo Exhibitions and Installations, 2009, 2010, 2011)
Villa Stuck (Solo Exhibitions and Installations, 1997)
VOOM Portraits (Solo Exhibitions and Installations, 2005, 2006, 2007, 2008)
Waco Door (Solo Exhibitions and Installations, 1997)
Walking (Solo Exhibitions and Installations, 2008)
Die Walküre (Theater Works, 2001 2005, 2006)
Wallpaper Magazine (Selected Publications, 2010)
Water Jug Boy (Solo Exhibitions and Installations, 1996)
Watermill (Film and Video Works, 1970)
Watermill (Performance/demonstration, Theater Works, 1971)
Watermill Quintet (Theater Works, 2011)
What Room: A Play for Three Minutes (Theater Works, 1990)
When We Dead Awaken (Theater Works, 1991)
White Raven (Theater Works, 1998)
White Town (Theater Works, 2003)
Wilson Wahn (Solo Exhibitions and Installations, 2001)
The Wind (Theater Works, 1998)
Wintermärchen (Theater Works, 2005)
Wings on Rock (Theater Works, 1998)
Winterreise (Theater Works, 2001)
Woyzeck (Theater Works, 2000, 2003)
Die wundersame Welt des Robert Wilson (Solo Exhibitions and Installations, 1992)
Z^2: the sleeping room of people who did not know each other (Solo Exhibitions and Installations, 2000)
Zeit Magazin (Selected Publications, 1991)

THEATER WORKS

All theater works are directed and designed by Robert Wilson unless otherwise noted; thus, Wilson's name is listed in production information only for additional functions he performed.

Full information on a production is given under the premiere date. Productions that continued into the following years (including tours) are listed under the year of the premiere, unless there is a significant gap in time between a premiere and later performances. Revivals and new productions are listed separately from the original production. For performance dates, spans only are given; performances may not have occurred on every date within the span.

2012 (scheduled)

Einstein on the Beach by Robert Wilson and Philip Glass; Lucinda Childs choreography. World tour January 1, 2012–January 31, 2013. The Power Center, University of Michigan, Ann Arbor, January 20–22 (preview). Opera Berlioz Le Corum, Montpellier, France, March 15 (preview), 17–18 (world premiere). The Barbican, London, May 4–13. Sony Center for the Performing Arts, Toronto, June 7–9. Brooklyn Academy of Music Opera House, Brooklyn, N.Y., September 14–23. Zellerbach Hall, Berkeley, Calif., October 26– 28. Het Muziektheater, Amsterdam, January, 5–12, 2013.

Macbeth by Giuseppe Verdi, Teatro Comunale di Bologna, dates to be announced.

2011

Il ritorno d'Ulisse in patria by Claudio Monteverdi. Director's collaborator, Giuseppe Frigeni; conductor, Rinaldo Allesandrini; scenic collaborator, Serge von Arx; costumes, Jacques Reynaud; lighting concept, Robert Wilson, design, A.J. Weissbard; dramaturg, Ellen Hammer. Teatro alla Scala, Milan, September 19_30, 2011.

The Life and Death of Marina Abramović. Concept Robert Wilson; co-creation, Marina Abramović; associate director, Ann-Christin Rommen; dramaturg, Wolfgang Wiens; music, Antony Hegarty; composer and music curator, William Basinski; costumes, Jacques Reynaud; lighting design, A.J. Weissbard; sound design, Nick Sagar. Manchester International Festival, Lowry Theater, Manchester, June 30–July 17, 2011.

Lulu by Frank Wedekind. Assistant director Ann-Christin Rommen; dramaturg, Jutta Ferbers; music, Lou Reed; costumes, Jacques Reynaud; scenic collaborator, Serge von Arx. Berliner Ensemble, Berlin, April 12, 2011 (premiere), Théâtre de la Ville, Paris, November 4–14, 2011.

I La Galigo (revival; see 2004 production). Fort Rotterdam, Makassar, Indonesia, April 23 and 24, 2011.

Snow on the Mesa (revival; see 1995 production). Lincoln Center, New York, March 15–20, 2011.

Watermill Quintet. Curation, Robert Wilson; music, Michael Galasso; lighting design, Robert Wilson and John Torres. Performers include Marianna Kavallieratos, Thanassis Akokkalidis, Derrick Ryan Claude Mitchell, Andrew Ondrejcak, Jason Akira Somma, and Carlos Soto. Guggenheim Works & Process, Guggenheim Museum, New York, March 13–14, 2011.

Norma by Vincenzo Bellini. Co-direction, Gudrun Hartmann; conductor Paolo Carignani; costumes, Moidele Bickel; lighting design, Robert Wilson; lighting A.J. Weissbard and Hans-Rudolf Kunz; scenic collaborator, Stephanie Engeln. Opernhaus Zürich, Zurich, February 27, 2011.

Madama Butterfly by Giacomo Puccini. Musical direction, Maurizio Benini. Opéra National de Paris, Paris, January 16–February 14, 2011.

2010

Makropulos Case by Karel Čapek. Co-direction, Ann-Christin Rommen; music, Aleš Březina; costumes, Jacques Reynaud; lighting design, Robert Wilson; lighting, A.J. Weissbard. Narodni Divadlo, Prague, November 18, 2010–February 1, 2011.

1433 – The Grand Voyage. Script, Ruo-Yu Liu; music, Ornette Coleman, Dickie Landry, and Chih-Chun Huang; costumes, Tim Yip; lighting concept, Robert Wilson; lighting design, A.J. Weissbard; aria design, Mei-Yun Tang; dramaturg, Sue Jane Stoker. Chiang Kai-Shek Cultural Center, Taipei, February 20–28, 2010.

Katya Kabanova by Leoš Janáček. Co-direction, Jean Yves Courregelongue; musical preparation and conducting, Tomas Netopil; chorus master, Martin Buchta; costumes, Yashi Tabassomi; lighting concept, Robert Wilson; lighting, A.J. Weissbard; dramaturgs, Beno Blachut and Ellen Hammer. Narodni Divado, Prague, June 26, 2010. Janáček Festival, Brno, Czech Republic, November 23, 2010.

30th Anniversary of Solidarność. Curation, Robert Wilson. Performers include Philip Glass, Sweet Honey in the Rock, Rufus Wainwright, Marianne Faithfull, and others. Gdańsk Shipyard, Gdańsk, Poland, August 31, 2010.

2009

Quartett (See 2006 version – same crew). 2009 Next Wave Festival, Brooklyn Academy of Music, New York, November 4–14, 2009.

L'Orfeo by Claudio Monteverdi. Direction collaborator, Giuseppe Frigeni; conductor, Rinaldo Allesandrini; costumes, Jacques Reynaud; lighting concept, Robert Wilson, design, A.J. Weissbard; scenic collaborator, Serge von Arx. Teatro alla Scala, Milan, September 19– October 6, 2009.

RUMI – in the Blink of the Eye. Ravenna Festival, Ravenna, July 15–17, 2009.

St. John's Passion by Johann Sebastian Bach. Musical direction, Rolf Beck; choreography, Lucinda Childs; costumes, Frida Parmeggiani; lighting Xavier Baron. Das Schleswig-Holstein Musik Festival, Opernhaus Kiel, Kiel, July 9, 2009.

Krapp's Last Tape by Samuel Beckett. Costumes, Yashi Tabassomi; lighting concept, Robert Wilson; lighting, A.J. Weissbard; performed by Robert Wilson. Spoleto Festival, Teatro Caio Melisso; Spoleto, June 28, 2009. Grand Théâtre de Luxembourg, Luxembourg, September 23, 2009. Teatro Mercadante, Naples, October 22–24, 2009. Teatro Comunale, Ferrara, November 18, 2009. Festival Internacional de Teatro de Bogota, Bogota, March 19–21, 2010. Teatro Mercadante, Naples, March 19–21, 2010. IME Theatre, Athens, May 8–9, 2010. National Theater of Korea, Seoul, September 24–26, 2010. Teatro Valle, Rome, October 10–11, 2010. Teatr Wielkl, Lodz, November 20–21, 2010. Teatro São Paulo, Porto Alegre, Brazil, September 23–25, 2011.

St. John's Passion by Johann Sebastian Bach; music director and conductor, Rolf Beck; Lithuanian National Opera and Ballet Theatre's symphony orchestra and chorus; costumes, Frida Parmeggiani; performance by Lucinda Childs. Vilnius Festival, Lithuanian National Opera and Ballet Theatre, Vilnius, June 14, 2009.

Der Freischütz by Carl Maria von Weber. Musical director, Thomas Hengelbrock; costumes, Viktor & Rolf; lighting, Robert Wilson. Festspielhaus Baden-Baden, Baden-Baden, May 31, 2009.

The Threepenny Opera by Bertolt Brecht. Music, Kurt Weill; performed by The Berliner Ensemble. Bergen International Festival, Bergen, May 30, 2009. Théâtre de la Ville, Paris, September 15–18, 2009. Pallas Theatre, Athens, January 14–17, 2010. Théâtre de la Ville, Paris, April 1–4, 2010.

KOOL – Dancing in my Mind. Guggenheim Museum, New York, April 17, 2009. Guild Hall, Easthampton, August 9, 2009. Akademie der Kunste, Berlin August 26–September 12, 2010. Jerome Robbins Theater, New York, December 9, 2010

Shakespeare's Sonnets (based on Shakespeare's *Sonnets*). Music, Rufus Wainwright. Berliner Ensemble, Berlin, April 12, 2009. Festival di Spoleto, Spoleto. June 25–27, 2010. Festival d'automne en Normandie, Rouen, November 22–23, 2010.

Götterdämmerung by Richard Wagner. Conductor, Phillipe Jordan; costumes, Frida Parmeggiani; lighting, Robert Wilson. Opernhaus Zürich, Zurich, March 15, 2009.

Siegfried by Richard Wagner. Musical director, Philippe Jordan; costumes, Frida Parmeggiani; lighting, Andreas Fuchs and Robert Wilson. Opernhaus Zürich, Zurich, March 8, 2009.

Orlando by Virginia Woolf. National Theater, Taipei, February 21–March 1, 2009.

Madama Butterfly by Giacomo Puccini. Musical direction, Vello Pahn; chorus direction, Alessandro Di Stefano. Opera National de Paris, Paris, January 29–March 4, 2009.

Aida by Giuseppe Verdi. Choreography, Jonah Bokaer; music conductor, Daniel Oren; chorus director, Andrea Giorgi; costumes, Jacques Reynaud. Teatro Dell'Opera di Roma, Rome, January 20–30, 2009.

2008

RUMI – in the Blink of the Eye. Teatr Wielki, Warsaw, February 22–24, 2008.

The Threepenny Opera by Bertolt Brecht. Music, Kurt Weill. Stavovské Divadlo, Prague, October 31, November 31, 2008. Spoleto Festival, Spoleto, July 5–6, May 24–25, 2008.

Das Rheingold by Richard Wagner. Opernhaus Zürich, Zurich, September 14, 19, 26, 2008. **Die Walküre**: November 20, 26, 2008.

Faust by Charles Gounod. Associate stage director, Jean-Yves Courregelongue; choreography, Jonah Bokaer; conductor, Gabriel Chmura; costumes, Jaques Reynaud with associate costume designer, Yashi Tabassomi; associate scenic designer, Serge Von Arx; performed by the Ballet and Orchestra of the Polish National Opera. Opera Narodowa, Warsaw, October 26, 2008.

Madama Butterfly by Giacomo Puccini. Conductor, James Conlon; associate conductor and chorus master, Grant Gershon. Los Angeles Opera, Los Angeles, October 1–18, 2008.

Happy Days [Oh les beaux jours] by Samuel Beckett. Costumes, Jacques Reynaud; lighting design, Robert Wilson; lighting, A.J. Weissbard. Grand Theatre du Luxembourg, Luxembourg, September 24, 26, 2008. Spoleto Festival, Teatro Caio Melisso, Spoleto, June 27, 2009. Teatro Metastasio, Prato, November 4–8, 2009. Teatro Comunale, Ferrara, November 19–22, 2009. Teatro Mercadante, Naples, November 25–December 6, 2009. Teatro Piccini, Bari, December 9 –13, 2009. Teatro Donizetti, Bergamo, December 15–20, 2009. Teatro Peroglesi, Jesi, January 15–16, 2010. Teatro Fraschini, Pavia, January 19–21, 2010. Teatro Sociale, Como, January 23–24, 2010. Landestheater, St. Polten, January 28–29, 2010. Teatro Giacosa, Aosta, February 3–4, 2010. Teatro Ponchielli, Cremona, February 6–7, 2010. Teatro Municipale, Piacenza, February 16–17, 2010. Teatro São Pedro, Porto Alegre, September 9–11, 2010. Théâtre Athénée, Paris, September 23–October 10, 2010, Teatro Stehler, Milan, November 9–14, 2010. Teatro Santiago de Mil, Santiago, January 27–30, 2011.

Madama Butterfly by Giacomo Puccini. Conductor, Alexander Vedernikov; chorus master, Valery Borisov. The State Academic Bolshoi Theatre of Russia, Moscow, September 18–21, 2008.

The Lady from the Sea by Henrik Ibsen. Adaptation, Susan Sontag; music, Michael Galasso; costumes, Giorgio Armani; lighting, A.J. Weissbard and Robert Wilson. Matadero, Madrid, March 27–April 27, 2008. Teatro Lope de Vega, Sevilla, March 12–15, 2008.

RUMI – in the Blink of the Eye (based on a poem by Mewlana Djalal-od-Din-Rumi). Original idea, Robert Wilson and Kudsi Erguner; assistant director and stage manager, Sue Jane Stoker; music, Kudsi Erguner; costumes, Christophe de Menil; lighting design, A.J. Weissbard and Robert Wilson; sound design, Peter Cerone; scenic and visual design collaborator, Serge von Arx. Teatr Wielki, Warsaw, February 22–24, 2008.

I La Galigo (based on Bugis' epic poem "Sureq Galigo"). Text adaptation and dramaturgy, Rhoda Grauer; assistant director, Rama Soeprapto; dance master, Andi Ummu Tunru; music, Rahayu Supanggah; costumes, Yusman Siswandi and Airlangga Komara; lighting concept, Robert Wilson; lighting design, A.J. Weissbard. Taipei International Theatre Festival, Taipei, Taiwan, August 7–10, 2008. Teatro degli Arcimboldi, Milano, February 12–17, 2008.

Die Frau ohne Schatten by Richard Strauss. Assistant directors, Giuseppe Frigeni and Marina Frigeni; musical director, Gustav Kuhn; choir master Alessandro di Stefano; costumes Moidele Bickel; lighting, Robert Wilson and Andreas Fuchs; scenic collaborator, Christophe Martin. Opera National de Paris, Paris, January 21, 2008.

2007

RUMI – in the Blink of the Eye. Pallas Theater, Athens, May 28, 2007.

The Temptation of Saint Anthony (based on Gustave Flaubert). Adaptation, Robert Wilson and Bernice Johnson Reagon. Teatro degli Arcimboldi, Milano, December 11–16, 2007.

Jo Kondo & Robert Wilson. Music, Jo Kondo; conductor, Charles Wuorinen; performed by Group for Contemporary Music. Guggenheim Museum, New York, November 18, 19, 2007.

Les Fables de La Fontaine (based on Jean de La Fontaine's *Anthology*). Associate baroque choreographer, Béatrice Massin; associate choreographer, David Krugel; music, Michael Galasso; costumes, Moidele Bickel; dramaturg, Ellen Hammer. Comédie-Française, Paris, October 17, 18, 2007.

The Temptation of Saint Anthony (based on Gustave Flaubert). Adaptation, Robert Wilson and Bernice Johnson Reagon. Arts Centre,–State Theatre, at the Victorian Arts Centre, Melbourne, October 11–14, 2007.

Les Fables de La Fontaine (based on Jean de La Fontaine's *Anthology*). Associate baroque choreographer, Béatrice Massin; associate choreographer, David Krugel; music, Michael Galasso; costumes, Moidele Bickel; dramaturg, Ellen Hammer. Lincoln Center Festival, New York State Theater, Lincoln Center, New York, July 10–15, 2007.

St. John's Passion by Johann Sebastian Bach. Music director and conductor, Rolf Beck; Lithuanian National Opera and Ballet Theatre's symphony orchestra and chorus; costumes, Frida Parmeggiani; performance by Lucinda Childs. Vilnius Festival, Lithuanian National Opera and Ballet Theatre, Vilnius, June 14–15, 2007.

RUMI – in the Blink of the Eye (based on a poem by Mewlana Djalal-od-Din-Rumi). Original idea, Robert Wilson and Kudsi Erguner; assistant director and stage manager, Sue Jane Stoker; music, Kudsi Erguner; costumes, Christophe de Menil; lighting design, A.J. Weissbard and Robert Wilson; sound design, Peter Cerone; scenic and visual design collaborator, Serge von Arx. Attiki Cultural Society's spring theater festival, Pallas Theater, Athens, May 28–31, 2007.

Madama Butterfly by Giacomo Puccini. Het Muziektheater, Amsterdam, March 9–April 11, 2007.

St. John's Passion by Johann Sebastian Bach. Music director and conductor, Rolf Beck. Théâtre du Châtelet, Paris, April 2007.

The Threepenny Opera by Bertolt Brecht. Music, Kurt Weill; assistant director Ann-Christin Rommen; dramaturg, Jutta Ferbers and Anika Bardos; musical direction, Hans-Jorn Brandenburg and Stefan Rager; costumes, Jacques Reynaud; lighting concept, Robert Wilson; lighting, Andreas Fuchs; assistant scenic designer, Serge von Arx. Berliner Ensemble, Berlin, September 27, 2007 (premiere).

2006

Quartett by Heiner Müller. Music, Michael Galasso; costumes, Frida Parmeggiani; lighting design, Robert Wilson; lighting, A.J. Weissbard; starring Isabelle Huppert. Odéon Théâtre de l'Europe, Paris, September 28–December 2, 2006.

Erwartung/Deafman Glance by Arnold Schöenberg. Musical direction, Daniel Barenboim; costumes, Moidele Bickel; lighting design, Robert Wilson. Staatsoper Unter den Linden, Berlin, September 2, 3, 10, 2006.

The Lady from the Sea by Henrik Ibsen. Direction and co-lighting, Robert Wilson; text adaptation, Susan Sontag; music, Michael Galasso; costumes, Giorgio Armani; lighting design, Robert Wilson; lighting, A.J. Weissbard and Robert Wilson. Dramatyczny Theater, Warsaw, May 16–19, 2006.

The Black Rider: The Casting of the Magic Bullets (based on *Der Freischütz* by August Apel and Friedrich Laun, and on *The Fatal Marksman* by Thomas de Quincey). Adaptation, Robert Wilson, Tom Waits (music/lyrics) and William S. Burroughs (text). Ahmanson Theater, Los Angeles, April 22–July 11, 2006.

Lohengrin by Richard Wagner, (revival; see also 1991 Zurich production). Musical direction, James Levine; costumes, Frida Parmeggiani; lighting, Heinrich Brunke. Metropolitan Opera, New York City, April 17, 20, 24, 29, May 3, 6, 2006.

Peer Gynt by Henrik Ibsen. Music, Michael Galasso; costumes and make up, Jaques Reynaud. Brooklyn Academy of Music, Brooklyn, New York, April 11, 13–16, 2006.

Aida by Giuseppe Verdi. Festspielhaus Winter Festival, Baden-Baden, February 22, 24, 26, 2006.

Der Ring des Nibelungen by Richard Wagner. Musical director, Christoph Eschenbach. Théâtre du Châtelet, Paris, **Das Rheingold**: March 30, April 8; **Die Walküre**: April 1, 10; **Siegfried**: January 26, 31 February 5, 8, April 3, 12; **Götterdämmerung**: January 28, February 2, 12, 15, April 6, 15.

Madama Butterfly by Giacomo Puccini. Performed by Patricia Racette and Vladimir Chernov, Los Angeles Opera, January 1–February 29, 2006. Performed by Liping Zhang/Hui He and Marco Berti, Opéra Bastille, Paris, January 21–February 28, 2006.

2005

I La Galigo (based on Bugis' epic poem). Lincoln Center Festival, New York, July 13–16, 2005. Teater Tanah Airku, Jakarta, December 10-12, 2005.

Parsifal by Richard Wagner. Conductor, Kent Nagano. Performance by Placido Domingo. Dorothy Chandler Pavilion, Los Angeles Opera, November 26, 30, December 3, 8, 11, 14, 17, 2005.

The Temptation of Saint Anthony (based on Gustave Flaubert). Adaptation, Robert Wilson and Bernice Johnson Reagon. Opera de Paris, Palais Garnier, November 24–December 16, 2005. European tour May 13–29, 2005.

Der Ring des Nibelungen: Das Rheingold and Die Walküre by Richard Wagner. Musical director, Christoph Eschenbach. Théâtre du Châtelet, Paris, **Das Rheingold**: October 19, 23, 25, November 1; **Die Walküre**: October 21, 27, 30, November 5, 2005.

Wintermärchen [A Winter's Tale] by William Shakespeare. Berliner Ensemble, Berlin, September 24 (premiere); March 10–12, 2005. Ruhrfestspiele, Recklinghausen, Germany, May 17, 18, 19, 20, 21, 2005.

Madama Butterfly by Giacomo Puccini. Bolshoi Theatre, Moscow, Russia, September 5, 6, 7, 8; April 10, 11, 12, 2005.

2 Lips and Dancers and Space. Choreography, Robert Wilson; music, Michael Galasso; costumes, Viktor & Rolf; text, Christopher Knowles; performed by Netherlands Dance Theater III. Forum am Schlosspark, Ludwigsburg, Germany, February 24–25, 2005. Het Muziektheater, Amsterdam, May 27–29, June 2, 3, 2005. Roman Theater, Verona, July 8, 9, 2005.

Peer Gynt by Henrik Ibsen. Music, Michael Galasso; costumes and make up, Jaques Reynaud. Det Norske Teatret, Oslo, February 19 (premiere)–April 23, 2005. Bergen International Festival, Norway, May 26–June 4, 2005.

The Black Rider: The Casting of the Magic Bullets (based on *Der Freischütz* by August Apel and Friedrich Laun, and on *The Fatal Marksman* by Thomas de Quincey). Adaptation, Robert Wilson, Tom Waits (music/lyrics) and William S. Burroughs (text). Sydney Theatre at Walsh Bay, Australia, January 8–22, 2005.

Les Fables de La Fontaine (based on Jean de La Fontaine's *Anthology*). Comédie-Française, Paris, November 12, 2004–March 3, June 6–20. September 13–January 28, 2006.

Leonce and Lena by Georg Büchner. Music, Herbert Grönemeyer. Berliner Ensemble Theater am Schiffbauerdamm, Berlin. 2005

2004

2 Lips and Dancers and Space. Choreography, Robert Wilson; music, Michael Galasso; costumes, Viktor & Rolf; text, Christopher Knowles. Theatre de la Ville, Luxembourg, November 10–11, 2004. Paleis voor Schone Kunsten, Brussels, November 18, 19, 2004. Städtische Bühnen Frankfurt, November 26–28, 2004.

The Temptation of St. Anthony (based on Gustave Flaubert). Adaptation, Robert Wilson and Bernice Johnson Reagon. Brooklyn Academy of Music, New York, October 19–24, 2004. Watermill Fall Benefit Performance, October 20, 2004.

Aida by Giuseppe Verdi. Théâtre de la Monnaie, Brussels, October 9 (premiere)–October 31, 2004.

Pelléas et Mélisande by Claude Debussy. Text, Maurice Maeterlinck; costumes, Frida Parmeggiani; lighting, Heinrich Brunke and Robert Wilson. Opéra Bastille, September 13 (premiere), 16, 20, 23, 25, 29, October 2, 2004.

Parsifal by Richard Wagner. Hamburg Staatsoper, September 12–October 10, 2004.

The Black Rider: The Casting of the Magic Bullets (based on *Der Freischütz* by August Apel and Friedrich Laun, and on *The Fatal Marksman* by Thomas de Quincey). Adaptation, Robert Wilson, Tom Waits (music/lyrics) and William S. Burroughs (text). Barbican Centre, London, May 17, 2004 (premiere). American Conservatory Theatre, San Francisco, August 26 (premiere)–October 10, 2004.

Die Zauberflöte by Wolfgang Amadeus Mozart. Opéra Bastille, Paris, June 23, 2004 (premiere).

I La Galigo (based on Bugis' epic poem). Esplanade Theatres on the Bay, Singapore Festival, Singapore, March 12, 2004 (premiere). Het Muziektheater, Amsterdam, May 12, 14, 15, 2004. Forum Barcelona 2004, Teatre Lliure, Barcelona, May 20–23, 2004. Festival Les Nuits de Fourvière, June 8–10, 2004. Ravenna Festival, Ravenna, June 18–20, 2004.

Madama Butterfly by Giacomo Puccini. Musical direction, Kent Nagano. Los Angeles Opera, February 12 (premiere), 15, 18, 21, 24, 26, 27, 29, March 4, 7, 12, 14, 2004.

Les Fables de La Fontaine (based on Jean de La Fontaine's *Anthology*). Comédie-Française, Salle Richelieu, Paris, January 30, 2004 (premiere).

Alceste by Christoph Willibald Gluck. Théâtre de la Monnaie, Brussels, January 23 (premiere), 25, 27, 29, February 1, 3, 5, 7, 10, 2004.

Leonce und Lena by Georg Büchner. Music, Herbert Grönemeyer. Berliner Ensemble Theater am Schiffbauerdamm, Berlin, Maifestspiele in Wiesbaden on May 26–27, 2004.

2003

Die Frau ohne Schatten by Richard Strauss. Opéra Bastille, Paris, December 9, 2003–January 8, 2004.

Aida by Giuseppe Verdi. Royal Opera House, Covent Garden, London, November 8 (premiere), 11, 14, 17, 20, 22, 26, 28, 2003.

Osud by Leoš Janáček. Teatro Real, Madrid, November 1 (premiere), 4, 6, 9, 11, 14, 16, 19, 2003.

White Town. Music by Hall Willner. Bellevue Teatret, Copenhagen, October 24–November 7, 2003.

Madama Butterfly by Giacomo Puccini. Het Muziektheater, Netherlands Opera, Amsterdam, October 1–23, 2003, January 13–31, 2004.

Woyzeck by Georg Büchner. Interpretation with music, Tom Waits and K. Brennan. The Barbican Centre, London, September 27–30, October 1–5, 2003. Romaeuropa Festival, Teatro Valle, Rome, October 11–13, 2003. MESS Sarajevo Festival, Sarajevo, Bosnia, October 18, 19, 2003. Brooklyn Academy of Music (BAM), New York, October 29–31, November 1–16, 2003. Freud Playhouse, UCLA, Los Angles, December 3–15, 2003.

The Temptation of St. Anthony (based on Gustave Flaubert). Ruhr Triennale, Gebläsehalle Duisburg Nord, Germany, June 20–July 6, 2003. Marseille, France, July 11–12, 2003. Festival di Ortigia, Amphitheatre, Siracuse, Italy, July 18–20, 2003. Festival di Perlada, Perlada, Spain, August 6, 2003. Festival de Santander, Palacio de Festivales de Cantabria, Santander, Spain, August 10, 2003. Sadler's Wells, London, September 11–15, 2003.

Leonce and Lena by Georg Büchner. Music, Herbert Grönemeyer. Berliner Ensemble Theater am Schiffbauerdamm, Berlin, May 1 (premiere), August 22–28, 2003, September 26–October 2, 10–12, 2003.

2002

Götterdämmerung by Richard Wagner. Musical direction, Franz Welser-Möst; costumes, Frida Parmeggiani; lighting, Robert Wilson and Andreas Fuchs. Opernhaus Zürich, Zurich, May 20, 2002 (premiere).

Osud. Music by Leoš Janáček. Musical direction, Jiři Bělohlávek; costumes, Jacques Reynaud; lighting, A. J. Weissbard. National Theatre, Prague, April 19, 2002 (premiere).

Doctor Caligari by Robert Wilson (based on the film *Das Kabinett des Dr. Caligari* by Carl Mayer, Hans Janowitz and Robert Wiene). Music, Michael Galasso; costumes, Jacques Reynaud; lighting, Urs Schönebaum and Robert Wilson. Deutsches Theater, Berlin, March 26, 2002 (premiere).

Aida by Giuseppe Verdi. Musical direction, Antonio Pappano; chorus direction, Renato Balsadonna; costumes, Jacques Reynaud. Théâtre La Monnaie, Brussels, January 30–February 20, 2002.

2001

Siegfried by Richard Wagner. Musical direction, Franz Weiser-Möst; costumes, Frida Parmeggiani; lighting, Robert Wilson and Andreas Fuchs. Opernhaus Zürich, Zurich, November 18, 22, 25, 29, December 2, June 6, 2001.

Winterreise. Music by Franz Schubert. Costumes, Yves Saint Laurent. Performed by Jessye Norman and Mark Markham. Théâtre du Châtelet, Paris, September 24–27, 2001.

Three Sisters by Anton Chekhov. Co-direction, Ann-Christin Rommen; music, Michael Galasso; costumes and makeup, Jacques Reynaud; lighting, Andreas Fuchs and Robert Wilson; sound, Ronald Hallgren. Stadsteater, Stockholm, September 12, 2001 (premiere).

Einstein on the Beach (non-Wilson production) by Robert Wilson and Philip Glass. Direction, Berthold Schneider; musical direction, Benjamin Meyers; exhibition concept, Veronika Witte; choreography, Tino Sehgal; costumes, Nina Thorwart. Staatsbank Französische Strasse, Berlin, August 22, 24, 26, 29, 31, 2001.

Die Walküre by Richard Wagner. Costumes, Frida Parmeggiani; lighting, Robert Wilson and Andreas Fuchs. Opernhaus Zürich, Zürich, May 27–June 22, 2001.

Prometheus by Robert Wilson. Music, Iannis Xenakis; musical direction, Alexandros Myrat; costumes, Franca Squarciapino; lighting, A. J. Weissbard and Robert Wilson; video images, Peter Cerone. Athens Concert Hall (Cultural Olympics 2001–2004), Athens, January 27–31, 2001. Peter B. Lewis Theater, Guggenheim Museum (Works and Process at the Guggenheim), June 28, 2001 [*Knee Play 2* and Act II only].

2000

Woyzeck by Georg Büchner. Adaptation, Wolfgang Wiens and Ann-Christin Rommen; music and lyrics, Tom Waits and Kathleen Brennan; costumes, Jacques Reynaud. Betty Nansen Teatret, Copenhagen, November 18, 2000–January 27, 2001. Berliner Ensemble, Berlin, September 1–8, 2001. Dramaten Theater, Stockholm, September 22–23, 2001. Gaiety Theatre (Eircom Dublin Theatre Festival), Dublin, October 3–6, 2001. Wroclaw, Poland, October 13–14, 2001. Teatro Zarzuela (Festival de Otoño), Madrid, November 2–4, 2001. TNT Théâtre de la Cité, Toulouse, November 9–11, 2001. Odéon-Théâtre de l'Europe, Paris, November 30–December 9, 2001.

Relative Light by Robert Wilson. Music by Johann Sebastian Bach and John Cage; violin solo, Nurit Pacht; costumes, Christophe de Menil; lighting, A.J. Weissbard. Le Manège (Via Festival), Maubeuge, France, March 23–25, 2000 [preview, titled *Commandment*]. Claustro de la Universidad de Valencia (Institut Valencià de la Música), Valencia, Spain, July 11–15, 2000. Auditorio Alfredo Kraus (Festival de Otoño de Teatro y Danza de Las Palmas de Gran Canaria), Las Palmas de Gran Canaria, Canary Islands, October 29, 2000 (premiere). Teatro Olimpico (Accademia Filarmonica Romana, Romaeuropa Festival), Rome, October 18–21, 2001.

Das Rheingold by Richard Wagner. Costumes, Frida Parmeggiani; lighting, Robert Wilson and Andreas Fuchs. Opernhaus Zürich, Zurich, October 8–November 17, 2000; May 24, June 1, 2002.

Hot Water by Robert Wilson. Performed by BARTO; costumes, Susanne Rauschig and Dorothée Uhrmacher; lighting design, Urs Schönebaum; video design, Chris Kondek; stage architect, Christophe Martin. Singapore Institute of Management Auditorium (New Inspiration, Singapore Arts Festival 2000), Singapore, June 14–22, 2000.

POEtry by Robert Wilson and Lou Reed. Based on the works of Edgar Allan Poe; text, lyrics and music, Lou Reed; costumes and makeup, Jacques Reynaud; lighting, Heinrich Brunke. Thalia Theater, Hamburg, February 13, 18–21, 24–27, 29, March 1, 3, 4, 5, November 23–26, 2000. Grande salle, Odéon Théâtre de l'Europe, Paris, December 12–22, 2000. Het Muziektheater, Amsterdam, May 9–12, 2001. Brooklyn Academy of Music, New York City, November 27–December 8, 2001.

1999

Orphée et Euridice by Christoph Willibald Gluck; musical direction, Sir John Eliot Gardiner; text, Pierre-Louis Moline (after Ranieri de' Calzabigi); costumes, Frida Parmeggiani; lighting, A.J. Weissbard. Théâtre du Châtelet, Paris, October 8, 11, 14, 17, 20, 23, 1999.

Alceste by Chrisoph Willibald Gluck, (revival; see also 1990 Chicago production, 1986 Stuttgart production). Musical direction, Sir John Eliot Gardiner; text, Roullet (after Ranieri de' Calzabigi); costumes, Frida Parmeggiani; lighting, A.J. Weissbard. Théâtre du Châtelet, Paris, October 9, 12, 15, 18, 21, 24, 1999.

THE DAYS BEFORE: death, destruction & detroit III by Robert Wilson. Texts, Umberto Eco and Christopher Knowles; music, Ryuichi Sakamoto; costumes, Jacques Reynaud. Teatro Comunale, Modena, June 19, 1999 (preview). New York State Theater (Lincoln Center Festival), New York City, July 7–10, 1999. Teatro de Madrid (Festival de Otoño), Madrid, November 18–21, 1999. Rivoli Teatro Municipal (Porto Natal Teatro Internacional), Oporto, Portugal, December 3–4, 1999. Büyük Salon, Atatürk Cultural Center (Istanbul International Theatre Festival), Istanbul, May 26–28, 2000. Auditorio de Galicia (Compostela Millenium Festival), Santiago de Compostela, Spain, August 12–14, 2000.

Scourge of Hyacinths. Music by Tania León; text, Tania León and Wole Soyinka (after the work by Wole Soyinka); costumes, Susanne Raschig; lighting, Andreas Fuchs and Robert Wilson. Salle Théodore Turrettini, Bâtiment des Forces Motrices, Genève, December 10, 1998 [Journée du 50e Anniversaire de la Déclaration Universelle des Droits de l'Homme, excerpts, with reading of text by Robert Wilson], January 17 [Geneva Opera Pool], January 19, 21, 23, 25, 27, 29, 31, February 1, 3, 4, 1999. Opéra de Nancy, Nancy, France, February 23, 25, 26, 1999. Festspielhaus St. Pölten, St. Pölten, Austria, March 19 (premiere). Palacio de Bellas Artes, Mexico City, March 6–8, 2001.

1998

70 ANGELS ON THE FAÇADE: Domus 1928–1998. Texts, Lisa Ponti and Christopher Knowles; costumes, Jacques Reynaud; lighting, A.J. Weissbard; sound, Peter Cerone; sets and images, Peter Bottazzi. Nuovo Piccolo Teatro, Milan, December 1–3, 1998.

Ett Drömspel [Dream Play] by August Strindberg. Music, Michael Galasso; costumes, Jacques Reynaud. Stadsteater, Stockholm, November 15, 19, 20–22, 26–29, December 4–6, 11–13, 26, 27, 1998; January 5–8, 13–15, 20, 21, March 20, 21, 27, 28, April 1, 5, 20, 21, 24, 25, 1999; October 19–22, 2000. Ruhr Festspielhaus (Ruhrfestspiele Recklinghausen, 9. Europäisches Festival), Recklinghausen, Germany, May 14 (preview), May 15–16, 1999. Théâtre de Nice, Nice, France, November 19–20, 1999. Burswood Theatre (Perth International Arts Festival), Perth, Australia, February 5–8, 2000. Salle Jean Vilar, Palais de Chaillot (Théâtre National de Chaillot), Paris, March 11–17, 2000. Brooklyn Academy of Music, Howard Gilman Opera House, New York City November 28–30, December 1–2, 2000. Moscow Art Theater (Theatre Olympics), Moscow, April 28–29, 2001. Barbican Centre, London, May 29–31, June 1–2, 2001.

O Corvo Branco [White Raven] by Robert Wilson and Philip Glass. Music, Philip Glass; text, Luísa Costa Gomes. Musical direction, Dennis Russell Davies; costumes, Moidele Bickel; lighting, Heinrich Brunke. Sala Júlio Verne, Teatro Camões (Expo '98), Lisbon, September 26, 28, 29, 1998. Teatro Real, Madrid, November 28, 30, December 1, 3, 4, 5. Carnegie Hall (American Composers Orchestra), New York City, February 27, 2000 [Act V, concert version only, with narration by Robert Wilson]. New York State Theater (Lincoln Center Festival), New York City, July 10–14, 2001.

The Wind (reading by Robert Wilson and Christopher Knowles). Text by Christopher Knowles. Longhouse, East Hampton, New York, August 15, 1998.

Dantons Tod [Danton's Death] by Georg Büchner (revival – see also Houston production, 1992). Text by Georg Büchner; mMusic, Thierry de Mey; costumes, Frida Parmeggiani; lighting, Heinrich Brunke. Landestheater (Salzburger Festspiele), Salzburg, July 25, 27, 28, 29, 31, August 3, 4, 6, 7, 8, 10, 12, 15, 17, 18, 20, 1998. Berliner Ensemble, Berlin, October 3–5, 1998.

Donna del mare [Lady from the Sea] by Henrik Ibsen. Text adaptation, Susan Sontag; music, Michael Galasso; costumes, Giorgio Armani; lighting, A.J. Weissbard and Robert Wilson; performed by Dominique Sanda, and others. Teatro Comunale di Ferrara, Italy, May 5–10, 1998. Teatro Storchi, Modena, May 14–17. Teatro Nuovo, Udine, May 21–24, 1998. Muhsin Ertugrul Sahnesi, (Istanbul International Theatre Festival), Istanbul, May 30–31, 1998. Nuovo Piccolo Teatro [Piccole Grandi Magie], Milan, June 5–20, 1998. Teatro Ariosto, Reggio Emilia, Italy, January 8–10, 1999. Teatro Grande, Brescia, Italy, January 13–17, 1999. Teatro della Celebrazioni, Bologna, January 21–24, 1999. Teatro della Corte, Genova, January 28–31, 1999. Teatro Manzoni, Pistoia, Italy, February 4–7, 1999. Teatro Bonci, Cesena, Italy, February 11–14, 1999. Teatro Pergolesi, Jesi, Italy, February 18–21, 1999. Teatro Biondo, Palermo, February 25–March 7, 1999. Teatro Verdi, Salerno, March 11–14, 1999. La Luna (Festival international de théâtre), Maubeuge, France, March 19–20, 1999. Grand Salle, Maison des Arts et de la Culture André Malraux (EXIT: Festival International), Créteil, France, March 25–28, 1999. Munye Theatre, Main Hall (Seoul Theatre Festival 2000), Seoul, South Korea, August 27–September 3, 2000 [performed by Korean cast].

Wings on Rock (based on *The Little Prince* by Antoine de Saint-Exupéry). Music, Pascal Comelade; costumes, Kenzo Takada. Performed by François Chat and Marianna Kavallieratos. Teatro della Fortuna, Fano, Italy [preview], April 21–23, 1998. Théâtre Gérard Philipe (Festival de St. Denis), Paris, June 15–20, 1998. Teatro Adrià Gual, Barcelona, October 6–8, 1998. Politeama Rossetti, Trieste, October 21–25, 1998.

Monsters of Grace: A Digital Opera in Three Dimensions by Philip Glass and Robert Wilson. Design and visual concept, Robert Wilson; music, Philip Glass; lyrics, Rumi; musical direction, Michael Riesman; sound design, Kurt Munkacsi; film and computer animation, Kleiser-Walczak Construction Company. Royce Hall (UCLA Center for the Performing Arts), University of California, Los Angeles, April 15–26, 1998. Barbican Theatre [BITE: 98], London, May 19–23, 1998. Festival Castell de Peralada, Catalunya, Spain, July 24–26, 1998. Wolf Trap, Vienna, Virginia, September 9, 1998. Teatro Massimo Opera House, Palermo, October 7–11, 1998. Teatro Olimpico (Romeuropa Festiva), Rome, October 13–18, 1998. Deutsches Theater, Munich, October 20–25, 1998. Teatro Storchi, Modena, Italy, October 27–28, 1998. Teatro Politema, Naples, October 30–November 1, 3–7, 1998. Het Muziektheater, Amsterdam, November 11–14, 1998. Theater & Musikgesellschaft, Zug, Switzerland, November 21, 1998. Barbican Theatre, London, November 23, 1998. Belfast Festival, Belfast, November 25–28, 1998. Brooklyn Academy of Music Opera House, New York City, December 9–20, 1998. Miami Light Project, Miami Dade Community College, Miami, January 23, 1999. Van Wezel Performing Arts Hall, Sarasota, Florida [concert version], January 25, 1999. University of Florida, Gainesville, January 27, 1999. University of North Carolina, Chapel Hill, January 29–30, 1999. American Music Theater Festival, Philadelphia, February 2–5, 1999. McCarter Theater, Princeton, New Jersey, February 6–7, 1999. Mershon Auditorium, Wexner Center for the Arts, Columbus, Ohio, February 10, 1999. Madison Civic Center, Madison, Wisconsin, February 12, 1999. Northrup Auditorium, University of Minnesota, Minneapolis, February 13, 1999. Hancher Auditorium, University of Iowa, Iowa City, February 15, 1999. University of Nebraska, Lincoln, February 18, 1999. Miller Auditorium, Western Michigan University, Kalamazoo, February 20, 1999. Lied Center, University of Kansas, Lawrence, February 28, 1999. Folly Theater, William Jewell College, Liberty, Missouri, February 27, 1999. Krannert Center, University of Illinois, Urbana, March 2, 1999. Chicago Theater, Chicago, March 5–6, 1999. Bass Concert Hall, University of Texas, Austin, March 16, 1999. Cullen Theater (Society for the Performing Arts), Houston, Texas, March 18–21, 1999. Performing Arts Fort Worth, Fort Worth, Texas, March 22, 1999. Centennial Hall, University of Arizona, Tucson, March 25, 1999. Gammage Center, Arizona State University, Tempe, Arizona, March 27, 1999. Royce Hall, UCLA, Los Angeles, March 29, 1999. Arlene Schnitzer Concert Hall, Portland Institute for Contemporary Art, Portland, Oregon, April 7, 1999. University of California, Davis, April 11, 1999. Zellerbach Auditorium (Cal Performances), University of California, Berkeley, April 13–17, 1999. Michigan Theater (University Musical Society), Ann Arbor, Michigan, April 22, 1999. Roy Thompson Hall, Toronto, April 24–25, 1999.

Lohengrin by Richard Wagner (revival; see also 1991 Zürich production). Musical direction, James Levine; costumes, Frida Parmeggiani; lighting, Heinrich Brunke. Metropolitan Opera, New York City, March 9, 13, 17, 21, 25, 28, April 2, September 30, October 3, 6, 10, 14, 17, 22, 1998.

Der Ozeanflug [Oceanflight] by Bertolt Brecht. Music, Hans Peter Kuhn; costumes, Jacques Reynaud. Berliner Ensemble, Berlin, January 28–31, February 21–24, March 6–8, 30, 31, 1998. Palazzo dei Congressi (Taormina Arte), Taormina, Italy, April 17–18, 1998.

1997

Saints and Singing by Robert Wilson and Hans Peter Kuhn, after Gertrude Stein. Text, Gertrude Stein; music, Hans Peter Kuhn; costumes, Hans Thiemann; lighting, A.J. Weissbard and Robert Wilson. Hebbel Theater, Berlin, November 4, 1997 (premiere). Broadcast [Hebbel Theater performance of November 4], on Arte, November 18, 1997. Maysfield Leisure Centre, Belfast, November 20–22, 1997. Schaubühne am Lehniner Platz, Berlin, February 18, 19, 24–27, March 3–5, 24–26, 29, April 3–5, 11, 12, 26, 1998. Theater am Turm, Frankfurt am Main, February 4–8, 1998. La Filature, Mulhouse, France, March 12–14, 1998. MC 93 Bobigny, Paris, France, June 12–14, 16–21, 1998. De Singel, Antwerp, January 7–10, 1999. Cankarjev Dom, Ljubljana, Slovenia, January 16–18, 1999.

Rescue (benefit concert/performance, part of *Laurie Anderson's Meltdown on the South Bank*). Direction, Laurie Anderson; featuring Laurie Anderson, Christopher Knowles, Lou Reed, Robert Wilson, and others. Purcell Room, Queen Elizabeth Hall, London, June 26, 1997.

Prometeo: Tragedia dell'ascolto. Music by Luigi Nono, text, Massimo Cacciari; costumes, Stefan Hageneier; sound environment, André Richard. Halles de Schaerbeek (Festival Ars Musica, produced by La Monnaie), Brussels, March 4, 5, 6, 8, 9, 11, 12, 13, 1997.

Pelléas et Mélisande. Music, Claude Debussy; text, Maurice Maeterlinck; costumes, Frida Parmeggiani; lighting, Heinrich Brunke and Robert Wilson. Palais Garnier (Opéra National de Paris), Paris, February 7, 10, 15, 19, 21, 26, 28, March 2, 1997. Grosses Festspielhaus (Salzburg Festival), Salzburg, July 21, August 2, 10, 18, 23, 1997. Palais Garnier (Opéra National de Paris), Paris, September 29, October 3, 5, 8, 12, 14, 1997; May 16, 18, 22, 24, 28, 30, June 2, 2000.

1996

Jessye Norman Sings for the Healing of AIDS (benefit concert). Direction, George C. Wolfe; design, Robert Wilson. Riverside Church, New York City, December 4, 1996.

Oedipus Rex by Igor Stravinsky, with "Silent Prologue" by Robert Wilson. Music, Igor Stravinsky; text, Jean Cocteau. Théâtre du Châtelet, Paris , November 12, 14, 19, 21, 23, 1996. Royal Festival Hall, London, November 26 (concert version only, with Robert Wilson narrating with the Philharmonia Orchestra). Opernhaus Zürich, Zürich, December 15, 17, 19, 21, 27, 29, 1996; March 13, 15, 18, July 4, 5, 1997 (paired with *Bluebeard's Castle*).

Orlando (English version; see also French version, 1993; Danish and German versions, 1989) by Virginia Woolf. Performed by Miranda Richardson. Royal Lyceum The atre (Edinbugh Festival), Edinburgh, Scotland, August 13–17, 19–21, 1996.

G.A. Story: Giorgio Armani: la sua storia, la sua moda by Robert Wilson. Stazione Leopolda, Florence, Italy, June 21, 1996.

Time Rocker by Robert Wilson. Text, Darryl Pinckney; music and lyrics, Lou Reed. Thalia Theater, Hamburg, June 12, 1996 (premiere). Odéon-Théâtre de l'Europe, Paris, January 7–9, 1997. Het Muziektheater, Amsterdam, May 14, 18, 17, 1997. Thalia Theater, Hamburg, June 11, 12, 13, 1997. Theater am Pfalzbau, Ludwigshafen, Germany, October Brooklyn Academy of Music, New York City, November 14, 15, 16, 18, 22, 23, 1997. Thalia Theater, Hamburg, January 18–19, 1998. Teatro Municipal, Rio de Janeiro, Brazil, June 19, 1998 (premiere). Thalia Theater, Hamburg, March 2–4, 1999.

La Maladie de la mort [The Malady of Death] (revival, in French; see also German production, 1991) by Marguerite Duras. Performed by Lucinda Childs and Michel Piccoli. Théâtre Vidy-Lausanne, Lausanne, May 7–26, 1996. Museumsquartier, Halle E (Wiener Festwochen), Vienna, June 9–11, 1996. Ruhr Festspielhaus (Ruhrfestspiele Recklinghausen), Recklinghausen, Germany, June 20–23, 25–30, 1996. Le Volcan, Le Havre, March 7, 8, 9, 11, 12, 1997. Espace des Artes, Chalon sur Saône, France, March 18, 19, 20, 1997. Le Carré Saint Vincent, Scène Nationale d'Orléans, Orléans, France, March 26–29, 1997. Opéra du Rhin, Strasbourg, April 4–6, 8–12, 1997. Teatro della Corte, Genova, Italy, May 7, 8, 9, 10, 1997. Thalia Theater, Hamburg, May 17–20, 1997. Théâtre de Caen, Caen, France, May 28–31, 1997. Cultureel Centrum Amstelveen (Holland Festival), Amsterdam, June 6, 7, 8, 10, 1997. de Singel, Antwerp, June 16–18, 1997. Falconer Teatret, Copenhagen, June 25–27, 1997. MC 93 Bobigny (Festival d'automne), Paris, September 23–October 26, 1997. Peacock Theatre (French Theatre Season), London, November 5, 6, 8, 1997. Bonlieu, Annecy, France, November 14–16, 1997. Théâtre National de Bretagne, Rennes, France, ov.November 22–December 5, 1997. Théâtre National Populaire, Villeurbanne, France, December 11–14, 1997.

Four Saints in Three Acts by Virgil Thomson, music, and Gertrude Stein, text. Costumes, Francesco Clemente; lighting, Jennifer Tipton. Brown Theater (Houston Grand Opera), Houston, January 26, February 3, 7, 9, 1996. New York State Theater (Lincoln Center Festival), New York City, August 1–3, 1996. Edinburgh Playhouse (Edinburgh Festival), Edinburgh, Scotland, August 29–31, 1996. Teatro Nacional de São Carlos, Lisbon, February 20–27, 2002.

1995

the CIVIL warS: a tree is best measured when it is down – Rome Section (concert version–see also 1984). Carnegie Hall (American Composers Orchestra), New York City, December 3, 1995.

Snow on the Mesa (dance). Text by, Paul Schmidt; costumes, Donna Karan; performed by the Martha Graham Dance Company. Eisenhower Theater, Kennedy Center, Washington, D.C., November 2–5, 1995. City Center, New York City, November 9–12, 1995. Creteil Maison de la Culture, Paris, December 6–10, 1995. Vígszínház (Budapest Tavaszi Fesztivál), Budapest, April 10–11, 1996. Het Muziektheater, Amsterdam, April 17–18, 1996. Pittsburgh, September 19–21, 1996. Joyce Theater, New York City (excerpt, as part of *Duets for Martha*), February 2–21, 1999.

The Golden Windows [Die Goldenen Fenster] by Robert Wilson [non-Wilson production, licensed by Robert Wilson; see also orignial production, 1982; revivals 1985, 1988)]. Direction, Jens Nüssle; music, Stefan Hänlein and Jens Nüssle. Theater Galerie, Neckartailfingen, Germany, October–December, 1995.

Bluebeard's Castle/Erwartung by Bela Bartók (*Bluebeard's Castle*) and Arnold Schönberg (*Erwartung*). Großes Festspielhaus (Salzburger Festspiele), Salzburg, August 24, 27, 30, 1995. (see also *Oedipus Rex*, 1996, paired with *Bluebeard's Castle*, Zürich).

Persephone. Texts by Homer, Brad Gooch, Maita di Niscemi; music, Gioachino Rossini and Philip Glass; costumes, Christophe de Menil; lighting, A.J. Weissbard and Robert Wilson. John Drew Theater, Guildhall, East Hampton, New York, July 28–30, 1995 (previews). Ancient Stadium of Delphi (International Meeting of Ancient Greek Drama, Theatre Olympics), Delphi, Greece, August 27, 1995. Théâtre du Manège (Visas festival), Maubeuge, France, March 29–31, 1996. Rumeli Fortress (International Istambul Theatre Festival), Istambul, May 17–18, 1996. Römisches Amphitheater Petronell-Carnuntum (Art Carnuntum Welttheater-Festival), Vienna, August 23–24, 1996. Théâtre National Populaire, Villeurbanne, France, November 5–9, 1996. Saitama Arts Theater (Sai-no-kuni Autumn Festival of Performing Arts), Saitama, Japan, November 30–December 1, 1996. Palazzo dei Congressi, Taormina, Italy, January 7, 1997. CRDC, Nantes, France, January 14–17, 1997. Teatro Romano, Fiesole, Italy, July 3, 4, 5, 1997 (broadcast on RAI, September 7, 1997). Tollwood Festival, Munich, June 20–July 13, 1997. Teatro Politema, Naples, January 9–18, 1998. Teatro Nacional La Castellana (Festival de Bogotá), Bogotá, Colombia, March 27–30, 1998. Moscow Art Theater, Moscow, May 18–20, 1998. Luzerner Theater (Internationale Musikfestwochen Luzern), Lucerne, Switzerland, August 31, September 1, 2, 1999. Teatro Avenida, Buenos Aires, September 23–26, 1999. Teatro Juárez (Festival Cervantino), Guanajuato, Mexico, October 12–15, 1999. Igrexa de San Domingos de Bonaval (Compostela Millenium Festival), Santiago de Compostela, Spain, August 8–10, 2000.

HAMLET: a monologue (based on the play by William Shakespeare). Adaptation, Robert Wilson and Wolfgang Wiens; music, Hans Peter Kuhn; performed by Robert Wilson (solo). Alley Theatre, Houston, May 19–23, 1995 (previews), May 24–27, 1995. Teatro Goldoni (Venice Biennale), Venice, Italy, June 20–21, 1995. Alice Tully Hall, Lincoln Center (Serious Fun! festival), July 6–8, 1995. MC 93 Bobigny (Festival d'automne), Paris, September 16–19, 1995. MC 93 Bobigny, Paris, February 10–17, 1996. Teatro Central, Seville, Spain, March 1–3, 1996. Hebbel Theater, Berlin, March 21–26, 1996. Helsinki, Finland, August 18–20, 1996. Vienna, Austria, September 1–2, 1996. Théâtre National Populaire, Villeurbanne, France, November 18–22, 1996. Teatro Lirico (Piccolo Teatro di Milano), Milan, May 9, 10, 11, 1997. Teatr Narodowy, Warsaw, May 22, 23, 24, 25, 1997. Het Muziektheater (Holland Festival), Amsterdam, June 28–30, 1997. Schauspielhaus, Zürich (reading by Robert Wilson only), July 8, 1997. LongHouse Foundation, East Hampton, New York (reading by Robert Wilson only), August 8, 1997. Granship Shizuoka Arts Theatre (Theatre Olympics), Shizuoka, Japan, April 16, 17, 18, 19, 1999. Shizuoka Performing Arts Center, Shizuoka, Japan, April 28–30, 2000.

Knee Plays and Other Acts: A Gala Benefit for The Kitchen (version of *Skin, Meat, Bones: The Wesleyan Project*, 1994) by Robert Wilson and Alvin Lucier. Music, Alvin Lucier. Hudson Theater, New York City, March 4, 1995.

1994

Der Mond im Gras: einmal keinmal immer by Robert Wilson (based on stories by the Brothers Grimm and Georg Büchner). Music, Robyn Schulkowsky. Münchner Kammerspiele, Munich, April 10–21, 1994.

Hanjo/Hagoromo: Dittico Giapponese by Yukio Mishima (*Hanjo*) and Zeami (*Hagoromo*). Music and libretto by Marcello Panni (*Hanjo*) and Jo Kondo (*Hagoromo*). Teatro della Pergola (Teatro Comunale di Firenze, Maggio Musicale Fiorentino), Florence, June 13–20, 1994. Opéra de Lille, Lille, December 1–3, 1994.

T.S.E.: come in under the shadow of this red rock by Robert Wilson. Text by T. S. Eliot, and others; music, Philip Glass. Case dDi Stefano (Orestiadi di Gibellina 1994), Gibellina, Sicily, September 3–10, 1994. Hetzer-Halle (Kunstfest Weimar), Weiemar, Germany, June 15, 16, 20, 21, 22, 23, 1996.

The Meek Girl [Une Femme douce] based on a story by Fyodor Dostoyevsky. Adaptation, Robert Wilson and Wolfgang Wiens; music, Stefan Kurt and Gerd Bessler; performed by Robert Wilson. Charles Chemin, Marianna Kavallieratos, and Thomas Lehmann. MC 93 Bobigny (Festival d'automne), Paris, October 11–23, 1994. De Singel, Antwerp, November
10–12, 1994. Stadthof 11, Zürich, November 24–27, 1994. Le Cargo, Grenoble, December 7–8, 1994. Das TAT (Theater am Turm), Frankfurt, Germany, January 5–8, 1995. Théâtre de Caen, Caen, France, January 13–14, 1995.

Skin, Meat, Bone: The Wesleyan Project by Robert Wilson and Alvin Lucier. Music, Alvin Lucier. Theater Center for the Arts, Wesleyan University, Middletown, Conn., November 20, 1994 (see also *Knee Plays and Other Acts*, 1995).

1993

Madama Butterfly by Giacomo Puccini. Choreography, Suzushi Hanayagi; costumes, Frida Parmeggiani; lighting, Heinrich Brunke and Robert Wilson. Opéra Bastille, Paris, November 19–December 10, 1993, September 29–October 1994. Teatro Communale, Bologna, Italy, March 21, 1996 (premiere). Opéra Bastille, Paris, June 9, 1997 (premiere); September 12, 14,17, 20, 23, 25, 28, 30, October 3, 7, 1998. ACT City (Theatre Olympics), Hamamatsu, Japan, June 5, 7, 1999. PalaFenice al Tronchetto (Fondazione Teatro La Fenice di Venezia), Venice, February 23–March 2, 2001.

Alice in Bed by Susan Sontag. Music, Hans Peter Kuhn. Hebbel Theater (Produced by Schaubühne am Lehniner Platz), Berlin, September 15–November 30, 1993.

Orlando [French version; see also Danish version (below), English version (1996), and German version (1989)], based on the novel by Virginia Woolf. Adaptation, Robert Wilson and Darryl Pinckney. Music, Hans Peter Kuhn; performed by Isabelle Huppert. Théâtre Vidy-Lausanne, Lausanne, Switzerland, May 9–June 6, 1993. Odéon-Théâtre de l'Europe (Festival d'automne), Paris, September 21–October 24, 1993. Théâtre de Colombes, Colombes, France, October 18, 1994. Teatro Lirico, Milan, November 16–18, 1994. Opéra du Rhin, Strasbourg, France, January 9–19, 1995. Quartz, Brest, France, February 3–5, 1995. Grande Auditório do Edificio Sede da Caixa Geral de Depositos (Culturgest Gestäao de Espaco Culturais), Lisbon, February 17–19, 1995. Théâtre de Nîmes, France, March 1–5, 1994. Théâtre National de Belgique, Brussels, March 14–19, 1995. Théâtre National de Bretagne, Rennes, France, March 28–April 7, 1995.

Orlando [Danish version; see also French version (above), English version (1996), and German version, 1989], based on the novel by Virginia Woolf. Adaptation, Robert Wilson and Darryl Pickney. Producer, Karen-Maria Bille; director Katrine Wiedemann; design, Christian Friedländer; performed by Susse Wold. Betty Nansen Teatret, Copenhagen, December 29–30 (previews), December 31, 1993–February 12, 1994; May 8–20, 1995.

1992

Alice (based on *Alice in Wonderland* by Lewis Carroll). Text by Paul Schmidt; music and lyrics, Tom Waits and Kathleen Brennan. Thalia Theater, Hamburg, December 19, 1992–January, 1993. Theater am Pfalzbau, Ludwigshaven, Germany, February 7–11, 1993. Centro Cultural de Belém, Lisbon, March 12–14, 1994. Teatro Vittorio Emmanuele, Massina, Italy, June 4–6, 1994. Brooklyn Academy of Music, New York City, October 6–8, 10–14, 1995.

Danton's Death (see also revival, Salzburg, 1998) by Georg Büchner. English version by Robert Auletta. Alley Theatre, Houston, October 27–November 15, 1992.

Don Juan Último by Vicente Molina Foix. Music, Mariano Díaz; costumes, Frida Parmeggiani. Teatro María Guerrero (Festival de Otoño), Madrid, September 26–December 1992.

Einstein on the Beach (revival of 1984 version; see also 1976 original version, 1988 new production and 2012–13 world tour) by Robert Wilson and Philip Glass. McCarter Theater, Princeton, New Jersey, July 24–25, 1992. Oper Frankfurt, August 19–22, 1992. State Theatre, Melbourne, September 17–20, 1992. Teatro del Liceo, Barcelona, September 29–October 3, 1992. Teatro de la Vaguarda, Madrid, October 7–10, 1992. Artsphere Performing Arts Center, Tokyo, October 18–25, 1992. Brooklyn Academy of Music, New York City, November 19–23, 1992. MC 93 Bobigny (Festival d'automne), Paris, December 11–21, 1992.

Dr. Faustus Lights the Lights by Gertrude Stein. Music, Hans-Peter Kuhn. Hebbel Theater, Berlin, April 15–26, 1992. Theater am Turm, Frankfurt, Germany, June 2–6, 1992. Teatro Goldoni, Venice, Italy, June 13–17, 1992. Teatro Argentina, Rome, June 22–28, 1992. Alice Tully Hall (Serious Fun! series), New York City, July 7–9, 1992. Szene Salzburg, July 27–30, 1992. Le Manege, Maubeuge, France, October 15–16, 1992. Théâtre de Gennevilliers (Festival d' Automne), Paris, October 22–31, 1992. De Singel, Antwerp, November 5–7, 1992. Teatro Lirico, Milan, May 26–29, 1993. Salle Pierre Mercure (Festival de Théâtre Amériques, University of Quebec at Montreal), June 10–12, 1993. Royal Lyceum Theatre (Edinburgh Festival), Edinburgh, August 25–28, 1993. Teatro D. Maria II (Encontros Acarte '93), Lisbon, September 10–12, 1993. Madách Szinház (Budapesti Tavaszi Fesztivál), Budapest, March 30–31, 1994. Divadle Archa, Prague, June 22–25, 1994. Lyric Theatre (Hong Kong Arts Festival), Hong Kong, February 17–19, 1995.

1991

The Malady of Death (German version–see also French version, 1996) by Marguerite Duras. Music, Hans Peter Kuhn. Schaubühne am Lehniner Platz, Berlin, December 21, 1991 (world premiere).

Grace for Grace (benefit). Staging, Robert Wilson. Saint John the Divine Cathedral, New York City, October 17, 1991.

Lohengrin by Richard Wagner (see also 1998 revival, New York City). Opernhaus Zürich, September 21–October 20, 1991; June 18, 22, 29, July 3, 6, 1997.

The Magic Flute [Die Zauberflöte, La Flûte enchantée] by Wolfgang Amadeus Mozart. Opéra Bastille, Paris, June 26–July 19, December 3–28, 1991; January 6–14, 1992; April 5–27, 1993; May 3–20, 1995; March 6, 8, 10, 11, 12, 13, 15, 16, 17, 20, 21, 23, 24, 25, 1998; March 6, 8, 10–13, 15–17, 20, 21, 23–25, 1999.

Parsifal by Richard Wagner. Hamburgische Staatsoper, March 21, 1991 (premiere). Wortham Theater Center (Houston Grand Opera), Houston, February 6–21, 1992.

When We Dead Awaken by Henrik Ibsen (English version by Robert Brustein). Adaptation, Robert Wilson; music, Charles "Honi" Coles. Loeb Drama Center (American Repertory Theatre), Cambridge, Mass., February 8–12, 1991 (previews), February 14–March 9, 1991. Cullen Theater, Wortham Theater Center (Alley Theatre production), Houston, May 22–28, 1991. Theatro Municipal de São Paulo (Bienal Internacional de São Paulo), São Paulo, October 8–10, 1991.

1990

Alceste (see also 1986 and 1999 productions) by Christoph Willibald Gluck. Civic Opera House (Lyric Opera of Chicago), Chicago, September 14–26, 1990, October 1–13, 1990.

Overture to the Fourth Act of Deafman Glance by Robert Wilson. Schloß Petronell, Carnuntum (Art Carnuntum), near Vienna, June 17, 1990.

What Room: A Play for 3 Minutes by Robert Wilson. Loeb Drama Center (American Repertory Theatre), Cambridge, Mass., May, 1990.

The Black Rider: The Casting of the Magic Bullets (based on *Der Freischütz* by August Apel and Friedrich Laun, and on *The Fatal Marksman* by Thomas de Quincey). Adaptation by Robert Wilson, Tom Waits (music/lyrics), and William S. Burroughs (text). Thalia Theater, Hamburg, March 31, 1990 (premiere), April 2–May 30, 1990, September 16–November 3, 1990 December (?), 1990, January 27–31, 1991, March 16–18, 1991. Theater an der Wien (Wiener Festwochen), Vienna, June 12–16, 1990. Théâtre du Châtelet (Festival d'automne), Paris, October 8–15, 1990. Het Muziektheater, Amsterdam, May 14–16, 1991. Schiller Theater (Theatertreffen Berlin, Berlin Festspiele), Berlin, May 25–27, 1991. Teatro Comunale dell'Opera di Genoa (Teatro Carlo Felice), Savona, Italy, June 23–28, 1992. Teatro Central Hispano (Expo '92), Seville, Spain, July 8–10, 1992. Brooklyn Academy of Music (Next Wave Festival), New York City, November 20–December 1,

1993. Thalia Theater, Hamburg, August 12–14, 16–18, 20–22, 1995. Hong Kong Academy for Performing Arts Lyric Theatre (Hong Kong Arts Festival), Hong Kong, February 10, 11, 13, 14, 15, 16, 1998.

The Black Rider: The Casting of the Magic Bullets [non-Wilson productions, licensed by Robert Wilson, et. al.] Schauspielhaus (Schauspiel Dortmund), Dortmund, Germany, October 8, 1994 (premiere). Großen Haus, Stadttheater (Theater Heilbronn), Heilbronn, Germany [directed by Lech Majewski, designed by Janusz Kapusta], March 18–28, 1995. Großes Haus, Deutsches National Theater und Staatskapelle, Weimar [directed by Christina Friedrich], May 31, 1995 (premiere). Kleines Haus, Hessischen Staatstheater, Wiesbaden [designed by Christian Schmidt], June 18–29, 1995. Kammerspiele, Bad Godesberg, Germany [directed by Frank Hoffman, designed by Christoph Rasche], November 24, 1995 (premiere). Theater Neumarkt, Zürich [directed by Stephan Müler, designed by Sigried Mayer], December 15, 1995. Junges Theater, Göttingen, January 1996 (premiere). Staatstheater, Kassel [directed by Jürgen Schwalbe, designed by Manfred Gruber], January 13, 1996 (premiere), additional performances November 28, 1996–April 19, 1997. Stadt Theater, Berne, Switzerland [directed by Thomas Münstermann, sets by Cornelia Gaertner, costumes by Catherine Voeffray], March 15–June 19, 1996. Schauspielhaus (Schauspiel Frankfurt), Frankfurt-am-Main [directed and designed by Alexander Brill], January 20, 1996–July 5, 1997. Stadttheatrer, Konstanz, June 12, 1996 (premiere). Altmark Theater, Stendal, August 31, 1996. Leverkusen, Germany [Schauspiel Frankfurt tour, directed by Alexander Brill], September 24–25, 1996. Staatstheater, Oldenbeurg, Oct 11, 1996–July 6, 1997. Wilhelmshaven, Germany [Oldenburgisches Staatstheater tour], October 16, 1996, February 17, 1997. Aurich, Germany [Oldenburgisches Staatstheater tour], October 29, 1996. Tiroler Landestheater, Innsbruck, November 2, 1996–January 22, 1997; February 28, March 19, 1997. Saarländisches Staatstheater, Saarbrücken, Germany, November 6, 1996–June 12, 1997. Theater Metropolis, Salzburg [directed by Josef E. Köpplinger], December 3, 12, 1996. Kleines Theater, Salzburg, February 1997. Staatsschauspiel, Dresden [directed by Klaus Dieter Kirst, designed by Kathrin Kegler], January 2, 1997–June 13, 1998. Halle 39, Theater am Lerchenkamp (Stadttheater Hildesheim), Hildesheim, Germany [directed by Ralf Knapp, designed by Susanne Balmus], February 11–May 3, 1997. Witten, Germany [Oldenburgisches Staatstheater tour], February 13, 1997. Stadtische Bühnen, Nürnberg [directed by Michael Blumenthal, designed by Robert Geiger], March 1, 1997–January 29, 1998. Théâtre Municipal, Luxembourg [Saarländisches Staatstheater tour], March 14–17, 1997. Schillertheater, Gelsenkirchen, April 1997 (premiere). Stadtische Bühnen, Freiburg, May, 1997 (premiere). Hans Otto Theater, Potsdam, May 1997 (premiere). Klostermine Limburg, Bad Durkheim, July 1997 (premiere). Junges Theater, Bremen, July 1997 (premiere). Landestheater, Tübingen, September 1997. Phönix Theater, Linz, Austria [dir. by Harald Gebhartl, designed by Dodo Deer], September 18, 19, 20, 22, 23, 24, 26, 27, 28, 30, October 5, 6, 1997. Stadtische Bühnen, Münster, October 1997 (premiere). Theater Phönix, Linz, Austria, October 1997 (premiere). Elverket Dramaten (Kungliga Dramatiska Teatern), Stockholm [directed by Einar Heckscher], October 2, 1997 (premiere). Bühnen, Kiel, December 1997 (permiere). Kleist Theater, Frankfut am Oder, December 1997 (premiere). Ulmer Theater, Ulm, January 1998 (premiere). Markgrafentheater, Erlangen, Germany [Schauspiel Frankfurt tour, directed by Alexander Brill], January 21–25, 1998. Bühnen der Stadt, Cologne, February 1998 (premiere). Landesbühne, Esslingen, May 1998 (premiere). Bad Hersfelder Festspiele, Bad Hersfeld, Germany [directed by Ingo Waszerka], June 9–August 2, 1998. ITV/Aqualta Stage 1, Arts Barns Open Space (Fringe Festival), Edmonton, Alberta [directed by Michael Scholar], August 14, 16, 19, 1998. Det Norske Teatret, Oslo, Norway [Noridska Strakosch Teaterforlaget tour, directed by Katrine Wiedemann, designed by Michael Kvium], September 4, 1998 (premiere). Renaissance Theater, Berlin [Bad Hersfelder Festspiele tour, directed by Ingo Waszerka], March 20, 1998 (premiere). Betty Nansen Teatret, Copenhagen [Noridska Strakosch Teaterforlaget tour, directed by Katrine Wiedemann, designed by Michael Kvium], September–November 1998. Landestheater Mecklenburg, Neustrelitz, Germany [directed by Mechtild Erpenbeck], September 19, 1998 (premiere). Theatre Network (Edmonton Fringe Holdovers) [directed by Michael Scholar], Edmondton, Canada, September 1998. Stadstheater, Braunschweig, September 1998 (premiere). Schauspielhaus, Hannover [directed by Hartmut Wickert, designed by Thomas Dreißigacker], October 24, 1998 (premiere). Metropol-Theater, Munich, October 1998 (premiere). Kammerspiele, Lübeck, October 1998 (premiere). City Theater, Helsinki, October 1998 (premiere). Theater Ingolstadt, Ingolstadt, Germany [directed by Dieter Gackstetter, designed by Erwin Bode], December 19, 1998 (premiere). Det Norske Teatre, Oslo, December 1998 (premiere). Grosses Haus, Theater der Landeshauptstadt, Magdeburg, MagdeburgGermany [directed by Manfred Repp, designed by Tom Presting], January 9, 1999 (premiere). Stadtische Bühnen, Osnabrück, March 1999 (premiere). Stadttheater, Bielefeld, April 1999 (premiere). Hoffmann Theater, Bamberg, May 1999 (premiere). Musicalensemble, Löhne, October 1999 (premiere). Theater Ingolstadt, Ingolstadt, Germany [directed by Dieter Gackstetter, designed by Erwin Bode], December 19, 1998 (premiere). Grosses Haus, Theater des Landeshauptstadt, Magdeburg, Germany [directed by Manfred Repp, designed by Tom Presting], January 9, 1999 (premiere). Stadttheater Pfrozheim (Theater Pforzhiem), Germany [directed by Ansgar Haag and Barbara Baumgärtel, designed by Klaus Hellenstein], March 30, April 8, 10, 22, 24, May 7, June 2, 13, 17, 19, 22, 1999. Store Scene, Aalborg Teater, Copenhagen [produced by Nordiska Strakosch Teaterförlaget, directed by Emil Korf Hansen, designed by Steffen Aarfing], May 7–June 12, 1999. Theater Hagen, Hagen, Germany [directed by Gil Mehmert, designed by Harald B Thor], May 15, 1999 (premiere). Grosses Haus, E.T.A. Hoffman Theater, Bamberg, Germany, May 15-June 20, 1999. Harry de Jur Playhouse, Henry Street Settlement (New York Fringe Festival) [produced by Michael Scholar, directed by Ron M. Jenkins, designed by Marissa Kochanski]), New York City, August 1999. Werretalhalle, Löhne, Germany [Musicalensemble Löhne production], September 11–19, 1999. Bürgerhaus Rehme, Bad Oeynhausen, Germany [Musicalensemble Löhne production], September 25, 1999. Das alte Kino, Vlotho, Germany [Musicalensemble Löhne production], October 23–24, 1999. Die Weberie, Gütersloh, Germany [Musicalensemble Löhne production], October 31, 1999. Stadttheater Herford [Musicalensemble Löhne production], November 6, 1999. Forum Ennigloh, Ennigloh, Germany [Musicalensemble Löhne production], November 13, 1999. Grosses Haus Altenberg, Altenberg, Germany [Altenberg-Gera Theater production, directed by Frank Matthus], November 20, 1999 (premiere). Residenztheater, Munich [directed by Andreas Kriegenburg], January 30, 2000 (premiere). Theater Senftenberg (Neue Bühne), Senftenberg, Germany, February 25, 2000 (premiere). Kulturhaus Wagram [Perpetuum series, directed by Fritz Humer and Susanne Denk, designed by Buster 49], St. Pölten-Wagram, Austria, March 17–April 16, 2000. Theater Baden-Baden, Baden-Baden, Germany [directed by Wolf Widder, designed by Sibylle Schmalbrock], April 4–May 5, 2000. Grosses Haus Gera, Gera, Germany [Altenberg-Gera Theater production, directed by Frank Matthus], May 5, 2000 (premiere). MTC Warehouse (Winnipeg Fringe Festival) [produced by Michael Scholar, directed by Ron M. Jenkins, designed by Marissa Kochanski]), Winnepeg, Canada, July 2000; Edmonton Fringe Festival, August 2000; Theatre Network (Edmonton Fringe Holdovers), September 2000. Meininger Theater (Südthüringisches Staatstheater) [directed by Dominik Wilgenbus], Meiningen, Germany, June 29, 2001 (premiere). Schleswig-Holsteinisches Landes Theater, Rendsburg, Flensburg, Schleswig, Germany, January 18–February 10, 2002.

King Lear by William Shakespeare. (see also 1985 workshop, Los Angeles). Bockenheimer Depot (Schauspielhaus, Frankfurt), May 26–June 17, 1990.

1989

Swan Song by Anton Chekhov. Münchner Kammerspiele, Munich, December 20–27, 1989; January 5–June 26, 1990. Tokyo Globe Theater (Mitsui Festival), Tokyo, June 1–5, 1990.

Orlando (from the novel by Virginia Woolf). [German version; see also French and Danish versions (1993), English version (1996)]. Adaptation by Robert Wilson and Darryl Pinckney; text, Virginia Woolf; performed by Jutta Lampe. Schaubühne am Lehniner Platz, Berlin, November 21–December 21, 1989; February 2 – June, August 31–October 14, 1990.

La Nuit d'Avant le Jour (Inauguration of the Opéra Bastille, Paris, in commemoration of the French bicentennial). Musical selections: Gounod, Meayerbeer, Massenet, Gluck, Saint-Saens, Bizet, and Berlioz. July 13, 1989.

De Materie by Robert Wilson. Music, Louis Andriessen. Het Muziektheater (Netherlands Opera), Amsterdam, June 1–17, 1989. Danstheater aan't Spui, The Hague, June 10, 1989. Roerdamse Schouwburg, June 24, 1898.

Doktor Faustus (based on the novel by Thomas Mann). Music, Giacomo Manzoni; costumes, Gianni Versace. Teatro alla Scala, Milan, May 16–20, 1989.

1988

The Forest. Text, Heiner Müller and Darryl Pinckney; music, David Byrne. Theater der Freien Volksbühne, Berlin, October 18–29, 1988. Deutsches Theater, Munich, November 5–12, 1988. Brooklyn Academy of Music, New York City, December 2–10, 1988.

Einstein on the Beach by Robert Wilson and Philip Glass (new non-Wilson production; see also 1976 original productions, 1984 revival, 1992, and 2012–13 production). Design and direction, Achim Freyer; music, Philip Glass. Ludwigsberg, Germany, October 8, 1988 (premiere). Grosses Haus, Staatstheater, Stuttgart, October 20, 1988 (premiere).

Cosmopolitan Greetings. Text, Allen Ginsberg; music, Rolf Liebermann and George Gruntz. Kampnagelfabrik (Hamburgische Staatsoper), Hamburg, June 11–July 1, 1988.

Le Martyre de Saint Sébastien by Gabriele d'Annunzio. Music, Claude Debussy; choreography, Robert Wilson and Suzushi Hanayagi. MC 93 Bobigny (Théâtre National, Opéra de Paris), Paris, March 28–April 16, 1988. Metropolitan Opera House, New York City, July 7–9, 1988. Palais Garnier, Paris, November 4–10, 1988.

The Golden Windows by Robert Wilson (University of Montréal production; see also 1982 and 1985). Direction, Diane Cotnoir; music, Gavin Bryars. Centre d'Essai (University of Montréal), January 21–24, 1988. Fifth International Festival of University Theater, Liege, Belgium, February 25–26, 1988.

Quartet. (U.S. version; see also German version *Quartett*, 1987), based on *Les Liaisons dangereuses* by Choderlos de Laclos. Text, Heiner Müller; music, Martin Pearlman. Loeb Drama Center (American Repertory Theater), Cambridge, Mass., February 10–March 6, 1988 (previews February 5–9).

1987

Parzival: Auf der anderen Seite des Sees by Robert Wilson and Tankred Dorst. Text, Tankred Dorst and Christopher Knowles; music, Tassilo Jelde. Thalia Theater, Hamburg, September 11, 1987–April, 1988.

Quartett (German Version; see also U.S. version 1988), based on Les Liaisons Dangereuses by Choderlos de Laclos. Text, Heiner Müller; music, Christoph Eschenbach. Schloßtheater Ludwigsburg (Theater der Welt festival, Stuttgart Schauspiel), Stuttgart, June 18–21, 1987, July 19, 30, 1987. Staatstheater, Stuttgart, June 18–21, 1987.

Overture to the Fourth Act of Deafman Glance by Robert Wilson. Performed by Robert Wilson and Sheryl Sutton. Ancient Stadium of Delphi (International Meeting of Ancient Greek Drama), Delphi, Greece, June 27, 1987. Alice Tully Hall (Serious Fun! series), New York City, July 17–18, 1987.

The Man in the Raincoat by Robert Wilson. (see also 1981) Direction, Rob Malasch; music, Laurie Anderson; performed by Michael Matthews. Het Muziektheater, Amsterdam, April 20, 1987.

Alkestis by Euripides. (German version; see also U.S. version, 1986). Translation, Friederike Roth and Ann-Christin Rommen; choreography, Suzushi Hanayagi. Staatstheater (Theater der Welt festival), Stuttgart, April 16–19, July, September 26–27, November 1, February 1988.

Death, Destruction, & Detroit II by Robert Wilson. Texts, Franz Kafka, Heiner Müller, Robert Wilson, Maita di Niscemi, and Cynthia Lubar; choreography, Suzushi Hanayagi; music/sound, Hans Peter Kuhn. Schaubühne am Lehniner Platz, Berlin, February 27–July 5, September 18–December 30, 1987.

Salomé by Richard Strauss. Based on the play by Oscar Wilde; costumes, Gianni Versace. Teatro alla Scala, Milan, January 11–23, 1987.

1986

Alcestis by Euripides. (U.S. version; see also German version, 1987). Adaptation, Robert Wilson; translation, Dudley Fitts and Robert Fitzgerald; additional texts, Heiner Müller; music/sound, Hans Peter Kuhn and Laurie Anderson; choreography, Suzushi Hanayagi. Loeb Drama Center (American Repertory Theater), Cambridge, Mass., March 12–23 (previews March 7–11), June 27–July 13, 1986. MC 93 Bobigny (Festival d'automne), Paris, September 18–28, 1986.

Hamletmachine by Heiner Müller (U.S. version). Translation, Carl Weber; music, Jerry Leiber and Mike Stoller. Mainstage Two (New York University, Tisch School of the Arts), New York City, May 7–June 15, 1986. Théâtre des Amandiers, Nanterre, France, October 1–10, 1987. Teatro Albeñiz, Madrid, October 14–17, 1987. Théâtre Jean Dasté (Théâtre Comedie de Saint-Etienne) Saint-Etienne, France, October 21–24, 1987. Théâtre de la Salamandre, Lille, France, October 30–31, 1987. Almeida Theatre, London, November 4–14, 1987. Comedie de Nice, France, November 18–21, 1987. Teatro Biondo, Palermo, November 26–27, 1987.

Hamletmaschine by Heiner Müller (German version; see also 1994). Producer, Thalia Theater and Hochschule für Musik und Darstellende Kunst; music, Jerry Leiber and Mike Stoller. Theater in der Kunsthalle, Hamburg, October 4–November 30, 1986, April 16–23, 1987. Theater Manufaktur (Berlin Festspiele Theatertreffen), Berlin, May 7–10, 1987.

Overture to the Fourth Act of Deafman Glance by Robert Wilson. Performed by Robert Wilson, and others. Teatro Grec, Barcelona, July 16–19, 1986. Teatro Romano, Malaga (Festival Internacional de Teatro), Spain, July 21–22, 1986.

Alceste by Christoph Willibald Gluck (see also Chicago production, 1990; Paris production, 1999). Based on the play by Euripides; choreography, Suzushi Hanayagi. Württembergischer Staatstheater, Stuttgart, December 5–21, 1986; June 18–22, 1987.

1985

King Lear by William Shakespeare (work in progress; see also 1990 Frankfurt production). Music/sound, Daniel Birnbaum. Stage One, Metromedia Square (UCLA Extension, Distinguished Artist in Residency program), Los Angeles, May 17–19, 1985.

Reading/Performance 1969–1984. Texts, Robert Wilson, Christopher Knowles, Ben Halley, Chris Moore, and David Byrne; performed by Robert Wilson. Colaiste Mhuire (Dublin Theatre Festival), Dublin, Ireland, September 28, 1985. Museum van Hedendaagse Kunst (Off Off Festival), Ghent, Belgium, October 30, 1985. Brattle Theatre, Cambridge, Mass. (music by David Byrne), February 22, 1986.

The Golden Windows by Robert Wilson (U.S. version; see also German version, 1982; Montreal version, 1988). Music, Tania León, Gavin Bryars, and Hans Peter Kuhn; costumes, Christophe de Menil; lighting design, Markus Bönzli. Carey Playhouse, Brooklyn Academy of Music (Next Wave Festival), New York City, October 22–November 3, 1985.

1984

The Knee Plays (from *the CIVIL warS*) by Robert Wilson and David Byrne. Music and texts, David Byrne; choreography, Suzushi Hanayagi. Walker Art Center, Minneapolis, April 25 (preview), April 26–28, 1985. Schauspielhaus (Theater der Welt '85 festival), Frankfurt, September 20–22, 1985. MC 93 Bobigny, Paris, October 3, 1985. Palacio de Exposiciones y Congresos (Festival de Otoño), Madrid, October 7–11, 1985. Teatro Malibran (La Biennale de Venezia, Festival Internazionale del Teatro), Venice, October 16–19, 1985. Teatro Sala Europa, Bologna, October 25–27, 1985. Schauspielhaus (Theater der Welt), Cologne, October 30–November 1, 1985. Loeb Drama Center (American Repertory Theatre), Cambridge, Massachusetts., September 19–October 5, 1986. Doolittle Theater, Los Angeles, October 14–19, 1986. Zellerbach Auditorium (UC Berkeley), Berkeley, California, October 24–25, 1986. Macky Auditorium, Boulder, Colorado, October 28, 1986. Kemo Theater, Albuquerque, New Mexico, October 31–November 2, 1986. University of Iowa, Iowa City, November 7–8, 1986. Music Hall, Detroit, November 13–16, 1986. Warner Theater, Washington, D.C.., November 19–22, 1986. Alice Tully Hall, New York City, December 2–3, 1986. Memorial Auditorium, University of Vermont, Burlington, December 6, 1986. University of Texas, Austin, May 11–12, 1987. Cullen Theater, Wortham Theater Center, Houston, Texas, May 15–16, 1987. Civic Theater, Chicago, May 17–29, 1988. Aura Hall (Mitsui Festival), Tokyo, June 15–17, 1988. Queensland Performing Arts Centre, Brisbane, Australia, July 7–9, 1988.

the CIVIL warS: a tree is best measured when it is down – Cologne Section (Act I, Scene A; Act III, Scene E; Act IV, Scene A and Epilogue) by Robert Wilson and Heiner Müller. Music by Philip Glass, David Byrne, Hans Peter Kuhn, Frederick the Great, Thomas Tallis, and Franz Schubert. Schauspielhaus, Cologne, January 19–21, 1984. Internationales Congress Centrum (Theater Treffen Berlin 84), Berlin, May 15–17, 1984. Loeb Drama Center, Cambridge, Massachusetts, (American Repertory Theater and Boston Institute for Contemporary Art), February 27–March 17, 1985.

the CIVIL warS: a tree is best measured when it is down – Rome Section (Prologue and Act V; see also 1995) by Robert Wilson and Philip Glass. Music, Philip Glass; text, Maita di Niscemi; choreography, Jim Self; costumes, Christophe de Menil. Teatro dell' Opera, Rome, March 25–31, 1984. City Center Theater, New York City, May 20, 1984 (concert version only). Dorothy Chandler Pavillion (American Music Weekend), Los Angeles, November 24–25, 1984 (concert version only). Netherlands Opera tour: Scheveningen, March 31, 1986; Utrecht, April 2, 1986; Eindhoven, April 5, 1986; Amsterdam, April 8–27, 1986. Brooklyn Academy of Music, Opera House (Next Wave festival), New York City, December 14–30, 1986.

the CIVIL warS: a tree is best measured when it is down – Marseille Workshop (Act II, Scenes A & B; Act III, Scenes A & B). Text, Etel Adnan; music, Gavin Bryars. La Sainte Baume, Marseille, France, February 13–25, 1984.

the CIVIL warS: a tree is best measured when it is down – Tokyo Workshop (Act I, Scene C; Act II, Scene C; Act III, Scenes C & D). February 10, 1984.

Médée by Marc-Antoine Charpentier (1693). Text by Thomas Corneille. Opéra de Lyon, France, October 22–November 8, 1984.

Medea by Robert Wilson and Gavin Bryars (see also Workshops, 1981). Based on the play by Euripides; music, Gavin Bryars; additional text, Heiner Müller and Vladimir Mayakovsky. Opéra de Lyon, France, October 23–November 9, 1984. Théâtre des Champs-Elysées (Festival d'automne), Paris, November 21–December 2, 1984.

Einstein on the Beach by Robert Wilson and Philip Glass (revival; see also 1988 new production, 1992 revival of 1984 production, and original version 1976). Texts, Christopher Knowles, Samuel M. Johnson, and Lucinda Childs; choreography, Lucinda Childs. Brooklyn Academy of Music, Opera House (Next Wave festival), New York City, December 11–23, 1984.

1983

the CIVIL warS: a tree is best measured when it is down – Rotterdam Section (Act I, Scene B) by Robert Wilson. Music, Nicolas Economou; choreography, Jim Self; costumes, Christophe de Menil; additional text, Maita di Niscemi. Schouwburg Theater, Rotterdam, September 6–11, 1983. Théâtre de la Ville (Festival d'automne), Paris, September 17–24, 1983. Théâtre Municipal (Opéra de Nîmes), Nîmes, France, September 28 October 1, 1983. Maison de la Culture, Grenoble, France, October 5–8, 1983. Théâtre National Populaire, Villeurbanne, Lyon, October 12–15, 1983. Nouveau Théâtre de Nice, October 19–22, 1983. Salle Jacques Thibaut, Bordeaux, October 26–28, 1983. Grand Théâtre, Lille, November 4–5, 1983. Maison de la Culture, Le Havre, November 9–10, 1983.

1982

The Golden Windows Die Goldenen Fenster by Robert Wilson (German version–see also U.S. version 1985; Montréal version 1988). Music by Tania Léon, Gavin Bryars, and Johann Pepusch. Münchner Kammerspiele, Munich, May 29, 1982 (premiere). Theater an der Wien (Wiener Festwochen), Vienna, June 5–6, 1983.

the CIVIL warS: a tree is best measured when it is down – Freiburg Workshop (second). Freiburg im Breisgau, Germany, June 26, 1982 ("Final Review" of four-week workshop).

Great Day in the Morning by Robert Wilson and Jessye Norman. Musical arrangements, Jessye Norman and Charles Lloyd, Jr. Théâtre des Champs-Élysées, Paris, October 12–23, 1982.

Overture to the Fourth Act of Deafman Glance by Robert Wilson. Performed by Robert Wilson, Carol Miles (Freiburg) and Chizuko Sugiura (Toga). Audimax-Universität, Freiburg, Germany, June 22 , 1982 (premiere). Japan Performing Arts Center (Toga Festival), Toga-mura, Japan, July 24–25, 1982.

1981

Medea (workshops) by Robert Wilson and Gavin Bryars (see also 1984). Musical Theater Lab, Kennedy Center, Washington, D.C. (first workshop), February 26–March 1, 1981. Aaron Davis Hall (City University of New York), New York City (second workshop), March 4–5, 1982.

Shirley, Keep Off. Arts Magnet High School, Dallas, Texas., April 30, 1981 (culmination of a week-long student workshop).

The Man in the Raincoat by Robert Wilson (see also 1987). Music, Hans Peter Kuhn; performed by Robert Wilson. Schauspielhaus Köln (Theater der Welt festival), Cologne, June 27–28, 1981.

the CIVIL warS: a tree is best measured when it is down (first workshop–see also Freiburg, second workshop, 1982). Bavarian State Opera, Munich, August, 1981.

Relative Calm by Lucinda Childs. Direction, Lucinda Childs; music, John Gibson; lighting and designs, Robert Wilson. Théâtre National de Strasbourg, France, November 16–17, 1981. SYGMA de Bordeaux, November 20, 1981. Théâtre Nouveau de Nice, November 25–28, 1981. Maison de la Culture de Grenoble, France, December 4–5, 1981. Brooklyn Academy of Music, New York City, December 18–20, 1981.

1980

Overture to the Fourth Act of Deafman Glance by Robert Wilson (see also 1982, 1986, 1987). Performed by Robert Wilson. Raffinerie Plan K, Brussels, February 25, 1980. Palais des Congrès, Liège, February 26, 1980. 42 ouest Av. des Pins (PERFORMANCE festival), Montreal, November 27, 1980.

DiaLog/Curious George by Robert Wilson and Christopher Knowles. Text by Christopher Knowles. Teatro Nuovo (Cabaret Voltaire, Rassegna Internazionale del Teatro d'Avanguardia), Turin, March 10–13, 1980. Festival of Ten Nations, Warsaw, May 21–23, 1980. Schouwburg Theater (Holland Festival), Rotterdam, June 1–4, 1980. Mitzi E. Newhouse Theater, Lincoln Center, New York City, June 24–29, 1980.

1979

Death, Destruction & Detroit: a play with music in 2 acts/a love story in 16 scenes by Robert Wilson. Music, Alan Lloyd, Keith Jarrett, and Randy Newman; additional texts, Maita de Niscemi. Schaubühne am Halleschen Ufer, Berlin, February 12, 1979 (premiere).

Edison by Robert Wilson. Additional dialog, Maita de Niscemi; music, Michael Riesman, and others. Lion Theater, New York City, June 19–24, 1979 (preview). Théâtre National Populaire, Villeurbanne, France, October 9–13, 1979. Teatro Nazionale (presented by Teatro alla Scalla), Milan, October 17–20, 1979. Théâtre de Paris (Festival d'automne), Paris, October 24–November 11, 1979.

1978

Prologue to Deafman Glance by Robert Wilson. Manhattanville College, Purchase, New York, July 12, 1978. John Drew Theater, Guildhall, East Hampton, New York, August 20, 1978.

1977

I was sitting on my patio this guy appeared I thought I was hallucinating by Robert Wilson. Co-direction, Lucinda Childs; music, Alan Lloyd; performed by Robert Wilson and Lucinda Childs. Quirk Auditorium (Eastern Michigan University), Ypsilanti, Michigan, April 2–3, 1977. Zellerbach Theater, Annenberg Center, Philadelphia, April 8–9, 1977. Paramount Theater, Austin, Texas, April 12, 1977. Bayou Building Auditorium (University of Houston), Clear Lake, Texas., April 14. Fort Worth Art Museum, Texas., April 16–17, 1977. Wilshire Ebell Theater, Los Angeles, April 19, 1977. Veterans's Memorial Auditorium, San Francisco, April 21–22, 1977. Walker Art Center, St. Paul/Minneapolis, Minn., April 26–27, 1977. Cherry Lane Theater, New York City, May 10–29, 1977. Théâtre de la Renaissance, Paris, January 16–29, 1978. Schouwburg Theater, Rotterdam, January 31, February 4, 1978. Royal Theater, The Hague, February 1, 1978. Staadsschouwburg Theater, Amsterdam, February 3, 1978. Theater II, Zürich, February 6–8, 1978. Théâtre de Carouge, Geneva, February 10–11, 1978. Piccolo Teatro die Milano, Milan, February 14–19, 1978., Theater des Westens (Theatertreffen '78), Berlin, May 26–30, 1978. Württembergische Staatstheater, Stuttgart, June 1, 1978. Royal Court Theatre, London, June 5–10, 1978.

DiaLog/Network by Christopher Knowles and Robert Wilson. Text by Christopher Knowles. Spazio Teatro Sperimentale, Florence, October 15–17, 1977. Münchner Theater Festival, Munich, October 20–23, 1977. Atelier Annick le Moine, Grand Palais, Paris, October 27, 1977. Institute of Contemporary Art, Boston, July 15–16, 1978. Mickery, Amsterdam, June 16–21, 1978. Walker Art Center, Minneapolis, August 4, 1978. Mo-Ming, Chicago, August 5–6, 1978. Palais des Beaux Arts (Kaaitheater), Brussels, April 29–30, 1979.

1976

DiaLog [3] by Robert Wilson and Christopher Knowles. Performed by Robert Wilson, Christopher Knowles, and Lucinda Childs. Whitney Museum, New York City, February 19, 1976. Douglass College, Rutgers University, New Brunswick, N.J., March 7, 1976. Corcoran Gallery, Washington, D.C., April 14, 1976.

Einstein on the Beach by Robert Wilson and Philip Glass (see also 1984 revival, 1988 new production, 1992, and 2012–13). Music, Philip Glass; text, Christopher Knowles, Samuel M. Johnson, and Lucinda Childs; choreography, Andrew de Groat. Video Exchange Theater, Westbeth Center, New York City (run-through), March 4–5, 1976. Museum of Modern Art, New York City (Knee Plays only), March 31, 1976. The Kitchen Center, New York City (musical selections only), March 19–20, 1976. Théâtre Municipal (Festival d'Avignon), Avignon, France (premiere), July 25–29, 1976. Teatro La Fenice (Venice Biennale), Venice, September 13–17, 1976. BITEF (Théâtre des Nations), Belgrade, September 22–23, 1976. La Monnaie, Brussels, September 28–30, 1976. Opéra Comique (Festival d'Automne), Paris, October 4–13, 1976. Deutsches Schauspielhaus, Hamburg, October 17–18, 1976. Rotterdamse Schouwburg, Rotterdam, October 22–23, 1976. Theatre Carré (Holland Festival), Amsterdam, October 26, 1976. Metropolitan Opera House, New York City, November 21, 28–28, 1976.

Robert Wilson Solo (including excerpts from **Deafman Glance, A Letter for Queen Victoria**, and **The King of Spain**). Salle Vilar, Maison de la Culture de Rennes, France, October 28, 1976. Malersaal, Deutsches Schauspielhaus, Hamburg, July 8–10, 1977. Kleine Zaal de Doelen, Rotterdam, July 12–13, 1977. Movie Star Club, Chiesa di S. Teresa, Capri, July 23–24, 1977. Salone Pier Lombardo, Milan, June 7–10, 1976. Teatro Comunale, Brescia, June 25, 1976.

Reconfirmation of Reservations (Robert Wilson solo). Salone Pier Lombardo, Milan, June 7–10, 1976. Teatro Comunale, Brescia, June 25, 1976.

1975

DiaLog/Sundance Kid by Christopher Knowles and Robert Wilson (reading). Performed by Christopher Knowles and Robert Wilson. St. Marks Church (St. Marks Poetry Project), New York, January 1, 1975.

A Solo Reading. Voice and drawings, Robert Wilson; music, Alan Lloyd. 147 Spring Street (Byrd Hoffman Foundation), New York City, February 2, 1975.

The $ Value of Man by Robert Wilson and Christopher Knowles. Texts, Robert Wilson and Christopher Knowles; music, Michael Galasso; choreography, Andrew de Groat. Lepercq Space, Brooklyn Academy of Music, New York City, May 8–11, 15–18, 1975.

DiaLog [2] by Robert Wilson and Christopher Knowles. Performed by Robert Wilson and Christopher Knowles. Connecticut College (American Dance Festival), New London, Conn., July 29, 31, 1975. Public Theater/Anspacher, New York City, August 7–9, 1975.

To Street: One Man Show. Performed by Robert Wilson. Kultur Forum, Bonn Center, Germany, September 20, 1975.

1974

DiaLog/A Mad Man A Mad Giant A Mad Dog A Mad Urge A Mad Face by Robert Wilson and Christopher Knowles. Performed by Robert Wilson, Christopher Knowles, and others. Villa Borghese (Contemporanea festival), Rome, March 3, 1974. Kennedy Center (Art Now series), Washington, D.C., May 30, 1974. Delgocha Gardens (Shiraz Festival), Iran, August 19–20, 1974. Galeria Ala, Milan, December 9, 1974.

Prologue to A Letter for Queen Victoria (gallery presentation) by Robert Wilson. Music, Kathryn Cation and Michael Galasso; choreography, Andrew de Groat. Six O'Clock Theater (Festival dei Due Mondi Spoleto), Spoleto, Italy, June 15–23, 1974.

A Letter for Queen Victoria by Robert Wilson. Additional texts, Christopher Knowles, Cynthia Lubar, Stefan Brecht, and James Neu; music, Alan Lloyd and Michael Galasso; choreography, Andrew de Groat; performed by Robert Wilson and members of the Byrd Hoffman School of Byrds. Teatro Caio Melisso (Festival dei Due Mondi Spoleto), Spoleto, Italy, June 15–22, 1974. Théâtre Municipal, La Rochelle, France, June 3–5, 1974. BITEF Festival, Belgrade, September 19–22, 1974. Théâtre des Variétés, Paris, December 5–31, 1974. Theater II, Zurich, October 16–18, 1974. Maison des Arts et Loisirs, Thonon-les Bains, France, October 21, 1974. Maison des Arts et Loisirs, Sochaux-Doubs, France, October 26, 1974. Théâtre Municipal, Mulhouse, France, October 29, 1974. Théâtre Huitième, Lyon, November 5–10, 1974. Palais de la Mediterranée, Nice, November 13–14, 1974. ANTA Theater, New York City, March 19–April 6, 1975.

1973

Workshop/Performance. Performed by Robert Wilson and Byrd Hoffman School of Byrds. Naropa Institute, Boulder, Colorado, 1973.

The Byrd Hoffman School of Byrds Spring Student Concerts. ncluded: Solos; Macrame Trio; Ramona's Engagemet [sic] Ring, by Jessie Dunn Gilbert; Lullabye, by Minda Novek; The Cradle Song, by Hope Kondrat; Orange Airplane, by Alan Lloyd; Memories, by Sue Sheehy; Reading, by Pontease Tyak; Solo Pablo Rimbaud; and Reception Play. Unknown location (probably 147 Spring St., New York City), May 7–12, 1973.

King Lyre and Lady in the Wasteland. Performed by Robert Wilson and Elaine Luthy. 147 Spring Street (Byrd Hoffman Foundation), New York City, May 12, 1973.

The Life and Times of Joseph Stalin by Robert Wilson. Music, Alan Lloyd, Igor Demjen, Julie Weber, and Michael Galasso; texts, Robert Wilson, Cynthia Lubar, Christopher Knowles, and Ann Wilson; choreography, Andrew de Groat; performed by Robert Wilson and the Byrd Hoffman School of Byrds. Det Ny Teater, Copenhagen, September 7–14, 1973 (previews). Brooklyn Academy of Music, Opera House, New York City, December 14–22, 1973. Teatro Municipal, São Paulo (under the title The Life and Times of Dave Clark), April 9–13, 1974.

1972

Overture [New York (Overture for **KA MOUNTAIN AND GUARDenia TERRACE**)] by Robert Wilson and the Byrd Hoffman School of Byrds. 147 Spring Street (Byrd Hoffman Foundation), New York, April 24–30, 1972.

Overture [Shiraz (Overture for **KA MOUNTAIN AND GUARDenia TERRACE**)]. Peformed by Robert Wilson and the Byrd Hoffman School of Byrds. Narenjestan Garden, Hkaneh-E Zinatolmolk, Shiraz, Iran, August 31, 1972.

KA MOUNTAIN AND GUARDenia TERRACE: a story about a family and some people changing. Direction, Robert Wilson, Andrew de Groat, Cynthia Lubar, James Neu, Ann Wilson, Mel Andringa, S.K. Dunn, and others; texts, Robert Wilson, Andrew de Groat, Jessie Dunn Gilbert, Kikuo Saito, Cynthia Lubar, Susan Sheehy, and Ann Wilson; music/sound, Igor Demjen; performed by Robert Wilson and the Byrd Hoffman School of Byrds. Haft Tan Mountain (Shiraz-Persepolis Festival of the Arts), Shiraz, Iran, September 2–9, 1972 (one continuous performance).

Overture [Paris (Overture for **KA MOUNTAIN AND GUARDenia TERRACE**)]. Design, Robert Wilson, Melvin Andringa, Kathryn Kean, Kikuo Saito, Ann Wilson, and others; music/sound, Igor Demjen; performed by Robert Wilson and the Byrd Hoffman School of Byrds. Musée Galliéra (Festival d'automne and Théâtre des Nations), Paris, November 6–11, 1972 (six-day exhibit with occasional performances). Opéra Comique (Festival d'automne and Théâtre des Nations), Paris, November 12, 1972 (titled "CYNDI"; texts, Robert Wilson, Cynthia Lubar, and Ann Wilson; music/sound, Igor Demjen; choreography, Andrew de Groat; set designs, Robert Wilson and Paul Thek (continuous 24 hour performance).

1971

Watermill (performance/demonstration). Music/sound, Melvin Andringa, Igor Demjen, Alan Lloyd, and Pierre Ruiz; performed by Robert Wilson, Andrew de Groat, Cynthia Lubar, and others. Morristown Unitarian Fellowship, New Jersey, March 16, 1971.

Program Prologue Now: Overture for a Deafman by Robert Wilson. Produced by Pierre Cardin and ALPHA. Espace Cardin, Théâtre des Ambassadeurs, Paris, June 8, 1971.

Demonstration/Lecture/Press Conference. Performed by Robert Wilson. Atelje 212 (BITEF Festival), Belgrade, September 14, 1971.

1970

George School Activity (lecture/demonstration). Conducted/performed by Robert Wilson. George School, New Hope, Pennsylvania, Spring 1970.

Handbill by Robert Wilson. Text, Kenneth King; music, Alan Lloyd and Julie Weber; performed by Robert Wilson, and others. New Museum (University Center for New Performing Arts), Iowa City, Iowa, November 13, 1970.

Deafman Glance by Robert Wilson. Music, Alan Lloyd, Igor Demjen, and others; performed by Robert Wilson, Raymond Andrews, Sheryl Sutton, and the Byrd Hoffman School of Byrds. University Theater (Center for New Performing Arts), Iowa City, Iowa, December 15–16, 1970. Brooklyn Academy of Music, February 25, March 5, 1971. Grand Théâtre de Nancy (Festival Mondial), France, April 22–23, 1971. Teatro Eliseo (Premio Roma festival), April 27–28, 1971. Théâtre de la Musique, Paris, June 11–July 3, 1971. Stadsschouwburg Theater (Holland Festival), Amsterdam, July 6, 8, 1971.

1969

The King of Spain by Byrd Hoffman (i.e., Robert Wilson). Performed by Robert Wilson and the Byrd Hoffman School of Byrds. Anderson Theatre, New York City, January 30–31, 1969.

Hauco–1941 (performance/lecture/demonstration). Performed by Robert Wilson and the Byrd Hoffman School of Byrds. New Providence High School, New Jersey, March 29, 1969.

The Life and Times of Sigmund Freud by Robert Wilson. Scenery, Fred Kolouch; performed by Robert Wilson and the Byrd Hoffman School of Byrds. Brooklyn Academy of Music, Opera House, New York City, December 18, 20, 1969; May 22–23, 1970.

1968

Alley Cats (duet performed in Meredith Monk's Co-op). Performed by Robert Wilson and Meredith Monk. Loeb Student Center, New York University, New York City, November 3, 1968.

ByrdwoMAN. Performed by Robert Wilson, S.K. Dunn, Kikuo Saito, Raymond Andrews, Hope Kondrat, Robyn Brentano, Meredith Monk, and others. 147 Spring Street, and Jones Alley, New York City, October 26, 1968.

Theater Activity [2] (including texts written and recorded by Buckminster Fuller). Performed by Robert Wilson, Devora Bornir, Kenneth King, and Hope Kondrat. American Theatre Laboratory, New York City, April 19, 1968.

Theatre Activity [1]. Performed by Robert Wilson, Andrew de Groat, Kenneth King, and others. Bleeker St. Cinema, New York City, March 7, 1968.

1967

Baby Blood [An Evening with Baby Byrd Johnson and Baby Blood]. Performed by Robert Wilson. 147 Spring Street, New York City, November, 1967.

Poles [outdoor sculpture, in conjunction with performances by Robert Wilson and others]. Grail Retreat, Loveland, Ohio, dates unknown.

1966
Clorox and Opus 2 (dance). Pratt Institute (Spring Recital of Dance Workshop), New York City, April 29–30, 1966.

1965
Modern Dance [four dances] by Robert Wilson. Performed by the "Ideas in Motion" youth theater program. Waco Civic Auditorium, Waco, Texas, July 29–31, 1965.

Silent Play. Performed by Robert Wilson, and others. San Antonio, Texas, Summer 1965.

America Hurrah by Jean-Claude van Itallie. Direction, Michael Kahn; setting, Robert Wilson; dolls designed by Robert Wilson and Tania Leontov. Cafe La Mama E.T.C., New York City, April 28, 1965 (premiere). Comediehuset, Copenhagen, October 18–November 5, 1965.

Duricglte & Tomorrow by Robert Wilson. Music, Praetorius. Memorial Hall, Pratt Institute (Spring Dance Recital), New York City, April 9–10, 1965.

1964
Dance Event at New York World's Fair. New York State Pavillion, New York City, ca. September 1964–June 1965.

Dance Pieces at Peerless Movie House. New York City, ca. 1964 (dates unknown).

Junk Dances by Murray Louis. Decor, Robert Wilson. Henry Street Settlement House (Murray Louis and Co.), New York City, November 27, 1964 (premiere).

Landscapes by Murray Louis. Decor, Robert Wilson. Henry St. Settlement House (Murray Louis and Co.), New York City, November 20, 1964 (premiere).

FILM AND VIDEO WORKS

For the series VOOM Portraits and Video Portraits, see "Solo Exhibitions and Installations," 2005–2011.

2009
KOOL – Dancing in my Mind. Direction, Richard Rutkowski. Screened at: Watermill Center, Watermill, NY, July 30, 2009; Akademie der Künste, Berlin, August 30, 2009; Sundance Channel, October 2010.

2006
Aida by Giuseppe Verdi. Directed by Benoît Vlietinck and produced by Benoît Jacques de Dixmunde. Stage direction, Robert Wilson; musical direction, Kazushi Ono. Recorded live at the Théâtre Royal de la Monnaie, Brussels, with the Symphony Orchestra and Choir of La Monnaie – De Munt. Release day May 29, 2006.

2005
Absolute Wilson (video documentary). Directed by Katharina Otto-Bernstein. Produced by Katharina Otto-Bernstein and and Penny CM Stankiewicz. Film Manufacturers Inc., 2005.

2003
Madama Butterfly by Giacomo Puccini. Directed by Misjel Vermerien and produced by Frank van Praag, for NPS Television and De Nederlandse Opera. Stage direction, Robert Wilson; music by Puccini, with recording by the Netherlands Philharmonic Orchestra, 2003.

2000
Alceste by Jean-Pierre Brossmann (based on Christoph Willibald Gluck's 1776 French version of **Alceste**). Directed for television and video by Brian Large and produced by Colin Wilson; co-produced with the Théâtre Musical de Paris – Théâtre du Châtelet with the support of Centre National de la Cinématographie. Stage direction, Robert Wilson. Release date February 24, 2009

1995
The Making of a Monologue: Robert Wilson's Hamlet (video documentary). Written and produced by Marion Kessel. Original Alley Theatre (Houston) production and video sponsored by the Caddell and Conwell Foundation for the Arts. Shown at: Salle Multi (Obscure), Quebec City, February 5, 12, 1996; Center for the Arts, Yerba Buena Gardens, San Francisco, November 11, 1996.

1994
The Tragedy of Hamlet, Prince of Denmark by Richard Rutkowski. Based on the play by Shakespeare. Performed by Heiko Senst, Robert Wilson, and others. Produced by See-No-Evil Productions, New York City. Filmed at Watermill Center, Long Island, New York. Shown at: Angelika 57 (Avignon/New York Film Festival), New York City, April 17, 1996.

The Death of Molière [La Mort de Molière] by Robert Wilson (on video HD). Scenario by Robert Wilson, Philippe Chemin, and Jan Linders. Texts by Heiner Müller and others. Music by Philip Glass. Produced by La Sept/ARTE, and Institut National de L'Audiovisuel (INA). Shown at: Festival International de Programmes Audiovisuels, Nice, January 17–22, 1995; Teatro Studio (Piccolo Teatro di Milano), Milan, June 22, 1995; Salle Multi (Obscure), Quebec City, February 5, 12, 1996; ARTE (broadcast throughout France and Germany), February 8, 1996; Magic Cinema (MC 93 Bobigny), Paris, February 12, 1996; Schweizerhof Hotel (Conference "Digital High Definition 16/9 and The Future of Film," sponsored by the International Film Festival of Berlin), Berlin, February 24, 1996; Whitney Museum of American Art (1997 Biennial Exhibition), March 20–June 15, 1997; Alabama: Kino auf Kampnagel, Hamburg, April 27, 1997; broadcast on RTP (Portugal), August 24, 1997; Spazio Officina Arti Electroniche (l'immagine leggera: Palermo International Videoart Festival), Palermo, Italy, October 1998.

1992
Don Juan Último. Text by Vicente Molina Foix. Produced by Telemadrid and Centro Dramatico Nacional. Shown at: Palazzo del Turismo (Rassegna Concorso Internazionale di Teatro per la Televisione e il Video), Riccione, Italy, May 26–29, 1994.

1991
Mr. Bojangles' Memory (made in conjunction with Wilson's exhibition at Centre Georges Pompidou). Produced by CCI/Centre Georges Pompidou. Shown at: Kijkhuis (10th World Wide Video Festival), The Hague, April 7–12, 1992; Salle Multi (Obscure), Quebec City, February 5, 12, 1996; Taormina Arte, Taormina, Italy, January 3, 1997; Alabama Kino auf Kampnagel, Hamburg, April 27, 1997; Spazio Officina Arti Electroniche (l'immagine leggera: Palermo International Videoart Festival), Palermo, Italy, October 1998.

1990
The Black Rider (video documentary). Directed by Theo Janssen and Ralph Quinke for German WDR television. Includes excerpts from the theatrical production of **The Black Rider**, from rehearsals in September 1989 to the premiere on March 31, 1990 at the Thalia Theater in Hamburg, Germany. Includes footage of interviews with Wilson, Waits, and Burroughs, as well as rehearsals and excerpts of scenes from the opening night performance.

1989
The Death of King Lear. Produced by Televisiòn Española. Shown at: Alabama: Kino auf Kampnagel, Hamburg, April 27, 1997; Spazio Officina Arti Electroniche (l'immagine leggera: Palermo International Videoart Festival), Palermo, Italy, October 1998.

La Femme à la cafetière. After a painting by Paul Cézanne. Co-produced by the Musèe d'Orsay, INA, and La September. Performed by Suzushi Hanayagi and Consuelo de Haviland. Shown at: Kijkhuis (Festivalkrant: World Wide Video Festival), The Hague, September 9–16, 1989; Festival de Programmes Audioviduels, Cannes, France, October 7–8, 1989; Biennale Festival of Cinema Art, Barcelona, November 1989; Festival de Video Art Plastique, Herouville St. Claire, France, November 30–December 3, 1989; Festival International du Film sur l'Art, Montreal, March 1990; International Video Festival, Saint-Herbin, France, March 22–25, 1990; Festival du Film d'Art, Paris, November 1990; Museo Nacional, Centro de Arte Reina Sofia (Bienal de la imagen en Movimiento '90), Madrid, Spain, December 12–24, 1990; The Kitchen (The Exploding Valentine: A Weekend of Video Romance and Revolt), New York City, February 14, 1992; Palazzo del Turismo (Rassegna Concorso Internazionale di Teatro per la Televisione e il Video), Riccione, Italy, May 26–29, 1994; Salle Multi (Obscure), Quebec City, February 5, 12, 1996; Taormina Arte, Taormina, Italy, January 3, 1997; Spazio Officina Arti Electroniche (l'immagine leggera: Palermo International Videoart Festival), Palermo, Italy, October 1998.

1986
Robert Wilson and the CIVIL warS. Directed by Howard Brookner and produced by Aspekt Telefilm, Hamburg, and Unisphere Pictures, New York.

1985
Einstein on the Beach: The Changing Image of Opera. Directed by Mark Obenhaus and produced by the Brooklyn Academy of Music, New York City.

1984
The Spaceman (video installation) by Robert Wilson and Ralph Hilton. Stedelijk Museum (part of exhibit "The Luminous Image"), Amsterdam, September 13–28, 1984.

1982
Stations by Robert Wilson. Directed and designed by Robert Wilson; music by Jacob Stern and Nicolas Economou; choreography by Jim Self. Produced by Lois Bianchi and the Byrd Hoffman Foundation in association with Zweites Deutsches Fernsehen (ZDF) and INA. Taped at Video Matrix, New York City. Shown at: Círculo de Bellas Artes de Madrid (Festival Nacional de Video), Madrid, June 11–16, 1984; Salle Multi (Obscure), Quebec City, February 5, 12, 1996; Spazio Officina Arti Electroniche (l'immagine leggera: Palermo International Videoart Festival), Palermo, Italy, October 1998; IV Gallery, Moscow, Russia, January 27, 1999; Cinema 2, Centre Georges Pompidou, Paris, February 18, 26, 2000.

1981
Deafman Glance [also called **The Murder**] by Robert Wilson. Designed and directed by Robert Wilson. Associate designer Tom Kamm. Produced by Louis Bianchi and The Byrd Hoffman Foundation, for the Corporation for Public Broadcasting. Taped at Matrix Studios, New York City. Shown at: Sequoia Theater (Mill Valley Film Festival), Mill Valley, California, September 25–October 2, 1986; Centre Georges Pompidou (L'epoque, la mode, la morale, la passion... series), Paris, May 21–August 17, 1987; Aarhus Videofestival '87, Aarhus, Denmark, September 5–13, 1987; Museum of Modern Art (Video and Dream festival) New York City, March 1990; University of Rhode Island (Video Art festival), Kingston, Rhode Island, March 27–April 13, 1990; Salle Multi (Obscure), Quebec City, February 5, 12, 1996; Alabama: Kino auf Kampnagel, Hamburg, April 27, 1997; Spazio Officina Arti Electroniche (l'immagine leggera: Palermo International Videoart Festival), Palermo, Italy, October 1998.

1978
Video 50 by Robert Wilson. Directed by Robert Wilson. Music by Alan Lloyd. Performed by Robert Wilson, and others. Produced by Film/Video Collectif, Lausanne, in association with ZDF. Taped at the Centre Georges Pompidou, Paris. Shown at: Círculo de Bellas Artes de Madrid (Festival Nacional de Video), Madrid, June 11–16, 1984; Grande Galerie, Centre Georges Pompidou (Féminin/Masculin series), October 26, 1995–February 12, 1996; Salle Multi (Obscure), Quebec City, February 5, 12, 1996; Spazio Officina Arti Electroniche (l'immagine leggera: Palermo International Videoart Festival), Palermo, Italy, October 1998; Le Manège (impact de l'image series), Maubeuge, France, May 17, 2000; 92Y Tribeca, New York, May 11, 2011.

1976
The Spaceman (video performance) by Robert Wilson and Ralph Hilton. Performed by Robert Wilson, Ralph Hilton, Christopher Knowles, Sue Sheehy, and others. The Kitchen, New York City, January 2–4, 1976.

1971
Overture for a Deafman (16mm film). 1971.

1970
Watermill (16mm film). 1970.

1965
The House (uncompleted). Featuring Jearnine Wagner. Filmed near San Antonio, Texas., Summer 1965

1963
Slant by Robert Wilson. For WNET – TV, c. 1963.

SOLO EXHIBITIONS AND INSTALLATIONS

2011
Mind Gap. Exhibition on brain research designed by Robert Wilson. Norsk Teknisk Museum, Oslo, April 16, 2011 (opening).

Video Portraits. Directed by Robert Wilson. Produced by Noah Khoshbin for Dissident Industries. Exhibited at: Portsmouth Museum of Art, Portsmouth, New Hampshire, January 16–April 29, 2011; Institutio Moreira Salla, Rio de Janeiro, February 15–May 15, 2011; Timken Museum of Art, San Diego, February 25–May 15, 2011; International Festival of Photography, Knokke-Heist, Belgium, April 9–June 13 2011; MdM Salzburg, Salzburg, July 16–October 16, 2011.

2010
Perchance to Dream: Roberto Bolle Video Portrait Exhibition. Center 548, New York, November 30–December 18, 2010.

Deafman Glance: Video Installation. Paula Cooper Gallery, NY, September 24–October 30, 2010.

Video Portraits. Directed by Robert Wilson. Produced by Noah Khoshbin for Dissident Industries. Exhibited at: Santander Cultural, Porto Algre, September 8–December 5, 2010; Jiri Svestka Gallery, Prague, November 12, 2010.

2009
Video Portraits. Directed by Robert Wilson. Produced by Noah Khoshbin for Dissident Industries. Exhibited at: Galerie Thaddaeus Ropac, Paris, France, January, 2009; Nasher Museum of Art, Durham, North Carolina, July 2–September 20, 2009; Groningen Museum, Groningen, Holland, 2009; Bernice Steinbaum Gallery, Miami, USA, February 7–March 7, 2009; The Fabric Workshop and Museum, Philadelphia, USA, February 13–March 12, 2009; Pasión & Francesas & San Benito, Valladolid, Spain, April 2–May 31; Neue Galerie am Landesmuseum Joanneum, Graz, Austria, 2009; Palazzo Reale, Milan, Italy, June 15–October 4, 2009; Hydra School Project, Hydra, Greece, June 15–September 30, 2009; Phoenix Hallen & Hamburger Kunsthalle, Hamburg, Germany, October 16, 2009–January 10, 2010.

Visions of the Frontier. Curated by Robert Wilson. Exhibition including works by Christopher Knowles, Andrea Crews/Maroussia Rebecq, Dash Snow, William Pope L, Matt Leines, Jonathan Meese, Megan Whitmarsh, Mark Manders, Japanther, Misaki Kawai Studio, Ed Templeton, PlanningToRock (Janine Rostron), and Vadim Fishkin. Institut Valencià d'Art Modern (IVAM), Valencia, Spain, May 28–November 15, 2009.

Egypt's Sunken Treasures. Curated by Franck Goddio. Designed by Robert Wilson. Soundscape by Laurie Anderson. Reggia di Venaria, Torino, February 7–May 31, 2009.

Writing Time. Performance and art installation for Montblanc and the launch of the "Montblanc Star Nicolas Rieussec Monopusher Chronograph." Directed by Robert Wilson. Music by Phillip Glass. Salon International de la Haute Horlogerie, Geneva, January 19–23, 2009.

2008
VOOM Portraits (High Definition Broadcast). Directed by Robert Wilson. Produced by Noah Khoshbin for VOOM HD Networks. Series includes portraits of Winona Ryder, Mikhail Baryshnikov, Robert Downey Jr., Jean Moreau, and Isabella Rosselini. Exhibited at: University of Iowa Museum of Art, Iowa City, February 2–March 30, 2008. CSPS Gallery, Cedar Rapids, February 2–March 30, 2008. Nasher Museum of Art at Duke University, Durham, February 23–July 6, 2008. International Festival of Films on Art (FIFA), Montreal, March 6–March 16, 2008. Joslyn Art Museum, Omaha, April 5–July 6, 2008. Bass Museum of Art, Miami Beach, May 1–August 3, 2008. Palazzo Leti Sansi (Spoleto Festival), Spoleto, Italy, June 29–July 3, 2008. National Museum of Singapore, Singapore, October 29–January 4, 2008. SESC Pinherios, San Paolo, Brazil, November 12–February 1, 2008. Devin Borden Hiram Butler Gallery, Houston, December–January, 2008. Art Miami (with Bernice Steinbaum Gallery), Miami, December 2–December 7, 2008.

Walking. Designed by Robert Wilson, Theun Mosk, and Boukje Schweigman. Terschellings Oerol Festival, Terschelling-Midland, The Netherlands, June 13–22, 2008.

Writing Time. Performance and art installation for Montblanc and the launch of the "Montblanc Star Nicolas Rieussec Monopusher Chronograph." Directed by Robert Wilson. Music by Phillip Glass. Salon International de la Haute Horlogerie, Geneva, April 7–12, 2008.

2007
VOOM Portraits (High Definition Broadcast). Directed by Robert Wilson. Produced by Noah Khoshbin for VOOM HD Networks. Series includes portraits of Winona Ryder, Mikhail Baryshnikov, Robert Downey Jr., Jeanne Moureau, and Isabella Rossellini. Exhibited at: Paula Cooper Gallery, New York, January 13–February 3, 2007. Phillips de Pury & Co., New York, January 17–February 14, 2007. Ace Gallery, Los Angeles, February 22–July 31, 2007. Triumph Gallery, Moscow, September 28, 2007. Ekaterina Foundation, Moscow, October 2–December 2, 2007. Museo D'Arte Contemporanea Donna Regina (MADRE), Naples, Italy, October 9–December 9, 2007.

2006
Never doubt I love 2 (installation). Drawings and sculptures by Robert Wilson. Music by Michael Galasso. Isola Madre, Italy, June 10–September 19, 2006.

The Glowing Wall (interactive LED installation). Designed by Robert Wilson and Tim Hunter Design. Orange County Performing Arts Center, Costa Mesa, Calif., September, 2006.

Giorgio Armani: A Retrospective (installation). Designed by Robert Wilson. Shanghai, China, opens April 1, 2006.

Isamu Noguchi: Sculptural Design. Japanese American National Museum, Los Angeles, February 5–May 14, 2006.

2005
VOOM Portraits (High Definition Broadcast). Directed by Robert Wilson. Produced by Noah Khoshbin for VOOM HD Networks. Series includes portraits of Winona Ryder, Mikhail Baryshnikov, Robert Downey Jr., Jeanne Moureau, and Isabella Rossellini. Exhibited at: PS 1 Contemporary Arts Center, New York, October, 2005.

A Space for Mozart (Mozarts Geburtshaus) (installation). Stiftung Mozarteum, Salzburg, December 5–31, 2006.

Isamu Noguchi (installation with works by designer Isamu Noguchi). Designed by Robert Wilson. Seattle Art Museum, Seattle, July 9–September 5, 2005.

Giorgio Armani: A Retrospective (installation). Designed by Robert Wilson. Mori Arts Center, Tokyo, April 2–June 5, 2005.

The Proscenium Eye: Drawings and Sculptures by Robert Wilson. Reilly Art Gallery, Providence College, Providence, May 3–6, 9–14, 19, 2005.

Aichi: In the Evening at Koi Pond. World Expo, Nagoya, Japan, March 25 (opening)–September 24, 2005.

2004

Exhibition: Wilson/La Fontaine. Foundation Pierre Bergé – Yves Saint Laurent, Paris, November 24 (opening)–July 31, 2005.

Exhibition of Drawings. Baronian Francey, Brussels, October 9 (opening)–November 20, 2004.

Exhibition of Drawings by Robert Wilson. Rena Bransten Gallery, San Francisco, September 1 (opening)–October 16, 2004.

Isamu Noguchi (installation with works by designer Isamu Noguchi). Designed by Robert Wilson. Noguchi Garden Museum, Queens, New York, June 12, 2004 (opening).

Imágines del Cuerpo (installation). Designed by Robert Wilson). Museu Barbier-Mueller d'Art Precolombi, Barcelona, June 3–October 31, 2004.

Giorgio Armani: A Retrospective (installation). Designed by Robert Wilson. National Museum of Roman Antiquities at the Terme di Diocleziano, Rome, May 6 (opening)–August 1, 2004.

Robert Wilson: Selected Works (exhibition of furniture and design). Ace Gallery, Los Angeles Opera, February 14, 2004 (opening).

2003

Moveable Seats. Galerie de France, Paris, November 7 December 31, 2003.

Giorgio Armani: A Retrospective (installation). Designed by Robert Wilson. Royal Academy, London, October 14 (opening)–February 15, 2003

Isamu Noguchi (installation with works by designer Isamu Noguchi. Designed by Robert Wilson. Maison de la culture du Japon, Paris, September 23–December 14, 2003.

Come in and go out (10 installations made in collaboration with students from art schools and universities in Copenhagen and Skåne). Exhibited at: Ny Carlsberg Glypototek and Thorvaldsens Museum, Copenhagen; The Museum of Contemporary Art, Roskilde; The Dinker Culture Centre, Helsingborg; Kulturen, Lund; Neon Gallery, Brösarp and Rooseum; Malmö, Konsthall; The Eastern Cemetery, Malmö, September 15–December 15, 2003.

The Temptation of St. Anthony. Galerie Hete A.M. Huenermann, Düsseldorf, June 21–23, 2003.

Isamu Noguchi (installation). Designed by Robert Wilson. Kunsthal, Rotterdam, May 17–September 2, 2003.

Robert Wilson (exhibition of furniture). Galleri Leivo, Stockholm, May 10, 2003 (opening).

Giorgio Armani (installation). Designed by Robert Wilson. Neue Nationalgalerie, Berlin, May 7, 2003 (opening).

Robert Wilson (installation). Galerie Nordenhake, Berlin, May 3, 2003 (opening).

Immaginando Prometeo (installation). Salone Internazionale del Mobile, Milan, April 8–May 11, 2003.

Chair Air. Galerie Ulrich Fiedler, Cologne, January 14–March 1, 2003.

Chair Chairs. Galleria Rossella Colombari, Milan, January 22, 2003.

2002

Never doubt I love (installation). Galeries des Galeries, Galeries Lafayette, Paris, January 22–February 23, 2002.

2001

Wilson Wahn. Theaterwissenschaftliche Sammlung, Universität zu Köln, Schloss Wahn, Cologne, September 14–November 4, 2001.

Robert Wilson: Russian Madness. Galerie Krinzinger, Salzburg, August 19, 2001 (opening).

Alberto Giacometti inszeniert von Robert Wilson (installation). Art Basel, Basle, Switzerland, June 13–18, 2001.

Isamu Noguchi: Sculptural Design. Organized by the Vitra Design Museum in co-operation with the Isamu Noguchi Foundation, Inc. Initial idea by Alexander von Vegesack. Curated by Katarina V. Posch and Jochen Eisenbrand. Collaborator Christian Wassmann. Light design by A. J. Weissbard. Sound design by Peter Cerone. Design Museum, London, July 20–November 18, 2001; Vitra Design Museum, Weil am Rhein, Germany, December 8, 2001–April 21, 2002; Reina Sofia Museum, Madrid, May 14–August 2, 2002.

Russian Madness (installation) Works included: Ludmila Bredkhina, Dmitry Bulnigin, Vladimir Duborssavsky, Vadim Fishkin, Vadim Fliagim, Ludmila Gorlova, Dmitry Gutov, Natalia Koudrianzeva, Oleg Kulik, Vladimir Kuprianov, Alexandre Lyachenko, Viacheslav Nizin, Anatoli Osmolovsky, Alexandre Ossachi, Dmitry Prigov, Konstantin Skotnikov, and Alexander Vinogradov. Reales Atarazanas (Valencia Biennial), Valencia, June 11–October 20, 2001.

Robert Wilson. Bernier/Gallery, Athens, January 28–February 10, 2001.

2000

Memory/Loss (revival of installation work for 1993 Biennale di Venezia). Galeria Krzysztofory (Festival Tadeusz Kantor), Cracow, Poland, December 9–30, 2000.

Robert Wilson: Zeichnungen 1971–1996. Galerie Fred Jahn, Munich, December 7, 2000–January 19, 2001.

Robert Wilson: recent sculpture. Paula Cooper Gallery, New York City, November 29, 2000 (opening).

Robert Wilson: three installations. Annemarie Verna Galerie, Zurich, November 24, 2000–January 27, 2001.

Anna Didn't Come Home That Night (installation). Det danske Kunstindustrimuseum, Copenhagen. November 22, 2000–February 25, 2001.

Robert Wilson on video: selected works in theatre, opera, film, video, and installation. Screenings organized by Bonnie Marranca. Location One, New York City, November 9–19, 2000.

Giorgio Armani. Exhibition designed by Robert Wilson. Curation by Germano Celant and Harold Koda. Lighting by A. J. Weissbard.Music by Michael Gelasso, lighting by A. J. Weissbard. Guggenheim Museum, New York City, October 20, 2000,–January 17, 2001. Guggenheim Museum, Bilbao, Spain, March 24, 2001 (opening).

Z2: the sleeping room of people who did not know each other (laser and video installation). Zürich Kosmos building, Vienna, June 6, 2000 (opening).

14 Stations (installation). Passionstheater, Oberammergau, Germany, May 21–October 8, 2000. Massachusetts Museum of Contemporary Art, North Adams, Massachusetts, December 8, 2001 (opening).

Le Tombeau de Suger (installation). Basilique de Saint-Denis [Festival de Saint-Denis], Saint-Denis, France, May 31–September 10, 2000.

A House for Edwin Denby and Edwin's Last Day (installation). Wanås Castle (Wanås Foundation), Knislinge, Sweden, May 27, 2000 (opening).

Anna's Room. Installation including performance by Ines Somellera. In Stanze e Segreti, Rotunda della Besana, Milan, April 11–May 7, 2000.

Robert Wilson: Time and Space. Itochu Gallery, Tokyo, April 21–July 8, 2000.

1999

Paul Landowski: le temple de l'homme (installation). Designed by Robert Wilson for the work of Paul Landowski. Petit Palais, Musée des Beaux-Arts de la Ville de Paris, December 7, 1999–March 5, 2000.

Robert Wilson: Rappel en Images (drawings from **Scourge of Hyacinths**). Galerie Papiers Gras, Geneva, November 18–27, 1999.

Chairs. Hiram Butler Gallery, Houston, October 31, 1999 (opening).

Robert Wilson: Time Rocker Knee Plays. The Norwood Gallery, Austin, Texas, October 29–November 27, 1999.

50 years Otto Versand (outdoor sculpture door for gala event). Otto Versand, Hamburg, August 28, 1999 (opening).

1998

Theater of Drawing: early artworks of Robert Wilson. Gund Hall Gallery, Harvard Graduate School of Design, Cambridge, Mass., October 5–29, 1998; Museum of Contemporary Art, Chicago, January 16–March 14, 1999; Museo del Pueblo (Festival Cervantino), Guanajuato, Mexico, October 2–31, 1999; Marion Koogler McNay Art Museum, San Antonio, Texas, March 12–May 19, 2002.

Bob Wilson: Relative Light. Palazzina dei Giardini, Modena, Italy, September 28, 1998–January 10, 1999.

Robert Wilson: A cidade e as estrelas: parte 5 (drawings from **O Corvo Branco/The White Raven**. Galeria Luís Serpa Projectos, Lisbon, September 26–November 7, 1998.

Robert Wilson: "Dantons Tod": Zeichnungen. Fördererlounge des Grossen Festspielhauses, Salzburg, July 25–August 30, 1998.

Carpets for a magical garden (Vorwerk carpet installation). Galerie der Herrenhäuser Gärten, Hannover, Germany, May 29, 1998.

1997

Robert Wilson/Villa Stuck (installation, also titled **Steel Velvet**). Museum Villa Stuck, Münich, November 25, 1997–February 8, 1998.

The Keir Collection of Medieval Works of Art (auction exhibition). Sotheby's, New York City, November 15–20, 1997.

Robert Wilson: Pelléas et Mélisande: Zeichnungen und Skulpturen. Schüttkasten Salzburg (sponsored by Galerie Thaddaeus Ropac), August 19–31, 1997.

Waco Door (permanent outdoor sculpture). Waco Art Center, Waco, Texas, April 18, 1997 (dedication).

1996

Water Jug Boy (installation). Art Cologne: Internationaler Kunstmarkt, Cologne, November 10–17, 1996.

Robert Wilson: Oedipus Rex: Nouveaux dessins. Galerie Thaddaeus Ropac, Paris, October–December 21, 1996.

Le Festival de la Mode par Robert Wilson (centennial installation). Galeries Lafayette, Paris, October 7–31, 1996.

Robert Wilson. Fotouhi Cramer Gallery, East Hampton, New York, July 13–August 4, 1996.

Robert Wilson: Survey of Drawings, 1973–1993. Modernism, San Francisco, June 20–August 17, 1996.

Robert Wilson. Galerie Lehmann, Lausanne, April 18–May 18, 1996.

Robert Wilson. Paula Cooper Gallery, New York City, March 30–April 27, 1996.

Robert Wilson (presentation of video and CD-Rom works). Salle Multi (Obscure Festival), Quebec City, Canada, February 5, 12, 1996.

1995

Erwartung: oeuvres sur papier. Galerie Thaddaeus Ropac, Paris, December 5, 1995–January 13, 1996.

H. G. (installation). Music/sound environment by Hans Peter Kuhn. Clink Street Vaults, London, September 12–October 15, 1995.

Robert Wilson: The Rooms of Seven Women, und Zeichnungen zu den Neuinszenierungen Blaubart/Erwartung. Karl-Böhmsaal des Kleinen Festspielhauses (sponsored by the Direktorium der Salzburger Festspiele and Galerie Thaddaeus Ropac), Salzburg, July 24–September 1, 1995.

Robert Wilson. Hiram Butler Gallery, Houston, May 20, 1995 (opening).

Dragons and Silk from the Forbidden City. Joyce (Joyce Ma Gallery), Paris, May 10–July 20, 1995.

Die Zauberflöte. Galerie Thaddaeus Ropac, Salzburg, Austria, January 20–March 15, 1995.

1994

Der Mond im Gras drawings. Gallery Biedermann (private showing), Munich, April 10, 1994.

Alice. Galeria Luís Serpa, Lisbon, Portugal, February 26–April 9, 1994.

Three Rooms. Akira Ikeda Gallery, New York City, January 22–February 26, 1994.

Disegni di Gibellina. Drawing exhibition in conjunction with the Italian Cultural Institute. Paula Cooper Gallery, New York City, January 13–27, 1994.

1993

Robert Wilson: Deafman Glance: A Video Installation. Paula Cooper Gallery, New York City, December 2–23, 1993.

Photographs of Robert Wilson Productions in Germany. Goethe House, New York City, November 2–December 3, 1993.

Robert Wilson: Memorie della Terra Desolata. Exhibition in conjunction with the performance of **T.S.E**. Baglio delle Case di Stefano, Gibellina Nuova, Sicily, September 24–November 7, 1993.

Monsters of Grace (installation). Galerie Franck+Schulte, Berlin, September 16–October 23, 1993.

Memory/Loss. Installation at the Biennale de Venezia, winner of the Golden Lion for Sculpture. Objects by Robert Wilson and Tadeusz Kantor. Sound score by Hans Peter Kuhn. Text by Heiner Müller. Granai delle Zitelle, Venice, June 13–October 10, 1993.

Portrait, Still Life, Landscape. Curated by Robert Wilson. Museum Boymans-van Beuningen, Rotterdam, May 15–September 9, 1993.

Draft Notes for a Conversation on Dante (presentation of a lithograph book). Galerie van Rijsbergen, Rotterdam, May 15–June 27, 1993. Galerie Thaddaeus Ropac, Paris, November 6–30, 1993.

Robert Wilson. Nathalie Beeckman Fine Arts, Brussels, March 29–April 31, 1993.

Robert Wilson: Furniture and Other Works. Waco Creative Art Center, Waco, Tex., February 18–April 11, 1993.

Mediale '93 (installation). Deichtorhallen, Hamburg, February 4–10, 1993. (See also Binnenalster Door, 1992, Hamburg).

1992

Binnenalster Door. Outdoor installation in conjunction with Mediale, February 4–10, 1993 Hamburg. Alster Lake, Hamburg, December–March 1993.

Robert Wilson: Works, 1972–1992. Raum für Kunst E.V., Hamburg, December 19, 1992–February 20, 1993.

La Flute Enchantée: Dessins. Galerie Thaddaeus Ropac, Paris, December 12, 1992–January 14, 1993.

Objects. Produzentengalerie, Hamburg, December 1992–February 1993.

Robert Wilson: Convidados de piedra. Video installation, in conjunction with performance of **Don Juan Último**. Sala Goya, Círculo de Bellas Artes (Festival de Otoño), Madrid, October 13–November 5, 1992.

Einstein on the Beach (drawings and furniture). Kamakura Gallery, Tokyo, October 12–31, 1992.

Robert Wilson. Exhibition of drawings and furniture/sculpture. Galeria Gamarra y Garrigues, Madrid, September 25–November 1992.

Robert Wilson. Installation of furniture, sculpture, and drawings, in conjunction with the performance of **Don Juan Último**. Instituto Valenciano de Arte Moderno (IVAM), Valencia, Spain, September 16–November 22, 1992.

Robert Wilson: Drawings for Alice in Wonderland. Laura Carpenter Fine Art, Santa Fe, New Mexico, July 18–August 5, 1992.

Robert Wilson: Drawings. Hiram Butler Gallery, Houston, Texas, February 1–March 31, 1992.

Robert Wilson: White Raven Drawings. Paul Cooper Gallery, New York City, January 1992.

1991

Robert Wilson: Zeichnungen-Zyklen: A Letter for Queen Victoria, 1971/72; Golden Windows, 1981/82: CIVIL warS, 1983: Swan Song, 1989. Galerie Fred Jahn, Munich, November 28–December 21, 1991.

Robert Wilson: Monuments. Kestner-Gesellschaft, Hannover, September 7–October 6, 1991. Bayerische Akademie der Schönen Künste, Munich, December 6, 1991–January 19, 1992.

Robert Wilson: Mr. Bojangles' Memory: og son of fire. Centre Georges Pompidou, Paris, November 6, 1991–January 27, 1992.

Robert Wilson: Lohengrin Drawings and Other Works. Annemarie Verna Galerie, Zürich, September 20–November 16, 1991.

Robert Wilson: Chairs for Marie and Pierre Curie, Sigmund Freud, Albert Einstein, A Table for Nijinski, and Parzival Drawings. Busche Galerie, Cologne, September 6–October 9, 1991.

Die wundersame Welt des Robert Wilson. Video presentation of **Video 50, Deafman Glance**, and **Stations**. Kino Arsenal (Freunde der Deutschen Kinemathek e.V.), Berlin, May 1–4, 1991.

Robert Wilson: Drawing and Sculpture. Drawings from **When We Dead Awaken** and **Lohengrin**. Barbara Krakow Gallery, Boston. Drawings from **When We Dead Awaken** with selected furniture and sculpture. Thomas Segal Gallery, Boston, March 2–April 13, 1991.

Robert Wilson: Die lithografischen Zyklen und Zeichnungen. Palais Stutterheim (Städtische Galerie), Erlangen, Germany, March 2–31, 1991.

Robert Wilson's Vision. Retrospective exhibition of drawings, paintings, furniture/sculpture, and video works from the past 20 years. Music/sound environment by Hans Peter Kuhn. Museum of Fine Arts, Boston, February 6–April 21, 1991. On tour: Contemporary Arts Museum, Houston, June 14–August 18, 1991; San Francisco Museum of Modern Art, September 12–December 1, 1991.

Robert Wilson: Sculpture, Furniture, Paintings and Drawings. Paula Cooper Gallery, New York City, January 26–February 23, 1991.

1990

Robert Wilson: Alceste Drawings and Furniture/Sculpture. Feigen Incorporated, Chicago, September 7–October 6, 1990.

Robert Wilson: Drawings, Sculpture and Furniture, the CIVIL warS. Virginia Lynch Gallery, Tiverton, R.I., July 29–August 23, 1990.

King Lear (drawings, furniture, and sculpture). Kunsthalle Schirn, Frankfurt, May 17–June 17, 1990.

Robert Wilson: Choreographie des Designs. Galerie AIDA, Hamburg, March 31, 1990 (opening).

1989

Swan Song (drawings). Galerie Fred Jahn, Munich, December 20, 1989–January, 1990.

Robert Wilson: Orlando: 22 Drawings and Furniture. Annemarie Verna Galerie, Zürich, October 28, 1989–January 27, 1990.

Robert Wilson: La Nuit d'avant le jour: Dessins. Yvon Lambert, Paris, September 9–October 14, 1989.

Erinnerung an eine Revolution (installation). Kunst-Buffet Basel Badischer Bahnhof (Galerie Fabian Walter), Basle, June 14–July 14, 1989.

Robert Wilson: Drawings for the Opera De Materie by Louis Andriessen. Stedelijk Museum, Amsterdam, June 2–July 16, 1989.

Robert Wilson Works, 1968–1989. Scuola d'Arte Drammatica, Milan, May 1989.

Robert Wilson: Zeichnungen und Druckgrafik. Galerie Lüpke, Frankfurt, April 21–May 27, 1989.

Robert Wilson: Die lithographischen Zyklen 1984–1986. Museum Morsbroich, Leverkusen, Germany, January 17–March 5, 1989.

1988

Dreams and Images: The Theatre of Robert Wilson (selections from Robert Wilson's papers). Rare Book and Manuscript Library, Butler Library, Columbia University, New York City, December 8–February 17, 1988.

Drawings. Marlene Eleini Gallery, London, November 1988.

Robert Wilson: Die lithographischen Zyklen, 1984–1986: Medea, Parsifal, Alceste. Galerie Fred Jahn, Munich, July 7–30, 1988.

Cosmopolitan Greetings (drawings). Galerie Harald Behm, Hamburg, June 1988.

1987

Robert Wilson: Die lithographischen Zyklen, 1984–1986: Medea, Parisfal, Alceste. Galerie Fred Jahn, Munich; Galerie im Theater der Stadt Gütersloh, October 30–November 30, 1988.

Robert Wilson: "Parzival" (drawings). Galerie Harald Behm, Hamburg, September 18–October 31, 1988.

Drawings. Galerie Biedermann, Munich, September 1988.

Robert Wilson: Erinnerung an eine Revolution (installation). Kunstgebäude am Schloßplatz, Galerie der Stadt, Stuttgart, July 3–August 16, 1988.

Robert Wilson: Drawings, Furniture and Props for Alceste, Alcestis, the CIVIL warS, Death, Destruction & Detroit II, Hamletmachine, Salomé. Paula Cooper Gallery, New York City, January 21–February 14, 1988; Aldrich Museum of Contemporary Art, Ridgefield, Conn., September 23, 1987–January 3, 1988.

1986

Robert Wilson: Drawings. University of Iowa, Iowa City, November 1–December 15, 1986.

The Knee Plays: Drawings. KiMo Gallery, Albuquerque, New Mexico, October 28–November 30, 1986.

Hamletmachine: Drawings. Theater in der Kunsthalle, Hamburg, October 4–November 15, 1986. Grey Art Gallery, New York University, New York City, May–June 1986.

Robert Wilson: Drawings for the Stage. Retrospective exhibition. Laguna Gloria Museum, Austin, Texas, July 10–September 7, 1986.

Drawings: the CIVIL warS: Robert Wilson. Hewlett Gallery, Carnegie-Mellon University, Pittsburgh, April 1–26, 1986.

Robert Wilson: Transmutation of Archetypes: Medea & Parsifal. Lehman College Art Gallery, City University of New York, New York City. Tour (possibly different titles): Hewlett Gallery, Carnegie-Mellon University, Pittsburgh, March 30–April 20, 1986; Kuhlenschmidt Gallery, Los Angeles, March 18–April 16, 1986.

Robert Wilson: The Complete Parsifal Portfolio: Drawings for Theatre Pieces. The Alpha Gallery, Boston, March 8–April 2, 1986.

Robert Wilson: Drawings: Alcestis. The Harcus Gallery, Boston, February 1986.

Robert Wilson: Drawings for the CIVIL warS. Rhona Hoffman Gallery, Chicago, January 10–February 1, 1986.

1985

Robert Wilson: Medea e Parsifal: Disegni, Incisioni, Video. Galleria Franca Mancini (Rossini Opera Festival), Pesaro, Italy, August 19–September 19, 1985.

Parsifal Lithographs. Werkraum der Münchner Kammerspiele, Munich, June 5, 1985; Institute of Contemporary Art, Boston, January 15–March 15, 1985.

1984

Robert Wilson: Drawings. Paula Cooper Gallery, New York City, December 4–22, 1984.

Robert Wilson's the CIVIL warS: a tree is best measured when it is down: Drawings, Models, and World Wide Documentation. Exhibition Center, Otis Art Institute, Los Angeles, June 11–August 15, 1984.

Robert Wilson, drawings for the CIVIL warS: a tree is best measured when it is down, and selected videos. Jones Troyer Gallery, Washington, D.C., May 29–June 16, 1984.

Robert Wilson: Dessins Pour Trois Opéras: Medea 1981; **Great Day in the Morning**, 1882; **the CIVIL warS, 1984**. ARCA (Centre d'Art Contemporain), Marseille, March 19–31, 1984.

Robert Wilson: Zeichnungen und Skulpturen. Kölnischer Kunstverein, Cologne, January 13–22, 1984. Walker Art Center, Minneapolis, April 25–May 25, 1984. Museo de Folklore, Rome, March 20–April 29, 1984.

1983

Robert Wilson: Dessins pour the CIVIL warS. Pavillion des Arts, Paris, November 15–December 11, 1983.

Robert Wilson: the CIVIL warS. Galerie Brinkman, Amsterdam, September 3–30, 1983; Museum Boymans-van Beuningen, Rotterdam, August 13–September 11, 1983; Raum für Kunst, Produzentaengalerie, Hamburg, June 9–30, 1983; Festival Mondial du Théâtre, Nancy, May 20–June 5, 1983.

Robert Wilson: Drawings. Gallery Ueda: Warehouse, Tokyo, May 10–30, 1983; Sogetsu School, Tokyo, May 6, 1983.

Drawings from the CIVIL warS. Leo Castelli, Richard L. Feigen, James Corcoran Gallery, New York City, May 3–June 11, 1983.

Works by Robert Wilson. Museum of Art, Rhode Island School of Design, Providence, January 14–February 13, 1983.

1982

Drawings for The Golden Windows. Marian Goodman Gallery, New York City, December 7–December 29, 1982.

Robert Wilson: dessins pour Medea/Great Day In the Morning. Galerie le Dessin, Paris, September 30–November 11, 1982.

Robert Wilson: The Golden Windows/Die Goldenen Fenster: Die Zeichnungen. Galerie Annemarie Verna, Zurich, August 31–October 2, 1982.

Robert Wilson: Die Goldenen Fenster: Zeichnungen. Städtische Galerie im Lenbachhaus, Munich, May 19–June 13, 1982.

1980

Robert Wilson/From a Theatre of Images. The Contemporary Arts Center, Cincinnati, May 15–June 29, 1980; Neuberger Museum, State University of New York, Purchase, July 13–September 21, 1980.

1979

Marian Goodman Gallery, New York City, 1979.

Skulima Gallery, Berlin, 1979.

Galeria Zwirner, Cologne, 1979.

Paula Cooper Gallery, New York City, 1979.

1978

Robert Wilson: Skulpturen. Galerie Folker Skulima (with the Berliner Festspiele), Berlin, May–June, 1978.

1977

Robert Wilson: Furniture. Multiples/Marian Goodman Gallery, New York City, November 22–December 31, 1977.

1976

Robert Wilson: Sculpture & Drawings. Iolas Gallery – Brooks Jackson, Inc., New York City, March 9, 1976 (opening).

1975

Galerie Wünsche, Berlin, 1975.

1974

Robert Wilson: Dessins et Sculptures. Musée Galliera, Paris, September 10–26, 1974.

1971

Willard Gallery, New York City, 1971.

SELECTED GROUP EXHIBITIONS

2010

Josef Svoboda – Robert Wilson. Museum Kampa, Prague, November 14, 2010–February 6, 2011.

2009

Stage Pictures: Drawing for Performance. MoMA, New York City, March 11–September 7, 2009.

2008

The Death of Molière. Directed by Robert Wilson. Texts by Heiner Müller. MoMA, New York City, March 1, 2008.

2005

Woman of Many Faces: Isabelle Huppert. Includes video by Robert Wilson. P.S.1 Contemporary Art Center, Queens, October 30–December 5, 2005.

2004

Connecting Collections – Four Perspectives (for Wall Street Rising). Co-curated by Robert Wilson, Diane von Furstenberg, Danny Simmons, Russel Simmons, Mikhail Baryshinikov. Wall Street, New York City, September 22 (opening)–December 10, 2004.

Design ≠ Art: Functional Objects from Donald Judd to Rachel Whiteread. Included objects by Robert Wilson. Cooper Hewitt Museum, New York City, September 10, 2004–February 27, 2005.

The International Festival of Films on Art. FIFA 2004 tribute to Robert Wilson's work. Montreal, March 11–21, 2004.

2002

Show people: downtown directors and the play of time. Exit Art, New York City, May 11–August 16, 2002.

2001

The inward eye: transcendence in contemporary art (included "Blue Geese."). Contemporary Arts Museum, Houston, December 8, 2001–February 17, 2002.

2000

Virginia Lynch: a curatorial retrospective. Rhode Island School of Design, Providence, September 28–December 23, 2000.

Chairs by the great for kids. Salone Internazionale della Sedia, Udine, Italy, September 9–12, 2000.

Acchrochage/Summer group show: works on paper. The Norwood Gallery, Austin, Texas, June 15–July 15, 2000.

Soft White: lighting designs by artists. Included Light Bulb from **Death, Destruction & Detroit**. University Gallery, University of Massachusetts, Amherst, April 7–19, 2000.

World stage design (drawings displayed in 1999 at the Prague Quadrennial). York Quay Gallery, Harbourfront Centre, Toronto, March 17–April 30, 2000.

1999

1999 Drawings. Alexander and Bonin, New York City, December 11, 1999–January 22, 2000.

Artists on line for ACOR. Gagosian Gallery, New York City, September 9–12, 1999.

Liebe, Blut und Pappmaché: Das Kabinett der Theaterrequisiten (included **Freud** hanging chair and table). Museum Bellerive, Zurich, November 6, 1999–January 23, 2000.

Visual artists salute Harvey Lichtenstein (included Forest Drop from **Alice**). Feigen Contemporary, New York City, June 1–5, 1999.

Comfort zone: furniture by artists (included **Stalin** chairs). New York City, Paine Webber Art Gallery (Public Art Fund), April 15–June 25, 1999.

1998

l'immagine leggera: Palermo international videoart festival. Screening of Robert Wilson videos: **Deafman Glance, The Death of King Lear, La Femme à la cafetière, Memory/Loss, La Mort de Molière, Mr. Bojangles' Memory, Stations, Video 50**. Palermo, Italy, October 2–8, 1998.

Countenance – Face, Head and Portrait in Contemporary Art. Included Bessie Smith Breakfast Chairs, Esmeralda Sofa, and Headrest for St. Theresa. Galerie Thaddaeus Ropac, Salzburg, July 19–September 1, 1998.

Amerikanische Zeichnungen. Galerie Tony Wuethrich, Basle, Switzerland, May 5–July 4, 1998.

Rund um Brecht: Portraits, Theaterbilder, Illustrationen (Oceanflight drawings). Galerie Pels-Leusden, Berlin (Charlottenburg), April 4–May 23, 1998.

Sculptors and their environments (included Doctor Procopius Chair from **Time Rocker**). Pratt Manhattan Gallery (Pratt Institute), January 31–February 26, 1998. Schafler Gallery, Pratt Institute, Brooklyn, New York, March 6–April 2, 1998. Rockland Center for the Arts, West Nyack, New York, October 17–December 10, 1999.

1997

Notable Notes: drawings by writers and composers. Joseph Helman Gallery, New York City, December 3, 1997–January 17, 1998.

Malerzeichnungen. Bayrische Akademie der Schönen Künste, Munich, November 25, 1997–January 18, 1998.

Tableaux. Contemporary Arts Museum, Houston, Texas, October 17–November 30, 1997.

Love Hotel: a National Gallery of Australia Travelling Exhibition (included Hanging Chair, 1977). Tour of five galleries in Australia, August 30, 1997–October 4, 1998.

Finders/Keepers (included Hanging Chair). Contemporary Arts Museum, Houston, May 10–August 3, 1997.

1997 Biennial Exhibition (included **Death of Molière** video). Whitney Museum of American Art, New York City, March 20–June 15, 1997.

Graphit auf Papie. Galerie Thomas von Lintel, Munich, February 6–April 5, 1997.

1996

The Chair Event (auction to benefit Friends in Deed). New York City, The Metropolitan Pavilion, December 13, 1996.

Puppets and Performing Objects in the 20th Century (included puppet from **the CIVIL warS – Knee Plays**). New York City, New York Public Library for the Performing Arts, June 11–September 28, 1996.

Black Grey & White. Düsseldorf, Galerie Bugdahn und Kaimer, May 29–August 23, 1996.

1995

Prints To Benefit the Foundation for Contemporary Performance Arts. New York City, Brooke Alexander Gallery, December 5–29, 1995.

Creative Arts Workshops for Kids. Mural with contribution by Robert Wilson. New York, 124th Street, between 2nd & 3rd Ave., 1995.

Un Cuore Per Amico. Triennale di Milano, Milan, Italy, October 30, 1995.

Féminin/Masculin (le sexe de l'art). Screening of **Video 50**. Centre Georges Pompidou, Grande Galerie, October 26, 1995–February 12, 1996.

Die Muse?: Transforming the Image of Woman in Contemporary Art [Les Muses? Transformation de l'image féminine dans l'art contemporain]. Gandolph Bibliothek, Galerie Thaddaeus Ropac, Salzburg, July 22–September 2, 1995; Galerie Thaddaeus Ropac, Paris, September 26–November 18, 1995.

The Art Show: Art Dealers Association of America, Paula Cooper Gallery section. Seventh Regiment Armory, New York City, February 23–27, 1995.

1994

Festival International des Jardins. Garden design by Robert Wilson. Chaumont-sur-Loire, France, July 1–October 16, 1994.

Dessiner: Une Collection d'Art Contemporain. Musée du Luxembourg, Paris, May 6–July 3, 1994.

Outside the frame. Performance and the Object: A Survey History of Performance Art in the USA Since 1950. Cleveland Center for Contemporary Art, February 11–May 1, 1994; Snug Harbor Cultural Center, Staten Island, New York, February 26–June 18, 1995.

1993

Magazin im Magazin: eine Ausstellung des Vorarlberger Kunstvereins–Magazin 4. Vorarlberger Kunstverein, Bregenz, May 29–June 26, 1993; Architektur Zentrum, Vienna, November 23–December 13, 1993.

The Teaching Tradition: A Sixtieth Anniversary Exhibition. New Jersey Center for the Visual Arts, Summit, New Jersey, November 14–December 31, 1993.

Seeing the Forest Through the Trees. Contemporary Arts Musem, Houston, Texas, August 14–October 10, 1993.

Drawing the line against AIDS. Peggy Guggenheim Collection (AMFAR, Venice Biennale), Venice, June 8–13, 1993.

Exploring Art in Contemporary Scale. Laguna Gloria Museum, Austin, Texas, January 24–February 1993.

1992

Drawings for the Stage. Stephen Solovy Fine Art, Chicago, January 11–February, 1992.

Summer Drawing Show. Galerie Fred Jahn, Stuttgart, July 1–July 22, 1992.

Six Operas: Six Artists (Alceste drawings). Marion Koogler McNay Art Museum, San Antonio, Texas., May 17–September 6, 1992.

Contemporary Masterworks. Feigen Incorporated, Chicago, May 15–June 20, 1992.

10th World Wide Video Festival (Mr. Bojangles' Memory video). Kijkhuis, The Hague, April 7–12, 1992.

The Exploding Valentine: A Weekend of Video Romance and Revolt (La Femme à la cafetière video). The Kitchen, New York City, February 14, 1992.

1991

Mara Eggert: Magische Augenblicke: Inszenierungen von Ruth Berghaus und Robert Wilson. Exhibition of performance photographs. Deutsches Theatermuseum, Munich, July 24–September 29, 1991.

Sélection: Oeuvres de la collection. FAE Musée d'Art Contemporain, Pully/Lausanne, June 10–October 13, 1991.

The Artist's Hand: Drawings from the BankAmerica Corporation Art Collection. San Diego Museum of Contemporary Art, La Jolla, California, June 8–August 4, 1991.

Interactions. Institute of Contemporary Art, Philadelphia, May 23–July 7, 1991.

Big Motion in Video. Medienwerkstatt, Vienna (Internationales Videotheater), May 7–8, 1991.

Danses Tracées: Dessins et Notation des Chorégraphes. Centre de la Vielle Charité, Musées de Marseille, April 19–June 9, 1991.

1990

Bienal de la imagen en Movimiento '90 (La Femme à la cafetière video). Museo Nacional, Centro de Arte Reina Sofiia, Madrid, December 12–24, 1990.

Second Harvest: Artists' Tribute to Paul Baker. The Art Center, Waco, Texas, July 10–August 19, 1990.

Art Against AIDS (Parzival drawing). 406 Seventh Street, Northwest, Washington, D.C., May 3–26, 1990.

Modèles Déposés–1. C.A.U.E., Limoges, France, April 20–May 26, 1990.

energieën [Salomé's Room]. Stedelijk Museum, Amsterdam, April 7–July 29, 1990.

Video Art (Deafman Glance video). University of Rhode Island, Kingston, March 27–April 13, 1990.

Black Rider: Robert Wilson/William S. Burroughs. XPO Galerie, Hamburg, March 3–April 28, 1990.

Video and Dream (Deafman Glance video). Museum of Modern Art, New York City, March 1990.

Festival International du Film sur l'Art (La Femme à la cafetière video). Montreal, March 1990.

International Video Festival (La Femme à la cafetière video). Saint-Herbin, France, March 22–25, 1990.

1989

Artists' Furniture. The Harcus Gallery, Boston, December 9, 1989–Jan 18, 1990.

Festival de Video Art Plastique (La Femme à la cafetière video). Herouville St. Clair, France, November 30–December 3, 1989.

Biennale Festival of Cinema Art (La Femme à la cafetière video). Barcelona, November 1989.

Bienal Internacional de São Paulo. Grand Prize for Best Event (**Parzival** and **Hamletmachine** furniture and drawings). São Paulo, Brazil, October 14–December 10, 1989.

La Rose des Vents: Soirée Bob Wilson. Presentation of Wilson videos. Café du Théâtre, Centre d'Action culturelle, Villeneuve d'Ascq, France, October 14, 1989.

Festival de Programmes Audiovisuels (La Femme à la cafetière video). Cannes, France, October 7–8, 1989.

Festivalkrant: World Wide Video Festival (La Femme à la cafetière video). Kijkhuis, The Hague, September 9–16, 1989.

Guest Artist in Printmaking. College of Fine Arts, University of Texas, Austin, September 1–29, 1989.

25 Jahre Video-Skulptur. Kongresshalle, Berlin, August 27–September 24, 1989.

Parachute Magazine Benefit. Galerie René Blouin, Montreal, August 19, 1989.

The Arts for Television. Contemporary Arts Museum, Houston (co-organized by the Stedclijk Museum, Amsterdam, and the Museum of Contemporary Art, Los Angeles), June 10–July 16, 1989.

Artist/Designer: Opening Exhibition. Artist/Designer, New York City, May 11–June 30, 1989.

1988

Zeichenkunst der Gegenwart: Sammlung Prinz Franz von Bayern. Staatliche Graphische Sammlung, Munich, September 21–December 18, 1988.

Focus on the Collection: Painting and Sculpture from the 1970s and 1980s. Neuberger Museum, Purchase, New York, January 31–March 27, 1988.

1987

Sculptors on Paper: New Work. Madison Art Center, Madison, Wis.consin, December 5–January 31, 1989. Kalamazoo Institute of Arts, Kalamazoo, Michigan, September 6–October 16, 1988. Pittsburgh Center for the Arts, May 28–June 19, 1988. Sheldon Memorial Art Gallery, University of Nebraska, Lincoln, March 14–April 30, 1989.

Lead. Hirschl & Adler Modern, New York City, December 3, 1986–January 16, 1987.

Ross Bleckner/Michael Byron/Roy Lerner/Barry Le Va/Will Mentor/ Deborah Remington/Gary Stephan/Keung Szeto/Gilbert & George: Pictures/Robert Wilson: Drawings. Aldrich Museum of Contemporary Art, Ridgefield, Connecticut, September 27, 1987–January 3, 1988.

Aarhus Videofestival '87 (Deafman Glance video). Aarhus, Denmark, September 5–13, 1987.

The Arts for Television (Deafman Glance video). Co-organized by the Stedelijk Museum, Amsterdam, and the Museum of Contemporary Art, Los Angeles. Stedelijk Museum, September, 1987. Institute of Contemporary Art, Boston, September 17–November 1, 1987. Museum of Contemporary Art, Los Angeles, October 6–November 15, 1987.

Art Against AIDS: A Benefit Exhibition. (the CIVIL warS drawings). Paula Cooper Gallery, New York City, June 4–July 4, 1987.

L'epoque, la mode, la morale, las passion... (Deafman Glance video). Centre Georges Pompidou, Paris, May 21–August 17, 1987.

Resolution: A Critique of Video Art. Los Angeles Contemporary Exhibitions, April 10–May 16, 1987.

Sculpture. Procter Art Center, Bard College, Annandale-on-Hudson, New York, March 1–18, 1987.

1986

Works from the Paula Cooper Gallery. John Berggruen Gallery, San Francisco, October 14–November 20, 1986.

Mill Valley Film Festival (Deafman Glance video). Sequoia Theatre, Mill Valley, California, September 25–October 2, 1986.

Die Maler und das Theater im 20. Jahrhundert: Schirn Kunsthalle, Frankfurt, March 1–May 19, 1986.

Public and Private: American Prints Today: The 24th National Print Exhibition (Parsifal print). The Brooklyn Museum, New York City, February 7–May 5, 1986. Flint Institute of Arts, Flint, Mich., July 28–September 7, 1986. Rhode Island School of Design, Providence, September 29–November 9, 1986. Museum of Art, Carnegie Institute, Pittsburgh, December 1–January 11, 1987; Walker Art Center, Minneapolis, February 1–March 22, 1987.

1985

Works on Paper. Joe Fawbush Editions, New York City, November 16–December 14, 1985.

The New Figure. Birmingham Museum of Art, Birmingham, Ala., October 4–November 17, 1985.

Contemporary American Prints: Recent Acquisitions. The Brooklyn Museum, New York City, September 27–December 30, 1985.

High Style (Stalin chairs). Whitney Museum, New York City, September 18, 1985–February 16, 1986.

Spatial Relationships in Video. MoMA, New York City, July 4–September 3, 1985.

New Works on Paper 3. MoMA, New York City, June 25–September 3, 1985.

Ed Grazda and Douglas Sandhage: Photographs of Robert Wilson's Deafman Glance, BAM 1971. Dance Theater Workshop, New York City, May 14–June 30, 1985.

Cinquante ans de dessins américains, 1930–1980 (Great Day in the Morning drawings). Ecole des Beaux-Arts, Paris, May 3–July 13, 1985. Städtische Galerie im Städtischen Kunstinstitut, Frankfurt (titled Amerikanische Zeichnungen), November 28–January 26, 1986.

Large Drawings. Traveling exhibition organized by Independent Curators, Inc., New York City. Bass Museum of Art, Miami Beach, Fla., January 15–February 17, 1985. Madison Art Center, Madison, Wis., August 11–September 22, 1985. Norman MacKenzie Art Gallery, University of Regina, Saskatchewan, November 8–December 15, 1985. Anchorage Historical and Fine Arts Museum, Anchorage, Alaska, January 15–March 1, 1986. Santa Barbara Museum of Art, Santa Barbara Calif., April 11–May 8, 1986.

1984

Familiar Forms/Unfamiliar Furniture. First Street Forum, St. Louis, Missouri, September 19–November 10, 1984.

Survey of Contemporary Painting & Sculpture. Museum of Modern Art, New York City, May 17–August 7, 1984.

Festival Nacional de Video (Video 50 and **Stations).** Círculo de Bellas Artes de Madrid, June 11–16, 1984.

1983

The Permanent Collection: Highlights and Recent Acquisitions. The Grey Art Gallery, New York University, New York City. November 8–December 10, 1983.

Der Hang zum Gesamtkunstwerk. Kunsthaus Zürich; Städtische Kunsthalle, Düsseldorf; Museum Moderner Kunst, Vienna; Grosse Orangerie, Schloß Charlottenburg, Berlin. Entire tour: February 11, 1983–April 30, 1984.

1982

The Next Wave. Paula Cooper Gallery (for the Brooklyn Academy of Music), New York City, November 5–27, 1982.

American Drawings of the Seventies. Louisiana Museum of Modern Art; Humlebaek, Denmark; Kunsthalle, Basle; Museum Lenbachhaus, Munich; Wilhelm-Hack Museum, Ludwigshafen, Germany, 1982.

1981

1981 Biennial Exhibition. Whitney Museum of American Art, New York City, January 20–April 12, 1981.

Other Realities: Installations for Performance. Contemporary Arts Museum, Houston, August 1–September 27, 1981.

Artifacts at the End of a Decade. Artist book including **The Golden Windows** set designs. Travelling exhibition sponsored by the Gallery Association of New York, including exhibition at the Frankfurter Kunstverein. 1981.

1980

Further Furniture. Marian Goodman Gallery, New York City, December 9–31, 1980.

1975

Paula Cooper Gallery, New York City, 1975.

1974

Ala Gallery, Milan, 1974.

AUDIO RECORDINGS

2005

Leonce und Lena by Georg Büchner. Produced by Robert Wilson. Hörsturz.

2004

The Temptation of Saint Anthony by Bernice Johnson Reagon. Co-produced by Ruhrtriennale and Change Performing Arts.

2003

I La Galigo by Rayahu Supanggah. Co-produced by Change Performing Arts and Bali Purnati Center for the Arts.

The Raven by Lou Reed. Written for POEtry, Wilson's stage adaptation of Edgar Allen Poe's "The Raven." RCA.

2002

Blood Money by Tom Waits. Written with Kathleen Brennan for Robert Wilson's production of Georg Büchner's **Woyzeck.** Epitaph Records.

Alice by Tom Waits. Written for Wilson's adaptation of **Alice's Adventures in Wonderland** and co-released with Waits' Blood Money. Epitaph Records.

1999

the CIVIL warS by Robert Wilson and Philip Glass. Nonesuch Records.

Other rooms, other voices: audio works by artists. Includes Robert Wilson reading works of Christopher Knowles. With publication edited by Daniel Kurjakovic and Sebastian Lohse. Radio project curated by Daniel Kurjakovic with Franziska Baetcke for Swiss Radio SR DRS2 (Zürich: Memory/Cage Editions, 1999).

1998

Saints and Singing. Music by Hans-Peter Kuhn. Co-produced by SFB, Hebbel Theater, and Arte.

Aquilarco by Giovanni Sollima. Includes Robert Wilson reading texts by Christopher Knowles. Point Music.

1993

Einstein on the Beach by Philip Glass and Robert Wilson. With the Philip Glass Ensemble, Michael Riesman, conductor. Elektra-Nonesuch.

The Black Rider by Tom Waits. Written for **The Black Rider** by Robert Wilson and William S. Burroughs. Island Records.

1985

Music for The Knee Plays by Robert Wilson and David Byrne: from Robert Wilson's the **CIVIL warS: a tree is best measured when it is down,** music by David Byrne. ECM Records. Re-issued as **The Knee Plays** by Nonesuch Records in 2007.

1979

Einstein on the Beach by Robert Wilson and Philip Glass. CBS Masterworks (originally released by Tomato Records).

1974

The Life and Times of Joseph Stalin. Byrd Hoffman Foundation, New York City.

Index of Illustrations

With the exception of Robert Wilson's personal selection of images for his "From Within" section, the photographs for this publication were chosen on the basis of their relevancy to content, importance in or representational value of Wilson's opus, chronological distribution and balance of images among works, beauty, and the availability and quality of high resolution photographs.

Images are listed in alphabetical order by nouns for all languages (i.e. the CIVIL warS is listed under "C"). Where multiple images of the same work appear on a page, the page number is given only once.

Contributors' Biographies

Marina Abramović

The diva of performance art whose use of the body as subject and medium helped pioneer the form. Her work in sound, photography, video, and sculpture has appeared in numerous solo exhibitions, including at documenta, Centre Pompidou, Whitney Biennial, and the Guggenheim Museum. Abramović's awards include a Golden Lion at the 47th Venice Biennale for her video installation – performance *Balkan Baroque* and a Bessie for *The House with the Ocean View*. In 2010 MoMA presented *The Artist is Present*, a major retrospective. She worked with Robert Wilson on *The Life and Death of Marina Abramović* (2011) and sits on the Selection Committee of the Watermill Center.

Laurie Anderson

Multimedia artist, poet, filmmaker, composer, and performer. She launched her music career with the chart-topping hit "O Superman" in 1980, and has since recorded a dozen albums. *The Record of the Time*, a retrospective of her genre- and medium-defying installation, audio, and visual work, toured internationally from 2003–2005. The author of six books and original scores for dance and film, Anderson is a recipient of a Guggenheim Fellowship and was awarded the 2007 Dorothy and Lillian Gish Prize. She was a narrative voice in *Einstein on the Beach* and *the CIVIL warS*, and her scores were used for *The Man in the Raincoat* and *Alcestis*; her sound installation accompanies Wilson's exhibition *Egypt's Sunken Treasures* (2009).

Pierre Bergé

Businessman and patron of the arts, co-founder and former C.E.O of Yves Saint Laurent Couture and current chairman of the Pierre Bergé – Yves Saint Laurent Foundation. A former director of Paris's Athénée Théâtre Louis-Jouvet, he served as President of the Paris Opéra from 1988–2000. Bergé is a UNESCO Goodwill Ambassador, the co-founder and president of Sidaction, and co-owner of the newspaper *Le Monde*. Among his honors are Commandeur des arts et des lettres, Officier de l'Ordre National du Mérite, and Commandeur de la Légion d'Honneur. A sponsor of Robert Wilson's work for 40 years, he is a member of the Board of Directors and the Advisory Board of the Watermill Center.

Anne Bogart

Stage director and head of the Graduate Directing Program at Columbia University. Co-founder and current Artistic Director of the ensemble SITI Company, she is the author of three books on theater and has taught at institutions including Trinity Rep Conservatory and Playwrights Horizons. Formerly President of the Theatre Communications Group, Bogart has served on the National Endowment for the Arts Overview Committee. Her awards include two Obies, the Villager Award, a National Endowment for the Arts Artistic Associate Grant, the ATHE Achievement in Professional Theater Award, and a Guggenheim Fellowship. Bogart's play *bob* is about the life and work of Robert Wilson.

Charles Chemin

Director, and film and stage actor. His performances include *Wonder/Lust* at New York's CSV Center, *Rimbaud* at the Comédie-Française, and an adaptation of Proust's *À la recherche du temps perdu* at the Athénée Théâtre Louis-Jouvet. *Girlmachine*, a performance piece developed by Chemin and Carlos Soto at the Watermill Center, and a top entry at Performa 09, had its European premiere at the Arts Arena/Door Studios in Paris. Chemin has known Robert Wilson since birth and performed in Wilson's *The Meek Girl [Une Femme douce]* and *Les Fables de La Fontaine*. In 2009–10, he was assistant director for Wilson's production of *Krapp's Last Tape*.

Daniel Conrad

Choreographer and director of site-specific dance films choreographed uniquely for the camera. Conrad's films, among them *Subways*, choreographed for and filmed in the subways of Prague, and *Seducing the Guard*, a documentary with five Nobel laureates, have won numerous awards at festivals such as the Locarno International, Montreal World, London International, and Hamburg Kurzfilm. Conrad's dance films have been widely broadcast and featured in museums, and have been purchased by film collections such as the National Gallery of Art in Washington, D.C., the Canadian Museum of Contemporary Photography, New York University, and the Princeton University Library.

Giuseppe Frigeni

Choreographer, director, scenographer, and lighting designer. He studied dance with Françoise and Dominique Dupuy, Carolyn Carlson, and Lucinda Childs. Since 1999, Frigeni has directed and designed the sets and lighting for his own operatic productions, including *Turandot*, *La Traviata*, Pascal Dusapin's *Passion*, and, in 2010, *Fidelio* at the Welsh National Opera. Frigeni began working with Robert Wilson in 1988 as co-director and choreographer. Their many productions together include *Alice in Bed*, *Four Saints in Three Acts*, *Look*, *Lohengrin*, *Alceste*, *Orphée et Eurydice*, *Das Rheingold*, *Die Walküre*, *The Magic Flute*, *Madama Butterfly*, *Pelléas et Mélisande*, *L'Orfeo*, and Monteverdi's *Il ritorno d'Ulisse in patria* at La Scala (2011).

Gao Xingjian

Nobel laureate in literature (2000), writer, translator, dramatist, critic, and artist. Born in eastern China, he made his theatrical debut in 1982 with *Signal Alarm*. After his work was banned in China in 1988, Gao came as a political refugee to France, where he later became a citizen and was named Chevalier des arts et des lettres by the French government. His literary opus includes the plays *Wild Man*, *The Other Shore*, *Snow in August*, the novel *Soul Mountain*, as well as poetry and many essays. Gao's ink paintings have been displayed in over 30 international exhibitions. He is the subject of one of Robert Wilson's Video Portraits.

Philip Glass

One of the most influential composers of the 20th century. Glass is the creator of more than 20 operas, among them *Satyagraha* and *Akhnaten*, eight symphonies and ten concertos, as well as numerous string quartets, solo works, and award-winning film scores. He was among the first recipients of a MacArthur Fellowship, and his many other recognitions include the 2010 National Endowment for the Arts Opera Honors award for lifetime achievement. In addition to *Einstein on the Beach*, Glass's collaborations with Robert Wilson include *the CIVIL warS*, *Persephone*, *White Raven*, and *Monsters of Grace*. He sits on the Board of Directors and the Advisory Board of the Watermill Center.

Sacha Goldman

Filmmaker and producer in the field of the arts and culture. A former UNESCO media adviser, he is Secretary General of the Collegium International, a think-tank that brings together state leaders, philosophers, and scientists. He met Robert Wilson in 1971 and worked on the international tour of *A Letter for Queen Victoria*. Goldman has filmed the happenings of the Watermill Center since its establishment in 1992. In addition to producing Wilson's Polaroid work, he presented a documentary on Wilson at the Holland Festival, and has completed a second film about Wilson's life and work, *Wilson, Waco, Watermill* (2011).

Jonathan Harvey

Among the world's foremost composers of electro-acoustic music. Pierre Boulez first commissioned him for IRCAM, where Harvey has completed a dozen commissions; other commissions include the Berlin Philharmonic. Harvey's work has been featured at the Scottish Symphony Orchestra, where he was resident composer, and the BBC Proms. A member of the Europea Academea, he has taught at Princeton, Stanford, Sussex, and Cambridge, where he is Honorary Fellow of St. John's College. He received the Britten Award for composition and the inaugural Giga-Hertz Prize. His *Body Mandala* won the 2008 Gramophone Award for Best Contemporary Recording. Harvey is the first British composer to be awarded France's Charles Cros Grand Prix du Président de la République (2010).

Isabelle Huppert

Stage and screen actress whose work with directors such as Claude Chabrol and Jean-Luc Godard has made her an icon of contemporary cinema. Her accolades include a César Award and twelve nominations, two Best Actress Awards from the Cannes Film Festival, a 2009 European Film Award for Outstanding European Achievement in World Cinema, and the Venice Film Festival's Special Lion. An Officier de la Légion d'Honneur, Huppert was President of the Jury of the 2009 Cannes Film Festival. She has appeared in Robert Wilson's productions of *Orlando* and *Quartett* (2006, 2009), and is a subject of Wilson's Video Portraits.

Stefan Kurt

Film and stage actor. Educated at the Conservatory of Music and Theater in Bern, he was a member of Hamburg's Thalia Theater ensemble between 1985–1993. Kurt's performance in Carlo Goldoni's *The Servant of Two Masters* won him a 1987 Boy Gobert Prize, awarded to young Hamburg stage actors; other awards include the Adolf Grimme Prize for his role in the film *Der Schattenmann*. He first collaborated with Robert Wilson on *The Black Rider*, and has since been featured in numerous Wilson productions such as *Alice*, *Time Rocker*, *Oceanflight*, *Leonce and Lena*, and *The Threepenny Opera* in Berlin, Paris, and New York City (2011).

Joseph V. Melillo

Executive Producer of the Brooklyn Academy of Music. Melillo arrived at BAM in 1985 as founding director of the Next Wave Festival, and since 1999 has been responsible for BAM's artistic direction. An Officier des arts et des lettres and recipient of an honorary OBE, he has served on the board of the Association of Performing Presenters and is a member of the International Arts Advisory Committee for the Wexner Prize. BAM's affiliation with Robert Wilson began with the 1969 premiere of *The Life and Times of Sigmund Freud*, and now includes among others, *Einstein on the Beach, the CIVIL warS*, and *Quartett*. Wilson chose to celebrate his 70th birthday at BAM with the American premiere of *The Threepenny Opera* (October 4, 2011).

Ivan Nagel

Theater theorist, critic, and director, Professor of History and Aesthetics at the Berlin University of the Arts. Formerly chief drama director of the Münchner Kammerspiele, director of Hamburg's Deutsches Schauspielhaus, and founder of the Theater der Welt festival, he is also a renowned scholar and author. A recipient of the Moses Mendelssohn Prize, the Order of Merit of Berlin, the German Federal Cross of Merit, the Ernst Bloch Prize, and the Heinrich Mann Prize of the Berlin Academy of Art, he was instrumental in bringing Robert Wilson's *the CIVIL warS* to Germany and in introducing Wilson to playwright Heiner Müller.

Jessye Norman

Legendary soprano who since 1969 has graced the world's major opera houses in roles from Berlioz's Cassandre to Mozart's Countess Almaviva and Bizet's Carmen. Celebrated for her work ranging from lieder to jazz, Norman has received a Kennedy Center Honor, the United States's highest award in performing arts; she is a member of the Royal Academy of Music, London, and Commandeur des arts et des lettres in France. In 2009 she was awarded the National Medal of Arts. She has collaborated with Robert Wilson on *Great Day in the Morning, Alceste*, and Schubert's *Winterreise* (2006), and sits on the Advisory Board of the Watermill Center.

Yvonne Rainer

Dancer, choreographer, and filmmaker. After studying at the Martha Graham School, she co-founded the Judson Dance Theater, whose postmodern style helped to introduce a new, non-narrative vocabulary into modern dance. She has choreographed more than 40 concert works, among them the influential *The Mind is a Muscle*, and directed numerous feature-length films; *Privilege* was awarded the Filmmaker's Trophy at the 1990 Sundance Festival. The recipient of two Guggenheim Fellowships, three Rockefeller Foundation grants, seven National Endowment for the Arts awards and a MacArthur Fellowship, she is currently Distinguished Professor of Studio Art at the University of California, Irvine.

Jacques Reynaud

Costume designer. Reynaud has worked at La Scala, The Lyric Opera of Chicago, the Salzburg Festival, the Piccolo Teatro in Milan, and has collaborated with directors such as Luca Ronconi and Hermann Broch. He has designed the costumes for numerous Robert Wilson productions, including all of those done at the Berliner Ensemble. Among the Wilson works he has designed are *Oceanflight, 70 ANGELS ON THE FAÇADE, Dream Play, THE DAYS BEFORE: death, destruction and detroit III, POEtry, Woyzeck, Doctor Caligari, Peer Gynt, Leonce and Lena, Wintermärchen, The Threepenny Opera, Shakespeare's Sonnets, Lulu*, and *Il ritorno d'Ulisse in patria* (2011).

Marc Robinson

Professor of English and Theater Studies at Yale University and Adjunct Professor of Dramaturgy and Dramatic Criticism at the Yale School of Drama. A specialist in American theater history, he was a regular contributor of criticism to *The Village Voice* between 1986–2003. Robinson's writing has appeared in *The New Republic, New York, Newsday*, and *The New York Times*, as well as numerous theater journals. His books include *The American Play: 1787–2000*, winner of the 2009 George Freedley Special Jury Prize given by the Theatre Library Association. In 2010, Robinson received the George Jean Nathan Award for Dramatic Criticism.

John Rockwell

Cultural critic and journalist. He began his career at *The New York Times* as classical music critic, then served as the paper's chief rock critic, European cultural correspondent, editor of the Sunday Arts and Leisure section, and chief dance critic. The founding director of the Lincoln Center Festival, he is the author of four books, a former member of the Board of Overseers of Harvard University, and Board Chairman of the National Arts Journalism Program. A Distinguished Visitor at the American Academy in Berlin and Chevalier des arts et des lettres, he sits on the Selection Committee of the Watermill Center.

Carlos Soto

Actor, director and performance artist. His work has been presented at numerous international venues including the Istanbul Biennial, Athens's Benaki Museum, the Moscow Museum of Modern Art, and London's Riflemaker Gallery. In 2008, he was artist-in-residence at the Kampnagel Theater in Hamburg. Soto has worked with Robert Wilson as an actor, costume designer, and assistant since 1997. As a resident artist at the Watermill Center, he developed and co-directed the performance piece *Girlmachine* with Charles Chemin, and designed the costumes for Wilson's *KOOL – Dancing in my Mind* at the Guggenheim Museum. He plays a young Marina Abramović in *The Life and Death of Marina Abramović* (2011).

Viktor & Rolf

Designers Viktor Horsting and Rolf Snoeren, the duo behind the Dutch fashion label Viktor & Rolf. Their work has been the subject of numerous museum exhibitions in the Netherlands, the U.K., Japan, Belgium, Germany, and the United States; Paris's Musée de la Mode et du Textile mounted a ten-year career retrospective in 2004. In 2009, they received MODINT's Grand Seigneur Award, Dutch fashion's highest distinction. They are also the authors of *Sprookjes*, a book of fairy tales. Viktor & Rolf designed the costumes for Robert Wilson's *2 Lips and Dancers and Space* and his production of Weber's *Der Freischütz* (2009).

Serge von Arx

Architect, exhibition and stage designer, Associate Professor and Artistic Director in the Scenography Department at the Norwegian Theater Academy of the Høgskolen i Østfold. He has written architectural criticism for the major Zurich daily *Neue Zürcher Zeitung* since 1998, and publishes widely on both architecture and scenography. Von Arx's collaboration with Robert Wilson began at the Thalia Theater, where he served as Wilson's stage design assistant. They have worked together on stage, exhibition, and installation designs for productions including *POEtry, Prometheus, Doctor Caligari, Osud, Leonce and Lena, Erwartung, RUMI, Faust, L'Orfeo, The Threepenny Opera, Shakespeare's Sonnets, Lulu*, and *Il ritorno d'Ulisse in patria* (2011).

Rufus Wainwright

"The greatest songwriter on the planet" (according to Elton John). Wainwright's "baroque pop" fusion of pop, rock, and opera has been recognized with Juno and GLAAD Media Awards for Outstanding Music Album and Outstanding Music Artist. *Rufus Does Judy at Carnegie Hall*, Wainwright's 2007 re-creation of Judy Garland's legendary concert, received a Grammy nomination, and his first opera, *Prima Donna*, premiered at the Manchester International Festival in 2009. In 2010 he played London's Royal Albert Hall, and in 2011, London's Royal Opera House featured five straight days of different Wainwright performances. Wainwright composed the music for Robert Wilson's *Shakespeare's Sonnets* and has performed with Jessye Norman and others at the Watermill Center's *Last Song of Summer* (2010).

Jörn Weisbrodt

Executive Director of Robert Wilson's RW Work Ltd. and Director of the Watermill Center. After studying opera directing, he became artistic production director at Berlin's Staatsoper Unter den Linden, working closely with Peter Mussbach and music director Daniel Barenboim. Weisbrodt spent a year at Berlin's Deutsches Theater and was one of the initiators of the *Zwischen Palast Nutzung e.V.*, developing cultural programming at the former home of the GDR Parliament. Formerly Wilson's personal assistant, he has worked with him at the Guggenheim Museum, Salzburg Festival, Paris Opera, Barbican Centre and many other institutions.

Robert Wilson

A "towering figure in the world of experimental theater," (*The New York Times*). Wilson's *Einstein on the Beach*, with Philip Glass, altered conventional notions of traditional operatic form, and he has also left his mark on classics from *Pelléas et Mélisande* to *Der Ring des Nibelungen* and *Madama Butterfly*, as well as masterworks of the modern repertory. Nominated for the Pulitzer Prize (drama), recipient of Venice's Golden Lion (sculpture), the National Design Award for lifetime achievement, and the 2010 Jerome Robbins Award, he is a member of the American Academy of Arts and Letters and Commandeur des arts et des lettres. Wilson is founder of the Watermill Center.

Editor, Margery Arent Safir

Professor of Comparative Literature, founder and director of the Arts Arena at The American University of Paris. She is the author, co-author, and editor of books and articles in English, Spanish, French, and German on major figures of contemporary Latin American literature, and has collaborated with distinguished scientists Stephen Jay Gould, Roald Hoffmann, and Evelyn Fox Keller on the interactions between science and literature. A 2007 Meymandi Distinguished Visitor at the National Humanities Center (US), she is a member of the board of Brazil's JACA Center of Art and Technology, and of the International Advisory Council of the Aspen Institute Global Initiative on Arts, Culture, and Society.

Photographic Credits

As a nonprofit organization, the Arts Arena is grateful to the photographers who in that same spirit generously waived their fees and contributed their images to this publication.

Every effort has been made to trace the copyright holders of the images contained in this book and we apologize in advance for any unintentional omission. We would be pleased to insert the appropriate acknowledgment in any subsequent edition of this publication.

For *The Black Rider* a discrepancy exists between the Robert Wilson archives and other sources; we have credited the city and photographer for which we received confirmation from two or more reliable sources.

Cover, *I La Galigo*, Singapore, 2004 ©Ken Cheung and Esplanade Theaters on the Bay /Singapore Festival.
p. *Peer Gynt*, Oslo, 2005, © Lesley Leslie-Spinks.
pp. 2-3: *Shakespeare's Sonnets*, Berlin, 2009, © Lesley Leslie-Spinks.
p. 4 top, *Einstein on the Beach*, New York City, 1976, © Babette Mangolte.
p. 4 bottom, A Space for Mozart (Mozarts Geburtshaus, installation), Salzburg, 2005, © Lesley Leslie-Spinks.
p. 5 top, Video portrait of Isabelle Huppert by Robert Wilson, 2005, © Robert Wilson.
p. 5 bottom, *Time Rocker*, Paris, 1997, © Florian Kleinefenn.
pp. 6-7, *The Threepenny Opera*, Berlin, 2007, © Lesley Leslie-Spinks.
p. 8, "Self-Portrait," Polaroid photograph by Robert Wilson, 1999, courtesy Sacha Goldman Collection.
p. 10, *Der Freischütz*, *Baden-Baden*, 2009, © Lesley Leslie-Spinks.
pp. 12-13, *The Forest*, Berlin, 1988, © Gerhard Kassner
p. 14-15, *1433 - The Grand Voyage*, Taipei, 2009, © The National Theater of Taiwan
pp. 16-17, *Norma*, Zurich, 2011, © Suzanne Schwiertz
p. 18 top, *Lulu*, Berlin, 2011, © Elisabeth Henrichs
p. 18 bottom, *KOOL – Dancing in my Mind*, New York City, 2009, © Pavel Antonov
p. 19, *Happy Days [Oh les beaux jours]*, Luxembourg, 2008, © Luciano Romano.
p. 19 bottom, *Death Destruction & Detroit II*, Berlin, 1987, © Ruth Walz.
pp. 20-21, *Einstein on the Beach*, New York City, 1976, © BHF.
p. 22, *Edison*, Paris, 1979, © Enguerand.
p. 23, *Les Fables de La Fontaine*, Paris, 2004, © Martine Franck.
p 24, *T.S.E.: come under the shadow of this red*, Gibellina, Italy, 1994, © Bruna Ginanni and © Armin Linke.
p. 26 top left, *St. John's Passion*, Paris, 2007, © Olaf Struck.
p. 26 top right, *The Threepenny Opera*, Berlin, 2007, © Lesley Leslie-Spinks.
p. 26 bottom, *the CIVIL warS – Knee Plays*, Minneapolis, 1984, © Richard Feldman.
p. 29, *POEtry*, Hamburg, 2000, © Herman Baus and © Clärchen Baus-Mattar.
p. 30, *POEtry*, Hamburg, 2000, © Herman Baus and © Clärchen Baus-Mattar.
p. 33 top, *Deafman Glance* [The Murder], video, New York City, 1981, © BHF.
p. 33 bottom, *DiaLog/Curious George*, New York City, 1980, © Leo van Velzen.
p. 34 top, *St. John's Passion*, Paris, 2007, © Olaf Struck.
p. 34 bottom left, *Relative Light*, Valencia, 2000, © Maque-Falgas.
p. 34 bottom middle, *Overture to the Fourth Act of Deafman Glance*, Hamburg, 1977, © Simon Friedemann.
p. 34 bottom right, *Overture to the Fourth Act of Deafman Glance*, Hamburg, 1977 , © Simon Friedemann.
p. 37, *Shakespeare's Sonnets*, Berlin, 2009, © Lesley Leslie-Spinks.
p. 38 top left, *The Threepenny Opera*, Berlin, 2007, © Lesley Leslie-Spinks.
p. 38 top middle, *The Threepenny Opera*, Berlin, 2007, © Lesley Leslie-Spinks.
p. 38 top right, *The Threepenny Opera*, Berlin, 2007, © Lesley Leslie-Spinks.
p. 38 bottom, *Shakespeare's Sonnets*, Berlin, 2009, © Lesley Leslie-Spinks.
p. 40, Rehearsal for *The Black Rider: The Casting of the Magic Bullets*, Hamburg, 1990, © Elisabeth Henrichs.
p. 41, Rehearsal, *The Threepenny Opera*, Berlin, 2007, © Lesley Leslie-Spinks.
pp. 42-43, *DiaLog/Curious George*, New York City, 1980, © Leo van Velzen.
p. 44, *Madama Butterfly*, Paris, 1992, © Florian Kleinefenn.
p. 47 top left, *Danton's Death*, Salzburg, 1998, © David Baltzer.
p. 47 top right, *Parisfal*, Hamburg, 1991, © Ralf Brinkhoff.
p. 47 bottom right, *Danton's Death*, Salzburg, 1998, © David Baltzer.
p. 49, *Oceanflight*, Berlin, 1988, © Brigitte Mayer.
p. 50 top, *A Letter for Queen Victoria*, La Rochelle, 1974, © Philippe Gras.
p. 50 bottom, *The Life and Times of Sigmund Freud*, New York City, 1969, © Martin Bough.
p. 52, Rehearsal, *Alcestis*, Paris, 1986, © Agence de Presse BERNAND.
p. 53, Rehearsal, *Happy Days [Oh les beaux jours]*, Luxembourg, 2008, © Luciano Romano.
p. 55 all, *The Black Rider: The Casting of the Magic Bullets*, Hamburg, 1990, © Ralf Brinkhoff.
p. 56 top, *Alice in Bed*, Berlin, 1993, © Wilfred Boing.
p. 56 bottom, *Alice in Bed*, Berlin, 1993, © Lutz Deppe.
p. 60, *The Magic Flute*, Paris, 1991, © Christian Leiber.
p. 62 all, *The Magic Flute*, Paris, 1991, © Christian Leiber.
p. 64, *Les Fables de La Fontaine* ,Paris, 2004, © Martine Franck.
p. 65 top, *Madama Butterfly*, Paris, 1992, unknown photographer.
p. 65 bottom, *Madama Butterfly*, Paris, 1992, © Florian Kleinefenn.
p. 69 all, *Lohengrin*, Zurich, 1991, © Schiegel & Egle.
p. 70 top and bottom, *Das Rheingold*, Zurich, 2000, © Suzanne Schwiertz.
p. 73 top, *The Malady of Death*, Lausanne, 1996, © Archie Kent.
p. 73 bottom, *The Malady of Death*, Berlin, 1991, © Archie Kent.
p. 74, *Quartett*, Paris, 2006, © Victor Pascal.
p. 76 left, *Overture to KA MOUNTAIN AND GARDenia TERRACE*, Shiraz, Iran, 1972, © Basil Langton.
p. 76 right top and bottom, *Overture to KA MOUNTAIN AND GARDenia TERRACE*, Shiraz, Iran, 1972, © Bahman Djalali.
p. 78 top and bottom, *Orlando*, Lausanne, 1994, © Absiag Tüllmann.
p. 83, Video portrait of Isabelle Huppert, 2006, © Robert Wilson.
p. 86, *Quartett*, Paris, 2006, © Victor Pascal.
p. 87 top and bottom, *Quartett*, Paris, 2006, © Victor Pascal
p. 88, *Robert Wilson Solo*, 147 Spring Street, New York City, 1974, © Carl Paler.
p. 91 middle left top, The Watermill Center, Water Mill, Long Island, c. 2001, © The Watermill Center, unknown photographer.
p. 91 middle left bottom, The Watermill Center, Water Mill, Long Island, 2009, © Louis Dengler.
p. 91 bottom left, The Watermill Center, Water Mill, Long Island, 2006, © Kali Vermès.
p. 91 right, Robert Wilson at Watermill, Water Mill, Long Island, 2001, © Kali Vermès.
p. 93, Robert Wilson at Watermill, Water Mill, Long Island, 2001, © Kali Vermès.
p. 96, *The Life and Death of Marina Abramović*, Manchester, 2011, © Lucie Jansch.
p. 98, Press conference, Robert Wilson and Philip Glass, Avignon, 1976, © BHF.
p. 100, *Einstein on the Beach*, Paris, 1992, © Federico Brandani and © Tilde Tullio.
p. 103 top left, *Einstein on the Beach*, New York City, 1976, © Philippe Gras.
p. 103 top right, *Einstein on the Beach*, New York City, 1984, © Philippe Gras.
p. 103 bottom, *Einstein on the Beach*, Venice, 1976, © Fulvio Roiter.
p. 104, *Einstein on the Beach*, Paris, 1976, © Anne Nordmann.
p. 105, *Einstein on the Beach*, New York City, 1984, © Lynn Kohlman.
p. 107 top, *Einstein on the Beach*, Paris, 1976, © Lynn Kohlman
p. 107 bottom, *Einstein on the Beach*, Venice, 1976, © Fulvio Roiter.
p. 108 *Phil/Watercolor*, 1977, © Chuck Close, courtesy The Pace Gallery.
p. 111 all, *White Raven*, Madrid, 1998, © Javier del Real.
p. 112 *Persephone*, East Hampton, N.Y., 1995, © Jeffrey Price.
p. 114 *Alcestis*, Cambridge, Mass., 1986, © Richard Feldman.
p. 116 top and bottom, *A Letter for Queen Victoria*, Paris, 1974, © Philippe Gras
p. 119, Rehearsal, *Alcestis*, Cambridge, Mass., 1986, © Paula Rhodes.
p. 120, *ByrdwoMAN*, New York City, 1968, unknown photographer.
p. 124, *The Man in the Raincoat*, Cologne, 1981, unknown photographer.
p. 125, *The Man in the Raincoat*, Cologne, 1981, © Simon Friedemann.
p. 126, *Einstein on the Beach*, Venice, 1976, © Fulvio Roiter.
p. 131, *Einstein on the Beach*, New York City, 1984, © Lynn Kohlman.
p. 132 top left, *Deafman Glance*, New York City, 1971, © Martin Bough.
p. 132 top right, *Deafman Glance*, Paris, 1971, © BHF.
p. 132 bottom, *Deafman Glance*, Paris, 1971, © Martin Bough
p. 134, *Deafman Glance*, New York City, 1971, © Douglas Sandhage.
p. 135, *Deafman Glance*, Paris, 1971, © J.P. Lenoir.
p. 136 top, *Deafman Glance*, Paris, 1971, © Clalude Derhan.
p. 136 bottom, *Le Martyre de Saint Sébastien*, Paris, 1988, © Rodolphe Torette.
p. 139, *Einstein on the Beach*, New York City, 1992, © T. Charles Erickson.
p. 140 all, *Woyzeck*, Copenhagen, 2000, © Eric Hansen.
p. 144 top and bottom, *The King of Spain/The Life and Times of Sigmund Freud*, New York City, 1969, © Martin Bough.
p. 146, *the CIVIL warS-Rome Section*, New York City, 1986, © Beatriz Schiller.
p. 147 top and bottom, *the CIVIL warS-Rome Section*, New York City, 1986, © Johan Elbers.
p. 149 top and bottom, *The Golden Windows*, New York City, 1985, © Debra Trebitz.
pp. 150-51, *Dream Play*, Stockholm, 1998, © Lesley Leslie-Spinks.
p. 152 all, *Dream Play*, Stockholm, 1998, © Lesley Leslie-Spinks.
p. 155, *Der Freischütz*, Baden-Baden, 2009, © Lesley Leslie-Spinks.
p. 156 top, Rehearsal for *The Forest*, Berlin, 1988, © Gerhard Kassner.
p. 156 bottom, *Death, Destruction & Detroit*, Berlin, 1979, unknown photographer.
p. 158, *DiaLog/Sundance Kid*, New York City, 1975, © Jacob Burkhardt.
p. 160, *Death, Destruction & Detroit*, Berlin, 1979, © Ruth Walz.
p. 161, *Death, Destruction & Detroit*, Berlin, 1987, © Ruth Walz.
p. 162, *Hamletmachine*, New York City, 1986, © Robert Marshak
p. 167 top, *Edison*, Paris, 1979, © Enguerand.
p. 167 bottom, *Doctor Faustus Lights the Lights*, Berlin, 1992, © Martin Steingraber.
p. 168, *I was sitting on my patio this man came along I thought I was hallucinating*, Ypsilanti, Mich., 1977, © Jacob Burckhardt
p. 171, *Video 50*, Paris, 1978, © Robert Wilson.
p. 174 all, *The Meek Girl [Une Femme douce]*, Paris, 1994, © Florian Kleinefenn.
p. 175 all, *The Meek Girl [Une Femme douce]*, Paris, 1994, © Florian Kleinefenn.
p. 177 top, *HAMLET: a monologue*, Berlin, 1996, © David Baltzer.
p. 177 bottom, *Krapp's Last Tape*, Rome, 2009, © Leslie Lesley-Spinks.
p. 178 *A Letter for Queen Victoria*, New York City, 1975, unknown photographer
p. 180 top and bottom, *A Letter for Queen Victoria*, Paris, 1974, © Beatrice Heyligers
p. 182, *Snow on the Mesa* (dance), New York City, 1995, © Jeffrey Price
p. 186, *The Life and Times of Joseph Stalin*, New York City, 1973, © Carl Paler
p. 188 top, *Death, Destruction & Detroit II*, Berlin, 1987, © Ruth Walz
p. 188 bottom, *the CIVIL warS – Rotterdam Section*, Rotterdam, 1983, unknown photographer
p. 192, *Hamletmachine*, Hamburg, 1986, © Simon Friedemann
p. 195, Rehearsal for *The Threepenny Opera*, Berlin, 2007, © Lesley Leslie-Spinks.
p. 197, Rehearsal for *Shakespeare's Sonnets*, Berlin, 2009 © Lesley Leslie-Spinks.
p. 199, *Winterreise*, Paris, 2006, © Marie-Noelle Robert.
pp. 200-01, *L'Orfeo*, Milan, 2009, © Lelli & Masotti.
p. 202, *L'Orfeo*, Milan, 2009, © Lelli & Masotti.
p. 205 all, *L'Orfeo*, Milan, 2009, © Lelli & Masotti.
p. 206, *Pelléas et Mélisande*, Salzburg, 1997, © Ruth Walz.
p. 207, *Pelléas et Mélisande*, Salzburg, 1997, © Ruth Walz.
p. 208, *Der Freischütz*, Baden-Baden, 2009, © Lesley Leslie-Spinks.
p. 209, *Der Freischütz*, Baden-Baden, 2009, © Lesley Leslie-Spinks.
p. 211, *Shakespeare's Sonnets*, Berlin, 2009, © Lesley Leslie-Spinks.
p. 213, *Dream Play*, Stockholm, 1998, Lesley © Leslie-Spinks.
p. 215 top, *Three Sisters*, Stockholm, 2001, © Lesley Leslie-Spinks.
p. 215 bottom, *Der Freischütz*, Baden Baden, 2009, © Lesley Leslie-Spinks
p. 219, *DiaLog/A Mad Man A Mad Giant A Mad Dog A Mad Urge A Mad Face*, Shiraz, Iran, 1974, © Mehdi Khonsari.
p. 221, *Shakespeare's Sonnets*, Berlin, 2009, © Lesley Leslie-Spinks.
p. 222 top, Preparatory drawings, *the CIVIL warS-Marseille Workshop*, 1984, © L. Giraudo.
p. 222 bottom, Preparatory drawings, *Doctor Faustus Lights the Lights*, Berlin, 1992, © Archie Kent.
p. 225 top, "Danton's Death," 1992, © Robert Wilson, courtesy Paula Cooper Gallery.
p. 225 bottom, "Doctor Faustus Lights the Lights," 1992, © Robert Wilson, courtesy Paula Cooper Gallery.
p. 228 top, "Medea, Act Two," 1983, © Robert Wilson, courtesy Paula Cooper Gallery.
p. 228 bottom, "Time Rocker," 1996, © Robert Wilson, courtesy Paula Cooper Gallery.
p. 231 top, "Salomé," 1986, © Robert Wilson, courtesy Paula Cooper Gallery.
p. 231 bottom, "Dream Play," 1998, © Robert Wilson, courtesy Paula Cooper Gallery.
p. 232 top and bottom, *RUMI – in the Blink of the Eye*, Warsaw, 2008, © Stefan Okolowicz.
p. 233, *Götterdämmerung* Zurich, 2002, © Suzanne Schwiertz.
pp. 234-35, *Shakespeare's Sonnets*, Berlin, 2009, © Lesley Leslie-Spinks.
p. 236, *The Forest*, Berlin, 1988, © Gerhard Kassner.
p. 237 top, *The Forest*, Berlin,1988, © Gerhard Kassner.
p. 237 bottom, *The Life and Times of Joseph Stalin*, New York, 1973, © Jennifer Merrin.
p. 238, *The Forest*, Berlin,1988, © Gerhard Kassner.
p. 239, *Doktor Faustus* (Manzoni), Milan, 1989, © Lelli & Masotti.
p. 240 top and bottom, *L'Orfeo*, Milan, 2009, © Lesley Leslie-Spinks.
p. 241 top and bottom, *L'Orfeo*, Milan, 2009, © Lesley Leslie-Spinks.
pp. 242-43, *Norma*, Zurich, 2011, © Suzanne Schwiertz.
p. 244 top left, *Three Sisters*, Stockholm, 2001, © Lesley Leslie-Spinks.
p. 244 top right, *The Threepenny Opera*, Berlin, 2007, © Lesley Leslie-Spinks.
p. 244 bottom left, *The Threepenny Opera*, Berlin, 2007, © Lesley Leslie-Spinks.
p. 244 bottom right, *Doctor Caligari*, Berlin, 2002, © Lesley Leslie-Spinks
p. 246, *Leonce and Lena*, Berlin, 2003, © Ralf Brinkhoff.
p. 247, *Leonce and Lena*, Berlin, 2003, © Ralf Brinkhoff.
p. 248, *Peer Gynt*, Oslo, 2005, © Lesley Leslie-Spinks.
p. 249, *Wintermärchen*, Berlin, 2005, © Lesley Leslie-Spinks.
p. 250, *Woyzeck*, Copenhagen, 2000, © Eric Hansen.
p. 251, *Peer Gynt*, Oslo, 2005, © Lesley Leslie-Spinks.
p. 253, *Shakespeare's Sonnets*, Berlin, 2009, © Lesley Leslie-Spinks.
p. 254 top and bottom, *Die Frau ohne Schatten*, Paris, 2002, © Christian Leiber.
p. 257, Video portrait of Jeanne Moreau, 2005, © Robert Wilson.
p. 259, "Watermill Dolmains," Polaroid photograph by Robert Wilson, 1999, courtesy Sacha Goldman Collection.
pp. 260, 261, Video portrait of Gao Xingjian by Robert Wilson, Rome, 2009, © Luciano Romano.
p. 262, *Jo Kondo & Robert Wilson*, New York City, 2007, © Pavel Antonov.
p. 263, Guggenheim Museum Works & Process, Robert Wilson and Jo Kondo, New York City, 2007, © Pavel Antonov.
p. 265, *La Femme à la cafetière* (video), Paris, 1989, © Gerard Sergent.
p. 266, *the CIVIL wars-Tokyo Workshop*, Tokyo, 1984, © Keisuke Oki.
p. 269 top, *the CIVIL warS – Rotterdam Section*, Rotterdam, 1983, © Georges Méran.
p. 269 bottom, *The CIVIL warS – Rotterdam Section*, Rotterdam, 1983, © Delahays.
p. 270, Rehearsal for *Orlando*, Taipei, 2009, unknown photographer.
p. 271, Rehearsal for *Orlando*, Taipei, 2009, unknown photographer.
p. 272, Video portrait of Steve Buscemi, 2004, © Robert Wilson.
p. 274, *Wintermärchen*, Berlin, 2005, © Lesley Leslie-Spinks.
p. 275, Rehearsal for *The Threepenny Opera*, Berlin, 2006, © Lesley Leslie-Spinks.
p. 276, *Time Rocker*, Paris, 1997, © Florian Kleinefenn.
p. 277, *Time Rocker*, Paris, 1997, © Florian Kleinefenn.
p. 279 top and bottom, *the CIVIL warS-Cologne Section*, Cologne, 1984, © Günter Beer.
p. 280 top left, *The Black Rider: The Casting of the Magic Bullets*, Hamburg, 1990, © Clärchen Baus-Mattar.
280, right top and bottom, *The Black Rider: The Casting of the Magic Bullets*, Hamburg, © Martin Eberle
p. 282, *The Threepenny Opera*, Berlin, 2007, © Lesley Leslie-Spinks.
p. 283, *The Threepenny Opera*, Berlin, 2007, © Lesley Lesley-Spinks.
p. 285, *Alice*, Hamburg, 1992, © Clärchen Baus-Mattar and © Herman Baus.
p. 287, Robert Wilson directing, *Wintermärchen*, © Lesley Leslie-Spinks.
p. 288, *The Life and Death of Marina Abramović*, Manchester, 2011, © Lucie Jansch.
p. 290, *Doctor Faustus Lights the Lights*, Berlin, 1992, © Gerhard Kassner.
p. 291 all, *Doctor Faustus Lights the Lights*, Berlin, 1992, © Gerhard Kassner.
p. 293, *Robert Wilson Solo*, Rennes, 1976, unknown photographer.
p. 295 top and bottom, Rehearsal for *The Life and Death of Marina Abramović* (press release), Madrid, 2010, © Anthony Crook.
p. 297 top and bottom, *The Life and Death of Marina Abramović*, Manchester, 2011, © Lucie Jansch.
p. 298 top and bottom, *The Life and Death of Marina Abramović*, Manchester, 2011, © Lucie Jansch.
p. 303 top and bottom, *The Life and Death of Marina Abramović*, Manchester, 2011, © Lucie Jansch.
p. 304 all, Robert Wilson, 1995, © Ruth Waltz.
p. 305, *Lucinda Childs*, 1977, © Robert Mapplethorpe Foundation. Used by permission.
p. 306, Christopher Knowles, 1974, © Robert Mapplethorpe Foundation.
p. 307, Terracotta figure of a Han dancer, courtesy Robert Wilson.
p. 308, Marlene Dietrich, 1941, © Horst, courtesy Robert Wilson.
p. 309, Edwin Denby, © Rudy Burckhardt, courtesy Robert Wilson.
p. 310, House for Edwin Denby, Sweden, courtesy Robert Wilson.
p. 311, Sharkskin shoe, courtesy Robert Wilson.
p. 312, Nazi, 1945, © Lee Miller, courtesy Robert Wilson.
p. 313, Albert Einstein, courtesy Robert Wilson.
p. 314, Painting by Clementine Hunter, courtesy Robert Wilson.
p. 315, Glasswork by František Vizner, courtesy Robert Wilson.
p. 316 top, *DiaLog/A Mad Man A Mad Giant A Mad Dog A Mad Urge A Mad Face*, Washington, D.C., 1974, © Carl Paler.
p. 316 bottom, Rehearsal for *Danton's Death*, Houston, 1992, © Jim Caldwell.
p. 321, Robert Wilson, Rehearsal for *Bluebeard's Castle*, Salzburg, 1995, © Ruth Walz.

Robert Wilson
From Within

The Arts Arena at the American University of Paris is a nonprofit initiative for the creative and performing arts and issues of culture and society. It serves as a laboratory for thinking and presenting the arts from a multicultural perspective and for energizing connections both across artistic disciplines and between the arts and business, cultural policy, sciences, technology, and development. Its exhibitions, performances, debates, colloquia, and lecture series are free to the public, and have taken place in Paris, London, and New York. Arts Arena publications are available internationally.

The Florence Gould Foundation is an American foundation devoted to French-American exchange and amity, and has consistently provided major support to French-American cultural initiatives. Florence Gould was born of French parents in San Francisco in 1895, and lived her life both in the United States and France. Central to that life was her interest in and dedication to arts and letters; at her death in 1933 she left the bulk of her fortune to the foundation that bears her name and continues her work.

Editorial Director: Margery Arent Safir
Assistant Editor: Alexandra Schwartz

Design: Herman Lelie and Stefania Bonelli
Copyediting: Alexandra Schwartz
Proofreading: Louise Stein
Photo Research: Suzanne Shaheen
Production: fandg.com
Color separation: Dexter-premedia
Printed in Italy by Graphicom

The Arts Arena   Flammarion, S.A.
The American University of Paris   87, quai Panhard et Levassor
31, avenue Bosquet   75647 Paris Cedex 13
75007 Paris, France   editions.flammarion.com
artsarena@aup.edu
www.aup.fr/arts
www.artsarena.org

ISBN: 978-2-08-020107-2

Dépôt légal: 10/2011
Cover image: *I La Galigo*, Esplanade Theaters
on the Bay/Singapore Festival, Singapore, 2004

Acknowledgements

THE ARTS ARENA
The American University of Paris

is most grateful to

the Florence Gould Foundation
whose generous support made this book possible.

I wish to express my personal gratitude to Alexandra Schwartz and Jörn Weisbrodt, whose contributions to this publication went well beyond the call of duty. Alexandra showed a maturity, capability, and commitment that were exceptional and far beyond what one would have expected from a young editor. It is in a very real sense that she can be called the Assistant Editor of this book.

Jörn Weisbrodt is at the very origin of *Robert Wilson from Within*. At the first spark of the idea for this book, he began to facilitate its becoming a reality. Without him, this book would not be on shelves today.

I am grateful also to Joseph Bradshaw, until recently Manager of The Robert Wilson Archive, who was a valuable consultant for this project; Louise Stein for undertaking the complicated proofreading; and Suzanne Shaheen for photo research. My thanks also to Julie Rouart and Kate Mascaro of Flammarion publishers for their work on the French and worldwide English editions of the book respectively, and to Todd Bradway of D.A.P./Distributed Art Publishers for his counsel, loyalty, and patience as this project found its final form.

Sean Kelly of the Sean Kelly Gallery, New York, was instrumental in providing access to artists who contributed to this publication, and in introducing me to designers Herman Lelie and Stefania Bonelli, whose engagement with the book has been total and critical. The number of extra miles they went is untold. Their work makes this book what it is.

Finally, I would like to thank the contributors who, working at the highest levels in their respective disciplines, nonetheless volunteered their time and talents for this publication. My gratitude to them and to the others mentioned here is not only for their work, but also for demonstrating by their example that the values of the arts world and academia can be exactly what they should be.

MAS